TRAVEL AND ADVENTURE

IN

SOUTH-EAST AFRICA

BEING THE NARRATIVE OF THE LAST ELEVEN YEARS SPENT BY
THE AUTHOR ON THE ZAMBESI AND ITS TRIBUTARIES; WITH
AN ACCOUNT OF THE COLONISATION OF MASHUNALAND
AND THE PROGRESS OF THE GOLD INDUSTRY
IN THAT COUNTRY

FREDERICK COURTENEY SELOUS, C.M.Z.S.

GOLD MEDALLIST OF THE ROYAL GEOGRAPHICAL SOCIETY

Introduction by Hammond Innes

W0006616

CENTURY PUBLISHING
LONDON

HIPPOCRENE BOOKS INC.
NEW YORK

Introduction copyright © Hammond Innes 1984

First published in Great Britain in 1893
by Rowland Ward and Co., Limited

This edition published in 1984 by
Century Publishing Co. Ltd,
Portland House, 12–13 Greek Street, London W1V 5LE

ISBN 0 7126 0445 6

Published in the United States of America by
Hippocrene Books Inc.
171 Madison Avenue
New York, NY 10016

*The cover painting is from the collection at the
Mathaf Gallery, 24 Motcomb Street, London SW1*

Reprinted in Great Britain by
Richard Clay (The Chaucer Press) Ltd,
Bungay, Suffolk

TO

ALL THOSE

WHO TOOK PART IN

THE EXPEDITION TO MASHUNALAND,

IN REMEMBRANCE OF

THE GREAT ENTERPRISE IN WHICH WE WERE ALL

PRIVILEGED TO TAKE A PART,

I DEDICATE

THIS BOOK

Yours very sincerely

F. C. Selous

INTRODUCTION

BLACK Africa has been so much in the news since colonial rule gave place to independence that it is difficult to realise how recently the interior was opened up, a century only separating the ox-drawn wagon train from the jumbo jet. Fred Selous was very much a part of that opening up, the second wave as it were after Burton, Livingstone, Speke, and all the other early explorers. He belonged to the Rhodes period. Indeed, this book is very largely set in that eastern part of Southern Africa that was to be called Rhodesia.

When he first went into this country it was ruled by the Mashona king Lo Bengula. Selous was barely nineteen then and the story is that when he asked permission to hunt in Mashonaland for ivory, the king laughed and suggested he go rabbit shooting rather than elephant hunting, and since he was of no account he could go where he liked. Selous was back in a few weeks with tusks weighing almost 500 lbs.

This was in the 1870s. *Travel and Adventure in South-East Africa* covers the years 1882 to 1893. By then Selous's reputation as a fearless hunter of big game was already established. He was, in fact, well on the way to becoming the boyhood hero of so many of the youngsters then being assiduously groomed in the smaller public schools as cadre for empire. At the age of 66, with a D.S.O. and the rank of major, he was shot by a German sniper at Beho Beho. This was in 1917 and three years later a statue of him was erected in the South Kensington Museum surrounded by big game trophies. He had shot at least thirty-one lions, some two hundred buffalo, innumerable elephant, and had become the prototype for all those boys' stories illustrated by pictures of a lone man firing at a charging elephant or a springing lion. Haggard must surely have had him in mind when creating his Allan Quatermain character.

At this point most thinking people will probably feel like throwing the book down, remembering the terrible slaughter committed by the hunters who followed in the wake of Selous. But Selous himself worked much of the time in close association with the Royal Geographical Society, particularly as regards the collecting of specimens. He was born very close to the London Zoo and this is probably the key to his life; also perhaps the fact that his father was chairman of the London Stock Exchange. He took very little account of money, except in so far as it was a necessary requirement in equipping his expeditions, most of which were run on a shoestring.

By the 1880s he was already conscious of what was beginning to happen to the great wealth of African fauna—" many forms of which are becoming scarcer, while some, alas! are already verging upon extinction.".

If he could have seen what would happen to Africa in the next hundred years, the explosion of population, the destruction of the wildlife that was so much a part of his existence, I don't think it would have made any difference. He belonged essentially to the Africa of the period in which he lived, tough men, Dutch and British, engaged in a tough scramble for gold, diamonds, land, ivory, everybody raiding everybody else, the last of the " Kaffir " wars leading to the Boer wars.

The quality of this book lies very largely in the observations of a man who travelled the interior with a live mind and an almost journalistic instinct for observation. And in a land where Chaka was so recently dead and Rorke's Drift only just fought, there was a great deal to observe. I remember Ian Player, the game warden whose name is chiefly associated with the white rhino, introducing me to an old Zulu whose father had heard Chaka address his impis. Incredibly, almost shockingly, the voice this old Zulu produced, the voice of Chaka speaking through his mouth, was falsetto, at times rising to a scream.

It was Lo Bengula himself who gave Selous an account of the relentless progress of the Zulu impis and the chapter describing the destruction of the wall-building Mashona on their high and fertile plateau explains the speed of European settlement and Fort Salisbury's subsequent growth. But he is not only an observer. His discussion of the origins of the " Zimbabwi " ruins, and of the Bantu people, shows a mind in tune with academic thinking.

There is so much of tribal history and political information in this book, such a great sense of belonging, that every observation, whether about archaeology or about the future of mining, particularly gold, or about animals or wild flowers, has an authoritative ring, the manner of his writing very much that of the explorers who had gone before. He was educated at Rugby and the fact that he had started out to be a doctor probably came in useful when dealing with both the people and animals of the country.

Selous was thirty-one when he fitted out the first of the expeditions covered by this book. He had spent a year in Germany soon after leaving school at the age of seventeen and this helped him with Afrikaans, so that he understood the Boers almost as well as the English. At the time he wrote this book he had spent more than twenty years in Africa and the picture he gives of the bush, the game and the people of that period makes it one of the continent's classics.

All of us who have been on safari in the less populated areas of Africa know the instant psychological metamorphosis that occurs when we leave the security of our vehicle, armed only with a camera, and start walking, particularly if we are near any of the " big five ". A herd of elephant rumbling and squealing in a bamboo thicket, a pride of lions resting in the upside-down cooling position under the shade of a tree—we feel suddenly naked and very vulnerable, and most particularly vulnerable if we know there's a black rhino or some buffs in the vicinity.

These are all animals that are now under threat, the moments of sighting becoming rarer. But when Selous was trekking into the interior the elephant herds were enormous and every form of game present in profusion, predators and scavengers everywhere. To experience anything like the equivalent today you must strike it as lucky as my wife and I did in the Serengeti and be there at the height of the migration when the wildebeest are calving. To drive out on to the plains through regiment upon regiment of zebra, battalion upon battalion of those fabulous bearded caricatures, hooves pounding all about the vehicle, and then the Grant and Thompson gazelles—a million beasts with their attendant lions, cheetahs, hyenas, vultures, eagles, even wild dogs, all living on the flesh and the afterbirth of the herbivores—this is one of the experiences of a lifetime.

There, and there only, you can still get a glimpse of what Africa was like in Selous's day. Selous, of course, had no safari truck, so just try it—try walking through that migration, from kopje to kopje across the plain. Or, as an alternative, join one of the Wilderness Trail expeditions, an imaginative idea started by Ian Player to introduce people to the wild.

In the hundred years since Selous was hunting in the highlands south of the Zambesi our attitude to wildlife has changed immeasurably. For instance, though I know the area where Selous hunted, have been driven miles into the Drakensberg in search of the black wildebeest, have lived with the migration in the Serengeti and followed Hugo van Lawick to his wild dog pack, have camped with the Adamsons on the Tana river and flown to the north of Lake Turkhana with Richard Leaky, I have only once in all my travels seen men going off to hunt. They roared past us in the dawn, scarves fluttering like pennants in the wind of their speed, their rifles raised as they shouted to us, the adrenalin running and their eyes alight.

But they weren't real hunters. They were game wardens going out to cage a black rhino that had found a way out of the reserve, and also to deal with some lions. This form of hunting can be extremely dangerous, particularly as they had told me the rifles would be bent if they were ordered to shoot " their " lions, a pride or two of lions being worth several game wardens and a deal of culling in the management of a reserve.

The real hunting now is of poachers, and the sad thing is that it is the unthinking stupidity of people in distant cities that is the cause of it all. If there were no market in wildlife products there would be no poachers, and no terrible lingering deaths in the bush. Anybody, in any city of the world, who buys anything of ivory is committing an offence against God—a wire snare round the leg of an elephant, worse still drawn tight round the trunk, too often the slow means of acquiring that ivory. As for those women in their leopard skin coats, the fur so immaculate because the animal has been netted and killed in a pit by red hot steel thrust up its anus . . .

There are men like Selous now in Africa, but they are game wardens, and just as our attitude to wildlife has changed, so I suspect has wildlife's attitude to humans, so many animals having learned to avoid man whenever possible. But when Selous wrote this book the climate of opinion was very different, his world still a place of pioneers, himself the spokesman of his period and his way of life.

Hammond Innes.

Kersey 1984

PREFACE
TO ORIGINAL EDITION

In the following pages I have written the story of the last eleven years of my travels in the interior of South Africa. During the first six years of that period, namely, from the beginning of 1882 to the end of 1887, I was principally engaged in collecting specimens of the magnificent fauna which once abounded throughout the land, but many forms of which are day by day becoming scarcer, whilst some, alas! are already verging upon extinction. My occupation naturally led me into parts of the country where game was still plentiful, and as in South Africa wherever there is game there are lions too, I now and then encountered some of these animals, and had one or two interesting experiences with them, of all of which I have given some account. The first nine chapters of the book deal with the experiences of these six years; but in addition to lion stories and hunting adventures, there will be found much matter of more general interest, such as some notes upon my own personal experiences amongst the South African Boers; accounts of the two expeditions sent against the Batauwani by Lo Bengula; the devastations committed by the Matabili in Mashunaland; notes upon the Bushmen etc.

Chapters XI., XII., and XIII. deal with accounts of journeys beyond the Zambesi to the countries of the Mashukulumbwi and Barotsi tribes.   My experiences amongst the former people were eminently unpleasant at the time, but have supplied me with the materials for two chapters that may be of interest to those of my readers who appreciate tales of adventure.

All the remaining chapters, with the exception of the last two, which are devoted to a narration of hunting reminiscences, some of which date back to many years ago, deal with the past history and present condition of Mashunaland.   The gold industry of Mashunaland is still in its infancy, but that the gold is there is, I think, no longer doubted in the best-informed circles of the London financial world.   Before this work is through the press the first section of the railway from the east coast to Mashunaland will be completed through the district infested by the deadly "tse-tse" fly, and will, it is to be hoped, be carried on from there into the heart of the country without delay.   Mining machinery will then be poured into the gold-producing districts, and it is not too much to hope and expect that before the end of this century large mining towns will have sprung up in each of the gold-bearing districts.   Each of these mining centres will support a large farming population, so that as the mining towns grow so will the land be occupied and cultivated, till at no distant date the homesteads of British and South African settlers will be scattered throughout the length and breadth of the breezy downs of Mashunaland.   That England owes the acquisition of this rich country—this new land of such great promise and such immeasurable possibilities—to the wisdom, foresight, and strength of purpose of Mr. Cecil Rhodes, the present Premier of the Cape Colony, is, I think, fully recognised in this country. The knowledge that many years of travel as a hunter and collector of natural history specimens had given me of the topographical features of the country, enabled me to play my part in the actual occupation of Mashunaland, and that I may yet live to see that far-off country, endeared to me by so many stirring reminiscences, grow and increase in prosperity until it has become a rich and prosperous portion of the British Empire, is my most earnest desire.

Some chapters of this book have already appeared in print in the shape of articles to the *Field* newspaper, and I have to thank the editor of that publication for his kindness in allowing me to reprint them here. My best thanks are also due to Messrs. Armour, Lodge, Whymper, and Wolf, for the care and trouble they have bestowed on the drawings depicting hunting scenes and phases of native life, with which the book is illustrated. The representations of hunting scenes and other incidents of adventure were all drawn from my own oral descriptions, and much care has been bestowed upon them. I am indebted to the kindness of the President and Council of the Royal Geographical Society for the map at the end of the book, which I hope will enable my readers to follow my routes; and also for some of the plates representing scenes on the Zambesi and in Mashunaland, which were originally produced by the Society to illustrate a paper written by myself, entitled " Twenty Years in Zambesi," which appeared in the

Geographical Journal for April 1893. My best thanks
are also due to Messrs. E. A. Maund, W. Franceys, and
W. Ellerton Fry, for the numerous photographs of views
taken by them in the interior of Africa, all of which
were generously placed at my disposal from which to
select suitable subjects for illustrations.

The manuscript of the book has been most carefully
read over by Mr. John Coles, F.R.A.S., the Map
Curator of the Royal Geographical Society, and travel-
editor of the *Field* newspaper, who has always taken
more than a friendly interest in my career as a hunter,
naturalist, and explorer. At his suggestion I have
adopted the spelling of native names recommended by
the Royal Geographical Society.

Finally my thanks are due to my publishers, Messrs.
Rowland Ward and Co., for the great pains they have
taken to turn out the book in the best possible manner.
The best artists procurable have been employed, and Mr.
Rowland Ward has himself spent much time in personally
supervising the many spirited drawings which cannot but
add to any value the book may have.

THE AUTHOR.

WARGRAVE.

CONTENTS

CHAPTER I

CHAPTER II

CHAPTER III

CHAPTER IV

CHAPTER V

CHAPTER VI

CHAPTER VII

CHAPTER VIII

LICHTENSTEIN'S HARTEBEEST HEAD.

LIST OF ILLUSTRATIONS

IN THE TEXT

CHAPTER I

WHEN on my way home to England in March 1881, I spent a few days with my old friend and companion of former years in the interior, Mr. Frank Mandy. At that time he was managing an ostrich farm near Port Elizabeth in the eastern province of the Cape Colony, and I found the details of his work most interesting, and saw too that with ordinary luck it was a very paying business. Indeed, no kind of industry has ever paid so well in South Africa as ostrich farming, before it became overdone, and the price of feathers sank so low that on most farms the cost of feeding the birds took all the profits. Then there was a general collapse, many farmers lost heavily, and ostriches could be bought for a fewer number of shillings than they had cost pounds only a short time before. After this ostrich farming found its proper level amongst the industries of the Colony, and in certain districts, where certain natural conditions exist, it still pays better than any other kind of farming. Finding Mandy so comfortably settled with every prospect of speedily becoming a well-to-do man, made me think seriously about my own future. I had already spent ten years of my life elephant-hunting in the interior, and every year elephants were becoming scarcer and wilder south of the

Zambesi, so that it had become almost impossible to make a living by hunting at all. Was the game worth the candle? and would it not be better to follow my friend's example, to bid adieu to savage beasts and barbarous men, and settle down and become a respectable citizen? These were the questions I asked myself, and when Mr. B——, a well-known merchant of Port Elizabeth, for whom my friend Mandy was managing the ostrich farm, offered me the management of another farm on which he wished to try cattle and donkey breeding, I agreed to return from England before the end of the year to settle down in the Cape Colony, and resolved that the wild wandering life of an elephant-hunter should be to me but a dream of the past.

I went home and spent some months in England, and of course often visited the Natural History department of the British Museum, where Dr. Günther and Mr. Oldfield Thomas showed me how old and dilapidated were many of the specimens of South African mammals, and how many noble forms were not represented at all; and I took a note of what I ought to get should I ever visit the interior again. But I did not intend to go; I was going to settle down on a farm; that was determined. I also received a lot of orders from a dealer in natural history specimens, which I made a note of, without any idea that I should ever be able to fulfil them.

In November 1881 I returned to the Cape, and the first thing I heard on landing was that Mr. B—— was dead, and that he had died a ruined man, having lost all his money in speculations on the diamond fields. Mandy was still on the farm, managing for the gentleman who had taken it over after Mr. B——'s death. Thither I went as quickly as the good steamer *Spartan* could take me. During the few months I had been away ostrich farming had reached and passed the meridian of its prosperity, the collapse had set in, and the effects of the sudden depression were being felt throughout the eastern province of the Cape Colony. I remained for a short time on my friend's farm, and one evening went in to Port Elizabeth to see an exhibition of mesmerism given by Professor B——. The hall was well filled, and the Professor commenced an interesting performance, aided by an assistant. Presently a man, who may have been a sailor in plain clothes, and who was certainly much the worse for liquor, insisted upon ascending the stage in order to test the genuineness of the Professor's power. He was of course objected to, but he was in that condition when a man is not easily gainsaid, and he ultimately overrode all opposition and seated himself in a chair on the stage, and soon afterwards sank into a semi-comatose condition. When aroused by the assistant approaching him and making some passes near his face, he had evidently quite forgotten his surroundings, and thought the mesmerist wanted to fight. Springing from his chair, he at once squared up to his adversary, and after first pouring an awful volley of language upon him, struck him a heavy blow in the face. The poor assistant was at first dazed, but he was a stout-built fellow, and, soon recovering himself, he threw off his dress-coat and waistcoat, and, turning up his shirt sleeves, squared up to the sailor, who had been waiting for him, but had never ceased to pour out a continuous flood of "language" all the time. There was now a general stampede in the stalls ; but cries of encouragement re-echoed from the gallery, and both the sailor and the mesmerist had many partisans. The latter was just closing with his adversary, than whom, to give him his due, he was much more fluent and easy with his oaths, when the curtain was let down. In company with some other men, I jumped on the stage and went behind the curtain, where we found the combatants in the grasp of policemen and others who had been hastily summoned. The wordy warfare, which was of a very strong character, continued as long as I remained there, and altogether I think I never saw a more amusing impromptu performance.

Whilst I remained with Mandy I did my best to try and get something to do, but a period of depression and retrenchment had set in, and nobody I knew could help me. Besides, they all said, " Oh ! you'll get tired of a quiet life in six months' time, and want to wander away into the interior again." Perhaps they were right. At any rate, the only way left for me to make a living was by obtaining the specimens of large animals for which I had received orders from the British, and South African Museums, and from the London dealer, so I determined to at once fit out an expedition for the purpose.

My first step was to proceed to Klerksdorp in the Transvaal, where I knew that my old friend Mr. Thomas Leask would give me every assistance in his power to carry out my plans. I reached Kimberley by rail and coach, and there met the late Mr. H. C. Collison, who had just come down from a hunting expedition in Mashunaland. He informed me that he had left his waggon-driver, a half-caste man named Norris, and several Matabili boys in Klerksdorp, who, as they all knew me, would be delighted to return with me to the interior. In Kimberley I bought a very fine young stallion, that was supposed to be " salted," as whilst in Bechwanaland the preceding year it had contracted, and recovered from the less virulent of the two forms of horse sickness prevalent in South Africa. These two forms of horse sickness are known as the "din ziekte" and the "dik-kop ziekte" (thin sickness and thick head sickness). The former is more prevalent than the latter in Griqua land, the south-western Transvaal, and in Southern Bechwanaland, whereas farther north the thick head type, in which the head swells, is the common form. The latter is the more deadly of the two, and should a horse contract it and recover from it he is thoroughly " salted," and you need have no fear of his con-tracting the milder disease. On the other hand, should a horse be " salted " only for the " thin sickness," and you take him to the northern Transvaal, or to the countries north of that state, he will very likely contract the " thick head sickness," to which he will in all probability succumb. Thus it was with my poor Diamond. I never owned a more likely young horse, and had he only lived he would have been invaluable to me, as when I bought him he was only four years old, a strong, well-made animal, with good bottom, and pretty fast, and withal the gentlest beast I have ever possessed. As he had grown up amongst the dynamite explosions continually going on in Kim-berley, he was never gun shy, and was an excellent shooting horse from the first. He fell a victim, however, a few months later to the fatal " dik-kop ziekte " at the River Tauwani beyond Bamangwato, and by that time I had grown so fond of him that I mourned his loss for many a day afterwards.

From Kimberley I rode up to Klerksdorp on Diamond, sending my baggage by transport waggon. I tied a blanket behind my saddle, and when the nights were fine, lay down

wherever I felt inclined, using my saddle for a pillow, and
having first put the hobbles on my horse, which never attempted
to stray but fed close round me all night.   On wet nights—for
it was the middle of the rainy season—I always managed to
reach one or other of the roadside shanties, where food and
shelter could be obtained, which even in those pre-Johannes-
burg days were fairly numerous along the Transvaal roads.   It
was on this journey that I met with the one single instance of
inhospitality that I have ever experienced from a South African
Dutchman, and after all I cannot blame the man, as after the
great influx of Europeans—not all good ones—into South
Africa, consequent upon the wonderful discoveries of diamond
and gold mines, the simple kindness and great hospitality for
which the Boers have always been noted was often shamefully
abused by unprincipled scoundrels, and it was no uncommon
thing for a Boer to wake up in the morning and to find that
the stranger, whom he had received as an honoured guest, and
who had eaten his bread and salt, had arisen in the night, and,
without wishing him good-bye, had gone off with the best horse
in his stable.   Such an experience would be enough to sour
the nature of a rude but kindly Boer, and prejudice him
against all " uitlanders " for ever.

One wild stormy evening between sunset and dark I rode
up to a large well-built farmhouse in the Free State, and
inwardly congratulated myself on having reached shelter before
one of the dense black masses of cloud, which were dissolving
in torrents of rain all round me, had burst upon and drenched
me to the skin.   Riding up to the front door, I greeted the
good-looking elderly Boer, evidently the owner of the farm,
with the usual " Good day, uncle," and at once asked him, " Kan
ik hier slaap van nacht? " ("Can I sleep here to-night? ").   I
was simply astounded when he commenced to make excuses,
saying his house was full, etc., for it was so very different from
the hearty " Kerl, saal maar aff, en kom binnen " (" Take your
saddle off, and come inside, my boy "), to which I had grown
accustomed throughout the Transvaal.   On first seeing me, no
doubt the old man thought that very probably I had stolen the
horse I was riding ; but noticing me more closely, and perhaps
feeling somewhat ashamed of himself, he so far relented as to

say, " Gij kan maar, darum aff saal " (" You may, however, saddle off ").   Had I done so, and talked with him and his wife for a bit, I have no doubt I should soon have overcome his suspicions and obtained all I required—a supper and a shake down, and a good feed for my horse ; but having, as I say, been accustomed to the unquestioning hospitality of my friends the Transvaal Boers, I was hurt and indignant at the old man's suspicions ; so, taking off my hat, I made him a low bow, without dismounting, and said, " Ik dank yo, om, voor yo groot vrijndlijkhet, maar lieberster zal ik in de regen gaan slaap, als in en huis waar ik niet welkom is " (" I thank you, uncle, for your great friendliness, but I would rather go and sleep in the rain than in a house where I am not welcome ") ; then turning my horse's head, I rode slowly away into the fast-gathering darkness of a stormy night.

Before long the rain commenced to fall, but not very heavily, though it soon grew very dark ; the road I was following was, however, well defined, and the frequent flashes of lightning would have enabled me to follow a much less well defined track.   After riding for about an hour, and no heavy rain having yet fallen, I met some waggons loaded with firewood for Kimberley, and learned from one of the drivers that there was an " hotel " about three miles ahead.   This place I presently reached, and found it to be a wattle-and-daub structure of the roughest description.   However, I was able to get something to eat, and a shake down, and Diamond was also put under cover and got a good feed of forage.   This, as I have said before, is the only time that I have ever met with inhospitality at the hands of a South African Boer, though experiences of the same kind are no doubt common along the main roads for the reasons I have given.   Wherever their confidence has not been abused, however, I say it without fear of contradiction, no people in the world can be more genuinely kind and hospitable to strangers than the South African Dutch, whether in the Transvaal, the Free State, or the Cape Colony ; and besides hospitality they possess in such an eminent degree so many of the qualities that Englishmen profess to admire, that, with a better knowledge of one another, the two races would, I feel sure, soon shake off their mutual prejudices, and agree to work together for the common good and advancement of the best interests of South Africa. So many writers on South Africa have written disparagingly of the Dutch without any real knowledge of the people themselves, their history, or their language, that I feel that I, who, during the twenty years which I have spent in that country, have been intimately acquainted with many Boer families, have a right to say something on the subject.

As a young man before going out to the Cape, I spent more than a year in Germany and Bavaria, and acquired a fair knowledge of German, which I found of great assistance to me in learning the Dutch patois spoken in South Africa. Thus I very soon was able to talk easily and fluently with the Boer hunters I met with in the interior. From the lips of some of the old "voortrekkers" I heard the story of the wrongs they suffered under the British administration of the Cape Colony, which, culminating in the emancipation of the slaves, and the payment to their owners of only about one-sixth of the value at which they had been estimated by the commissioners employed for that purpose, plunged the whole country into grief and dismay. Then the sterner spirits resolved to submit no longer to uncongenial laws, administered by officials who had no sympathy with the people they governed. The great trek of 1836 was organised, and hundreds of brave Dutchmen trekked away with their wives and their families, their flocks and their herds, into the unknown wilderness beyond the great Orange river, carrying with them a bitter hatred of British rule, which still animates their descendants at the present day. The history of the emigrant Boers, during the first few years after they left the Cape Colony, is one of the most romantic interest, and no people, in whose veins had run a less heroic blood than the Boers had inherited from their Dutch and French Huguenot ancestors, could have held their own against, and finally triumphed over, the manifold difficulties they had to encounter. Weinen (the place of weeping) in Natal and Leydenberg (the hill of sorrow) in the Transvaal are the names of two townships, laid out by the emigrant Boers, which tell their own tale of the grief and suffering caused by the massacres they suffered at the hands of the Zulus after the

treacherous murder of Pieter Retief and his comrades by
Dingan. The name of Blood river was given to the stream on
whose banks an army sent by the Zulu king to exterminate the
Boers was defeated by them with great slaughter on the 16th
of December 1838. Something of all these matters I have
heard from old men in the Transvaal, and I soon conceived a
strong sympathy for the simple kindly people who had so
sternly refused to submit to uncongenial laws, which feeling
became genuine admiration when I heard how they had rallied,
after the massacres perpetrated on outlying families by the
Zulus and the Amandibili, and had finally conquered Dingan,
and driven Umziligazi beyond the Transvaal.

A most interesting and carefully accurate book has been
written by Mr. G. Macall Theal entitled *History of the Boers in
South Africa*, which I would advise all my readers to study,
if they wish to know something of the people, in preference
to taking the opinion of some prejudiced Englishman on the
subject, who may have lived years in a place like Johannesburg
or Kimberley and yet know absolutely nothing about the Boers,
or understand a word of their language. No generous-minded
man can read this story without acknowledging that it is the
history of a people possessing all the qualities required to build
up a great nation. What the Boers want is education and
knowledge ; they have plenty of good natural qualities. Where,
I would ask, will you find more courteous or kindlier gentlemen
than amongst the educated Dutch of the Cape Colony ? many
of whom are nearly related by blood to the rough frontiersmen
of the northern Transvaal. I always think that the ordinary
tourist in South Africa, who after a six weeks' rush through the
country by rail and coach comes home and writes a book, gets
altogether a false idea of the country. He visits Cape Town,
Kimberley, and Johannesburg, in none of which places does he
meet perhaps with any one who was not born in Europe ; he
sees nothing but English newspapers, and hears nothing but
English or German spoken. Of the Boers he sees nothing at
all, unless he goes into the markets, where he will find some of
them in charge of the produce waggons with their long teams
of oxen ; and he comes home again impressed with the idea
that the English language is superseding the Dutch, and think-

ing that before long the Dutch element will be swamped in South Africa by the English. These conclusions are altogether wrong. Throughout South Africa the people who live in the towns such as Kimberley, Cape Town, and Johannesburg, are English, Scotch, Germans, and Jews. The Dutch throughout the country live out on their farms, and are not seen at all by many tourists. In the whole of the Malmesbury district close to Cape Town, one of the principal agricultural centres in the Colony, there is not one single English or Scottish farmer, and in the eastern districts the poorer farmers of British descent seem to me to prefer to speak Dutch rather than English. In 1876 I travelled through the Colony from Port Elizabeth to Graaf Reinet by waggon, in company with several transport riders, all of them the sons of farmers in the eastern province, and all of them English or Scotch by blood. They could all speak English perfectly well, but amongst themselves they never used any language but Dutch, and their children may possibly not learn English at all. The South African Dutch, too, are one of the most prolific races in the world, and very large families of from twelve to sixteen children are not uncommon ; so that I feel convinced that in South Africa the Dutch element will never become swamped as it has been in America. However, the South African of the future will have no cause to be ashamed of his ancestry, whether they be English, Scotch, Dutch, or French Huguenot. I myself have always got on so well with the Boers, and Englishmen and Dutchmen are really so much alike in thought and feeling, that I feel sure that all that is required to make them work harmoniously together is a better knowledge of one another than at present prevails. There are good and bad amongst all nations, but it is as unreasonable to say that the Boers are a nation of inhuman brutes because one of them may have committed a brutal crime (and this has been often done), as to take Mr. Deeming or Jack the Ripper as a fair specimen of an Englishman. The greater part of the Boers I have known have been kind masters to their servants, though they are severe with them if they offend. They treat the natives, as do all colonists, as an inferior race, not as equals, and there can be no doubt that they are perfectly right in doing so. Granted that certain Kafirs are better men than certain white men, the fact remains that as a whole the Kafirs are an inferior people, and in their present state of development are with some few exceptions only fit to be hewers of wood and drawers of water. However, this is a difficult question, and one which I am not competent to discuss. I will only say that in my opinion the average Dutch Boer treats the natives in South Africa quite as well as the average Englishman.

When I first went out to South Africa I used to play a little Bavarian instrument—the zither—and I kept up my playing for many years, and when travelling through the Transvaal my musical talents used to keep me in butter, milk, and eggs. When we outspanned near a Boer farm, Edwin Miller, a young colonist who was usually with me, and who was thoroughly at home with the Boers, used to go up to the house, and in the course of conversation ask the goodwife if she was fond of music, and then tell her about my little instrument, when of course I was asked to play, and my pathetic Bavarian airs used to be much appreciated, and the old illustrated Bible was usually brought down, and the drawing of the " Harp that David played " compared to my zither ; and then I was offered milk, eggs, butter, and fresh bread if it was baking day. Miller, at my suggestion, always brought up an immense bucket for the milk, with many apologies because we had nothing smaller ; for the goodwives in the Transvaal do not care about parting with much fresh milk, as they want it for butter-making. However, if you bring up a big bucket, they are obliged to pour a good deal in to make any kind of show at all. Once we came to a farm on a Sunday morning, and Miller at once tried to open negotiations for obtaining milk and fresh butter. The ladies were most anxious to hear the music, but the old Boer had scruples of conscience, it being Sunday, and it was only when Miller pointed out that my zither was the same instrument as the harp that David used to play that he consented to have it brought up to the house. When I had tuned it up he insisted that nothing must be played but hymns ; so I played him the Danube Waltz, and noticing his astonishment, assured him that it was a French hymn. He seemed puzzled, but only muttered that it did not sound like a hymn. I then played him " Il bacio," when he jumped up, and striking his hand on the

THE AUTHOR PLAYING ZITHER IN BOER FARMHOUSE.

"When I had tuned it up he insisted that nothing must be played but hymns; so I played him the Danube Waltz. . . . With the help of the ladies of his family we persuaded him that it was an Italian hymn, and he took all the rest quietly, and his wife and daughters set us up again in butter, milk, and eggs."

table, said, " Nay, verdommt, daats geen Psaum niet, daats en yodlepijp " (" No, damn it, that's no hymn, that's a hornpipe "). With the help of the ladies of his family we persuaded him that it was an Italian hymn, and he took all the rest quietly, and his wife and daughters set us up again in butter, milk, and eggs.

After this long digression I will now again resume my narrative.

On reaching Klerksdorp I found that Mr. Collison's boys were still there waiting for a chance to get back to the interior, and I at once engaged the whole lot, including Norris the waggon-driver, and Laer, a young Griqua lad, who had been my friend's " after-rider," and who became most useful to me, as I taught him to help me in skinning and preparing skins for Museum specimens.   I bought a large roomy buck-waggon from Mr. Leask, with a half tent, or covered-in compartment to sleep in at the back, and laid in a sufficient stock of provisions, trading goods, etc., to last me for a year's trip.   I also bought from Mr. Leask the fine span of oxen that had belonged to Mr. Collison, which greatly delighted my driver Norris, as he knew them thoroughly, and understood all their little idiosyncrasies. Just the day before I was ready to start, Mr. Frederick Arnot rode into Klerksdorp from Potchefstroom.   Mr. Arnot, who has since gained for himself an honourable name amongst the missionary pioneers who have carried their gospel into Central Africa, was then quite a young man, and had only lately left Scotland.   He was very anxious to proceed at once to the interior, in order to commence his work amongst the natives, so I offered him a passage in my waggon as far as˙Bamang-wato, where I proposed to put him in the hands of the London missionaries.   I found Mr. Arnot a very pleasant, good-tempered companion, and he bore with cheerful equanimity all the dis-comforts of waggon travel in the rainy season.   Several times we stuck hopelessly fast, had to unload the entire waggon, and carry everything for a considerable distance to firm ground, and were then able to drag the empty waggon through the mud to the goods, which were then again packed on to it.   Before reach-ing the northern frontier of the Transvaal, however, the rainy weather suddenly ceased, and it became very dry and hot, and as we went north the country became drier and drier, so I took the best watered of the roads leading to the Marico river, passing through the farm of one of the old voortrekkers, Friedrich de Lange by name.

I am not quite sure, but I think the old man was no longer living at this time. He had been the possessor of a very curious snake-stone, which I first saw in 1875. I was then travelling with an old interior trader named John Cruickshank, who took me to De Lange's farm on purpose to see the stone. I saw it on several occasions afterwards, and for the last time in 1884. This stone old De Lange kept carefully packed away in cotton wool in a small box; and this box was in an old desk, which he kept locked. He certainly believed himself in its efficacy, and said he would not part with it on any consideration. Mr. Cruickshank offered him £50 for it in my presence, but he refused to sell it. He told us then that the value of the stone was well known in the district, as it had saved the lives of so many people—whom he named—and several horses. Amongst other names he mentioned that of a daughter of an old elephant-hunter named Antony Fortman, who, he averred, had been bitten by a cobra some years before when quite a child. As the stone had to be sent for, it had only reached her, he said, just in time to save her life. Two years later, in 1877, this story at any rate met with a curious confirmation. At that time Antony Fortman was at Tati in Matabililand with his family, his eldest daughter being a girl about sixteen years of age. I had quite forgotten about the snake-stone, when one day the conversation turning on snakes, Antony Fortman said to his daughter, " Turn up your sleeve and show Mr. Selous where the snake bit you." This she did, and on the girl's left arm near the shoulder was a very large and ugly scar, as if a piece of flesh had sloughed away and the wound had then skinned over. Fortman then proceeded to tell me how the girl had been bitten some years before in Marico, when quite a child, and that a horse had been saddled up at once and a messenger despatched for De Lange's snake-stone, how the little girl had become insensible and turned nearly black before the stone arrived, and that it had been twice applied before it drew out the snake poison. The stone itself was, as far as I remember, of a very light porous substance, round and flattish, an inch or so in diameter, and about one-third of an inch in thickness.   Its upper surface was smooth and polished, with blackish and grayish mottlings, its under side being rough and unpolished.   However, it is so long since I last saw it that I will not vouch for the complete accuracy of this description.   The more important point is that both De Lange and Fortman described the action of the stone in the same way.   The rough side, they said, when applied to the punctures made by the snake's teeth, adhered to the wounds, until a certain amount of poison had been absorbed, when the stone fell off.   It had then to be placed in a glass of ammonia, or its most obvious substitute, when the poison, looking like a thin white thread, they said, was seen to come from the stone, and rise to the surface of the glass.   When nothing more came from the stone, it was taken out of the glass, and again placed on the wound, until all the poison was extracted.   Friedrich de Lange told me that he brought this snake-stone with him from the Cape Colony, and that it had been an heirloom in his family for some generations.   In all probability it was originally brought from India, and it is at least remarkable that this stone was believed by the Boers in Marico to have the same powers attributed to certain snake-stones in India.   That Friedrich de Lange himself believed in its powers I think there can be no doubt ; otherwise he would not have treasured it so carefully, or have refused the £50 Mr. Cruickshank offered him for it.

A few days after leaving De Lange's farm we reached the Marico river, and followed it to the junction with the Limpopo or Crocodile river.   A drought had now set in in the middle of the rainy season, and the heat was so great that the young grass soon commenced to look withered and shrivelled up.   As it was still early in the season, and I had plenty of time in hand, I travelled very slowly along the Crocodile river, hoping that the weather would change, and rain would fall before I reached the spot beyond the Notwani junction, where the road leaves the river and strikes northwards through a very waterless stretch of country to Bamangwato.   The drought had driven all the game in the district to the neighbourhood of the river, and by riding out every morning at daylight I often came across some antelopes not far away from the water, and shot and preserved the skins of several hartebeests, wildebeests, etc. Diamond I found to be a splendid shooting horse, but another very good animal that I had bought in Klerksdorp, though an excellent horse for a journey, was so gun shy I could do nothing with him after game at this time, though ultimately I made a very good shooting horse of him, and he did me splendid service for some years—indeed until the end of 1888, when I sold him to Lewanika, the chief of the Barotsi tribe on the Upper Zambesi. About a month later than the time I am speaking of, and soon after I had passed Bamangwato on my way to Matabililand, both my horses, Diamond and Nelson, contracted the fatal horse sickness. Poor Diamond died, but Nelson just pulled through ; however, he had become so thin and weak during the progress of the sickness that it was some months before I could ride him again.

During the very hot weather we experienced on the Crocodile river I only travelled at nights, so as to save the bullocks as much as possible. My days I spent in shooting and preserving antelope skins for mounting in museums, or in collecting butterflies, for I may say that I have made extensive collections of these beautiful and interesting insects in all parts of Central South Africa, all of which collections I have presented to the South African Museum in Cape Town, where they have been catalogued and described by my friend, Mr. Rowland Trimen, the curator of the Museum, who not only has a most comprehensive knowledge of every branch of natural history, but is besides the best living authority on African lepidoptera. It is now a very hard matter, as I can vouch, to catch a butterfly that Mr. Trimen does not know, but it is a real pleasure to get him a new species, for he is so delighted to see it.

One day whilst walking along the bank of the Crocodile river with my net, I thought I heard a kind of moaning noise in the river, and pushing my way through the scrub which here clothed the bank, I found one of my best oxen with his fore-legs stuck fast in the mud, and the rest of his body under water. A huge crocodile that had been tearing at the poor animal, and inflicting the most excruciating torture upon him, rushed away through the water at my approach, and disappeared. When the cattle had gone down to drink, by a steep path, one of them had been pushed into deep water, and had swum down under the bank, unnoticed by the herd-boy. He had then tried to get out where the bank was muddy, and had stuck fast, and in this position had been attacked by the crocodile. We soon got him out with the help of two other oxen and a yoke and chain, which was attached to "reims"[1] made fast round his horns. The poor animal had been very badly bitten. There were deep wounds on the top of his back near the kidneys, and near the root of the tail, and other deep wounds in his flank, and it certainly looked as if a very large crocodile had taken the entire thickness of the ox's body in his gape. However, as this was a large Transvaal ox weighing quite 1000 lbs. as he stood, I can hardly believe that it can have been so, and yet I do not know how otherwise to account for the depth of the wounds, as, had they been mere surface nibblings, they ought not to have been dangerous. Whilst I was attending to the ox, and syringing out the wounds with strong carbolic lotion, Mr. Arnot went down to the river and watched for the reappearance of the crocodile, and presently got a shot at the ugly-looking head of a very large one, and thought he hit it; but one does not often recover a crocodile shot in deep water, as they sink to the bottom, and do not rise for some days. Although the Limpopo or Crocodile river is by no means a large river above its junction with the Tuli, I think that crocodiles are more numerous in it than in any other river that I have visited, with the exception of the Botletlie. They are, too, dangerous at times, and every year kill a lot of calves, and sheep, and goats, belonging to Khama's people. Mr. W. Rowles, an interior trader, told me that on one occasion whilst he was swimming a herd of goats through the river a few miles below the Notwani junction, three of them were seized and pulled under water by crocodiles. In 1876, too, a Boer hunter named Berns Niemand was killed by one of these reptiles lower down the river, and as I have often heard the story from Solomon Vermaak and Pieter Swart, who were with him and witnessed the catastrophe, I will relate it :—

---

[1] Raw hide thongs.

A party of Boer hunters were returning from a hunting expedition to Umzila's country, and trekking up the Crocodile river, which they wished to cross at a certain ford they knew of. On reaching this place they found the river pretty full of water, so Berns Niemand, Pieter Swart, and Solomon Vermaak stripped and went in to test the depth. Vermaak told me that the water was about up to his shoulders, and that he had just crossed it followed by Swart, when, looking round, he saw that Niemand was standing in the water up to his shoulders near the bank on which the waggons were standing and facing that way. Suddenly he saw the head of a large crocodile appear above the water and quickly approach his friend. " Pass op voer yo, Berns ! " (" Look out, Berns ! ") he shouted out, but too late, for, as the unfortunate man turned his head to see what danger threatened him, it was seized by the horrid reptile, and he was never seen again, either alive or dead : the crocodile took care of that. The horror and consternation caused in the hunters' camp by such an untoward event may be imagined, especially as poor Berns left a wife and children to mourn his loss.

In spite of everything I did my poor ox died on the third day after he was bitten, having first swelled up to a great size. I think his kidneys had been injured by the crocodile's teeth.

CHAPTER II

ON 5th March, travelling slowly northwards, we reached the
junction of the Notwani with the Limpopo or Crocodile river,
about seventy miles south of Bamangwato. Although it was
the rainy season we had now been having a spell of excessively
dry hot weather, that had already lasted for more than a
month, and the consequence was, that all the pools of water
lying on the road between the river and Bamangwato, which
had been filled during the early part of the rainy season, had
again dried up, and the young grass, which had attained to
about a foot in height, had been scorched and withered away
by the intense heat of the sun. As my bullocks had a journey
of over five hundred miles before them, I did not care to take
them through this seventy miles of waterless country in the
intense heat if I could avoid it; nor did I feel inclined to
remain where I was and wait for the rain; for, although at this
season of the year it was sure to fall before long, I might still
have been delayed for some time. Under these circumstances I
determined to ride in to Bamangwato during the night, and ask
the Chief Khama to allow me to trek along the Limpopo, and
then up the Mahalapsi river, rejoining the main road to the

Matabili country at the ford of the latter river. If I could
take this route, I knew I could get water for my bullocks
every day, whether it rained or not ; but as I was well aware
that Khama was very averse to new roads being made through
his country, and as he had always treated me with the greatest
courtesy and consideration, I did not wish to do anything to
displease him, though I had little doubt that he would grant
my request when preferred. Having once made up my mind
about undertaking the ride, I determined to start that very
evening as soon as the moon rose, which would be about seven
o'clock, as it was just one day past the full. I had no
preparations to make, for I intended to reach Bamangwato
within twelve hours, and so had no occasion to carry either
food or water ; and as I knew it would be a close, hot night, I
did not even take a coat. One thing, of course, I took with
me, and that was my rifle, together with a few cartridges ; not
that I thought there was any probability of my making use of
them, but in a wild country one never likes to be without a
rifle. A few nights previously we had heard lions roaring on
the opposite bank of the river, but, as these animals were
then already very scarce in this part of the country, I thought
the few that might still be about were sure to be in the vicinity
of the river, where, owing to the drought, all the game were
necessarily collected. Moreover, the moon was so bright that I
should have had no hesitation about riding through a country that
I knew to be infested by lions, as these animals are essentially
lovers of darkness, and seldom very bold on moonlight nights.

It was, I suppose, about seven o'clock when I mounted my
horse and bade good-bye to Mr. Arnot. As I did so the
moon rose gloriously (still almost a perfect orb) above the tree-
tops to the east, and I at once set out on my journey. The
road from the Notwani Ford just led me for about four miles
along the Limpopo, and then, finally leaving the river, bore
away due north towards Bamangwato. My horse—I was
riding Nelson, who, as I have said before, was a first-rate hack
—was in very good order for a journey, and got over the
ground at a very fair pace, alternately cantering and walking
with a quick springy step. The moon soon rose well above
the trees, and cast a soft white light over the forest-covered

country through which my road led. It was a hot sultry night, without a breath of wind, and the fine dust stirred from the sandy road by my horse's hoofs remained suspended in the air in clouds behind me. An intense stillness prevailed, unbroken by the cry of either bird or beast, or the hum of the tiniest insect—the death-like stillness of the waterless forests of south-western Africa.

After having ridden for about an hour and a half, I passed the large "vley"[1] of Moruling, which is seldom without water at this time of year, but was now as dry as a bone. By this time I had realised that, however romantic it may be in theory to ride by moonlight, alone, through wild African forests, it is uncommonly slow and dreary work in practice. However, as I had undertaken the ride, I was bound to go through with it ; and at any rate I knew I had a good horse under me that would carry me without fail to my destination. It must have been about ten o'clock, I suppose, when I reached a place known as the Brack Reeds. This is a valley in which there is an old river-bed, in former times doubtless a running stream, and a tributary of the Limpopo, but in which, at the present day, there are only to be found a few pools of brackish water, at which it is dangerous to let cattle drink, as it often brings on severe purging. It was here that I had determined to off-saddle for the first time, so, turning my horse from the road, I loosened his girths and eased him of his burden ; then, laying my rifle on the saddle, I put on him a pair of hobbles, that I had brought for the purpose, to prevent him from straying. Behind me were a few scattered thorn-bushes, towards which my horse at once betook himself, by a series of little jumps, in search of grass. In front of me lay the open valley of the Brack Reeds, covered with grass only a few inches in length, which, scorched and shrivelled by the blistering sun, looked almost white in the moonlight. I intended to give my horse about half an hour's rest and then continue my journey, so I walked to one of the thorn-bushes behind which he was now feeding, and stretched myself flat on my back with my hands beneath my head and my large slouched hat pulled over my face to keep the moon out of my eyes.

---

[1] A hollow which holds water during the rainy season.

I had been lying thus upon the ground for perhaps a couple of minutes, listening to the slight noise made by my horse as he cropped the short dry herbage. Suddenly the sound' ceased. For a few seconds I lay dreamily wondering why it did not recommence ; but as there was still silence, I rolled quickly over on my stomach, and, looking under the bush to ascertain why my horse had stopped feeding, I saw that he was standing in an attitude of fixed attention, with ears pricked forward, intently gazing towards the road. I instantly turned and looked in the same direction, and as instantly saw on what the horse's eyes were fixed. There, not thirty yards away, and right in the open, a lioness, looming large and white in the brilliant moonlight, was coming up at a quick and stealthy pace, and in a half-crouching attitude. In an instant I was on my feet, and the lioness, probably observing me for the first time, at once stopped and crouched perfectly flat on the ground. The saddle and rifle lay out in the moonlight right between me and the lioness, though nearer to me than to her. It was not a time to hesitate. I knew she must be pretty keen set, or she would have retreated upon seeing me ; and I felt that if I remained where I was, she would resume her journey towards my horse, which might end in my having to carry the saddle back to the Notwani. Obviously the only thing to be done was to get hold of my rifle ; so I walked quickly forward into the moonlight towards where it lay against the saddle. I must confess that I did not like advancing towards the lioness, for I knew very well of what hungry lions are capable ; and there is nothing like experience to damp the foolhardy courage of ignorance. However, whilst I took those dozen steps she never stirred ; but just as I stooped to grasp my rifle she sprang up with a low purring growl, and made off towards some thorn-bushes to her right. I fired at her as she ran, and, though I certainly ought to have hit her, I must have missed, as she neither growled nor changed her pace. But I was fairly well pleased to have driven her off, and lost no time in loosening my horse's hobbles and saddling him again.

My idea is that this lioness had come a long distance on my horse's spoor—perhaps all the way from the river, as when I saw her she was just leaving the road at about the spot where

I had turned off it with the horse ; and he no doubt observed her as soon as she came in sight on the road, whilst, being amongst the bushes, he himself was invisible to her. At any rate, had I lain quiet for another ten seconds, she would have been on my horse, and I should probably have had to trudge back to my waggon with the saddle on my back. All things considered, I thought myself well out of the adventure, though it certainly would have been much more satisfactory had I killed the lioness. Nothing further occurred to disturb the monotony of my long night ride, and about seven o'clock the following morning I reached Bamangwato, having done the seventy miles—much of it over very sandy ground—within twelve hours.

Khama, with the courtesy which he is always ready to extend to all those who have not abused it, at once gave me leave to take the road I wished to travel ; but, as it turned out, there was no need to do so. The weather suddenly changing, heavy rains set in, which refilled all the dried-up "vleys," and soon coaxed the withered herbage back to life. So, getting a friend in Bamangwato to take me out in a light waggon to where I had left my own at the Notwani (for to have ridden back again in the rainy weather that had now set in would have been anything but pleasant), I was able to travel by the ordinary route, and find abundance of water for my cattle at every outspan.

More than five hundred miles to the north-east of the scene of the adventure last narrated, on the banks of a small stream, a tributary of the River Bili, and in the midst of the well-watered valleys and verdant forests of Northern Mashunaland, I formed a hunting-camp early in June of the same year, 1882.

On 20th June I returned to camp after an absence of ten days. I had been away buying maize for my horses from Lo Magondi's Mashunas, and nearly fifty of them had followed me back to camp in the hope of getting some meat. On the day after my return I employed these men in strengthening the fences enclosing my camp and cattle kraal, which adjoined one another ; in the former of these stood my waggon, to which my horses were tied at night, and a hut occupied by some of my boys.

My waggon was of the kind known as a buck waggon, on the hinder part of which stood a tilt or tent where I slept when in camp, the front part being used to pack stores, specimens, etc., while over the whole was stretched a large canvas sheet, in the shelter of which, and under the waggon, slept my driver, Norris, and the Griqua lad Laer. When I went to buy corn I had taken the wheels and "understel"[1] from the waggon, and by putting in a short "langwaggon"[1] and making a false bed-plank, constructed a small light vehicle, whereon I could carry a couple of thousand weight, which could be easily drawn by eight oxen. This, with the bags of corn still upon it, was standing just at the gate of my camp, the body of the large waggon within the camp being supported on strong piles driven deep into the ground.

On the day of which I am speaking, and whilst most of the Mashunas were at work strengthening my camp, I rode out with the rest of them and my own boys to try and get some meat, and shot three sable antelopes—a big bull and two cows. As they were all fine animals, and this being the cold season their glossy black coats were in excellent order, I determined to prepare them for specimens, and so carried back their skins, skulls, and leg-bones with me to camp. When I got home it was too late to prepare them that day, so, as at this time of year there was no fear of their going bad if left for a night, I folded them up to keep them from getting dry, and laid them down inside my camp, behind the waggon, where the high thick fence shaded them entirely from the afternoon sun. As I had an hour to spare, and as the boys who had remained in camp whilst I was away buying corn had told me that the hyænas were very bold and troublesome and came prowling round the place every night, I thought I would set a gun for their benefit. By sundown I had my gun ready set alongside of an ant-heap about two hundred yards from camp. I then tied up my dogs, lest they should smell the bait and meet with the fate intended for a hyæna. Though, as a rule, I seldom have less than ten dogs with me in the hunting veld, and often more than twenty, this season I possessed only three. One of these was a fine

[1] Understel is the lower part of a South African waggon upon which the body is supported. The langwaggon is a portion of the understel.

large mongrel named Blucher, an excellent watch-dog, very plucky, and altogether about the best of his kind that I have yet seen in Africa. The other two were mere puppies, not more than six months old, but Blucher had already made very sharp watch-dogs of them. The waxing moon was about four days old and already gave a pretty good light until it set, which, I suppose, was about ten o'clock, so I did not expect

ANT-HEAP.

the hyænas to come about before that time. However, I had scarcely finished my evening meal—and it could not have been later than eight o'clock—when the set gun (an old six-to-the-pound, heavily loaded with a charge of slugs) went off with a tremendous report, and I made sure that a hyæna must have lost the number of his mess. Followed by Norris, Laer, and nearly all the Kafirs, I at once ran out to see what had happened, but we found nothing lying dead at the ant-heap, as I had expected. I then sent for a light, and told some of my boys to let the dogs loose. But we could find no trace of blood, nor could there have been any about, for had there been Blucher would have discovered it. What happened I think is this : a jackal had come to the bait instead of a hyæna. Had it been the latter animal, he would have taken the whole lump of meat into his mouth, and, as this was tied over the muzzle of the gun, would most certainly have had his head blown to pieces, but a jackal might just have seized the meat below the barrel, and, by pulling at it, exploded the gun without receiving the charge. If this was so, I think that jackal must have been startled. Thinking, however, that the same thing might happen again, I did not reset the gun, but, regaining the waggon, turned in, and lighting a candle, began to read.

Before proceeding farther, let me mention two things to which I shall refer later on. First, about ten yards from the entrance to my camp (which was just a gap in the fence, about three feet wide) there stood a large open packing-case, in which had been stowed the trading goods which I had made use of in buying corn. These I had removed, but in the bottom of the case were still lying an adze, an axe, several augers, and other tools. Secondly, inside my camp I had made a rough platform, the ends of the poles forming which at one side rested on the rail of my waggon. On this platform were packed several dried skins of large antelopes, all of them preserved for mounting, with the leg-bones attached. The three fresh antelope hides were lying, as I have said before, rolled up on the ground within the fence.

I had just left off reading and had blown out my candle, when Blucher and the puppies commenced a most furious barking, several hundred yards down the valley on the edge of which my camp was situated ; but I could hear that they kept coming nearer, as if retreating before an enemy. Pulling a blanket over my shoulders, I got up and stood on the rail of the waggon, listening. The moon was now down and the night very dark, and the barking of the dogs, which had never once ceased, was steadily and constantly approaching. Norris came out from under the waggon, and I asked him what he thought the dogs were barking at. He replied in Dutch, "Sir,

it must be a lion ; Blucher would not retreat like that before a
hyæna." As the dogs were now close at hand I got down
from the waggon, and, followed by Norris, walked to the gap
in the camp fence. Just as we reached it Blucher's deep bark
suddenly ceased, and some heavy animals came galloping past
us in the open ground between my camp and the stream
below, while at the same instant the two puppies rushed in
between our legs. Then everything was still except for the
occasional angry yapping of the puppies behind us ; but
Blucher's deep voice we heard no more, and I felt sure that he
was dead, and had, moreover, been killed by a lion, having
been caught in the rush we had heard. I wondered how it
was that he had not given a yelp when he was caught, but
concluded he must have been seized by the head and killed
instantaneously. Two of my Matabili boys, whose sleeping-
place was on the other side of the kraal, now came to me,
having made their way through the cattle, and reported that
some animal was crunching bones on the other side of the
camp. Immediately after, one of the Mashunas came running
in from their camp—which was just at the side of mine—
carrying a torch of blazing grass, and calling out, " Shumba,
Shumba ! lion, lion ! the lion has caught the big dog ! " which
I could have told him myself. He said that when the dogs
approached, barking and evidently retreating before something,
he and his comrades made up their fires, as they thought the
pursuers might be lions ; but that when they heard the rush
and the subsequent silence of Blucher, they felt sure that there
was one of these animals about, and that the dog had been
caught. After this, however, and just before he came to call
me, he said that he and his companions had heard something
walking over the dead leaves close behind their encampment.

I now took a double-barrelled 10-bore rifle which I had in
the waggon, and went back with the man to his camp, where I
found all the fires burning brightly, and the Mashunas sitting
up talking in low tones. Several of them asserted that they
had heard some animal walking stealthily among the dead
leaves with which the ground was strewn, just behind their
encampment ; so, accompanied by the man who had called me,
I went round to the back of their fence. Here we squatted

down, with our backs close against the fence, and peered intently into the darkness before us ; but for some time we neither saw nor heard anything. After sitting perfectly quiet for perhaps a quarter of an hour, I began to get very cold, and as the whole camp was now perfectly still, and the puppies had ceased barking, I thought the lion was probably satisfied with catching Blucher, and had withdrawn ; so I crossed to my camp, a distance of less than twenty yards, and again turned in. The boys sleeping in the hut within my camp had now made up a large fire, and one of them was sitting in the entrance behind it. I suppose I had been lying in the waggon for perhaps half an hour, and was just dropping off to sleep, when the puppies once more commenced to bark outside the encampment, and then came rushing through the gap in the fence. At the same moment the Kafir sitting by the fire, one of Khama's people, called out, " Here's the lion ! here's the lion ! he has taken the skin ! " I thereupon jumped out of the waggon again to find out what had happened. The Kafir boy whose cry had roused me had retreated into the hut, but came out when I called him. He said that a lion had come in through the opening in the fence, close behind the dogs, had stood for an instant in the full light of the fire, then seized one of the fresh-killed antelope skins and gone out with it. I went and looked, and, sure enough, there were now only two instead of three skins ; that of the bull was gone. Neither of my horses had stirred, though the lion must have been within ten yards of one of them when he seized the skin, and both of them must have seen him. I now loosened them, and Norris and I led them round to a small clear space behind the waggon, and there tied them up to the fence.

I thought that the lion would now be satisfied, for there is a good deal of eating in the skin of a sable antelope bull, and he had had the dog besides, by way of an entrée ; so, believing there was nothing more to be done, I again turned in. But on this night I was not destined to enjoy much sleep, for certainly within an hour of the last depredation, during the whole of which time my two young dogs had kept up a desultory barking, they again came suddenly rushing through the fence, and I felt sure that the lion was once more behind them. I heard Norris say to Laer, "It's the lion that's driving the dogs in again;" but none of the Kafirs in the hut spoke, and, with the exception that the dogs kept on growling and barking, everything remained quiet. Again I got out of the waggon, and saw that the fire in front of the hut had burned quite low, and that the Kafirs, having barricaded the entrance with logs of wood, were apparently asleep within. On calling to them I found, however, that this was not so, but that they were wide awake.

I now went to look at the sable antelope skins, and found there was only one left, proving conclusively that the lion had again come in and carried off the other. Being determined not to lose the third and last, I picked it up and threw it on to the waggon, and then, not knowing what else to do, went to bed again. I now felt no inclination to sleep, so lit the candle and commenced to read, wishing for daybreak, that I might come to conclusions with the lion or lions. I felt very vexed at the loss of my dog, and was determined to exact vengeance if possible. I now felt pretty sure that more than one lion was about, and feared they might yet get into my cattle kraal, which no doubt would have happened before this, if the fence had been in the same condition it was in on the previous day; but the Mashunas had luckily made it very high and strong, and the gate was blocked by thick thorn-bushes. My horses were in the safest place it was possible to find for them, so there was nothing more to be done but await events.

I had been reading for perhaps an hour, when the large empty packing-case which, as I have said before, was standing just outside the entrance to my camp, was violently moved, so that the augers and other tools lying on the bottom of it began to rattle loudly. I sat up and listened, hardly knowing what to make of it. "Master, master, hear the lion," called out Norris from beneath the waggon. Seizing my rifle, I jumped out, and proceeded cautiously to the entrance, followed by Norris. On looking out I could see the shadowy form of the large white case being moved about, whilst the tools in it rattled loudly. The lion must have been standing over it, and probably clawing about inside it, in the hope of finding something to eat. Look as I would, I could not in the darkness make out the form of the beast; however, there was no doubt about his being there, so I let go one barrel of the 10-bore right into the case. The lion at once apparently left it, as for an instant after the shot it was still; but he immediately returned and sent it rolling over, on which I instantly fired the left-hand barrel. I knew that I had missed him, or else shot him through the brain, with the second shot, for had I wounded him he would have growled; but up till now, he or they had never by the faintest purr betrayed what sort of animal it was that had been thus keeping me from my natural rest.

After sitting for more than half an hour at the entrance, gazing intently into the darkness, and getting very cold, I again got into the waggon, still keeping my candle alight; but for a long time everything remained perfectly quiet, and it seemed as if the lion or lions were at last satisfied with their investigations, and did not intend to trouble us further. My confidence was, however, misplaced. The dogs, now tired out and lying inside the camp by the fire, recommenced barking suddenly, and almost at the same instant the waggon was slightly shaken, and there was a disturbance among the dried skins, followed by a continuous rattling, first inside and then outside the camp. What had happened was this. For the third time the lion had entered the camp, and this time, finding nothing on the ground, had seized one of the dried skins which were packed on the platform I have before described. To do this he must either have jumped on to the platform or else reared himself on his hind legs, with his fore paws resting on it. When he took the skin he must have been within six feet of Norris and Laer, and only separated from them by the canvas sheet which hung down all round the waggon. Had they been accessible, he would probably have preferred one of them to a dry hide. Of course, directly I heard the noise I was out of the waggon again, and went round to the entrance. The leg-bones, which were attached to the feet, now kept rattling continually against the hard dry skin, as the lion, I suppose, tore at it with his teeth. From the sounds he seemed to have settled down to work right in

front of the camp, and, as far as I could judge, not more than
thirty yards off. Norris was standing beside me, and kept
asserting that he could see the lion, and wanted me to let
him fire ; but, as I was quite sure he was mistaken, I would
not do so, though, as the rattling noise continued, I thought
I would fire a shot myself as near as I could at the spot
whence the sounds appeared to issue. This I did : the noise
at once ceased.   Then, after a few moments' pause, the silence
which had followed immediately upon the shot was broken by
a single roar or growl, which, had there been any doubt about
it before, would at once have settled the question as to what
kind of animal it was that we had to deal with. This was the
first and the last sound to which the lions gave utterance
during the whole of this eventful night. My shot, I fancy,
must have gone very near the animal, and slightly disturbed
his equanimity, for, after having expressed his annoyance by
this single growl, he retreated, dragging with him the skin,
which rattled as he went, towards the stream which ran down
the valley about one hundred and fifty yards below the camp.

During the remainder of the night nothing further occurred.
I did not turn in again, but dressed and then sat by the fire
and had some coffee made.   Every now and then I could hear
the noise made by the lions down by the water, as they gnawed
at the hard skin and rattled the leg-bones ; but they seemed
satisfied with the very tough nut they had to crack and not
inclined to revisit the camp.

When it was near daydawn I cleaned my rifle and had
two horses saddled up, one for myself and the other for
Norris.   At last day really began to break, and a rosy tinge
in the eastern sky showed where the sun would presently
make his appearance ; and as the darkness gradually gave
way to a dim grayish light, through which objects rapidly
became more and more distinguishable, I walked to the
gap in my fence and looked across the valley before me.
At first I could see nothing, but presently, on the open
ground close down to the water, I thought I could distinguish a something, which might have been a small ant-heap
or a little bush, but that I knew nothing of the kind existed
there.   Presently I saw another something, longer and lower

than that I had first seen ; but what these somethings were it
was impossible to say, until, as slowly but surely the light grew
stronger, I descried with tolerable distinctness two lions, or rather
a lion and a lioness, lying on the open ground close to the bank
of the stream, and not more than one hundred and forty yards
or so from where I stood. The lioness was lying with her head
raised, looking straight towards the camp, and the lion about
ten yards to one side of her, broadside on, with his head on the
ground, perhaps still gnawing at the skin. I raised my rifle
and looked along the barrel, but not being able to see the
sights, I would not yet venture to commence the attack.
Another minute or two went by, and the lions did not move,
but still the light was not strong enough to enable me to see
the sights. Then the lioness stood up, and turning round,
walked slowly to the bank of the stream and disappeared,
followed, as I then first saw, by either two or three small cubs.
The lion at once rose and followed her. Although I could
still only see my rifle sights indistinctly, I was afraid to wait
any longer, for, except where I had burnt it off just round
my camp, the whole country was still covered with the long
summer grass, which, although scanty beneath the forests, was
in the open valleys about three feet high. I thought the lions had
gone into the bed of the river to drink, and that they would lie
there, and delay a little time before finally retreating. As the
banks of the stream were steep, I thought I might get a shot
at them before they became aware of my proximity. I had on
this occasion a single 450 Express by Henry of Edinburgh,
for, although my favourite little Metford, by Gibbs of Bristol,
was in the waggon, I had not been able to get the cartridges
for it up to the Transvaal in time to bring with me on the
present expedition. Norris carried the double 10. As soon
as the lions disappeared from view, I told Norris to get on his
horse and lead mine, keeping pretty close behind me, but not
so close as to spoil my chance of a shot ; I then advanced
quickly but cautiously to the bank of the stream, fully expecting to surprise them and get a very close shot ; but when,
having reached the point from which I could command a view
of the bed of the stream, I saw no signs of the lions, my disgust may be better imagined than described.

Running back to my horse, I hastily mounted, and telling
Norris to cross the stream and keep down the opposite bank,
cantered along the near side.   However, it was of no use, and
although we rode backwards and forwards, first along the
stream and afterwards in the forest skirting the valley, we saw
no more of the lions that day ; indeed, without dogs to follow
the spoor, it would have been by the merest chance had we
come across them.   They must have walked down the river
bed under the shelter of the bank, without pausing, when I saw
them disappear, and had probably emerged again a few
hundred yards down the valley in the long grass, and so made
their way into the forest.

They had won the first match, though I hoped I might yet·
turn the tables on them in the return.

On getting back to camp I found the lions had eaten all
the thinnest part of the dry hide, though the bulk of it was
still intact ; it had been cured with arsenical soap, but I do not
suppose they had swallowed enough of the poison to affect
them.   Of the wet sable antelope skins I could find no
trace but the leg-bones, and of poor Blucher no remnants whatever could be discovered.

I felt pretty sure that, unless the lions caught game in the
meantime, they would pay me another visit ; and as, until I
had come to an understanding with them, I could not leave
my camp on a hunting trip ; and as, even if I could find them
by daylight, the fact of the country being still everywhere
covered with the long summer grass would render the result of
the encounter extremely doubtful,—I determined to set guns
for them, and occupied the afternoon in constructing an enclosure with two openings, each protected by a gun.   In this
enclosure I placed a large lump of meat and the dried sable
antelope hide which the lion had destroyed.   I felt pretty
certain that if they returned they would endeavour to seize the
meat and infallibly come to grief.   Just about sundown I
heard one of the Kafirs call out, " Here's the big dog," and
running out, was immensely surprised to see poor Blucher,
whom I had mourned as dead, coming up slowly and with
hung-down head from the river.   The poor brute was in a
sorry plight, and I never saw either man or beast with a more

woebegone expression of countenance, though, when I spoke to him, he wagged his tail feebly.   His flank was torn open, the entrails in one place protruding, and he had several wounds on the neck.   On examining him I found that there were four holes through the skin of his neck, two on each side, but that the muscles beneath did not appear to be injured.   My idea is that the lion had seized him by the neck, but that the loose skin slipping up, the four large canine teeth had simply made four holes through the scruff of his neck, and perhaps, when the lion opened his mouth to get a better hold, the dog managed to make his escape, getting a claw wound as he did so.   What I cannot understand is that he never yelped when he was seized.   Can it be that the terror inspired by his dreadful position—a terror that caused him, when escaping, to rush away into the forest, and there lie hidden for nearly twenty-four hours before returning to camp—made him powerless to use his voice ?   Such a thing sometimes happens to human beings, so why not sometimes to dogs ?   I may here mention that about fifteen months after the events I am now describing, one of the two puppies I have spoken of, and which I still possess, was carried off from outside my camp at the River Manyami by a leopard.   She gave tongue lustily, and the other dogs—about a dozen in number—at once going to her assistance, drove the leopard off.   As, however, we saw no more of Ruby that night, and the next morning could find no trace of her, we thought she had been carried off and eaten, but on the evening of the following day she suddenly made her appearance, very badly bitten about the neck, and also with several claw wounds, having been away in the bush for more than forty hours after her escape from the leopard.   But to resume. I at once syringed out poor Blucher's wounds with strong carbolic lotion, and then, after pushing back the exposed intestine, sewed up the cut in his flank.   Although these wounds at last healed up, the poor dog seemed never to be himself again ; but, becoming thinner and thinner, and almost altogether refusing food, at last died a mere bag of bones.

In the evening I tied up the puppies lest they should go down to where the guns were set, and then, there being nothing more to do but await events, settled myself down for a read.

I did not expect that the lions would put in an appearance before the moon set, and was afraid hyænas might come before them. This was just what did happen. About an hour before the moon went down, one of the guns went off, but, as no sound whatever followed the report, I felt pretty sure it was not a lion that had disturbed the line ; so, accompanied by Norris, Laer, and a lot of Kafirs, I went down to see what had happened, and found a large spotted hyæna (*Hyæna crocuta*) lying dead in front of one of the guns. He had got the entire charge of buckshot beautifully, some through the shoulder, which must have pierced his heart, but the major part a little high behind the shoulder, so that his lungs must have been blown to pieces, and probably his backbone broken, which made him fall in his tracks. There was no doubt that the gun was well set, and had it only been a lion instead of the hyæna he would have got the charge just in the right place. Not knowing what to do with the carcase of the hyæna, I had it dragged within the enclosure, and then reset the gun, which, as the recoil had broken some of the fastenings and altogether deranged it, took me some time. We then returned to camp, hoping again to hear a gun go off, followed by the growl a lion would be sure to give when he received the charge. The night, however, passed over without any further disturbance from either lions or hyænas.

The next day I rode out with my own Kafirs and a lot of Mashunas to get some meat, taking Laer also with me. I was riding a very good shooting horse lent me by Lo Bengula,[1] with the single defect that he had but one eye, and Laer was mounted on a fast but bad-tempered pony that I had purchased in Bamangwato, of which animal I never succeeded in making a good shooting horse. During the morning I saw no game, but in the afternoon, on the way home, we came across a small herd of Tsessebe antelopes, three of which I shot. By the time we had skinned and cut them up it was getting late, and as, having started soon after sunrise, we had not yet breakfasted, Laer and I rode on in front of the Kafirs. After some time Laer stopped and said, " Sir, the Kafirs are shouting behind us." Reining in, I listened, and thought I too could just hear them.

[1] Lo Bengoola (Bengula), son of Umziligazi, and present king of the Amandibili.

I imagined they must have viewed either elephants or rhinoceroses, and, telling Laer to follow me, galloped back as hard
as I could towards the Kafirs.   Soon I could plainly hear them
shouting, and presently saw one of them standing on an ant-
heap in the middle of an open space between two belts of
forest.   The ground was covered with grass, not the long rank
grass of the moist valleys, but growing thinly and not more
than a foot in height.   Galloping up to Umlizan, the Kafir on
the ant-hill, I called out, " What is it ? " to which he answered,
" A lion ! a lion ! "   Whilst speaking I had gone some distance
past him.   " Where is he ? " I asked.   " There ! there ! close
in front of you, lying flat on the ground."   I instantly saw him
—a male lion, crouched perfectly flat, with his head on his outstretched paws, and certainly not more than twenty yards from
me.   I was too close to feel inclined to dismount, especially
as I was riding a steady shooting horse.   To rein in, turning
my horse at the same time, and to raise my rifle, was the work
of a moment.   My horse, however, would not keep perfectly
still ; and as I was trying to get the sight on to the lion's nose
below the eyes, I saw him draw in his forelegs, which had been
stretched out, under his chest ; then his whole body quivered.
I knew what these signs portended, and that he was on the
point of charging.   Just then I fired, and made a very lucky
shot, as, owing to the slight movements of the horse, I could
not get a steady one.   Seeing what was coming, I just touched
the trigger as the sight crossed the lion's face, and, luck being
on my side, the bullet struck him exactly between the eyes.
Had I been standing on the ground, the bullet would probably
have glanced from his skull, but firing as I did from the
horse's back, it drilled a small hole through the frontal bone
where it struck, and blew off a large piece at the back of the
brain-pan.   This lion's skull I sent to Mr. Alexander Henry
of Edinburgh, the maker of the rifle with which it was shot,
and have no doubt that he still has it in his possession,—at
any rate he sent me a letter of thanks for it.   Death, of course,
was instantaneous, and I at once set to work to skin him.
He was a fair-sized male, with a coat in very good order, but
without much mane ; his long perfect teeth showed he was in
the prime of life, but he was in very low condition—a rather

curious circumstance, as, although game was not particularly
plentiful in this part of the country, still it was by no means
scarce. The pads of his feet were worn quite smooth, as if he
had lately done a lot of travelling. I suppose he had had a
turn of ill-luck. Whether this lion was one of those that were
at my camp I do not know ; but I hardly think so, as we could
find no signs of sable antelope hide in his stomach. As soon
as we had skinned him, Laer and I again started on in front,
but were closely followed by the Kafirs. I carried the skin
with the paws attached folded round my waist and hanging
down behind me on each side, and the skull was tied in front
of Laer's saddle.

We had just entered the belt of forest on the farther side
of which ran the valley where my camp was situated, when
Laer, who was some thirty yards in front of me, his pony
having a quick ambling pace that my horse could not keep up
with, stopped, and turning round, beckoned to me. I thought
he had seen game on ahead, but, as I did not want to shoot
anything more, I did not hurry up to him. As I came near I
said, " What is it, Laer ? "—" It's another lion, sir," he answered.
" Where ? " I asked, dropping the reins and working as hard as
I could to unfold the skin that was twisted round my waist,
while at the same time I sought everywhere with my eyes in
front of me. However, I could not make him out ; but just as
I got the skin loose and let it drop to the ground, up jumped
a lion with a loud purr some fifty yards in front of me, and
went off through the forest as hard as he could.

Luckily, between the stems of the trees there was but little
underwood and the grass was nothing like so long and thick as
in the valleys, except indeed at the bases of the enormous ant-
heaps with which these forests are studded, where the grass
always grows longer and thicker than anywhere else. As the
lion made off I dug my spurs into my horse's ribs, and after a
race of three or four hundred yards, the lion, finding that he
could not get away from me, stopped suddenly at one of the
large ant-heaps I have just spoken of, faced round, and stood
with glaring eyes and open mouth, his head held low between
his shoulders, looking as savage as he could, growling hoarsely,
and twitching the end of his tail from side to side. Pulling in

my horse, I tried to fire again from his back, but he was excited by the gallop, or perhaps the growling of the lion disconcerted him, and he would not stand still at all. My antagonist looked so nasty that I scarcely liked dismounting, as I was pretty close to him, and when a lion is driven to bay as this one was, it is impossible to tell at what instant he may make up his mind to charge. If he will wait till you are on the ground, of course you have a very nice shot ; but he may make his rush just as one is dismounting, and neither on the ground ready to shoot nor on the horse ready to gallop off. But this day the luck was all in my favour. I dismounted, and taking a quick but steady sight, planted a bullet just between his neck and shoulder, on receiving which he reared himself up with a loud roar, and fell over sideways, while I inwardly said to myself, " I've got him." The lion was lying half in and half out of the long grass, but my horse having twisted right round as I fired, I had to take my eyes off him to remount, and when, on regaining the saddle and turning the horse's head, I again looked at the same spot, the lion was gone ! I felt sure I had given him a dead shot, and thought he must have just managed to wriggle himself into the long grass, and might be lying there dead. I rode closer, then right up to the grass, which stood just in a patch round the base of the ant-heap, but was over six feet in height and very thick. I could, however, neither see nor hear anything. Presently Laer came up with Umlizan and some of the Mashunas, for whom he had had to wait, as the pony would not allow him to put the skin of the lion first shot on its back. As soon as they came up I again rode close to where the lion had disappeared, and called to Umlizan to come and climb a tree close by, from the top of which I thought he might be able to see the lion lying in the grass, probably dead. However, though he went to the top, and said he could see well into the grass, he could not discover the creature's whereabouts.

The sun was now very nearly if not quite down ; I did not wish to lose the lion, or leave him to be eaten by hyænas during the night, and at the same time I did not half like going into long grass after him when I was not quite sure that he was really dead. However, after a little more hesitation, I resolved to take the bull by the horns, and so, dismounting, walked into the grass, holding my rifle cocked and ready for action.   I soon found out that the lion was not there, either dead or alive, and the blood track showed me where he had gone out the other side.   Here again the grass was short and sparse, and by the dull evening light I could see a whitish line through it, that marked the lion's track, which I could not have seen by sunlight.   Mounting my horse, and followed by Laer, I went rapidly along this track.   About one hundred yards farther on there was a patch of longer grass, and as soon as I neared it I walked my horse very slowly, as I fully expected to find the wounded beast lying in it.   Nor was I mistaken, for on reaching it I saw him lying, as I thought, dead, about five yards in front of me.   He was lying stretched on the ground, not flat on his side certainly, but half on his side, with his hind quarters nearest me, and certainly dying, although he was not, as I thought, dead.   "Here he is," I called out joyfully to Laer, under this impression.   Hardly were the words out of my mouth than the lion was on his feet and round on me with marvellous quickness, growling savagely ; but at the first movement I had wrenched my horse round, and dug the spurs into him and was at once in full flight closely pursued.   He did not come more than twenty or thirty yards, his strength probably failing him, and I pulled up at once, as I saw that an accident had happened to Laer.   He was some ten yards behind me when the lion charged out, and turned his pony and galloped off parallel with me ; but about twenty yards beyond where the lion stopped I suppose the pony shied at something, for I saw his rider fall off, and at once reined in.   Laer, let me here say, had a strong thong fastened to his waistbelt at the one end, and to a running loop on the bridle at the other, in imitation of the thin thong which I generally use, but which I always arrange in such a way that I can loosen it in an instant.   He, however, had simply tied it in a knot to his waistband, and was fast bound to the horse.

The position was now this : the lion was standing with open mouth, from which blood was flowing, growling savagely, and looking like nothing but a wounded and furious lion, whilst right in front of him, and within thirty yards, stood Laer's

refractory pony, backing towards the lion, and pulling with him
Laer, who, of course, was looking full into his open jaws, which
he did not seem to admire. I think I shall never forget the
momentary glimpse I had of his face. He was at that time
only a lad of about fifteen or sixteen years of age, and there
is no wonder that he was frightened—but frightened he most
certainly was ; his hat had fallen off, his mouth was wide open,
and his eyes staring, and he was pulling desperately against the
horse, which was steadily dragging him nearer to the lion. I
was a little to the right of Laer and a little farther from
the lion, but not much, and he looked alternately at the two
of us. I am sure it was simply want of strength that prevented him from coming on and mauling either Laer or the
pony, for before I could raise my rifle he sank down on the
ground, but still kept his head up, and, with his mouth
wide open, never ceased growling or roaring (I do not know
which is the better word). Of course I fired as quickly as
I could, the circumstances not admitting of any delay. I
aimed right for his open mouth, and at the shot his head fell
so suddenly, and in such a way, that I knew the bullet had
reached his brain.

The whole of this scene, which has taken so long to
describe, was, of course, only a matter of a few seconds. On
going up to the lion I found that my bullet had struck him
in the right eye, which was, of course, wide open at the time,
and had not touched or injured in any way the lid or eye-
lashes either above or below—not a very good shot, as I aimed
for his open mouth at not more than forty yards, but a very
effective one. We could now hear the two young dogs
barking at the waggon, from which we were distant about
a quarter of a mile, and by the time the lion was skinned it
was quite dusk. There was no doubt about his being one of
those that were at the camp two nights before, as on cutting
him open we found large pieces of sable antelope skin still
undigested in his belly. Like the lion first shot, he was an
animal in the prime of life, in very good hair, but without
much mane. As the spot where we first saw him was less
than half a mile from my camp, I feel sure that had we not,
by mere chance, ridden right on to him and killed him, he

LAER AND THE LION.

"The lion was standing with open mouth, from which blood was flowing, growling savagely, and looking like nothing but a wounded and furious lion, whilst right in front of him, and within thirty yards, stood Laer's refractory pony, backing towards the lion, and pulling with him Laer, who, of course, was looking full into his open jaws."

would most certainly have paid us a second visit the same night.

Where the lioness was I do not know, but I expect she was not far off when we first saw her mate. I fully expected that, in spite of his death, she would come smelling round the waggon, and my first care on getting back was to see that the guns were properly set. However, though another hyæna came and got shot, she did not put in an appearance, and I think she must have been scared by the death of her companion and left the district, as, during the remainder of the hunting season, neither she nor any other of her kind ever troubled me again. From this date (22nd June) until the following December I was continually hunting and travelling, and during that period went on foot to the old Portuguese town of Zumbo, situated at the junction of the Loangwa and Zambesi rivers, and was during the whole time in a country where lions were always prowling about, though nowhere plentiful ; yet, though I sometimes heard them at night, I never got sight of another, and I consider it a most extraordinary instance of good luck to have chanced upon two single lions in one day as I have described.

CHAPTER III

DURING the following six weeks I shot and preserved a great
many fine specimens of the larger African antelopes, some of
which may be seen in the New Natural History Museum at
South Kensington, whilst others are in the collection of the
South African Museum at Cape Town.   By the beginning of
August I had got all the specimens it was possible for me to
carry on my waggon ; so as it was too early in the year to
return to Matabililand, I determined to cross the Hanyani
river (or Manyami as it is called by the Mashunas), and then
make my way down to the Zambesi.

Whilst I had been hunting, my old friend Mr. George
Dorehill had come into the country on a shooting trip, together
with his wife and two young children, and I think that Mrs.
Dorehill was the first English lady who travelled in Mashunaland, though the wives of several Boer hunters had previously
been in the country.   Mr. Dorehill had formed a camp not
many miles away from mine, and the first time I visited him,
as I was following his waggon track, I came suddenly upon

LEOPARD FEEDING ON RHINOCEROS CARCASE.

"The leopard was so much occupied with the business he had in hand that he neither saw nor heard my horse approaching, and I reined in and shot him through the shoulders before he knew I was near him."

the remains of a black rhinoceros he had shot, and saw a leopard feeding at the carcase, a lot of vultures sitting on the ground all round, but at a respectful distance. The leopard was so much occupied with the business he had in hand that he neither saw nor heard my horse approaching, and I reined in and shot him through the shoulders before he knew I was near him. He fell to the shot, and died almost immediately ; and I at once took off his skin and carried it to my friend's waggon. This leopard must, I presume, have been excessively hungry to have come out and fed at a carcase in broad daylight, as I found him doing ; but though not fat, he was not at all emaciated, and his skin was in very good order.

When I started on my journey to the Zambesi, I again slept at Dorehill's waggon, and the following morning crossed the Hanyani. At that time (1882) this river had long been almost the " Ultima Thule " of travellers and hunters whose expeditions had set out from the British colonies of South Africa, my friends George Westbeech and George Phillips—who in 1868 accompanied a Matabili army to Wata's mountain, and visited the upper course of the Mazoe—being the only Europeans who had ever been more than a day's walk in that direction. Unfortunately they did not take any notes of their journey, or map out their route, and as Mr. Thomas Baines never crossed the Hanyani, the whole country to the east of that river was either left a blank on the best maps or very erroneously filled in. For this reason I was anxious to travel through the country to some known point, such as Tete or Zumbo on the Zambesi, and map out the intervening country.

On 6th August I crossed the Manyami, and slept at Manyanga's, the chief of a small Mashuna village, and made a final start to the north-east early the following morning. My party consisted of Laer (who had become a very useful, handy, little fellow, and who, as he had been born and brought up in the interior, possessed a good knowledge of several native languages, besides speaking Dutch), two Matabili boys, two of Khama's people from Bamangwato, and three Mashunas. In addition to this rather mixed lot I also had a pack donkey, a strong, useful animal, whose services, however, it was not ordained that I was long to enjoy.

After leaving Manyanga's (the little village where we had slept), we travelled during the forenoon through thick Mahobo-hobo forests, crossing two small streams running to the north-west, tributaries of the Manyami. There appeared to be no game whatever in this district, as we saw no spoor of any kind. Whilst breakfasting, a pair of those rare and beautiful rollers (*Coracias spatulatus*), first discovered on the central Zambesi by my friend Dr. Bradshaw, came and perched upon the tree beneath which I was sitting. They were so close that I could see plainly their two long tail feathers, broadened out or spatulated at the extremity in the form of a paddle, which is the main feature which distinguishes them from their southern congener. Not having a shot gun with me, I was unable to shoot and preserve these rare and handsome birds, as I should have liked to have done. All this portion of the country had, at no very distant date, been thickly populated, almost every valley showing traces of old rice-fields, whilst large patches of thick forest had been cleared for the cultivation of maize, pogo corn, sweet potatoes, etc. Every cluster of rocks had been the site of a Mashuna village, many of which had not been long deserted. But the ever-present fear of invasion by the cruel and bloodthirsty Matabili had caused the natives of this rich and fertile tract of country to desert the homes of their fore-fathers and retreat towards the east and north.

Towards evening, having travelled continuously in a north-easterly direction, we reached a rocky hill standing conspicuously in the midst of an open country, on the highest rocks of which was perched a still inhabited Mashuna village. As soon as we saw the huts I sent my own Mashunas on in advance, to tell the people of my approach and friendly intentions. Otherwise, as I knew from experience, every man, woman, and child would have bolted, and I should not have been able to obtain from them the provisions I needed. The abject state of fear in which the inhabitants of this part of Africa were then living can scarcely be comprehended by the members of any society living under a powerful and settled government, and must have made their lives a misery to them. My whole party, including myself and the donkey, only numbered ten ; yet, after crossing the Manyami, until I passed the extreme limit of the Matabili raids, the people everywhere fled precipitately at our approach, the old women running from the cornfields, wailing and shouting, and the cattle and goat herds leaving their flocks to shift for themselves. It was often, indeed, with the greatest difficulty that my own Mashunas, after a lengthened parley, were able to persuade the villagers to come to my camp with provisions. They soon, however, gained confidence when they learnt who and what I was—an Englishman on a journey to the Basungos (Portuguese) on the Zambesi ; and then every man, woman, and child crowded round the camp ; myself—the first white man

NATIVE VILLAGE, MASHUNALAND.

any of the women and children had ever seen—and the donkey, an equally strange sight to them, being the great attractions. The name of the hill near the base of which we encamped was Ushamba, that of the head man being Umfan-ee-chee-ha. We were now close to the western end of the Umvukwi hills, and on their northern side. This range of hills, I found, commencing in a series of low wooded ridges, extends for a considerable distance from the Manyami towards the Zambesi, and forms a watershed, all the streams flowing from its northern slope running either into the Manyami or Zambesi, whilst those from its southern side flow into the Mazoe. As the natives here said there were lots of elands about, which fed every night through their cornfields, and were very insistent that I should try and shoot one, and as I myself would also have been glad to get a little fat for cooking, I resolved to stand over a day and see what I could do.

The following morning, therefore, I was early astir, and, under the guidance of the Mashunas, made a long round. However, we saw no elands, for, although there was much spoor in their old cornfields, none of it was that night's, and none, consequently, fresh enough to follow. Late in the afternoon we came upon a small herd of sable antelopes, of which I shot the bull. He was a fine, handsome animal, but carried a small pair of horns ; being in good condition, however, his meat was excellent. The Mashunas brought every fraction of the animal (intestines included, of which they are very fond) into camp, and I then gave about half the meat to the town, and with part of the rest bought some rice and ground nuts.

On 9th August I again resumed my journey, travelling in a general direction somewhat to the north of east, our route running parallel to the great range of Umvukwi. During the morning we crossed the River Umkwasi, a tributary of the Manyami, a pretty little purling stream, whose limpid waters ran noisily over a pebbly bed. Both before and after crossing the Umkwasi, we passed several native villages, all perched amongst small detached rocky hills. The inhabitants, however, must have seen us from afar and fled at our approach, as, although the fires were still burning (on some of which pots were left cooking), we saw neither man, woman, nor child. Some of them were doubtless watching us as we looked about amongst the huts, examining their household utensils, yet, although my fellows shouted lustily that we were not Maziti (Matabili), but a party of peaceful travellers, no one mustered up sufficient courage to come near us. The country about here is undulating and well watered, open glades and patches of forest alternating.

In the evening, after a hard day's walk, we reached Chikasi's hill. On this day the sun set exactly west-north-west by compass. Chikasi's hill is one of many very remarkable rocks about here, immense blocks of stone rising sheer from the level

plain to a height of several hundred feet. The huts and store-
houses for rice and corn were built on the very summit of this
huge rock, which must be altogether impregnable to such foes
as the Matabili, as on the one side it is a sheer precipice
several hundred feet in height, and on the other can only be
scaled by its inhabitants in certain places by the help of rude
ladders. The daily labour entailed in carrying up wood and
water for cooking to the summit of this rock—a duty which
devolves entirely upon the women—must be very great, and
shows the state of terror in which these poor people were living.
Judging from the number of well-worn footpaths which we were
continually crossing, leading in all directions, and the utter
absence of game of any kind whatever, the country about here
must have been thickly inhabited. These people were formerly
very rich in cattle, sheep, and goats, the greater part of which,
however, had been swept off by the ferocious Matabili, so that
at the time of my visit they had but very few left. During the
day's walk I noticed in the open glades, where the young grass
was already several inches high, a great profusion of wildflowers, all of which might have passed for those one sees at
home in an English meadow. What I mean is, that though
many of them were very beautiful, yet there was nothing grand
or luxuriant about them to remind one that the soil on which
they grew lay far within the tropics. To all intents and purposes, however, owing to its altitude, this is a temperate country,
although the level descends continuously from the Manyami.
The temperature during the winter months is about that of
a fine English June during the day, though much colder at
nights.

It was nearly dark by the time we had completed our
camp, which we pitched beneath a large spreading tree, and
close to a fine spring of water, which, welling out of the rich
black soil, poured its waters into a clear stream that flowed past
the foot of Chikasi's hill. By this time we had established
friendly communications with the inhabitants—after a great
deal of cross-questioning and explanation, all shouted backwards and forwards between the summit of the rock and my
camp—and we were soon surrounded by all the villagers, who
at our invitation had brought ground nuts, pumpkins, and maize

(for the donkey) for sale. The head man, Chikasi, a venerable barbarian, with a placid and dignified expression of countenance, presented me with a hen and several eggs, and later on sent me three plates of prepared food, and seemed much pleased with the beads with which I, on my side, presented him.

My donkey now refusing to eat the maize which I had had cooked for him, and the natives assuring me that lions were unknown in this part of the country, I hobbled him, and turned him loose to graze during the night, as there was a nice patch of young grass round the spring, close alongside of our camp.

It must have been about an hour before daybreak when I heard the donkey clattering over a large flat stone just behind the camp. Surmising that something was behind him persuading him to run like this (for he was fast hobbled), I jumped up and ran out to try and get in front of him; but the short, sharp stubble of the burnt-off grass cut my naked feet so cruelly that I was soon obliged to halt. At this moment the donkey gave a cry—something between a bray and a scream—which sounded quite unearthly in the stillness of the night, and I knew the poor brute was in trouble. I now shouted to my Kafirs, and, as they came running up, we again heard the donkey making most distressing noises not far off, and whilst I returned to camp to get my shoes they ran to his assistance, as we already guessed he was attacked by hyænas. Almost immediately afterwards my boys returned with the news that they had reached the poor animal too late, having found him upon the point of death, a wretched hyæna having torn his entrails out. It was now very near daybreak, so I sat by the fire until it was just getting light, and then, taking my rifle, went to where my poor donkey lay, in the hope of finding his destroyer still at the carcase. The loathsome brute, however, had never returned, after having been scared away by my boys, and so had only killed the donkey, without eating a morsel of the meat. He had seized the unfortunate animal from behind, between the legs, and tearing open his belly, had dragged out the entrails. It was whilst undergoing this dreadful torture that the poor creature must have shrieked out in his agony.

About an hour after sunrise the following morning we again made a start, and, travelling to the north-east, reached the pretty little River Mutiki, after a walk of about three hours. This river, like the Umkwasi, so the natives told me, pours its waters into the Manyami.   After breakfast we again pushed on, and presently reached a large town, the inhabitants of which had only deserted it a few days previously.   As I wanted to purchase food, we followed on their tracks, which led us about ten miles to the north, considerably out of our way.   When we at last came up with them the sun was nearly down.   We found them busy building a new town, and chopping down the forest all round to make clearings for their cornfields.   These people had a considerable herd of cattle, and I was enabled to buy a potful of delicious milk from them.   We were now beyond the farthest point ever reached by a Matabili marauding expedition, and might therefore have expected to find the people on ahead in possession of cattle in some numbers.   The country through which we had travelled this day was very hilly, not to say mountainous, and to the north and east, as far as we could see, it appeared to be very rough and broken.   The name of this town, or of its head man—I am not sure which—was Se-fu-pi.   There appeared to be no game whatever in this part of the country.   On the following day we travelled to the north-east, getting close to the mountain range of Umvukwi towards evening.   In the course of the day we saw a wart-hog and a small herd of zebras ; but they got our wind, and I was not able to get a shot.   After leaving Se-fu-pi the country was at first very rough and hilly, becoming more undulating as we neared Umvukwi, and well wooded throughout.   Late in the afternoon we crossed the Dandi, another tributary of the Manyami river.   A couple of hours' walk the next morning brought us to the base of the Umvukwi range, which we struck at the foot of a bare precipitous crag, called Inyambari.   Here we found numbers of small native towns, perched upon the hills, lying in every direction ; in fact, there was a large native population in the neighbourhood, who seemed very comfortably off, and were in possession of numbers of cattle and large flocks of goats.

After breakfast we continued our journey, but, getting into

a maze of stony hills, were forced to go off our course a good deal. Just after sundown we reached a small stream, the Savakaranga, where we slept. There was said to be tse-tse fly here.

On 13th August we continued our journey for about two hours in a general northerly direction, through a succession of steep stony hills, until the footpath we were following brought us to a small village at their foot. From this village a flat forest-covered country stretched away as far as one could see to the north and north-east. The head man of the district was named Garanga. He seemed a friendly old man, and said that if I would remain at his town for a day, he would give me two boys to show me the way to the Portuguese on the Zambesi (for a consideration, of course); so, as my feet were rather sore from walking over the stony hills during the last two days, I agreed to do so.

We had now descended into the Zambesi valley, and both birds and insects were more numerous than amongst the rugged hills we had just left. I saw here, amongst others, the beautiful scarlet-winged plantain-eater (*Corythaix porphyreolopha*), so conspicuous both for the beauty of its plumage and its loud harsh cry of Glock-glock-glock. I also noticed along the little river which ran beneath the village three species of kingfishers: . the great African (*Ceryle maxima*), the common black and white (*Ceryle rudis*), and the lovely deep blue one (*Alcedo semitorquata*), somewhat similar to, though larger than, our English bird. The very small blue kingfisher (*Corythornis cyanostigma*) so common on most African rivers I did not see, though it, too, is doubtless a native of these parts. I also saw what was to me a new species of bee-eater, the body dark green, and head, throat, and breast red, with no long feathers in the tail. A whole colony of them had taken possession of a high bank for a nesting station, and drilled it with holes in a manner that reminded me of the nesting-places of sand martins at home. I caught here several (to me) new species of butterflies, one a very handsome species of Vanessa, I think. My old friend, the tse-tse fly, was also now commencing to make his presence disagreeably felt.

Early next morning I left Garanga's, with three of his men

as guides.   At first we took a path that led north-north-east as far as the little River Kadzi, where we breakfasted.   We then held a better course for the rest of the day to the east-north-east, crossing a tributary of the Kadzi, the Ma-ovi, soon after breakfast. The path we were following now took us along the Kadzi for the rest of the day, and we camped on its bank.   The country is quite flat about here, and covered with open Mopani forests. Along the river there is a great deal of palm scrub, and I was often reminded, in the course of the day, of the country along the banks of the upper Chobi.   In the morning I saw two small herds of zebra and a few Impala antelopes, and along the Kadzi there was a good deal of buffalo and black rhinoceros spoor ; I also noticed the tracks of a fine herd of elephant bulls, which had crossed the river a few days before.   In the evening I shot a wild pig (wart-hog), which was the first head of game I had bagged, or had had a chance of bagging, for some days.   The tse-tse fly swarmed along the River Kadzi, and was a great pest, keeping one in a perpetual state of irritation all day long.

The next day we made about fifteen miles to the north-east, and slept at the little River Biri.   As we reached our camping-place some time before sundown, I went out to see if I could not shoot anything ; but, though I saw a herd of waterbuck and wounded one of them, I lost it in the bush, and eventually got back to camp long after dark, tired and dis-appointed.   That night a lion roared close to us.

On 16th August I started before sunrise, and, after a hard walk of over three hours, reached a small stream of water. From here, about another five miles brought us to the River Umsengaisi, which, where we crossed it, was about two hundred and fifty yards broad, with a sandy bed, over which the water ran with a good current, nowhere more than knee deep.   Here I shot two Impala antelopes, so I determined to remain over for the rest of the day.   This river swarmed with the accursed tse-tse flies, which gave us no peace.   In the afternoon I took a stroll down the river catching butterflies, and saw herd after herd of graceful Impala antelopes coming down to drink. They were very tame, but, as I had meat enough, I did not attempt to molest them.   I also saw a good deal of spoor of

black rhinoceros ; these animals only come down to the river
to drink at nights, lying asleep during the day at some distance
off, where there is thick covert.   From where we were camped
this day we could see a range of hills, on the other side of the
Zambesi, apparently about fifteen miles to the north-east,
among which was one very high peak called Degoza.

Early the following morning we once more resumed our
journey, and at first followed the course of the Umsengaisi to
the north-east for about five miles, when we left it, and took a
footpath trending slightly to the south of east, which we followed
for about three hours ; we then turned again to the north-east,
and presently nearly due north, and, just at sundown, after a
hard day's walk over a very roundabout road, reached Chabonga,
as it is called by the Portuguese, a native town on the banks
of the Zambesi.   The chief of this place was an educated black
man, who had been brought up, I suppose, at Tete by the
Portuguese.   His name, he told me, was José Miguel Lobo,
but by the natives he was called Chimbuna.   He received me
very kindly, gave me the best dinner I had had for some
time, and a stretcher to sleep on in one of the empty
chambers of his low roomy house.   He was an elderly man,
and had been a great traveller in his time, knowing the
whole of the Zambesi country well, and having been by
steamer to Mozambique.   He told me that he had met with
Dr. Livingstone in the land of Cazembi, far to the north of
the Zambesi.

The following day, 18th August, I remained at Chabonga
with old Lobo, and bought a goat and a little tea and sugar
from him.   I was now enabled to get some definite information
as to my whereabouts, for although I knew I was somewhere
between Tete and Zumbo, I had but little idea how far I was
from these places respectively.   I first tried to carry on the
conversation in Kafir, but although, through my boys, I was
able to command three native dialects, neither of these was
altogether intelligible to old Lobo himself, or to any of the
men he produced as interpreters, and I finally found that I
could get on better with the very small stock of Portuguese of
which I was master.   My host informed me that I was only
four days' walk from Zumbo, whilst it would take me eight to

reach Tete, and, moreover, that the road to the latter place led
for much of the way through a very rough and hilly country.
Although I should have preferred going to Tete, and getting
back from thence to the Mashuna country along the course of
the River Mazoe, two reasons decided me to make for Zumbo
instead, and then ascend the Panyami, until I got somewhere
near to Lo Magondi's country, whence I could strike straight
for my waggon.   The first reason that led me to adopt this
plan was the dilapidated state of my one pair of " veldschoon,"
which were already in such a state of disintegration that I felt
sure they would never hold out through eight days of rough
walking to Tete ; and the second was the time that such a
journey would occupy, for, as my waggon was standing all
alone in the Mashuna country, with no one to look after my
property but some Kafir boys, I did not care about remaining
too long absent.   Having finally decided to start the following
day for Zumbo, I set to work to patch up my shoes with some
Impala skin, which occupied me for the greater part of the day.
The heat of the sun was now very great here, although the
nights were still cool and refreshing.   I noticed in the fields
round the town great quantities of tomatoes ; and old Lobo
told me that he raised a good quantity of wheat along the river,
and was always able to supply the Portuguese passing up or
down with as much as they wanted.   Just opposite here, on
the northern bank of the river, was a high flat-topped mountain,
called Matemwi.

On 19th August, after having breakfast with old Lobo, I
bade him adieu, and started westwards towards Zumbo, getting
as far that day as the mouth of the River Umsengaisi, near the
farther bank of which we slept.   Just where this river emptied
itself into the Zambesi, and on the eastern bank, there was a
small native town, with a couple of square houses with broad
verandahs standing out conspicuously among the round native
huts.   This town belonged to a half-caste Portuguese named
Perizengi, who at the time of my visit was absent on a slave-
trading and hunting expedition to the Senga country, north of
the Zambesi.   At this village I noticed three women tied
together by their necks, newly-caught slaves doubtless ; but at
this time, although illegal by Portuguese law, slavery on the

central Zambesi was by no means a thing of the past, as some
people would have had one believe.

The following morning, after pursuing the course of the
Zambesi for some distance, we got into a well-beaten footpath
striking obliquely away from the river, and thinking that it
would prove to be a short cut across one of the large bends,
we took it and followed it for several miles, until at last, as it
began to trend more and more to the south, we became convinced that it would not lead us back to the Zambesi at all,
but would probably take us to some native town miles out of
our course. We now left the path and struck straight back
for the river, having to make our way through a lot of rough,
thorny bush and over several stony ridges intersected by
ravines full of brambles. In this thick bush we continually
came upon black rhinoceros spoor, much of it so fresh that I
expected every moment to see one of the animals themselves.
The black rhinoceros is still very plentiful throughout a large
tract of country along the southern bank of the central
Zambesi, as it doubtless is also in many other parts of the
interior of Africa, and it will be many years, perhaps centuries,
before it is altogether exterminated ; whilst its congener, the
large, white, grass-eating rhinoceros, whose range was always
much more limited, as it was entirely confined to those parts
of Southern, South-eastern, and South-western Africa where
were to be found the open grassy tracts necessary to its
existence, is upon the verge of extinction without there being
a single specimen, or even the head of one, in our national
museum. When we at last reached the Zambesi again, it was
just getting dusk, and we were all of us, I think, pretty tired.
Just where we struck the river a herd of hippopotami were
disporting themselves, and as long as I was awake I could hear
them snorting and bellowing.

The next day we made an early start, and, finding a well-
beaten footpath along the river's bank, got over a good deal
of ground during the day, reaching Matakania's town, which
was situated close to the mouth of the Manyami river (here
called Panyami), just after sundown. During the day I shot a
large crocodile and an Impala antelope. A little after dark,
when we had made a comfortable camp, and just as I was

about to make an attack upon my evening meal, a lot of Matakania's people came down and insisted upon my coming up to the town to sleep. At first I refused to do so, protesting that I was much more comfortable where I was ; but, upon their making a great fuss, and saying that I would not come to the town because I had a Matabili army behind me, and had come on to spy out the land, and that they would beat their war drums and summon the people from all the surrounding villages if I remained where I was, I thought it would perhaps be as well to humour them and avoid any chance of misunderstanding. Upon going up to the town I found that Matakania was away to the north of the Zambesi, in the Luisa country, somewhere near Cazembi, on a slave-trading and elephant-hunting expedition. No doubt, had he been at home, he would have treated me as well as did old Lobo ; as it was, the man he had left in charge of his town offered us no food, and only a dirty old hut to sleep in ; but, upon my refusing to enter a place only fit for dogs and Kafirs, they gave me a stretcher under the verandah of Matakania's large square house.

At daylight the following morning I packed up my traps ready for an early start ; but, upon going down to the river where the women were already getting water, I saw a hippopotamus about eighty yards from the shore, lying with its head and part of its back above the water, calmly looking at the people as they came down to the river. It was lying in a sort of backwater, out of the stream, so, knowing that if I killed it the current could not carry it away, I went and fetched my rifle, and, sitting on the bank, took a steady aim between its eyes as it lay stolidly gazing at me. The bullet struck it fair, and it gave one plunge forward, and disappearing from view, never rose again, so that I felt sure, as did all the Kafirs who were looking on, that it was dead. Knowing that the carcase would not rise to the surface for several hours, perhaps not till late in the afternoon, I unpacked my things again and made breakfast, intending to wait and see if I could not get any fat for cooking.

Whilst I was engaged upon my scanty meal, one of Matakania's daughters, a nice-looking young girl, came and paid me a visit, bringing as a present a piece of bacon and a plate of biscuits made from wheat grown on the banks of the river. About an hour later three large boats, of the kind called "escalere" by the Portuguese, flat-bottomed and built of planks, and capable of carrying about three tons of cargo, hove in sight, coming rapidly towards us from the direction of Zumbo, which was only about fifteen miles off. They were propelled not by oars but by paddles, four or five on each side, the blades of which flashed in the sunlight at every stroke. The crews sang merrily as they came towards us, keeping time to the music with their paddles. I was told they were "soldados" who had been on duty at Zumbo, and were now going down to Quilimane, and was in hopes that there might be a white Portuguese officer with them. When they arrived, however, I was disappointed to find that the man who seemed to be in command was as black as any of his crew. In the stern of one of the boats, beneath an awning made of bent saplings thatched with grass, a pretty though languid-looking mulatto, or rather quadroon girl, was reclining upon some mats. She was, I presume, the daughter of one of the Portuguese at Zumbo, and was probably going down to Tette or Quilimane to be educated. The three boats' crews only made a stay of a few minutes, and then, embarking again, departed singing blithely as before.

I now began to grow impatient, and eventually, as the presumably dead hippopotamus showed no sign of coming up, I once more tied up my things, and resumed my journey along the river's bank, hoping that night to reach one of the towns of Kanyemba, from whom I knew I should be able to get a boat to take me across the river to Zumbo. About ten minutes after leaving Matakania's town we crossed the mouth of the Manyami or Panyami, here a broad river, with but little water above its sandy bed, presenting a very different appearance from what it does near its source in the Mashuna country, where it is a succession of deep blue pools flowing swiftly amongst great boulders of rock, along the banks of which I have often roamed. Prior to my visit in 1882, the mouth of this river was always placed in the best maps a little to the west of Zumbo, whereas it really enters the Zambesi some fifteen miles or so to the east of that place.   This mistake, I suppose, arose through wrong information having been given to Dr. Livingstone as to the real position of the mouth of the river, when he first passed down the Zambesi, and again when he returned with his brother Charles Livingstone and Dr. Kirk in 1861.   As upon both those journeys he travelled along the northern bank, and therefore could not have seen the mouth of the Panyami himself, and as, in the twenty years that had elapsed since that time, no other Englishman had visited this part of the Zambesi, the error had remained unrectified.

After leaving Matakania's town we walked hard for the rest of the day along a well-worn footpath, and late in the evening, just as it was growing dusk, reached a small village, not far from one of Kanyemba's towns.   Here we slept. Just before reaching this village I shot a waterbuck, and the people went out and brought in all the meat.   The head man turned out a very good fellow.   He was an immense man, a good deal over six feet high, and very big and broad. He was deeply pitted with smallpox, and had, too, a wall eye, yet, in spite of these disadvantages, he had a rollicking, jovial expression of face.   His wives had just brewed a great quantity of strong beer, and he presented me with three enormous pots, each holding about ten gallons, besides some meal, and a hen with eight eggs.   My Kafirs naturally all got very drunk, and even then could not get through half of the beer.

Early the following morning I again pushed on, and reached Kanyemba's first town after about an hour's walk, and another two hours brought us to the village where he was then residing.   He knew me at once, for this was the same man I had met four years before on the Kafukwi and in the Manica country.   He at once agreed to put me across the river in one of his large boats, but asked me to stop and have breakfast first, which I was only too glad to do.   He was busy building a fine large new house at the time of my visit.   Amongst the people working were nine slaves (doubtless just caught in some recent raid) all chained together, an iron ring round their necks, and about five feet of strong heavy chain between each two. The chain was very new-looking, clean, and bright—which was doubtless a great consolation to the poor wretches. This town of Kanyemba's was on the banks of a small stream, a tributary of the Zambesi, but several miles from the great river itself.

After breakfast, Kanyemba, having first given me a sheep and a large basketful of meal, told off five Kafirs to take me across the river to Zumbo. It took us quite two hours to get down to the boat, which was about four miles above Zumbo, and from the point of embarkation we had a very pleasant trip down the river. Just above Zumbo the Zambesi emerges from a deep gorge in the mountains, and broadens out into a fine sheet of dark blue water, with only here and there a sandbank cropping up above the surface. About a mile above the town the River Loangwa, coming from the far north, pours a fine broad stream of water into the Zambesi. We passed a herd of hippopotami just before reaching Zumbo, and there was also a big old bull disporting himself within a hundred yards of the landing-place. As we stepped ashore one of the five white men (Portuguese) who were then living at Zumbo—Senhor Joaquim Andre Gourinho—came down, and, bidding me welcome, offered me the use of one of the many unoccupied houses, for the accommodation of myself and Kafirs during my stay—which was, however, only to be of a few days' duration—and I subsequently found him most kind and hospitable.

All the Portuguese here were mere wrecks of men—frail, yellow, and fever-stricken—and offered a strong contrast to the robust and powerful figures of the natives. Yet one would not imagine that the country about was very unhealthy, as both banks of the river were very dry and barren, and there was no appearance of marsh or swamp in the neighbourhood. The trade of Zumbo is confined to ivory alone, all of which comes from the countries to the north of the Zambesi, on both sides of the River Loangwa. Senhor Gourinho, who was the principal merchant at the time of my visit, and was also, I fancy, the agent for a house in Quilimane, had a good deal of fine ivory in his storehouse, and told me that not long before my arrival he had sent off two large boat-loads (10,000 lbs.) to Quilimane. I was told that six days' journey up the Loangwa there were plenty of elephants still, and fancy that Zumbo would not be a bad place for an enterprising hunter to fix upon as his basis for hunting expeditions to the north of the Zambesi. The Portuguese, however, whom one meets on the Zambesi are no sportsmen, and not only never hunt, but never even travel by land unless carried in a palanquin, nor even leave their houses in the middle of the day without an umbrella to protect them from the sun, exposure to the heat of which, they say, gives them fever.

The tse-tse fly swarms on both sides of the river in the immediate vicinity of Zumbo, so that cattle cannot be kept there ; but the Portuguese keep great quantities of lean, long-snouted pigs, which, being fed regularly every evening, and enclosed in yards at night, do not wander far from the houses. Goats are also plentiful at Zumbo, and fairly cheap. I was surprised to find that neither Senhor Gourinho nor any of his countrymen had thought of planting fruit-trees of any kind along the river, although he told me that he had been living there for eight years. He had, however, a very good and fruitful vegetable garden, which was watered by hand every morning and evening, and during my visit I revelled in peas, beans, tomatoes, and onions. He also grew his own wheat. During my visit to Zumbo I amused myself and passed the time in collecting butterflies along the banks of the Zambesi and Loangwa rivers ; it was, however, too early in the season, and I did not reap a very rich harvest. What I got, however, I subsequently forwarded, together with my Mashunaland collection, to Mr. Rowland Trimen, the well-known naturalist and energetic curator of the Cape Town Museum.

One day I took a stroll with Senhor Gourinho down the river to look at the ruins of the old town of Zumbo. Nearly two hundred years ago Zumbo was a flourishing place, it seems, with a governor, a Catholic church, and a college—the ruins of the two latter edifices being the only ones whose solid stone walls have in some places resisted time's all-destroying hand. The great trade of the country, my informant told me, was at that time in gold dust ; and it is difficult to understand why this trade should have so entirely collapsed as it has done, for the same forces that in days of yore brought the gold, grain by grain, from the mountains to the plains below are still at work ; and if there was payable gold in the river's sands then, so, one would think, there must be still.   Yet the only trade now carried on is in ivory, and the natives seem to have lost all knowledge of even the most primitive processes employed by their forefathers to extract the golden grains from the soil.

On 28th August I bade adieu to Senhor Gourinho and his fellow-exiles, all of whom had been most kind to me during my visit, and, getting across the river by ten A.M., soon left Zumbo and the fair Zambesi far behind me.   Striking pretty well to the south, we reached the banks of the Panyami, about ten miles from its junction with the Zambesi, and after a hot walk through dreary, parched-up, leafless Mopani forests.   As I went down for a bathe in the river I saw a pair of the great African kingfishers, and a handsome kinghunter (*Semi cærulea*, I think).   I had also seen during the day, whilst still near the ˙Zambesi, a flock of parroquets, or mouse birds, of a species unknown to me.   They were of a pale green colour, with rose-coloured heads and long tails.   I remember having seen a flock of the same birds once before on the northern bank of the Zambesi, near the mouth of the Kafukwi river.   As my friend Mr. Thomas Ayres of Potchefstroom, by far the most experienced, but at the same time the most modest and unassuming, of South African ornithologists, is unacquainted with this bird, I presume it is a species not yet known to science.

All round the spot where we pitched our camp for the night jasmine bushes were growing wild, and their uncultured blossoms smelt as sweetly as those of the creepers we are accustomed to see covering our walls at home.   The next morning we were up at daybreak, and made an early start in the cool of the morning, and when, after a steady tramp of more than three hours we called a halt, we had put a good piece of country behind us.   We followed native footpaths from one village to another along the banks of the river. These people are of a tribe called Matandi, who tattoo their

stomachs.   In the course of the morning I saw some koodoos
and Impalas, and also a wild pig, but, having food with me, did
not shoot.   Farther on we crossed the fresh spoor of a few
elands and of a large herd of buffaloes, and I also saw several
of the handsome purple plantain eaters, with bright scarlet
wings.   In many places along the banks of the river the whole
air was impregnated with a strong fragrant perfume, proceeding from the sweet-scented blossoms of a flowering shrub, growing plentifully in this district, that I had not met with elsewhere.   The tse-tse fly, too, was swarming, and we found it, as
usual, an intolerable plague.

Just where we breakfasted, a large river, the Angwa, ran
into the Panyami from the south-south-west ; it was over
three hundred yards broad, with a sandy bed but little water,
though during the rains it must become a large river.   After
breakfast we followed its course for about an hour and a half,
and then, crossing it, took a native footpath running due south,
which, after a three hours' walk through dry and dreary Mopani
forest, again brought us to the banks of the Panyami at a
small village, the name of whose head man was Inyonangwa.
In the evening we walked on to another village about three
miles distant, where we slept.   The head man of this village
was one Shangwi.

The following morning we walked about eight miles to
the south-south-west before breakfast, soon after which we
crossed the Panyami, at a place where our guide said there
were some hippopotami ; but, as we could see nothing of them,
I presume they must have travelled farther up the river.   Our
guide now wished me to remain here, that I might look for the
hippos, protesting that the nearest water was too far off for us
to reach that day.   Perceiving that there was something amiss,
and that the ingenuous youth had only come thus far with us
in the hope that I would shoot something, and would now
take the first opportunity to make a bolt home, leaving us to
find our way through the wilderness as best we might, I
insisted upon his going on until he brought us to the path
leading into the mountains, which were still some fifteen miles
in front of us, telling him that, if he did so, as he had agreed
to do when he started in our company, I would pay him well,

but that otherwise I was quite prepared to use force to make
him stick to his bargain ; and, seeing that I meant what I said,
he once more sulkily took the lead.   Half an hour's walk now
brought us to the little river Dandi, although our lying guide
had sworn we should not reach water that day, and we had
filled all the calabashes in consequence.   I said nothing, but
made him trudge along briskly in front.   We now kept amongst
the windings of the Dandi, until late in the afternoon, when we
took a large footpath leading a little more to the east, which
brought us at sundown to a deserted native village, just under
the hills.   Here were two deep pits, which the natives had dug
for water, but they were quite dry.   We then followed a small
watercourse coming from a gap in the hills, at the foot of which
we were, until it grew quite dark ; and it became a difficult
matter to make our way through the thick bush and giant,
tangled grass, the stems of which were as thick as one's finger.
Our guide now averring that we should find water in the next
gorge, we again moved on.   Suddenly (I was walking close
behind him) he made a dash through a patch of bush, sprang
into a small ravine and was gone, carrying off a calabash and
some other trifles belonging to one of my Kafirs.   I rushed
after him, as his desertion left us in no very enviable position ;
but in the darkness, the bush, and the long grass he soon disappeared.

   We held along under the hills for another hour, hoping to
find a stream issuing from them, or a native footpath leading
into them ; but crossing several of the former, all dry, and
fearing to cross the latter in the darkness, I called a halt, and,
lighting a fire, resolved to pass the night where we were.   We
had now been many hours without water, and the heat of the
sun had been, as it always is in the Zambesi valley, terrific, so
that we were all suffering from thirst.   Before lying down I
called a council of war, and debated with my boys as to what
would be the best course to follow on the morrow ; whether
we should retrace our steps to the Dandi, rest a bit there, and
then fill the calabashes and make a fresh start ; or, thirsty as
we were, strike forward into the hills, trusting to chance for
water ; and at length we decided upon the latter course.

   Before dawn we were up and stirring, and had everything

tied up and ready for a start as soon as day should break.   At
the first sign of dawn we struck for a gorge in the hills close
to us, and found a well-beaten native track leading into it.
Following this path, which climbed right up the very steep side
of the mountain, we came, after an hour's scramble, and when
close to the summit, upon a spring of water running out of a
little boggy hollow.   I need hardly say that we here called a
halt and made breakfast, not a very substantial one certainly,
as it only consisted of a little rice, but as we had been four-and-
twenty hours without food, even this and a cup of warm tea
was by no means to be despised.   After breakfast we again
followed our footpath, but it soon became very indistinct, and
before long disappeared altogether.

In front of us, to the south, there now lay nothing but a
mass of rugged hills, very high and steep, but as there was
nothing for it but to make our way over them, we set about it
without delay.   We crossed three chains running parallel to
one another about east and west, and then at last got amongst
some smaller hills, and in the afternoon struck a native footpath.   The labour entailed in climbing over these excessively
steep and stony hills under a burning tropical sun can hardly
be exaggerated.   This evening I was seized with an attack of
fever, the result of over-exertion during the last three days in
the broiling heat of the sun.   Could I have taken the proper
medicines and rested for a day or so, I have little doubt, from
former experience, that I should have shaken off this attack
without difficulty.   As it was, however, I had not a grain of
any sort of medicine, and to remain where I was for the sake
of rest meant starvation, as we were reduced to our last day's
food, having reckoned upon reaching the first Mashuna villages
the previous day.   So the next morning, 1st September, after
passing a feverish and unrefreshing night, I was obliged, in spite
of feeling very unwell, to push on again.   We kept to a native
footpath that we had struck the previous day, and, following it
for about eight miles, reached the River Dandi, after crossing
which we kept along its banks until we reached a cluster of
small villages, the name of whose head man was Shipurero.
Having ' rested for an hour here, and purchased some food, we
again pushed on, and a walk of about two hours brought us

to the little river Umpingi, where we slept. I had felt very
unwell all day, and in the evening was seized with a violent
attack of fever, which lasted the greater part of the night.
Towards morning, however, I broke out into a profuse perspiration, and soon felt much better, though excessively weak.

Before the sun rose we again made a start, so as to get the
full advantage of the coolness of the early morning. For about
two hours and a half I struggled on, but was then again seized
with fever and forced to lie down and coil up in my blanket.
All day long I was excessively ill—so ill, indeed, that I did not
think it would be possible for me to walk for some days to
come ; so I sent two of my boys back to a native village we
had passed that morning, to buy food. When they returned
four Mashunas came with them, who said they were going in the
same direction as ourselves, and would travel with us. Still
feeling very ill, and so weak that I did not think it would
be possible for me to walk for a day or two, I offered them
liberal payment if they would make a light stretcher and
carry me for three days. This they agreed to do, saying that
they would go back and sleep at their village that night,
and return early in the morning. During the night the fever
again left me ; I slept well and perspired tremendously, and on
the following morning, although I still felt as weak as a child,
and my head ached a bit, felt at any rate several hundred
per cent better than I had done on the preceding day.

About an hour after sunrise the four Mashunas came and
said they were ready to carry me, and my own boys having
made a light stretcher the preceding evening, everything was
ready. However, Shipurero's men now refused to carry out
their agreement, unless I paid them beforehand, demanding at
the same time a most extravagant price for their services. To
such extortion I determined not to submit, and resolved to
try once more what my own legs could do for me ; so, after
cursing them in five languages, I bade my own boys get everything ready, and again made a move forwards. I can imagine
nothing harder than having to walk thus in the hot sun, day
after day, when weak and ill with African fever, but there was
no alternative, as I was still a long way from my waggon in
the Mashuna country.

Being once on my legs, which were now thoroughly accustomed to walking, I got on as far as the little river Mabari,
quite six or seven miles, before taking a rest.   Where we
crossed it there was a pretty little cascade rushing over a solid
block of rock.   After a rest and a cup of tea, I again pushed
on, but the intense heat of the sun soon began to make me feel
ill again, and I did not get very far before I was obliged to lie
down.   That evening two of my Kafirs (one a Matabili and
the other a Mangwato) were knocked over with fever, and lay
groaning all night.

As I was now well beyond the limit of the tse-tse fly, and
within four days' walk, for a healthy man, from my camp
beyond the Manyami, I determined to send Laer on to the
waggon, with a couple of the Kafirs who were still well, for the
horses, and in the meanwhile remain where I was for the sake
of the rest ; and they started accordingly at daylight the following morning, 4th September.

About mid-day on 10th September Laer returned, bringing
with him one of the Matabili boys whom I had left in charge
of my cattle at the waggons, riding the spare horse.   I was
indeed rejoiced to see him, having spent a pretty miserable
time of it, waiting, and waiting, and waiting, for seven livelong
days and sleepless nights : for I had been excessively ill the
entire time, and had only broken out into a perspiration and
taken a turn for the better the night before his arrival.   My
two sick boys, too, were still both very bad, and professed themselves utterly unable to walk.   For my part, I was so utterly
tired of the camp in which I had lain so long inactive, that I
at once set about making preparations for a start, leaving the
Matabili boy who had just arrived, and the Mangwato
lad who had remained with me whilst Laer was away, to look
after their sick comrades, and come on with them by slow
stages as soon as they were able to travel.   Laer and I,
accompanied by my two Mashunas, saddled up the same
afternoon, and just at nightfall reached Chikasi's hill.   This
hill, it may be remembered, is the place where my donkey
was killed the preceding month as we were on our way to the
Zambesi.

As from this place we followed the same route we had

travelled before, and which I have already described, it would be superfluous to give any further account of it: suffice it to say that on 14th September I once more arrived at my camp, where, however, I was without medicine, and still about two hundred and fifty miles from the nearest white men (the missionaries and traders of the Matabili country). However, I had now quite got the better of the fever, and although I had a few subsequent relapses, they were slight and of short duration. The two boys whom I had left behind sick did not get to the waggon till the end of the month, and even then remained in a very precarious condition for a long time afterwards ; eventually, however, they both recovered. When Laer came back for me with the horses he had told me that the evening he had arrived at the waggons the two Kafirs who had accompanied him—the one a Matabili and the other a Mashuna—had been seized with fever, and on my arrival there I found them still very ill, and shortly after this Laer also got a sharp attack, which lasted him, off and on, until we reached the Matabili country ; so that, of our whole party of nine who had made the journey to Zumbo, only three—one Mangwato boy and two Mashunas— entirely escaped the fever. This fever was, I believe, entirely brought on by constant exposure to the intense sultry heat of the mid-day sun in the Zambesi valley, to which none of us were accustomed. In all other parts of tropical South Africa —both in the very hot, but at the same time intensely dry deserts of the west, and the well-watered uplands of the east— I have never found that exposure to the sun, even in the hottest weather, did me any harm ; but then, in those parts, the elevation was always about three thousand feet and upwards above sea-level, whilst the elevation of the Zambesi valley at Zumbo is, I believe, less than one thousand feet, which will perhaps account for the difference.

With my arrival at my waggon my little journey through unexplored country came to an end. Early in October I left my hunting camp in Mashunaland, and after an uneventful journey of about a month's duration, reached the Matabili country just as the rainy season was setting in. I did not remain there long, but journeyed down to Klerksdorp in the

Transvaal, and packed and despatched my collections to Cape Town and England. Then, after laying in a fresh stock of provisions and trading goods, I again set out for the interior, and in May 1883 pitched my camp on the banks of the Manyami river in Mashunaland.

ROCK PAINTINGS IN MASHUNA-
LAND.

CHAPTER IV

Prepare for journey to the Mazoe and Sabi rivers—Lichtenstein's hartebeest—Shoot
wart-hog and Tsessebe antelope—Shoot roan antelope cow with fine horns—
Eland hunting—Large wart-hog shot—Cross the Manyami—Fine country—
Devastations of the Matabili—Ostrich shooting—Find ostrich's nest—Wound
cock ostrich—A cold wet night—Resume my journey—Roan antelope shot—
Reach Sadza's villages—Eland hunting—Hyæna carries off eland skin—
Hyæna killed—Another eland shot—Skin spoilt by the natives—Reach the
Sabi—Description of natives of this district—Search for Lichtenstein's hartebeest
—Mount Gato—Cross the Masheki—Large baboon shot—Scarcity of game—
Cross the Sabi—Black rhinoceros shot—Lion heard at night—Return to main
camp.

IT was during the year 1883 that, after first having made an
unsuccessful search for elephants to the north and west, I pre-

pared for a journey across the Manyami to the head waters of the River Mazoe, and from thence to the eastern bank of the River Sabi, or Shabi, where I hoped to obtain specimens of the white rhinoceros (*R. simus*) for the British Museum, and at the same time of a species of hartebeest which I knew to be an inhabitant of this district of South-eastern Africa.

This hartebeest is the *Alcelaphus lichtensteini* of Dr. Peters, and was first met with by him in the neighbourhood of Sena on the lower Zambesi. I had myself seen and shot these animals near the Kafukwi river, to the north of the Zambesi, and believe it to be the common species of hartebeest met with in South-Central and Eastern Africa. However, with the exception of the specimens obtained by Dr. Peters which were in the Museum of Natural History at Berlin, and a couple of skulls purchased from myself by the British Museum, this animal was at the time of which I am writing unrepresented in all European collections ; and I was, therefore, anxious to get a few good specimens for mounting.

It was already the 11th of July before I was able to make a start. I took with me the lightest of my two waggons, pulled by fourteen oxen, and my two best shooting horses, and was, of course, accompanied by crowds of meat-hungry Mashunas. The first day I shot during the morning a wart-hog and a Tsessebe antelope, and in the afternoon a very fine roan antelope bull with a beautiful pair of horns, measuring thirty inches over the curve. The following day an incident occurred which is perhaps worth relating. I had been the whole morning engaged in trying to get hold of some elands, which during the preceding night had been feeding in the corn-fields of some Mashunas living close to where my waggon was standing ; but after having followed them for several hours, they had finally got my wind in some thick bush at the foot of a range of hills, into which they had retreated, and as I did not care to have my horse's feet knocked about, I left the spoor and rode home, reaching my waggon about three o'clock in the afternoon. After a good meal of cold wild pig's head, washed down with tea, I got restless again, and so called for my second horse, having resolved to take a ride by myself round a range of hills to the west of the camp, in the hope of

coming across elands in the evening, since I was anxious to
shoot one for the fat.   As I had not much time to spare, I
rode away at a canter, taking no Kafirs with me.   About a
couple of miles from camp, in an open valley between some
low hills, I came upon a large herd of zebras and sable
antelopes feeding together; but as they were not what I
wanted, I did not trouble them, but rode past.   A little later I
shot a fine oribi antelope, which I wanted for a specimen, and,
after disembowelling it, I fastened it securely behind the saddle.
It was here that I lost my knife—a loss which I only discovered later on.

The sun must have been nearly down, and I was riding at
the base of some wooded hills, and not more than a couple of
miles from camp, when I thought I saw something move
amongst the open forest a few hundred yards in front of me.
Reining in my horse behind a bush, I looked anxiously from
behind it and made out an eland cow, while a second glance
showed me there were others behind her feeding down from the
hills.   The first thing to be done was to detach the oribi from
the horse; this I at once proceeded to do, and then, pushing
the carcase in under a bush, threw a little grass over it to
hide it from the sight of vultures, etc.   I now became aware
that I had not got my cartridge belt round me, and knew that
I must have left it on the ground where I had shot and dis-
embowelled the oribi antelope.   I had thus only the one cartridge that was in my rifle.   At first I thought of riding back
to look for my belt, but it was already very late, and as I felt
pretty sure I could find it the following day, I resolved to try
to drive one of the elands up to the waggon and despatch her
there.   With this intention I rode out from behind the bush,
and the elands, seeing me, turned and made for the hills at a
trot.   There were six of them, three full-grown cows and three
younger animals.   I at once let my horse out and tried to cut
them off, and keep them on level ground; but it was no good,
as the distance was too short, and in spite of my utmost efforts
they gained the steep stony hillside, and clambered up it like
goats.   Although it was rather a foolish thing to do, as I risked
laming my horse, I followed them.

The elands soon reached the summit of the range of hills,

and I was not far behind them.   Here the ground was level though stony, and after trotting across it they descended on the opposite side.   At the base of the range lay a broad open plain, and beyond it a second range of stony hills, and I saw that I must head my eland before she crossed the valley and reached this second range.   How my good horse got down the descent without falling or breaking his legs I do not know, but when I reached the level ground the elands were not more than two hundred yards ahead of me.   I now raced them, and was soon alongside of the finest cow, a beautiful animal, striped almost as distinctly as a koodoo.   I did my best to turn her towards my waggon, but she would not swerve from her course, and when I got slightly in front of her she shot past behind my horse and resumed her way.   There was now nothing to be done but to shoot her at once before she got into the hills which we were fast approaching, so, passing her again, I reined in, and as she came by gave her my only bullet.   She fell at once to the shot and lay quite still.

Walking up to her, I found that I had struck her just behind the shoulder, but a good deal too high ; in fact, the ball must have jarred her backbone, causing her to fall so suddenly. I saw, however, that she was not dead, but only paralysed, and she soon began to raise her head and forequarters, but her whole body seemed powerless behind the bullet wound. Nevertheless, I felt pretty sure that during the night, if left alone, she would recover ; and as, besides being fat, she was a beautiful specimen of a striped eland, one that would do very well for the British Museum, I resolved to despatch her at once. Feeling for my knife, I now discovered for the first time that it was gone, and knew I must have left it on the ground after disembowelling the oribi.   What was to be done ?   I had not another cartridge with which to kill her, nor even a knife.   The only thing I could think of was to bind her hind legs securely together with the thong which in South Africa one always has round one's horse's neck.   This I at once set about doing, and as I thought, soon bound her hind legs together just above the hough in such a way that, struggle as she might, she would not be able to get them loose.   All this time the eland had been struggling desperately with her forequarters, but her hind

legs seemed paralysed.   My victim being at last, as I thought,
secured, I made the best of my way to the waggon, intending
to return at once with one of my Kafirs in order to despatch
her, and then leave the boys to sleep at the carcase.   However, it was farther than I thought from camp, and it was
nearly dark when I got there, so, thinking it then too late to
return, I decided to put it off until the following morning,
trusting that neither lions nor hyænas would interfere with my
prize during the night.

The next morning before the sun was up I was on my way
back to the eland accompanied by a lot of hungry Mashunas
all eager to get a little meat.   I rode straight to where I had
left the animal on the preceding evening, and, as she had fallen
right in the open, I knew that I ought to have seen her when
still some distance off.   But see her I certainly did not, and
there was soon no doubt in my mind that, wherever she was, she
was not where I had left her.   Scarcely crediting my senses, I
now looked for the exact spot where I had left her lying, and
soon found it.   There was the place where she had fallen,
marked by a little dry blood, and the traces of the struggles
she had made during the night to regain her legs.   She had
evidently got on her feet at last, with her hind legs still fast
bound, as we could see by the spoor left by the two hind feet
being close together.   We now followed her track, which led
us into the thickly-wooded and stony hills just in front of us,
making sure of coming up with her before long.   However, we
were mistaken, for, after following the spoor slowly and laboriously right up to the top of the range, and then all along the
crest of the ridge for miles, until after mid-day, I finally gave
it up, feeling sure that the thong must have worked loose or
broken.   Thus I was done out of fat meat, as well as my museum
specimen, and I only hope my would-be victim recovered from
the effects of her bullet wound, as I imagine she probably did,
for I think no vital part had been injured.

On my way back to camp I rode round behind the hills
where I had shot the oribi, and taking my horse's spoor, found the
spot and recovered my knife and cartridge belt.   I had scarcely
remounted when a very large wart-hog trotted out from a
patch of bush a short distance in front of me.   One of my best

"My dog Punch tried to seize him by the ear."

dogs had followed me from the camp, and wishing to see whether he would tackle so big a pig alone, I gave chase, calling to the dog to come on.   A wart-hog can go well for a few hundred yards, but the one I was after was a very big heavy old boar, and, my horse being a fast one, I soon overhauled him.   Just as I came up on the one side, my dog Punch was on him on the other, and tried to seize him by the ear.   The old boar seemed just to give a sudden twist with his head without stopping for an instant, but he sent the dog rolling yards away.   Punch soon picked himself up, and nothing daunted, came rushing to the attack once more, but as he did so I saw that the blood was pouring from a large gash in his shoulder, and not wanting him to get further hurt, I jumped off and rolled his antagonist over just as Punch was about to seize him for the second time.   He proved to be a very fine specimen of a wart-hog, and was one of the largest I have ever seen, possessing, too, a perfect pair of tusks.   He was also very fat—and let me say here that a fat wart-hog is excellent eating. As he was such a fine specimen, I skinned and preserved him carefully, and his mortal remains may now be seen in the South African Museum at Cape Town.   My dog, I found, had got a very pretty cut three inches long, down the shoulder, but it was only a flesh wound, and although it bled a good deal was not at all dangerous.   On returning to camp I washed it out with a weak lotion of carbolic acid, and then put a couple of stitches in it, and though poor Punch was stiff and lame for a few days, he was very soon himself again.

The following morning I crossed the Manyami with a good deal of trouble, as the ford was deep and the banks of the river very steep, and during the afternoon shot a roan antelope bull. I was now upon the high open downs in which the Manyami and Mazoe rivers take their rise.[1]   These open grassy downs extend over a large tract of land, and without doubt form the finest country for European occupation in South Africa.   Owing to their elevation above sea-level (which is from 4500 to 6000 feet) the climate is delightful for the greater part of the year,

[1] The following passages were written in my diary in 1883, long before any one ever dreamed that Mashunaland would one day become a British colony.   I reproduce them just as I wrote them ten years ago.

though during the months of June and July it is rather bleak
and cold. This high plateau is intersected in every direction
by running streams that never dry, and, as the fountains
which supply them well out from the highest portions of the
downs, a large area of country might be put under irrigation.
The whole year round, a cool wind blows almost continually
from the south-east—a wind which in the winter months becomes so keen and cold that it seems to come direct from
the frozen seas of the Antarctic Circle. This, in fact, is a
country where European children would grow up with rosy
cheeks, and apples would not be flavourless. Although these
downs are very open, still one is never out of sight of patches
of forest trees, so that the luxury of a good log fire at night
can always be enjoyed—a luxury which will be appreciated
by South African travellers who have journeyed through the
treeless wastes of the Cape Colony, Orange Free State, and
Transvaal.

There is another point about the Mashuna uplands well
worth noting. In all other portions of South Africa with which
I am acquainted, whether in the Transvaal, Bechwanaland, or
the Matabili country, when the long summer grass is burnt off,
which usually happens about June or July, the country remains
a blackened, dreary, grassless waste until the following rainy
season commences. Or, say that precautions are taken, and
the grass is not burnt off, well then it becomes dry as tinder,
all nourishment being scorched out of it, cattle invariably
get into a very low condition, and should the season be a late
one, very many die of starvation. Now on the Mashuna
plateau, when the long summer grass is burnt off, a short sweet
grass at once springs up in the moist valleys which, after
attaining to about a foot in height, seeds, and on this grass
cattle and horses thrive well.

Some fifty years ago this fine country must have been
thickly inhabited, as almost every valley has, at one time or
another, been under cultivation. The sites of villages are also
very numerous, though now only marked by a few deep pits
from which the natives obtained the clay used by them for
plastering their huts and making their cooking-pots, and also
the presence usually of a cluster of huge acacia-trees, which

grow to a far greater size on the sites of old villages than anywhere else.   On the summit of every hill may be found the
walls, in more or less perfect preservation, of what, I think,
must have been cattle kraals.   These walls are very neatly
built of squared stones, nicely fitted together, but uncemented
with any kind of mortar.   The peaceful people inhabiting this
part of Africa must then have been in the zenith of their prosperity.   Herds of their small but beautiful cattle lowed in
every valley, and their rich and fertile country doubtless
afforded them an abundance of vegetable food.   About 1840,
however, the Matabili Zulus, under their warlike chief Umziligazi, settled in the country which they now inhabit, and very
soon bands of these ferocious and bloodthirsty savages overran
the peaceful vales of the Mashuna country in every direction.
The poor Mashunas, unskilled in war, and living, moreover, in
small communities scattered all over the country, without any
central government, fell an easy prey before the fierce invaders,
and very soon every stream in their country ran red with their
blood, whilst vultures and hyænas feasted undisturbed amidst
the ruins of their devastated homes.   Their cattle, sheep, and
goats were driven off by their conquerors, and their children,
when old enough to walk and not above ten or twelve years of
age, were taken for slaves ; the little children too young to
walk were, of course, killed together with their mothers.   In a
very few years there were no more Mashunas left in the open
country, the remnant that had escaped massacre having fled
into the mountainous districts to the south and east of their
former dwellings, where they still live.   Thus, in a short time
an immense extent of fertile country, that had, perhaps, for
ages past supported a large and thriving community, was again
given back to nature : and so it remains to the present day—
an utterly uninhabited country, roamed over at will by herds of
elands and other antelopes.

In the north-eastern corner of this high country, in the bed
of the River Mazoe and its tributary streams, the natives obtain
alluvial gold, not very much it is true, but as they only work in
the most primitive way they cannot wash much ground in a
day.   Whether a rich alluvial gold-field will or will not eventually be opened up in this district is a point upon which I will

not hazard an opinion, as I know nothing whatever about gold-digging.   All I do know is that alluvial gold is obtained by the natives from all the streams here by very primitive processes, and that there is splendid water-power to assist the scientific gold-digger.

At mid-day on 16th July I found myself on the edge of the broken country in which the Mazoe takes its rise.   In the morning I had chased and shot a hen ostrich, and missed a fine cock, although the latter gave me by far the easiest chance. In the afternoon, after first starting my waggon, having given my driver instructions to hold to the south-east, and to keep on the high ground, I again rode out to look for ostriches, feeling rather sore at having missed the chance I had in the morning of shooting a fine cock.   It was a very cold bleak day, with a biting wind sweeping over the downs from the south-east ; the sky, too, was overcast and looked very much like rain, although it was now the middle of the dry season. However, it is seldom that a year passes without winter rains falling in this part of the country.

It was getting late in the afternoon when I suddenly de-scried a black speck, which looked like an ostrich, far away in the distance.   Pulling in my horse I looked intently at it.   As I did so it suddenly disappeared.   I felt sure that it had lain down in the grass, and knew that if it really had been an ostrich it was very probable that it had a nest there, for it was the breeding season for these birds.   I accordingly rode steadily in the direction where whatever it was I had seen had dis-appeared, and at length began to think that I had overridden it, when up jumped a hen ostrich from a little patch of long grass about eighty yards in front of me, and ran away slowly, with outstretched, drooping wings and lowered neck.   I might have had a splendid shot at her, but from the way she ran I knew she had got off her nest, and so did not fire, as I felt sure that if I now went the right way to work, I should in all probability be able to secure the cock bird.   Riding up to the patch of grass from which the ostrich had risen, I saw she had a nest there containing thirteen eggs.   These I did not disturb, but at once looked about for a suitable spot close at hand, and within easy range of the nest, to make what is known in

OSTRICH AND NEST.

colonial parlance as a "hock," that is, some sort of shelter in which to lie hidden in order to shoot the cock bird on his return to the nest.

My idea was to prepare a hock immediately, and then to get back to the waggon before dark, and leave the shooting of the ostrich to the following day, it being now very late, and dense masses of black clouds, drifting up from the south-east, warning me that a heavy storm of rain was coming up apace. There being no cover of any kind within a radius of a mile from the nest, and the grass being all burnt off, with the exception of the one small patch, it was rather difficult to know how to make a shelter of any kind that would not attract the attention of such a wary bird as an ostrich. About a hundred yards away, however, one solitary tuft of long grass had escaped the fire, and here I resolved to make my hiding-place. I first sent all the Kafirs who were with me away with the exception of two, telling the former to go and wait for me in the shelter of some forest about a mile and a half away, as I knew that the cock bird might come on at any moment, and was afraid that if he saw a crowd of people close to his nest he might take fright and desert it altogether. We now began to make the shelter as quickly as possible. First we cut a lot of long grass from the patch where the nest was, and brought it to the single tuft, and my boys set to work to dig a little circular trench a few inches in depth, in which we planted the grass, which was about three feet high, and nearly as thick in the stem as straw. We had only completed about a quarter of the circle when in the far distance I suddenly saw an ostrich approaching, which I felt pretty sure was the mate of the bird that had left the nest. Meantime the dark banks of cloud had been drifting up, and soon a cold sleety rain began to fall.

That the ostrich we had seen was the master of the nest was soon placed beyond doubt, as he was fast approaching and had been joined by the hen. He would come on at a run for a hundred yards or so, then stand and evidently examine the ground. My two boys and I were by this time fairly well concealed, as we had about a third of the circle of grass up, and were crouching behind it ; but my horse with the saddle and bridle still on him was grazing only a little distance behind us, and of course in full view on the open ground. However, the cock bird came nearer and nearer, not continuously, but by fits and starts. Whenever he advanced he came on at a run, but then would stand still for a long time, and evidently felt uneasy about the horse. If he could have got a good view of him, I daresay he would have taken fright, but it was raining so hard that we could only see very indistinctly, and my idea is, that the bird took the horse for some sort of game, which he was anxious to drive away from the vicinity of his nest. He had now approached to within four hundred yards, the hen being some distance behind him, and from here he came in one run right up to the nest, and stood there within a hundred yards of where I lay. Now was my time, so, pushing the barrel of my rifle cautiously out between the grass, I prepared to fire. The rain was coming down in a perfect deluge, and, moreover, was being driven by a strong wind right into my eyes, so that, although the ostrich was so near, he looked shadowy and indistinct, and I could not for the life of me tell at what angle his body was towards me. However, I dared not delay. There he was, close to me at any rate, and I was afraid he might take fright and go off at any moment. I thought he was standing about broadside to me, and so, getting the sight as well as I could into the centre of his body, I touched the trigger and heard the bullet tell loudly. At the shot he opened his wings and rushed off; I thought he would fall every instant, but when he had covered three hundred yards, and still kept on running strongly, I knew that his heart and lungs were untouched, and guessed that I had struck him a little too far back. However, as the bullet which had struck him was an expanding one, I knew that he had received a wound from which he could never recover, and made sure I should get him.

Almost immediately after I had fired the heavy rain ceased, so that we could see the wounded ostrich more plainly. After running for about five hundred yards he commenced to walk, and before long stopped and stood still, and the hen bird then joined him. I ought now to have left him alone, as he would doubtless soon have lain down and died during the night. However, I was over anxious to get his feathers, and as it was impossible to remain where we were and watch him, the sun having set and darkness fast coming on, I jumped on my horse and galloped towards him, thinking that wounded as he was I should be able to run him down before dark. As I mounted he saw me, and at once went off with a long start. I chased him until I felt that my horse was getting done, but could not gain on him, and soon saw that I had made a mistake in chasing him at all. I now marked him enter a strip of timber that ran out from the point of a solitary hill,[1] which stands alone, a conspicuous landmark on these downs, and determined to return and take his spoor here on the following day. I then rode back to my boys, feeling very crestfallen, and we at once made a start for home ; it was quite dusk and the rain was again pouring steadily down.

According to our calculations we ought not to have been very far from where the waggon had outspanned for the night, as we thought that it had taken a course nearly parallel with our own. We therefore struck across the downs to the eastward, and every now and again I fired a shot ; we were wet through, the rain fell steadily, and a cold biting wind blew across the open moorland. Luckily for them my boys all had their blankets with them, otherwise I do not know how they would have stood it. I had a warm jumper over my cotton shirt, but in spite of this my teeth soon began to chatter with the cold, so I dismounted and led my horse. Every now and then I fired a shot, hoping to hear an answering shot from the waggon.

After proceeding some two or three hours we began to get among stony ridges, and knew that we were on the edge of the hilly country which skirts the eastern side of the plateau, and I felt certain that we had either overshot the waggon, having crossed the track in the dark, or else that the waggon had gone more to the eastward than I had intended, and got down amongst the hills. Could we have lit a fire I would have done so, and remained where we were till daylight ; but, soaking wet as everything was, it was impossible. Neither did staying where we were all night, wet through and exposed to

[1] Mount Hampden.

the cutting wind, offer any special attractions, so I determined
to try to get back to the place where we had last outspanned,
and then follow the waggon spoor until we got up to it.
Although it was a dark rainy night this was not so difficult as
it might at first appear ; we had been travelling the preceding
day and that morning along a large deep-worn native path, so
that in reality we had only to strike this footpath to find our
waggon spoor.   I had brought with me from Khama's country
two Bushmen, splendid hands at finding their way, and as
soon as they had settled between them the exact direction they
ought to take, they stepped out confidently enough.   It must
have been nearly midnight, I think, when we at last struck the
path, and although we could not see it, we could feel the
waggon spoor with our hands.

The rain, which all this time had been falling without
cessation, now began to hold off, and the moon, too, was
up, though the sky was so overcast that it did not do
much to dispel the darkness.   We were, as it turned
out, to the east of where we had last left the waggon ;
at any rate we were on the track, and all we had to do was to
stick to it.   We now kept along the deep-worn path, my boys
every now and then feeling for the spoor.   After an hour or
so we commenced to descend into the hills which skirt the high
plateau, and I wondered where on earth my driver had got
to with the waggon.   At the bottom of the slope we came to
some native cornfields, and here we lost the spoor altogether.
As I knew by the presence of the cornfields that we were
close to a village, I determined to hold the footpath, and
having done so for another half-hour we reached a small
village.   After a good deal of talking my own Mashunas
induced a man to appear.   On asking him where my waggon
was he said it was not far off the cornfields where we had
lost the spoor, so I asked him to guide me to it.   He at first
objected that it was night-time and very black (which, as it
was two A.M., was true enough), and then offered me a hut to
sleep in.   However, I was determined to get to my waggon
that night if possible ; so, after getting over his scruples by
promising him a small present, we once more made a move,
and about three o'clock in the morning reached the waggon at

last. I at once took off my wet things, put on a dry shirt, and sitting over the fire wrapped in a warm blanket, had some meat fried and coffee made, and was soon comfortable enough as far as my bodily wants were concerned, though still bitterly sore at heart at not having secured the ostrich, for, with all the rain that had fallen during the night, I did not think there would be much chance of following its spoor in the morning.

My boy, I found, had kept along the footpath after first inspanning, thinking he would be able to turn away from it before reaching the hills, but getting involved amongst some stony ridges, had kept on it till he got right off the open country, and then, trying to turn back, had again got amongst stones and hills and there outspanned. He said he had fired several shots during the early part of the night to attract my attention, but of course we were then miles away, and had heard nothing of them.

The next day was fine and bright after the heavy rain, and I ought to have gone and had a look for my wounded ostrich, but I was tired after the night's walk, and delayed starting till after breakfast; then a lot of Mashunas came up to the waggon with all sorts of things to sell, including two nice little cows, and a few quills of alluvial gold, and it ended in my deciding not to go at all, as I concluded that the heavy rain had very likely obliterated the spoor, and thought I should very likely have had a long ride for nothing. As it turned out, had I gone I should in all probability have found the bird, for the following day a Griqua hunter in my employ, who was looking for ostrich nests on the downs, saw from the top of the hill near which I had left off chasing my wounded bird some vultures and crows settling in a patch of bush, and going down, found them busily engaged on my cock ostrich. That it was mine there was no doubt, as he found the solid end of my little Express bullet in the body. He plucked out all the feathers and took them with him to my main camp, and stowed them away in his own hut, together with those of other two cock birds which he had himself shot. Unfortunately, by some mischance, before I returned from the Sabi the hut got alight and all the feathers were burnt, which I was the more sorry for as, besides the direct loss entailed, my man told me that the feathers of the bird I had shot were remarkably fine.

On the 18th of July I was again ready to make a move, and finding a practicable road, trekked up on to the high country again, and held away across the downs to the south. In the afternoon I shot a fine roan antelope bull, and the following morning a cow carrying the finest pair of horns I have ever seen, as they measure two feet seven inches over the curve. On the 20th we crossed the River Ruwa, one of the main tributaries of the upper Manyami, close to a cluster of Mashuna villages under a head man named Entakwasheki, and the following day reached See-kwanka's, near which we slept, having passed other towns about mid-day. There was little or no game to be found in this part of the country as there were a good many natives in the district. After leaving See-kwanka's we held away in a southerly direction, crossing the heads of numerous small streams flowing to the eastward. Though the country appeared to be very suitable for game, there was nevertheless very little to be seen, a few hartebeests and an odd roan antelope being apparently the only surviving species. During the morning I came across a solitary old roan bull, but he was very wild, and went off at a great pace when I was still a long way from him. However, after a sharp gallop I got a shot at him as he was crossing a small stream, and breaking his hip had him at my mercy. After killing him with a bullet through the lungs, I brought the waggon to the carcase and loaded up every scrap of the meat, as I wanted it all to buy rice and maize from the Mashunas on ahead.

About mid-day on the 23rd we reached a lot of villages under a petty chief named Sadza. Here I determined to remain for a couple of days, in order to rest the oxen and buy provisions from the natives. As they told me there were plenty of elands in the neighbourhood, I rode out the following morning in search of them, and as luck would have it, came across a small herd of these fine animals within two miles of my camp. The herd consisted of a magnificent old bull, two younger bulls, and four cows, two of which had small calves with them only a few days old—beautiful little creatures of a reddish-fawn colour, profusely banded with perpendicular white stripes. I shot the old bull and the two younger ones, and as the former was a magnificent animal, prepared his skin for setting up, and hoped some day to see him in the British Museum,[1] set up in a manner that would recall to my mind, in some degree, the splendid creature he looked when alive, though I was fully aware how difficult it must be to mount these large skins so as to do them justice.

To give an idea of the size and bulk of a large eland bull, I think I cannot do better than record a few measurements of this particular animal, taken on the spot with a tape-line. Standing height at withers, five feet nine inches ; girth of neck midway between jaw and shoulder, five feet one inch ; depth of body, measured over the curve behind the shoulder from the wither to the middle of chest, four feet one inch ; breadth of chest between the forelegs, one foot two inches. These last three measurements were taken on the naked carcase after the skin had been removed.

I also wanted a well-striped cow and a young calf for the museum ; but although I might have got them this day, after slaying the three bulls I did not care about shooting any more ; and indeed, had it not been that I wanted a lot of meat for the crowds of Mashunas who had accompanied me, I should only have killed the one.

The following day I was busy preparing the big eland's skin with arsenical soap, melting down the fat, and buying provisions from the Mashunas.

During the two previous nights that we had been here a hyæna had been prowling round the camp trying to get hold of something ; but as the moon was not long past the full, the nights had been light, and the dogs had kept him out. This evening, however, as the moon did not come up much before ten o'clock, there were some hours of darkness after the sun went down. My whole camp was fenced in, the waggon standing in the centre, and my two horses being tied on the farther side. Beside them, spread out on the hide of one of the young eland bulls, lay their feed of boiled maize cooling, as it was just hot out of the pot. It must have been about

---

[1] This hope has been realised, and this magnificent animal may now be seen in our national collection.

eight o'clock, and the thirty or forty Mashunas, sitting round
the blazing fires on my side of the camp, not ten yards
from the horses, were talking, laughing, and making such a
noise as only Kafirs can when revelling in an abundance of
meat, porridge, ground nuts, and other delicacies dear to the
African stomach, when suddenly a hyæna, having crept through
a break in the fence, appeared in the full light of the fires,
seized the eland skin that was spread out close to one of the
horses, and was through the fence again before one could count
five. As he had come up under the wind the dogs had not
scented him, but they saw him (as did I myself and most of the
Kafirs), and immediately gave chase, barking furiously.

Seizing my rifle, and accompanied by several of the Kafirs,
some carrying bundles of blazing grass, I followed, guided by
the barking of the dogs. By the light of the blazing grass we
could see quite plainly the broad track left by the heavy eland
skin as it had been dragged rapidly along, and, after crossing
a stream which flowed just below our camp, at length came up
to the dogs ; they had managed to drive the hyæna off, and
were keeping guard over the skin. This skin, it must be
remembered, was the green hide of an eland bull (it only
having been shot the previous day), and must have weighed at
least forty pounds, probably more, and it will give some idea of
the strength of the South African spotted hyæna, when I relate
that this beast had been able to drag such a weight at such a
pace that my dogs were not able to overtake him before he had
got to a distance of at least three hundred yards from the
camp, for, as the dogs saw him seize the skin and make off with
it, and followed on the instant, he only had a few yards' start.

Having recovered the skin we returned with it to the camp.
Such impertinence, however, could not be passed over, for
although we had not lost the skin, my horses' feed had been
scattered to the winds, so as I knew that the enterprising
beast would be sure to return before long, I determined to give
him a warm reception. I was sure he would come back on
the spoor of the eland skin again under the wind, so having
tied up the dogs, I took my rifle and went and sat behind a
little bush about twenty yards outside the camp fence. The
night was very dark, and I knew that I should not see him at all

until he was so near me that I could hardly miss him. I had sat for about half an hour when I fancied I saw near me a darkish object that had not been there before, but as it was quite stationary I could not make it out ; for some minutes there was no movement visible in this darkish mass, but then it came palpably nearer, and I knew that it was the hyæna. I let him come on until he was within seven or eight yards of me, and then feeling sure that I could not miss him, although I could see nothing more definite than a something blacker than the surrounding darkness, levelled my rifle and fired. It seemed to me that the animal fell to the shot, struggled a moment, and then regaining his legs went off at a slow pace. I ordered the dogs to be loosed, and the Kafirs coming out with torches of blazing grass, I examined the ground along the track he had taken and soon found blood. The dogs now came up, and at once taking the spoor, bayed the hyæna in a patch of long grass about one hundred yards ahead. Upon our setting light to this he bolted, and closely attended by the dogs, got across the open ground between the long grass and the river, and being evidently very nearly done for, jumped into a pool of water, where he stood half immersed, snapping at the dogs as they tried to seize him by the ears. He was now at a terrible disadvantage, as the Kafirs, coming up with blazing grass, plunged their assegais into him from the high bank above, and he was soon disposed of. We then got him out of the pool, and dragged him up to the camp. He was a fine large male hyæna, and had done lots of damage in his time no doubt, as the Mashunas say that he had lately killed three of their little cattle, besides a number of goats.

During the night the sky became overcast, and when morning broke we found ourselves enveloped in a thick mist which presently became a fine rain. About ten o'clock, however, the mist cleared off, and though the sky still remained dark and overcast, it looked as if the sun would presently get the better of the rain, so I determined to inspan and hold on my course to the south. After starting the waggon I made a round on horseback to the eastward in search of game, and passed several Mashuna villages perched amongst the rocks of the little stony hills which here stud the country, but saw no game whatever.

Just before sundown I got back to my waggon, which I found outspanned close to the River Caringwi, a tributary of the Ruzarwi.

The following morning we crossed the former river just at its junction with the latter. About here there is an outcrop of enormous masses of bare rock, gigantic, smooth, rounded boulders, one of which reminded me of a Brobdingnagian hippopotamus lying asleep. On a pile of rocks some two hundred feet in height, at the foot of this immense block, there was a small Mashuna village, the huts being built upon the ledges, and some of them upon the highest rocks, while several of the chasms between two large boulders had been bridged over with logs. As the waggon approached, the whole population of this quaint-looking village sat in groups, squatting on their hams upon the flat rocks, reminding me irresistibly of a troop of baboons. When we came close beneath their abode they all came down and ran alongside of the waggon and horses, talking and gesticulating in a state of intense excitement and wonder. The sight of the white man mounted on a strange-looking quadruped, and the waggon with its revolving wheels and long span of oxen, no doubt formed a topic of conversation amongst them for some time, as I was the only European that had ever passed that way.

A couple of miles beyond the town we came to the little river Chingi-Ka, and, as we could not immediately find a ford, I ordered the waggon to outspan on the northern bank whilst I went to look for one. This I soon found, and crossing the river and riding a little beyond it, came upon a small herd of elands consisting of a beautiful young bull and three cows, two of them accompanied by their new-born calves. The sun was already down, and it was fast becoming dusk, but I determined to have the young bull—in the first place because I wanted fresh meat, and in the second because I could see that he was very finely marked. As I approached, the elands stood looking wonderingly at the first horse, I suppose, they had ever seen, but upon getting my wind they came bounding past at about one hundred and fifty yards' distance in splendid style. Taking aim well in front of the bull I fired as he was passing at a slashing pace, and breaking his shoulder, at once disabled him, and then despatched him with a bullet through the lungs. This was really a most beautiful animal. He had not yet attained the immense neck or the large bunch of black bristly hair on the forehead that are only found on an old bull eland, but on the other hand, whereas the old bulls have never much hair upon their bodies, this younger animal possessed a splendid coat, the ground colour being of a rich, warm reddish-fawn, with a broad black line running down the centre of his back from the mane on the wither to the tail, while on each side he was banded with nine broad white stripes, quite as distinct as those on a koodoo. He had also a splendid long even pair of horns measuring two feet seven inches in length, whereas in an old bull the horns, being worn down, seldom exceed twenty-eight inches. Altogether he was a most beautiful specimen, and I determined to preserve him for setting up.

It was now too late to do anything, but I had three Mashunas with me who agreed to sleep at the carcase to keep off any prowling hyænas that might be about. I gave them the most strict orders not to touch the eland before my return with the waggon the next morning, as of course they could not be expected to know how to skin him properly for setting up. As one of them went with me to the waggon, which was quite close, in order to get a fire stick, I there again told him through my own boys, who spoke his language well, and whom he thoroughly understood, that he was not to touch the eland until my arrival with the waggon in the morning.

As I was anxious to get early to work upon the eland, I inspanned before sunrise the following day, and, crossing the river, trekked up to where I had shot him. Being on horseback I rode a little in advance, and what was my surprise and rage upon coming up to the carcase to find that the Mashunas had skinned and cut it up during the night. A glance at the skin showed me that they had destroyed it for the purpose for which I wanted it. I was—and naturally I think—very exasperated, and as I came towards the rascals who had played me such a trick they saw that my intentions were not friendly and bolted in different directions, leaving their assegais, bows and arrows, etc., behind them. These I at once seized, and smashing them over my knee threw one after the other upon the fire. My waggon now came up, accompanied by a long string of Mashunas who were following me for meat. They all belonged to the same clan as those who had cut up and destroyed the eland's skin contrary to my express orders, and I determined that they, at any rate, should get none of it. I could not put the entire carcase on the waggon, so, after cutting off all I wanted, I collected the rest into a heap, and then, making the Mashunas bring pile upon pile of dry wood, made an immense fire over it. As the wood burnt away I kept adding fresh fuel, until everything was charred to a cinder. To those who do not know the Mashunas, their intense eagerness for meat, and what they will do and undergo in order to obtain it, it will be difficult to understand how exasperating this proceeding was to their feelings. The greater part of them, when they saw that I was about to commit so horrible a crime, after looking on for a few minutes with faces expressive of agony and astonishment, and probably thinking that a man capable of such a deed would be capable of anything, turned upon their heels and left at once for home.

By mid-day, the meat being all consumed, I again inspanned and resumed my journey, shooting a roan antelope bull on the way. Towards evening we neared the hills through which runs the River Sabi.

On 29th July I reached a small native village a few miles to the south of a conspicuous mountain called Wedza, and in the afternoon rode down through a gorge in the hills to have a look at the River Sabi, which I found here to be about one hundred yards broad, its waters flowing in several channels amongst masses of rocks and stones. As the country to the south now looked very rough and mountainous, and as the natives said that Lichtenstein's hartebeest (which they called " Unkwila nondo ") was to be found about two days' journey farther on, I determined to leave my waggon in charge of the head man of the village and go on with the horses. It did not take me very long to arrange matters. Early the following morning I again set out, under the guidance of a man who professed to know the country well, and attended by a crowd of natives eager to get a little meat. Our route at first led through hills, some of them rocky and precipitous, others undulating and wooded from top to

bottom.   Before we had proceeded far we came upon a small
herd of elands, one of which I shot, sending most of the meat
back to the waggon.

In the afternoon we crossed the little river Impali, a tributary of the Sabi.   Perched high upon a rocky crag overhanging
this river was a Mashuna town, a short distance beyond which
we encamped for the night.   Most of the natives in this part
of the country carried bows and arrows, which one now seldom
sees amongst the Mashunas farther north.   The women were
tattooed on the forehead, cheeks, breasts, and stomach; some of
them were fairly good-looking, and all seemed fat and well fed.
The dress of the girls consisted of a small skin apron behind
and a very tiny one in front, the married women wearing
leathern skirts reaching to their knees.   Some of the young
girls' aprons were very neatly ornamented with beads, always
in a zigzag Vandyke-like pattern.   Were it not for the invasions of the Matabili from the west and Umzila's Zulus from
the south, these people would live happily enough.   They
possess cattle and goats in considerable numbers, and grow an
abundance of vegetable food, amongst which may be mentioned
maize, rice, pogo corn, Kafir corn, ground nuts, beans, pumpkins, and sweet potatoes.

The following day I continued my journey southwards,
parallel with and not far away from the Sabi, crossing the
little river Muti-a-shiri.   We saw no game, but in traversing
some open glades noticed the spoor either of Tsessebe or
Unkwila nondo antelopes.   My guide said it was the spoor of
the latter animals, and I think he was right, as the footprints
appeared to be a little smaller than would have been those of
Tsessebe antelopes.   I wanted to stop and hunt for them, but as
my guide said they were much more plentiful farther south, and
was anxious to get on, I let him have his way, and we resumed
our journey.   Shortly before mid-day we reached a small native
village, where we breakfasted.   It was close here that three
years previously the Jesuit priests, Fathers Law and Wehl, had
crossed the Sabi on their ill-fated journey from the Matabili
country to Umzila's kraal, and the natives pointed out to me
whereabouts they passed in the valley below.   This village was
situated at the foot of a stupendous mass of rock called Gato,

which rose sheer from the plain in the form of a sugar loaf, a gigantic naked mass, nearly a thousand feet in height. It would be a conspicuous landmark for many miles around were it not that there are other similar masses of rock in this district.

A couple of miles after passing Gato we crossed the River Masheki, a pretty little stream of crystal-clear water about sixty yards broad, and from two to four feet deep, flowing rapidly over a sandy bed. Shortly after crossing this river we saw two koodoos, one of which I shot, and a few miles farther on came to a small stream, on the banks of which my guide advised me to make a camp from which to hunt for Unkwila nondo antelope. As there was still an hour's sun when we got here I took my rifle and made a round on foot, but saw nothing whatever in the shape of game. Whilst returning just at dusk, and when not more than two hundred yards from camp, I met an enormous old male baboon coming up from the water. He was walking along very slowly with his head turned towards the camp listening to the Kafirs talking, and never saw me. I looked at him coming and he seemed to me to be the very largest baboon I had ever seen, and, as I wanted the head of a very large male, I prepared to shoot him. As he stalked slowly past, chewing the wild fruits of which his mouth was full, I fired, and the bullet going right through both shoulders killed him on the spot. He just fell on his face perfectly dead and never moved again. When I came to examine him I was astonished at his size and the great length of his face from the eyes to the tip of his nose, which was eight inches. He was so old that he had no canine teeth with the exception of one broken fang, so that his head was useless to me. But the Kafirs carried him into camp, and one of them took his skin, and thus his life was not sacrificed altogether for nothing.

On the following day, 1st August, I had a long day's ride in search of Unkwila nondo antelopes, but though I saw a little spoor, I did not come across any of the animals themselves. In the course of the day I shot a wart-hog, the only living creature I saw. Several times during the day we came across the tracks of a herd of buffaloes, which animals seemed to frequent this part of the country; the freshest spoor, was, however, several days old.

Following the advice of my guide I now resolved to cross
to the western side of the Sabi, and, leaving our camp at sunrise the next morning a two hours' ride brought us to the banks
of the river close to the Rukwi kwi Hills.   We saw no living
animal on the way, and indeed, game of all kinds seemed to
have been all but exterminated by the natives in this part of
the country.   Where we crossed it the Sabi is a really fine
river, with a running stream of beautifully clear water over one
hundred yards wide, though the full breadth of the river's bed
from bank to bank was more than three hundred yards.   It is,
however, only full from bank to bank during the rainy season.

After crossing the river we travelled to the south-west and
camped on a small stream to the south-east of Se-bum-bum's
mountain.   Taking a ride up the valley in the evening I met
an old rhinoceros bull of the black or prehensile-lipped species.
I had only my little 450-bore rifle with me, but disposed of
him with three shots, all running ones, as he got my wind and
made off just as I saw him.   After giving him the first shot
I galloped close up to him to try to turn him down towards
our camp, but he resented this and chased me for some distance,
and at a great pace, snorting furiously the while.   After sus-
taining another chase I gave him a second shot and disposed
of him with the third.   He seemed a very old animal, and his
horns, though massive, were short, and evidently much worn
down.   As I had no boys with me I left him as he was for
the night, intending to return in the morning to chop off his
horns and take some of the hide for sjamboks.   Shortly after
dark a lion roared loudly close behind our camp, the first I
had heard for more than a month.   I was in hopes that he
might smell the dead rhinoceros, and, thinking I might possibly
find him there early the next morning, made a start for the
carcase as soon as it was light.   However, the lion was not
there, nor had he been there during the night ; so, leaving
some of the Kafirs to cut up the rhinoceros, I made a big round
with the rest, not getting back to camp till sundown.   The
only game we saw during the day was a herd of roan antelope.

I was now close to the edge of the " fly " country, which
at this time extended from here southwards along both banks
of the Sabi, and I was therefore unable to proceed any farther

in that direction with my horses. When I left my camp at the Manyami I had hoped to find white rhinoceroses and also Lichtenstein's hartebeests outside the "fly" country, but I now felt convinced that the former animal was only to be met with in the "fly" country, whilst the latter, although it still existed beyond this limit, was, at any rate, scarce and difficult to get hold of. I had now been so long away from my main camp that I was anxious to get back again, and so resolved to recross the river, have another hunt there for Lichtenstein's hartebeest, and then, whether I obtained specimens or not, to return to my waggon and travel back to my camp on the Manyami as quickly as possible.

As it turned out, I was very unlucky this year, and never saw a single specimen of Lichtenstein's hartebeest. On my way back to the Manyami I followed my own waggon track as far as Sadza's villages, and then striking farther westwards, struck the Inyachimi river near its source, and followed it down to its junction with the Manyami. I then passed through a district which had been devastated by the Matabili only a few months before, and reached my main camp after an absence of six weeks.

CHAPTER V

EARLY in the year 1883 the first of the two expeditions that were sent by Lo Bengula against the Batauwani of Lake Ngami was undertaken. This was a very bold enterprise, as the marauders had to traverse nearly four hundred miles of desert country, entirely uninhabited except by Bushmen ; a country in which game too was very scarce, and throughout which water was only to be found in pools, often widely separated one from another. Although not a complete failure, as was the subsequent expedition, this raid was only partially successful, as the Batauwani, though partly taken by surprise, managed to keep the marauders in check with a small body of mounted men armed with breech-loading rifles, whilst their women and children crossed the Botletli river in canoes. The Matabili succeeded in capturing a considerable number of cattle, and also burnt down the large native town in which the Batauwani had been long living in peace and security. With the exception, however, of murdering a good many Bushmen, and capturing some of the children of these wild people for slaves, the expedition was, through no fault of theirs, a singularly bloodless one.

I have often noticed men of a very advanced age taking part in the most arduous raids made by the Matabili upon the surrounding tribes, and I will adduce one very remarkable instance, which seems to show that savages sometimes retain their vigour for a very long period of time. One of Lo Bengula's men who took part in the first expedition to Lake Ngami, and survived the long march of eight hundred miles there and back, was present at the attack on the Boer camp at Vechtkop, between the Rhenoster and Wilge rivers, in what is now the Orange Free State. This attack is historical, and took place in October 1836[1] under the leadership of Kalipi, one of Umziligazi's

UMHLAMELA, DAUGHTER OF LO BENGULA.

favourite generals. The Boers beat off their assailants, and Captain, afterwards Sir, Cornwallis Harris has described his meeting with the discomfited warriors, who were carrying their wounded comrades on their shields. My tough old friend, the Matabili, has often described the fight to me, and shown me the marks he bore on his person, the effect of a charge of slugs in the stomach, which he had received from one of the Boers' old muzzle-loading guns. He always maintained that at this time he was an " indoda," *i.e.* a full-grown man, and not an " ee-ja-ha," or young soldier. But say that in 1836 he was only twenty-three, in 1883 he must have been seventy years of age—a great age indeed at which to undertake the hardships of a protracted marauding expedition.

The second expedition sent by Lo Bengula to Lake Ngami was a most disastrous one. The Batauwani got information concerning the impending attack from some Bushmen, and had time to remove all their women and children, and to drive all their cattle to beyond the Botletli river. They then lay in ambush amongst the reeds which fringed the river's bank, and awaited their foes, and when they appeared gave them a very

---

[1] See Theal's *History of the Boers in South Africa*, p. 76.

warm reception with their breech-loading rifles. Many of the
Matabili were shot, including Pulinglela, one of the king's
brothers, and many other men of note. Many more were
drowned in trying to cross the Botletli, on a bed of water-plants,
which grew so thickly on the surface of the river in one place
that they thought it would support their weight. Possibly the
thickly-growing vegetation might have supported the weight
of a few men at a time, but as the bold attempt was made by
a large number at once, their united weight broke through the
bed of weeds, and they were all precipitated into deep water, where
many of them being unable to swim were drowned. Baffled
and beaten, the marauders had now to commence their retreat to
their own country through four hundred miles of desert, under
the most disadvantageous circumstances. As is usual, they had
only brought with them a sufficient number of cattle to serve as
food during the time occupied by the journey from Matabililand
to Lake Ngami. Once there, it was their business to capture
and take back to their king the flocks and herds of their enemies
—a certain number of which would have been slaughtered every
evening for their consumption. On this occasion they did not
capture a single animal, and with starvation staring them in
the face, commenced their long march homewards.

The horrors of that journey have often been described to me
by survivors. A few head of game were shot, and a few Bushman
encampments were looted, but many hundreds of Lo Bengula's
fiercest warriors died from starvation, thirst, and exhaustion on
their return from this disastrous expedition. Towards the end
of the journey ever-increasing numbers died daily round every
pool of water on the line of march. Parched with thirst, and
exhausted with starvation and fatigue, they would lie flat down
and drink their fill, and day after day, I have been told, numbers
died in this position. Only the remnant of the army got back
to Matabililand, and of the fine regiment of the " Intembi "
but few survived to tell the tale of their unsuccessful raid to
Lake Ngami.

One portion of the army several hundreds strong fared
better than the main body. Instead of returning home by the
way they had come they kept more to the north, and when
near the Mababi river were fortunate enough to surprise a

waggon of Khama's in charge of one of his hunters, who had
with him a valuable shooting horse belonging to his chief.
This man was surrounded by the Matabili, who seized and
bound him and would certainly have killed him if he had not
escaped very cleverly.   After they had secured him his captors
tried to catch his horse, but the animal being frightened would
not allow them to do so.   Seeing this Khama's man said, " Let
me catch the horse for you ; he knows me, and will allow me to
do so."   The Matabili, never dreaming that the man would be
able to ride without saddle and bridle, allowed him to make the
attempt ; but their would-be victim had determined to make a
bold bid for life, and so shouting to them not to come too near
him, or they would again frighten the horse, he first caught the
animal and then hastily fastened the thong, with which it had
been knee-haltered, in its mouth, so that it would serve as a
makeshift bridle.   The Matabili, seeing that he had caught the
horse, were now closing in, but before they got near him he
sprang on the horse's back, and urging it on by voice and heel,
galloped through them, unhurt by the assegais that were thrown
at him, and got clean off.   Eventually he reached Bamangwato
safely after a ride of several hundred miles.   However, as all
the Bushmen and Makalaka in the country he travelled through
were Khama's people, he was everywhere kindly treated, and
supplied with food of one kind or another.   The Matabili took
Khama's span of oxen (which furnished them with a good
supply of food), and burnt his waggon.

   At Khama's waggon they also captured a Bushman, and
told him his life should be spared if he would guide them
to Pandamatenka.   They struck the waggon track which
runs from Bamangwato to the Zambesi, close to Gazuma
" vley," and about fourteen miles to the north of Pandamatenka.
Many of them then knew where they were, so, as they
had no further need of their guide, they assegaied him.
Three years afterwards, in 1888, I was shown the spot where
his remains had long lain at the foot of an ant-heap, just at
the side of the waggon track.   An old half-caste elephant-
hunter named Africa, who was in the employ of Mr. Westbeech,
was at this time living at Gazuma with a boy named Charley
(who was afterwards in my service), and several families of

Bushmen.   When the Matabili came filing out in long lines across the open plain in which Gazuma is situated, the Bushmen all ran away into the forest, with the exception of a few who took refuge in Africa's hut.   One man and his wife, a woman with a young child at her breast, remained outside, in the enclosure which surrounded the principal hut, saying that the Matabili would not interfere with "Georos's" (Mr. Westbeech's) dogs, as "Georos" was Lo Bengula's friend.   The day before the arrival of the Matabili, Africa had shot a fat eland bull, the meat of which was hanging up all round his hut, cut in strips to dry.   The sight of this meat put the hungry savages in good humour.   They took it all, also a bag of Kafir corn that he had, but as they knew Africa to be one of George Westbeech's people they were civil enough to him and Charley, and did not even go into the hut, in which several Bushwomen had taken refuge, and where they were hiding under skins. Presently, however, Charley told me, one of the endunas asked Africa where all the Bushmen were whose household goods were lying about the camp, and being told that they had all fled away into the forest as soon as they saw the Matabili appearing in the distance, got angry and said, not a dog of them should have lived if he had seen them.   He then seemingly for the first time noticed the man and woman with the child, who were both standing near him, and without saying another word plunged his assegai through the body of the baby and into the breast of the woman, killing them both with the one thrust.   He then stabbed the man through the arm and the muscles of the chest just as he turned to run, calling out at the same time, "Kill that dog."   No one, however, paid any attention to him, as they were all too busy with the eland meat, and the Bushman escaped with his life.   Game being fairly plentiful between Pandamatenka and Matabililand, this division of the Matabili army reached home in good order, as they suffered no great privations or hardships.

As in the foregoing pages I have frequently spoken of Bushmen, I will take this opportunity of saying a few words concerning these curious and interesting people.   The Bushmen of the interior of South-western Africa are called "Masarwas" by the Bamangwato, and "Amasiri" by the Matabili.   It is difficult to make out their true race affinities, but their language is undoubtedly nearly allied to that spoken by the Koranas and Namaquas living along the Orange river. I make this statement on the strength of the following facts. In 1871 a Korana boy named John entered my service, and went to the interior with me the following year ; and as he had previously learned to speak Dutch from a Griqua master, I could converse freely with him. In 1873, when elephant-hunting in the Linquasi district to the west of Matabililand, we saw a great many Masarwas (Bushmen), and noticing that their language, full of clicks and clucks and curious intonations of the voice, was similar in character to that I had heard spoken by the Koranas on the banks of the Orange river in 1871, I asked John if he could understand them ; but he only laughed and said " No, sir." During the next two years, however, John had a lot to do with the Masarwas, and one day towards the end of 1874, as we were returning from the Zambesi to Matabililand, I heard him conversing quite familiarly with some of these people. " Hullo ! John," I said, " I thought you told me that you couldn't understand the Bushmen ?"—" Well, sir," he answered, " at first I thought I couldn't, but gradually I found that I could understand them, and that they understood me ; and in fact I can say that with a few slight differences these Bushmen speak the same language as my people (the Koranas) on the Orange river." A Griqua family, too, the Neros, who have for many years past been living in Matabililand, all speak Sasarwa (the language of the Masarwas) with perfect fluency, and they have all assured me that they had no difficulty in learning it, as it was only a dialect of the Korana.

Physically, however, speaking generally, the Masarwas whom I have met—and they are many—although they differ essentially from the Kafir tribes by whom they are surrounded, also differ very considerably from the Koranas and Hottentots. Usually, though not invariably, they are lighter in colour and slighter-built men than the Kafirs ; but they are not so short in stature as the Koranas and Hottentots, the greater part of them being from five feet six inches to five feet nine inches in height, and some of them standing over six feet. Occasionally, however, one notices men amongst them of a distinctly Hottentot type, short and stout-built in figure, with high cheek-bones, oblique eyes, and peppercorn hair.   Altogether, I am inclined to think that the Masarwas were originally a people allied in race to the Koranas and Hottentots, but that from a constant infusion of foreign blood, brought amongst them by refugees from different Kafir tribes, they have to a great extent lost the physical characteristics of that race, though they still retain their ancient language almost intact.

The native weapons of the Masarwas are, or rather were, bows and arrows ; for in some parts of the country they have entirely discarded these weapons, and now use guns in their stead. Bows and arrows were still, however, in common use in quite recent times amongst the Bushmen living in the desert country bordering the Botletli river.   Their bows are so small and weak-looking that they seem rather toys than the deadly weapons they really are.   Their arrows are short and unfeathered, being made of light reeds, into the end of which bone heads are inserted.   These bone arrow-heads are always thickly smeared with poison, which is apparently made from the body of a cater-pillar, or grub, mixed with gum.   At least in the quivers of all the Bushmen whose belongings I have examined, I have always found, besides their arrows and fire sticks, a kind of small bark box containing the bodies of grubs or caterpillars preserved in gum, and have invariably been told that these grubs contained the poison which they smeared on their arrows.   I do not know whether the language of the Bushmen who used to infest the mountainous parts of the Cape Colony, the Free State, and Natal is allied to that of the Masarwas, but I presume it must be more or less, and, at any rate, the habits and mode of life of both these wild peoples were very similar ; the weapons, too, of the Bush-men of the Cape Colony—now almost an extinct race—were tiny bows and poisoned arrows.   It would be interesting to learn whether there is any affinity between the languages spoken by the pigmy races of North-western Africa and the dialects used by the Bushmen of the south-western portion of the continent. Their habits, and customs, and mode of life would seem to show that they are all very closely allied.   The Niam-niam dwarfs described by Schweinfurth, as well as the pigmy race of Monbuttoo, skeletons of whom have been sent to Europe by Emin Pacha, use bows and poisoned arrows, as also do the unpleasant little savages encountered by Stanley in the forests bordering the Aruwimi. The Bushmen are probably the direct descendants of the earliest type of man that appeared in Southern Africa; and they probably came from the north and spread down the western side of the continent, long before the black races appeared upon the scene.

Possibly the first appearance of this primitive race of men in Northern Africa was contemporaneous with the migrations into that continent of the original ancestors of the rich and varied fauna by which it is now inhabited; all the more highly specialised forms of which are descended from prototypes, which, as that distinguished naturalist Mr. A. R. Wallace has shown, were originally evolved in the northern hemisphere, and gradually spread southwards on the approach of the last glacial period, penetrating into Africa hundreds of thousands of years ago, before that continent was divided from Europe by the Mediterranean Sea. The curious ant-eaters (earth pigs and pangolins) are probably relics of an earlier fauna, which have survived owing to their nocturnal habits. Many other forms were doubtless exterminated, as Mr. Wallace has pointed out, by the large carnivora of the later period. Be this as it may, we have proof positive that a form of man from whom the Bushmen are in all probability descended, inhabited Southern Africa at a very remote period of the earth's history.

In an interesting paper on " The Antiquity of Man in South Africa," by Dr. A. P. Hillier of Kimberley, it is clearly shown that ages upon ages ago a race of savages existed in that part of the world, who were closely allied to the Bushmen still lingering in certain parts of the country. Speaking of a skull that was found in one of the " kitchen middens or refuse-heaps " on the banks of the Buffalo river, of considerable, though not vast, antiquity, Dr. Hillier says, " It is a small round skull with a low contracted brow, and is of great thickness. It is like the skull of a Bushman or Hottentot, and in all probability is the skull of an individual of one of these races, or of some race very nearly allied to them." Farther on, and speaking of the refuse-heap where this skull was found, Dr. Hillier says, " Whatever the age of this mound, and no unprejudiced observer will

deny that it is considerable, it is but a thing of yesterday
compared to the antiquity of those implements left on the
water's edge when the river[1] stood seventy feet higher than it
now does, or than it did when the foundation shell of this huge
mound was laid." Much interesting information will be found
in this paper concerning the implements here referred to, and
the evidences of their extreme antiquity. The general conclusions of the writer are, that at an immensely remote period
of time a race of men of a very low type migrated from the
north, down the western side of the continent, and that these
people, who were in all probability the progenitors of the
modern Bushmen, penetrated to the southernmost parts of Africa.

But to return to the Masarwas. As trackers and assistants
in the hunting veld they are unrivalled, and they are more
docile and less assertive than Kafirs. To be seen at their best
they must be hungry, and lightly indeed must the wounded
animal tread that hopes to escape from a half-starved Masarwa,
but as soon as they get fat, they become lazy and careless, like
dogs. The life these people lead is a hard one, and I have
often seen them reduced to the last stage of emaciation by
slow starvation, when they have been living for a long time on
very innutritious food. Their faces then looked like skulls over
which yellow parchment had been tightly stretched, and the
muscles of their limbs had wasted away to such an extent
that the bones of the knees had the appearance of great knobs
in the middle of their legs. In such cases their stomachs were
always enormously distended, the result of living upon very
innutritious food, an enormous quantity of which was requisite
to sustain life at all. Such seven-eighths-starved Bushmen are
splendid fellows as assistants in tracking game. In spite of
their emaciated condition they can stand an extraordinary
amount of fatigue, and are exceedingly keen, as their very lives
may depend upon the successful issue of the hunt; should
elephants, however, or other large game be killed, you won't
get your Bushmen any farther. They will at once fetch their
women and children, and the whole tribe will then settle down
alongside of the carcases, and there they will remain, until they
have eaten every scrap of the meat, by which time they will

[1] The Buffalo.

have become quite fat and lazy. There is one faculty which the Bushmen possess in an extraordinary degree, and that is the sense which enables them to find their way, by day or by night, through level pathless forests, where there are no landmarks whatever, to any point which they wish to reach, where they have ever been before. This sense is often well developed in oxen and horses, and elephants possess it in perfection, and will travel immense distances by night in a direct line, to a certain patch of dense bush, where they wish to stand during the heat of the day, or to a pool of water, which has not been visited by them, or by any other elephants, for months or perhaps years previously. Amongst highly-civilised races this sense is conspicuously wanting, and I should say that the greater part of our most profound philosophers would make very poor backwoodsmen. Amongst the various Kafir tribes with which I am acquainted, the sense of locality and direction is, as a rule, not nearly so well developed as with the Bushmen, though some individuals are certainly very good at finding their way in the bush.

When the first Matabili expedition that was sent against the Batauwani returned from Lake Ngami in 1883, they brought back with them some Masarwa children that they had captured in the desert. About a dozen boys were handed over to the king, the eldest probably not being more than ten years old, whilst most of them were little mites of only five or six. They were very thin on their arrival at Bulawayo, but being well fed, as the king's slave-boys always are, they soon got fat, and seemed quite contented with their lot. At night they slept round the fires in the king's courtyard, within the high palisades by which it is enclosed, the entrance to it being of course blocked up. One morning it was discovered that the little Masarwas were gone. Search was at once made for them, and as some of the children were so young it was expected that they would soon be discovered and brought back. However, they were never seen again in Matabililand. When Lo Bengula told me about the escape of these little Bushmen, he wound up his account by saying, "Asi ubantu, Amasiri ; inyamazana gōdwa" ("The Bushmen are not human beings ; they are only wild animals").

In 1884 I made a journey with my waggon from Bulawayo to the Mababi country, taking pretty well the same line that had been followed the previous year by the Matabili army, and after crossing the waggon road from Bamangwato to the Zambesi, began to get among the Bushmen. I made a point of inquiring about the captured children who had made their escape from Bulawayo, and was assured that all but one, who had died of exhaustion on the way, had found their way home in safety. As long as they were amongst the Matabili kraals and cattle posts, they had only travelled at night, and lain in hiding during the day. They had lived on berries and lizards and tortoises during their long journey through the desert. It was on this same journey, when near the pool of " Metsi butluku " (the bitter water), that on my return to the waggon one day from a giraffe hunt, I found an old Bushwoman seated by my fire, talking with the boys I had brought with me from Khama's country. The old creature, who had been captured the previous year, and taken by some unusually humane Matabili as a household drudge for his wife, must have been at least sixty years of age ; yet she had managed to make her escape from the centre of Matabililand, travelling, like the little children, by night, and hiding by day, and like them always holding a true course towards her distant desert home. She told me she had watched the waggon for three days before daring to approach it, as she feared there might be Matabili there. At last, seeing that my cattle-herd wore the Mangwato dress, she had mustered up courage to speak to him, and had then come to the waggon. After this the old lady had an easy time of it. I gave her a blanket, as the nights were bitterly cold, and food from my own pots every day. Whenever we outspanned the old lady was very active in collecting wood for the fire, and getting water. One day, after she had travelled about ten days with the waggon, she disappeared. The Bushmen told me her own people were living at a water-hole not far away, and she had gone to them. The wild creature left me without warning and without thanks, but I have no doubt she felt grateful, and told her people of the kind treatment she had received at the white man's waggon.

Besides the Masarwas there is another tribe of wild people

inhabiting the eastern portion of the Kalahari, who are called
by the Bechwanas, Bakalahari (they of the desert). These
people are as a rule blacker than the Masarwas, and are believed
by ethnologists to be degenerated Bechwanas, who were driven
into the western deserts by more powerful tribes encroaching
from the east. Though they most of them speak Sechwana as
well, yet amongst themselves they speak a Bushman dialect
full of clicks and clucks, and they are probably a mixed race
formed by the fusion of Bechwana refugees with the aboriginal
desert tribes. In some parts of the country these nomads still
use bows and poisoned arrows at the present day. Many of
the Bakalahari, in the districts to the north and west of
Bamangwato, have, under the kind and just rule of Khama,
attained to a certain degree of civilisation, and now form an
interesting illustration of a people in a transition stage from
utter barbarism to a more advanced condition. A generation
ago all the Bakalahari lived the life described by Dr. Livingstone and others. They wandered continually under a burning
sun, over the heated sands of the Kalahari, without any fixed
habitation, and ever and always engaged in a terrible struggle
for existence ; living on berries and bulbs and roots, on snakes
and toads and tortoises, with an occasional glorious feast on a
fat eland, giraffe, or zebra caught in a pitfall ; sucking up
water through reeds and spitting it into the ostrich egg-shells
in which they were wont to carry it, and altogether leading a
life of bitter, grinding hardship from the cradle to the grave.
In fact they were utter savages—joyless, soulless animals—
believing nothing, hoping nothing, but, unlike Bothwell, fearing
much ; for they were sore oppressed by their Bechwana masters,
and often became the prey of the lions and hyænas that
roamed the deserts as well as they. Now, many of these wild
people have been induced by Khama to give up their nomadic
life. He supplied them with seed-corn, and as may be seen at
Klabala and other places, some of the Bakalahari of the
present day hoe up large expanses of ground, and grow so
much corn that, except in seasons of drought, they know not
the famine from which their forefathers were continually
suffering. In addition to this, Khama and his head men have
given them cattle, sheep, and goats to tend for them, from

which they obtain a constant supply of milk. So that it may be said that Khama has successfully commenced the work of converting a tribe of miserable nomadic savages into a happy pastoral people.

At the conclusion of the last chapter I spoke of passing through the country of Chameluga, which had lately been devastated by the Matabili, and I will now relate the tragic death of the wizard of Situngweesa.

Chameluga had long had the reputation amongst his own people of being a powerful sorcerer, and his fame must at last have spread to Lo Bengula, who used to profess the firmest belief in his supernatural powers, and who for many years treated him with great consideration. In 1878 I wrote of Chameluga that, "unlike most other Mashuna chiefs, who are the victims of continual depredation, he is not only left in the quiet enjoyment of his own, but often receives presents of cattle, young girls, etc., from Lo Bengula. It is very probable, however, that his majesty (to use one of his own phrases) is only fattening this false priest, and that one day he will pounce down upon and massacre him and all his people, and take his cattle and the ivory, of which it is said he has a considerable store. This is only surmise, but even thus did Umziligazi, his father, put to death, at one fell swoop, a whole bevy of Makalaka molimos,[1] to whom up till that day he had always shown great favour."

Chameluga, however, retained the ascendency he had gained over Lo Bengula for five years after this was written, and during that time his people, who had for many years enjoyed an immunity from the attacks of the Matabili, grew rich, and became a very prosperous community. Their villages were called collectively Situngweesa, and were situated in the fertile, well-watered country between the Umfuli and Manyami rivers. Early in 1883, however, this period of prosperity came to a sudden and disastrous termination ; for in that year their aged chief was murdered by the order of Lo Bengula, their kraals were destroyed, and they themselves were driven into the hilly country beyond the Mazoe.

The army which was sent to destroy the people of Situng-weesa left Matabililand and travelled eastwards about the

---

[1] Gods.

same time that the first of the two expeditions I have already spoken of went westwards towards Lake Ngami.

Chameluga was, however, not killed in his own country, but in Matabililand, and I heard the story of his death from one of the youngest of his wives, who was an actual eye-witness of the event. This girl, Bavea by name, was born in Matabililand of slave parentage, and was sent by Lo Bengula as a present to Chameluga in 1880. When quite a child she had previously been apprenticed to Mrs. Helm (the wife of the well-known missionary in Matabililand) by the king's sister, and had been brought up in her house, and during that time had learnt to understand and speak English quite fluently. In 1880, as I have said above, very much against her will, she was taken away from Mrs. Helm, and sent for a wife to the wise man of Situngweesa. Early in 1883 Lo Bengula, for the last time, sent presents and friendly messages to Chameluga, at the same time requesting that he would pay him a visit at Bulawayo. Such an invitation was tantamount to a command, and the old man set out on his last earthly journey, accompanied by a small party of his own people, amongst whom were the girl Bavea and one of his sons (a boy of about fifteen years of age). Some time after despatching his messengers to Situngweesa to summon Chameluga, Lo Bengula sent out the greater part of the fighting men from the eastern side of his country to meet his visitor on the road. The orders given to his general appear to have been—" Meet the wizard at the Tchangani river, kill him and all who are with him, and then hasten on and destroy all his people at Situngweesa, and bring back their cattle and ivory." Thus when Chameluga and his little party reached the Tchangani river, the Matabili were already there. The warriors, however, kept out of sight, and only a few head men came forward as if to greet the chief. As they advanced Bavea said to her aged husband, " They are going to kill you ; I know the Matabili. Run ! run ! I see blood in their eyes ; run ! run !" But the old man answered, " Child, I am too old to run. If his day has come, Chameluga does not fear to die ; but bid my son, who is young and swift of foot, creep away in the bushes whilst there is yet time, and carry the news to my people."

The girl was right; she knew the Matabili only too well. Very soon the little party were surrounded by Lo Bengula's savage warriors, and one more of those tragedies took place which are so common in the interior of Africa that they excite but little attention. Chameluga and his whole party were murdered, with the exception of Bavea, who was taken back to Matabililand. Her life amongst the Mashunas must, however, have been to her liking, as she subsequently ran away, and in 1887 I saw her amongst Lo Magondi's people in North-western Mashunaland, and it was then that she told me this story. But the boy had escaped, having crept away just before the attack without attracting notice, and even as the massacre proceeded he was fleeing fast to the north-east. Fear lent him wings, and in an incredibly short space of time,

MATABILI WARRIOR.

having escaped being killed by lions—a very real danger in this part of Africa—he carried the news of the murder of his father to Situngweesa. The people did not require to be told that the Matabili, having killed Chameluga and his party, would be sure to come on in order to destroy his towns with all their inhabitants and take their cattle. They fled at once across the Manyami river, and down into the hilly country between the Mazoe and Inyagui rivers. So hurriedly, indeed, did they leave their homes, that they left most of their grain stores and a small herd of cattle behind them.

When the Matabili, a couple of days later, arrived upon the scene, eager for slaughter, and expecting to find their would-be victims in blissful ignorance of the fate which had befallen their chief, they found all the towns deserted. They captured the small herd of cattle that had been left behind, and which were still feeding close to one of the villages, and they also killed a small party of Mashunas who were coming from a distant kraal on a visit to Situngweesa, and who, unfortunately for themselves, arrived there on the very same day as Lo Bengula's warriors. These men were certainly out of luck, and they were all assegaied. Four months later, in the month of August, on my return from the Sabi, I visited the deserted towns of Situngweesa. Some of the villages had been burnt, but others were still standing; and although all the corn-bins had been overturned, many of them were still full of maize. I saw the remains of two of the murdered Mashunas. In the fields surrounding the villages the rice and " pogo " corn had been harvested before the flight of the people, but there were great quantities of ground nuts and sweet potatoes still in the ground at the time of my visit. The Matabili at once followed on the spoor of the escaped tribe, and raided part of the country of Umsa-washa, near the head waters of the Mazoe river. As, however, the inhabitants were on the look-out for them, they were not very successful, and returned without having killed many people or captured many cattle. On their way home to the Matabili country this "impi"[1] passed the kraals of a tribe of Mashunas living on the head waters of the Bembisan river, under the petty chiefs Musigaguva and Madabuga. These Mashunas had long before been taken under the protection of Umziligazi, Lo Bengula's father, and had been tributary to the Matabili for many years. They had large herds of Matabili cattle in their keeping, many of them wore the Matabili dress, and most of them spoke the language of their conquerors. Why they were destroyed is to me a mystery to this day, nor have I heard any reason given by any of the Matabili who took part in the massacre, except that it was the king's command.

With the Matabili army of which I am now speaking was a man of the waggon-driver class named John Matoli, who many years previously had accompanied Sir John Swinburne to Matabililand as a waggon driver, and who, having

[1] Army.

since settled and married there, is sometimes forced into
military service. John Matoli speaks English well, and I
have known him ever since 1872, and always found him a
very reliable man, and as the destruction of Musigaguva's
kraals is an undeniable fact, I see no reason to question his
account of the tragedy, which is as follows. When the impi
came to Musigaguva they camped close to the Mashuna kraals,
the inhabitants of which brought down food and beer for the
Matabili soldiers, who seemed on very friendly terms with
them, they on their side suspecting nothing. On the day of
their arrival everything remained quiet, but the following
morning the Matabili, acting on the orders of their endunas,
suddenly surrounded the different small kraals, and then at
once fell upon the unsuspecting inhabitants. None were spared,
but men, women, and children were ruthlessly slaughtered,
many of the infants, according to John Matoli, having been
seized by the ankle and their brains dashed out against stones.
It was in April 1883 that this cruel massacre took place, and
towards the end of the following November, on my way back
to Matabililand, I passed through the country, and, camping
one night amongst the ruins of the deserted kraals, saw with
my own eyes the devastation that had been wrought.

CHAPTER VI

Break up camp—Waggon breaks down—Send Laer to Grant's camp for another
wheel—Follow on horseback—Laer meets five lions—Return to my waggons
—Shoot a leopard—Oxen attacked by a lion at the Umfuli—Laer kills the lion
—Move camp to the River Zweswi—Shoot another large lion—Return to Matabililand—The Sea-Cow Row—Unjust treatment at the hands of the Matabili.

EARLY in November 1883 I broke up camp on the banks of
the River Manyami, in Northern Mashunaland, and turned my
face to the south-west. I had not seen a white man since
leaving the Matabili country in the previous April; but I
knew that two hunters, an Englishman and a Boer, were camped
near the River Zweswi, three days' journey from me, and so
resolved to make for their camp and spend a few days with
them and enjoy the pleasure of speaking my own language
once more.

The day after leaving the Manyami, whilst crossing a
tributary of the River Sarua, in a very rough, stony place, the
right hind wheel of the smaller of my waggons collapsed, the
spokes all breaking short off at the nave. I had all the tools
with me necessary for re-spoking it, and one of my drivers, a
Griqua named Samuel, who had been brought up amongst the
Boers, was quite equal to the job; but as I knew that it would
take several days to chop the wood, make and fit the spokes,
pull on the tire, etc., I determined to first try to get my
waggons on to my friends' camp and do the work there. It
was a mere question of whether the hind axle of either of my
friends' waggons was the same size as mine. If it was, I had
only to bring a wheel over from their camp and fit it on to my
waggon in place of the broken one. I at once measured the
length and circumference of my axle, and started Laer off with

LAER MEETS FIVE LIONS.

"The whole five of them then emerged on the other side and walked away, continually stopping and looking round by the way, towards the forest skirting the valley."

a couple of Kafirs and eight oxen, with yokes, chain, etc., to
drag the wheel back on a bush, if it should prove to be the
right size.   I told them to sleep at the River Umfuli, and go on
to Zweswi the following day, I myself intending to ride through
on horseback.   The next morning I made an early start.   I
did not follow the waggon track—one of my own making—
but took a bee-line across country, crossing the Umfuli some
miles above the usual ford.   When I again struck the track I
saw that I had passed my boys, as my oxen's spoor was not in
the road.   I did not follow it for more than a quarter of a
mile, and, then again leaving it, rode straight across country
for the hills, near which I knew, from native report, that my
friends' camp was situated.

About four o'clock I rode up to the waggons, but found
that both Grant and Karl Weyand were away hunting ; however, their people made me comfortable, and I was soon
drinking a cup of tea, the usual tipple of South African
hunters and travellers.   A little before sundown Laer turned
up with the oxen, and with his help I at once took the hind
wheel off Grant's waggon and measured his axle, which I
found was of the same make, and exactly of a size with mine.
We then chopped a thick bush, and fastening the wheel
on it, made everything ready for an early start back to my
waggons on the following morning.   Laer and my two Kafir
boys told me that just beyond where I had left the track they
had come across five lions.   Just here there is a watercourse
running down an open valley, and these lions, it seems, had
killed an eland and dragged it into the creek to eat.   They
must have heard or smelt the oxen coming along the road, and
two of them, a large male and a female, jumped on to the
bank and came trotting towards them, but seeing Laer and the
Kafirs, stopped, and then walked back and entered the creek
again.   The whole five of them then emerged on the other
side and walked away, continually stopping and looking round
by the way, towards the forest skirting the valley.   According
to Laer and the Kafirs, this family party consisted of a large
male and a young male, and three full-grown females.   The
big one seems to have been a magnificent animal, as Laer—
who, although quite a youth, has grown up in the wilds, and

has seen many lions—said he thought it had a finer mane than
he had ever seen before.   Chukuru, one of the Matabili Kafirs
with him, describing the incident to me, said, "Maimamo!
wasn't it awful ('Sa be ka').   Such an enormous one ('Um ka
la gata').   He looked as if his shoulders were loaded with
bundles of grass, and behind he was so small he looked hungry.
When I saw him coming towards me in the open my heart
died, and I gave thanks when I saw him turn back."   I was
terribly vexed when I heard that, if I had kept along the
waggon track for another mile or so, I should have come across
these lions.   I was well mounted and had a good rifle with me,
and had I only sighted them in so open a part of the country
I think I should have added at least the skin of the big male
to my collection of hunting trophies.

At daylight the following morning, leaving Laer to come
on with the wheel, I rode on ahead, as I intended to reach my
waggons the same evening, but knew that my boys would have
to sleep on the road.   I now followed the waggon track, as I
thought it just possible that I might still find the lions along
the creek where they had been seen the day before.   However,
on reaching it a flock of vultures sitting on the bank and others
flying overhead showed me where the carcase of the eland lay,
and at the same time assured me that the lions themselves had
finally abandoned their prey.   I now left the waggon track
and rode along the creek, intending to follow it to its junction
with the River Lundaza, a tributary of the Umfuli, and then
take a bee-line for my waggons.   I had not proceeded very
far when I saw, a considerable distance ahead of me, a smallish
animal emerge from the forest and cross the open ground extending along the creek.   It very soon reached the bank, and,
going down to drink, at once disappeared.   On first sighting it
I had seen that it was some cat-like animal, and as it was too
small for a lioness, had guessed it to be a leopard.   As soon as
it was in the creek and well out of sight, I galloped as hard as
I could in order to get up to it before it had finished drinking.
However, it must have heard me, and came up the bank again
when I was still about one hundred and fifty yards distant from
it.   I saw at once that it was a fine leopard, but had little time to
examine him, as, after glancing towards my rapidly-advancing

horse for the briefest time possible, he bounded away across the open towards the forest which skirted the valley.   He had not very far to go, but, instead of keeping up his pace he soon changed from a gallop to a trot, so that I gained upon him fast, and, pulling in and jumping off, got a shot just as he was entering the bush.   The bullet, as I afterwards found, struck him in the right thigh, breaking the bone, and passed out on the left side behind the ribs.   He did not stop or turn round, but, with a loud snarl and a flourish of his tail, galloped in among the trees.

Hastily remounting, without having taken my eye off him, I was soon close up again, when he ran into a patch of grass at the foot of a large bush and became invisible.   I did not know at this time that his right thigh was broken, but I knew that a wounded leopard is a very dangerous animal to deal with (as savage as a lion and as agile as a cat), and so rode cautiously, completely round the bush beneath which he lay, to see if I could not get a sight of him.   However, he was so well concealed by the grass that I could see absolutely nothing of him, although, being on horseback, my eyes were well above the ground.   I now rode nearer and began to think he was dead or dying, as he allowed me to come to within twenty-five yards before making a sign.   When at about this distance, however, he suddenly raised his head with a loud snarling grunt, and gave me a fine view of his open mouth garnished with a very serviceable-looking set of teeth. Thinking he was coming, I instantly jerked my horse half round ; but the apparition disappeared, and I could see nothing again.   However, I had seen whereabouts he was lying, and so determined to fire a shot or two to make him show himself ; but before I could do so he again raised his head with another snarl, and immediately after came straight out at me, and at such a pace, that before I could turn my horse and get him started the leopard was right under his tail.   He chased me for some sixty or seventy yards before he stopped, coming right into the open, and keeping close up the whole time.   I pulled in as quickly as I could, and before the plucky little beast regained the bush gave him a second shot, which quickly proved fatal. When charging and chasing me this leopard growled or grunted

or roared exactly like a lion under similar circumstances, and
made just as much noise.   And had it not been for his broken
thigh I believe he would have clawed the horse.   He proved
to be a fine male, and I was better pleased at shooting him
than I should have been with killing a lioness, as he only made
the third of these handsome animals that have fallen to my rifle
during all my wanderings.   I soon removed his skin, and after
tying it securely behind the saddle, rode on my way ; and,
crossing the Umfuli shortly after mid-day, reached my waggons
about four o'clock in the afternoon.

Awaking at daylight the next morning, and looking out of
my waggon, the first thing I noticed was one of the oxen
which had been sent with Laer to fetch the wheel standing
amongst the others with a broken riem[1] hanging from its
horns.   It was evident that the animal had got loose from
wherever it had been tied up on the previous evening, and
come all along the road back to the waggons during the night.
I at once surmised that a lion was at the bottom of the
business, and thinking that the rest of the oxen might have
been scattered in the night, and Laer left in a fix, I determined to ride back at once and see what had really happened.
I was soon ready, and only waiting to drink a cup of coffee,
saddled up and proceeded on my way.   A couple of hours'
ride brought me close to the Umfuli, and when near the ford
I heard the crack of a whip, and soon saw Laer with six oxen
in the yokes coming on with the wheel.   On riding up the
first thing I noticed was the skin of a fresh-killed lion lying
over the wheel, the grim head and great paws still attached,
and the yellow eyes, even in death, still full of fiery light.
" Well, Laer," I said, " what has happened, and who shot the
lion ?"—" I did, sir," he answered, evidently feeling very proud
of himself, and proceeded to tell me all about it.

It appeared that he had reached the Umfuli late the
preceding evening, and that by the time he had pulled the
wheel across the river, and outspanned and tied up the cattle
(along the side of the old kraal we had made here some
months previously), lighted a fire, and got things ship-shape
for the night, it was nearly dark.   Laer and one of the Kafirs,

---

[1] Riem, the thong used in South Africa for tying up cattle.

a Mangwato boy named April, were engaged in making up
the fire and boiling the coffee kettle, when Chukuru, the
other lad, who was breaking dry wood from the kraal fence,
was heard to call out "Maimamo! Siluan, siluan!" ("Lion,
lion"), and immediately after he came rushing up to them
with a lion grunting loudly close behind him. The fearsome
beast, Laer said, came up to within a short distance of them;
so near, indeed, that he was plainly visible by the light cast by
the fire. I asked him why he had not fired at this juncture.
"I was so frightened," he answered, "that I forgot all about
my rifle," but he added that both he and April had shouted
as hard as they could, and waved burning brands which they
caught up from the fire, Chukuru, thoroughly frightened,
crouching behind them the while. The lion now retired into
the darkness, and the three frightened boys built up the fire,
and bringing all the kraal fence away from alongside the
oxen, built a hedge behind themselves, extending from the
bush on which the wheel lay to the old fence on the other
side of the fire. The eight oxen were tied two by two to
the chain attached to the bush that carried the wheel, and
allowing three yards of chain for each pair of oxen, the two
farthest off must have been under fifteen yards from the
fire. They had scarcely completed these preparations for the
night, and again replenishing the fire, taken their places
behind it, when they all three saw the lion emerge from the
darkness, and coming rapidly past the front oxen, seize one
of the second pair and drag it to the ground. It must have
been at this moment that the one which turned up at the
waggons during the night had broken his riem and run off.
By the light of the fire the boys could see pretty well what
was going on, and Laer was preparing to fire at the lion,
when April said: "Let me shoot! you're only a child," and
taking the rifle from him—a Martini-Henry—fired, but without any apparent result, as the lion still hung on to the ox.
Laer then put in another cartridge, and tried a shot with
much more effect, as the marauder at once released his victim,
and fell all of a heap, and without a moan, to the ground,
being, in fact, stone dead, for this lucky shot had broken
his neck just behind the head, and of course killed him

instantly. It was some time before the boys could believe
he was really dead ; but, as he did not move, they gradually
became convinced that he was, and, approaching him cautiously with lighted torches of dry grass, at last went close up
and pulled him back to the fire. Laer said that although
some of the cattle had pulled violently at their riems when
the lion first seized the ox, they soon ceased to manifest
alarm, and were all quite quiet when the dread beast lay dead
in their midst.

Upon several other occasions I have seen cattle evince
very little alarm with a lion in their immediate vicinity ; and,
again, I have known them to be seized with a regular panic,
under the influence of which they have fled for miles. As a
general rule, however, I think it is a mistake to say that
oxen and horses have an instinctive fear of the smell of a
lion. I have always found that a shooting horse trained to
carry meat will allow you to pack a reeking lion skin upon
him with as much indifference as an antelope hide, so long as
he has never been frightened or mauled by one of the former
animals ; this, at least, is my experience.

On examining the wounded ox, which April was driving
on slowly behind the team, I found that the lion had seized
him by the muzzle with one paw, fixing the claws of the
other paw in his left shoulder, and biting him at the same
time at the back of the neck. However, he might possibly
have recovered from these wounds, but April, in firing at his
assailant, had unfortunately shot the ox through the hind leg,
just grazing the bone, but nearly severing the tendon, and
of course laming him badly. On examining the lion skin
I found it was that of a fine young male, with a splendid
set of teeth and good claws, and, riding back to look at the
carcase, found it to be by no means in bad condition. Had
Chukuru been a little farther away from the fire the hungry
beast would most assuredly have caught, killed, and eaten
him. I now gave orders to Laer to come on with the wheel,
and told April to bring the wounded ox on as far as he
could, but to leave him as soon as he lay down or refused
to proceed, since I had made up my mind to send Samuel
back with some boys as soon as I reached the waggon, to

kill him and cut up the meat.   This I did, and so ended this experience.

Laer always was a most lucky boy for coming across lions.   I remember in 1882 I sent him out to Matabililand, in the early part of the hunting season, with some of the skins of the antelopes I had already preserved, as I saw I was getting so many that I should never have been able to have carried them all at once, on my one waggon, at the end of the hunting season.   Laer travelled with the small waggon I had made by taking the wheels off my big buck waggon and then putting in a short langwagen.[1]   He only had a double-barrelled shot gun with him with which to shoot guinea-fowls along the road, as I had no spare rifle to lend him.   One night he was camped at the Umniati river, the ten oxen being tied up, two by two, to the yokes as usual.   Laer and the two Kafir boys who were with him were lying inside a fence which they had built behind them, and which ran out at right angles from the hind wheel of the waggon.   A large fire was burning at their feet, which cast a good light for some distance round it.   Suddenly Laer heard a commotion amongst the cattle, and jumping up simultaneously with the two Kafir boys, they all saw a large lion emerge swiftly from the gloom of the night, advance rapidly, and seize one of the two oxen that were standing just in front of the two tied to the disselboom.[2]   The grim beast stood in the full light of the fire, with one paw over the shoulder of the ox, and the other holding the poor animal by the muzzle, the lion's hind feet being planted firmly on the ground all the time.   Laer then very pluckily fired a charge of shot into him at less than ten yards' distance.   He told me, in relating the adventure, that the lion, on being hit, gave a loud roar, and instantly quitting the ox, bounded off into the darkness, and did not return. Possibly he died from the effects of the wound.   The ox that had been attacked had to be driven loose from the Umniati river to Matabililand, and eventually died from the effect of the bites he had received in the back of the neck.

[1] A particular portion of a South African waggon.   [2] Waggon pole.

The next day, after fitting Grant's wheel on to my axle, I started for my friends' camp, which I reached the following evening. Both Grant and Karl Weyand were now at their waggons, and busy making preparations to trek out to the Matabili country, as the rains were beginning to fall. There being no good wood for spokes just round their camp, it was resolved that we should move all the waggons to the bank of the River Zweswi, where there was plenty, and remain there whilst the work was being done, and then all travel together to Matabililand. As the river was only three or four miles off, it was decided that Karl Weyand and I should trek down to the ford early the following morning, and then send Grant's wheel back to bring on his waggon. Accordingly that evening we made everything ready and tied the oxen in their places, and at daylight inspanned and started, reaching the Zweswi before the sun got warm. I rode on horseback just in front of the waggons, thinking I might get a shot at something ; but I saw nothing, except that I noticed the fresh track of a large lion in the soft sand of the river's bed.

I had outspanned the waggons, chopped a bush, and sent the wheel back to Grant, and was busy making preparations for breakfast, when two of my men who had been hunting elephants in the " fly " country to the north came up and said, " Sir ! sir ! we have just seen a big lion close by, just on the other side of the river ; he is very vicious, and stood and growled at us." These two men, I forgot to say, I had found the previous evening at Grant's camp, where they had arrived the day I left with the wheel, and hearing that I was coming on with the waggons, had waited there for me. This morning they had taken a round with their guns, and coming up along the river to where we were outspanned, had walked right on to the lion when they were actually within sight of the waggons—doubtless the same animal whose fresh spoor I had seen whilst crossing the river. To my inquiries they replied that they had really seen the lion just on the other side of the river, and wondered that I had not heard the animal growling. When I asked one of them, who was a very good shot, why he had not fired at the lion, he said that he would have done so, but his chum prevented him, saying, " Let him alone : don't you see how vicious he is ? If you miss him he is sure to come and bite," and that whilst they were talking the lion had retreated amongst some bushes behind an ant-heap. As they said he was a large lion with a fine mane, I was very anxious to get him, and so had all my dogs caught and tied up at once. I knew that he would not go far, but would just lie in the patch of bush where my men had seen him, waiting for night to pay a visit to my camp ; and so, as breakfast was nearly ready, I had something to eat before starting in pursuit.

As soon as I was ready I had my best horse brought up, and, having all the dogs led, proceeded to where my men had seen the lion some half-hour previously. Here we took up the spoor, and I gave strict orders to the boys leading the dogs not on any account to let them loose until we actually sighted the quarry. The ground was not very favourable for tracking so soft-footed an animal as a lion ; still, by looking carefully it could be made out, and we followed it, step by step, through the first patch of bush into a narrow valley covered with soft green grass. Here it was impossible to see anything ; but this opening in the forest, down which ran a little rill into the Zweswi, was not more than twenty yards broad, and beyond it lay another patch of bush in which I felt pretty sure the lion was then lying. Still holding the line the spoor had led us, and crossing the grass to the sandy soil in which the trees grew beyond it, I told my men to look carefully for the tracks, whilst I rode on a little ahead, bidding them on no account to come on until they had got the spoor. I now rode slowly on by myself, keeping as sharp a look-out as possible both in front and on each side of me. The bush consisted of small saplings with very little underwood, but as the trees were already mostly in leaf, I could not see very far.

I had ridden perhaps one hundred yards in this way when suddenly, with the corner of my eye, as it were, I saw a something, and, turning my head, instantly became aware that it was the lion. He was lying exactly at right angles to the course I was riding, and was watching me intently. His hind legs were doubled in under him, and his head placed flat upon his outstretched paws, just in front of which lay the fallen trunk of a small dead tree, some eight or ten inches in diameter. When I first saw him, lying at a distance of about forty yards, I had a perfectly clear view of him from my horse's back, and, pulling in instantly, tried to fire from the saddle. However, the horse would not stand, but moved on, bringing a tree in the line of fire ; this I let him pass, and, getting another good view beyond it, again pulled in, but, as the perverse animal would not keep still, I dismounted. All this time the lion had never moved, nor did he now, but lay watching me intently with his yellow eyes. Nothing stirred but his tail, the end of which he twitched slowly, so that the black bunch of hair at its extremity appeared first on one side of him, then on the other. As I raised my rifle to my shoulder I found that the fallen tree-trunk interfered considerably with the fine view I had had of him from my horse's back, as it hid almost all his nose below the eyes. In the position in which he was now holding his head I ought to have hit him about half-way between the nostrils and the eyes, which was impossible ; anywhere above the eyes would have been too high, as the bullet would have glanced from his skull, so that it required a very exact shot to kill him on the spot. However, there was no time to wait, and trying to aim so that the bullet should just clear the fallen log and catch him between the eyes, I fired. With a loud roar he answered the shot, and I instantly became aware that he was coming straight at me, with open mouth and flaming eyes, growling savagely. I knew it was hopeless to try to get another cartridge into my single-barrelled rifle, and utterly useless to try to mount, more especially as my horse, startled by the loud hoarse grunts and sudden and disagreeable appearance of the charging lion, backed so vigorously that the bridle (to a running ring on which a strong thong was attached, the other end being fastened to my belt) came over his head. I had a strong feeling that I was about to have an opportunity of testing the accuracy of Doctor Livingstone's incredible statement that, for certain reasons (explained by the Doctor), a lion's bite gives no pain ; but there was no time to think of anything in particular. The whole adventure was the affair of a moment. I just brought my rifle round in front of

"Just within the bush the dogs again brought him to bay alongside a large ant-hill, and I galloped round in front of him."

me, holding the small of the stock in my right hand and the barrel in my left, with a vague idea of getting it into the lion's mouth, and at the same time yelled as loud as I could, " Loos de honden, loos de honden," which being translated means, " Let loose the dogs." In an instant, as I say, the lion was close up to me. I had never moved my feet since firing, and, whether it was my standing still facing him that made him alter his mind, or whether he heard the noise made by my people, who, hearing my shot, immediately followed by the loud growling of the lion, were all shouting and making a noise to frighten the lion from coming their way, I cannot take upon myself to say ; but he came straight on to within about six yards of me, looking, I must say, most unpleasant, and then suddenly swerved off, and passing me, galloped away.

I tried to keep my eye on him and get the bridle back over my horse's head at the same time, but he was thoroughly frightened and kept on backing. At this instant the dogs came up, and Punch and Ruby took the spoor, followed by the others ; but by the time I had quieted and mounted my horse both lion and dogs were out of sight. I now galloped in the direction they had taken, and soon heard a dog bark, immediately followed by the growling of the lion. Then there was a perfect chorus of barking and growling and I knew that the dogs were on to him, and that, bar accidents, his skin was mine.

Putting spurs to my horse, I soon came up with the dogs, just as they were going through an open valley with their grim opponent, a great gaunt, hungry-looking lion, but with a fine mane. My pack were all round him, barking furiously, Punch and one of the young dogs going sometimes dangerously near. Just as the lion entered the bush he faced round at the dogs and I jumped off for a shot ; but he turned again, and only gave me a chance from behind. I fired, and knew I had hit him by the growl he gave, and I afterwards found that the bullet had passed through his left thigh without breaking the bone and out through his flank. Just within the bush the dogs again brought him to bay alongside a large ant-hill, and I galloped round in front of him.

As soon as he saw me he paid no further heed to his canine foes, but stood, with his eyes fixed on the most dangerous of his assailants, growling hoarsely, and with his head held low between his shoulders—just ready to charge, in fact. I knew my horse would not stand steady, so jumped off, and taking a quick aim fired instantly, as it does not do to wait when a lion is looking at you like this, and when he may make up his mind to come at any moment. Usually they jerk their tails up over their backs, holding them perfectly stiff and rigid, two or three times before charging. They sometimes charge without doing this, but they never do it without charging. My bullet inflicted a mortal wound, entering between the animal's neck and shoulder and travelling the whole length of his body. He sat down like a dog on his haunches immediately after, and was evidently done for, as he lolled his tongue out of his mouth and growled feebly when the dogs bit him in the hind quarters.

Not wishing to spoil the skin I would not fire again, and was standing by my horse waiting for him to give up the ghost, when a rifle was discharged from behind me, and over the lion rolled. This shot was fired by John Slaipstein, one of the two men who had first seen him, and when I found that, firing at a distance of about fifteen yards, with a 10-bore rifle, he had knocked a hole through the lion's skin about the size of a shilling, I was naturally vexed, and abused him very freely. My own bullets, being solid 450's, had scarcely marked the skin at all.

I now examined the dead beast, and could find no sign of his having been hit by my first shot, but on his cheek a patch of hair had been knocked off and blood was oozing from the skin, and what happened I think is this: my first bullet must have struck the fallen tree, and, glancing off, missed the lion, but knocked a splinter of wood into his face with sufficient force to tear some hair off and make the skin bleed. This made him growl and come out at me. Had he been really wounded, and then charged, I do not believe he would have swerved off as he did. He was a fine large lion, and must have been a very fine animal when in his prime: but he was evidently very old and in low condition, and his teeth were much worn and broken. His skin, however, was in good order, and he had a very nice mane. I have no doubt that he would have paid a visit to my camp that night had he not been seen and hunted up, for he must have been suffering from extreme

hunger.   His pegged-out skin measured ten feet eleven inches in
length, and he was in fact the second largest lion, judging by the
length of the pegged-out skin, that I had killed up to that time.
I have since killed two more whose dimensions were greater.

About the middle of December I reached Matabililand,
and for the first time received unjust treatment at the hands of
Lo Bengula, though I believe that I have to thank Ma-kwaykwi,
the head enduna of Bulawayo, for all the trouble and annoyance I was put to.   I will briefly relate what occurred, as it
will give stay-at-home people some idea of the injustice white
men sometimes have to put up with amongst savage tribes.
Certainly the remembrance of what is known in Matabililand
as the " Sea-Cow Row " still calls up very bitter memories in
me ; and though the resentment I felt against the king at the
time, and for long afterwards, has now very much toned down,
I have never forgiven Ma-kwaykwi for rounding on me as he
did, after having for years previously pretended to be my friend.
It gave me a lesson which I shall never forget, the moral of
which is—never believe you know the workings of a savage
man's mind sufficiently to enable you to trust him implicitly.

It has long been known by the white men resident in
Matabililand that the people do not like hippopotami to be
killed indiscriminately, though they do not object to one or two
being shot for food.   They have some superstition on the subject, and profess to believe that a drought will follow the
slaughter of a large number of these animals, unless their bones
are thrown back into the river.   I have always respected this
superstition, and never shot any of these animals in Lo
Bengula's country except when I wanted food, and then
usually after having asked his express permission.

Well ! in 1883, hippopotamus hide sjamboks being in great
demand in the Cape Colony and the Transvaal, a trader in
Matabililand, whose name it is unnecessary to mention, was
foolish enough to employ several Griquas and colonial natives
who had settled in Matabililand, and who were all expert
hunters, to shoot hippopotami for him and cut up their hides
into sjamboks ; thinking, of course, that the king would not
hear of it.   These men slaughtered about fifty hippopotami,
however, and as enormous numbers of untrimmed sjamboks

were continually being brought in to M——'s store at
Emhlangen, the king soon got to hear of what had been going
on, and was naturally very angry.   M—— was summoned to
Bulawayo, and was still there on my arrival from the hunting
veld in December.   I left my waggons at Emhlangen and
rode over to Bulawayo to see Lo Bengula, and the same evening walked up to the kraal with my old friend Mr. James Fairbairn to see him.   As I came up to the large brick house
which has been built for him, M—— was just leaving, and I
heard the king say, " You have sinned, you have sinned greatly
(' onili kakulu '), and you shall pay for it."   When I came up he
greeted me in the most friendly manner, and asked me all
about my hunt ; and he then told me how angry he was that
so many hippopotami had been killed.   I told him that I
thought it was a great shame, and further said that I had not
even seen a hippopotamus the whole year, but I also told him
that one of my waggon drivers (practically one of the king's
own people, as he belonged to the kraal of the Amazizi) had
shot one hippopotamus for food for himself and his boys, low
down the course of the Manyami river, beyond the farthest
limits of Matabililand.   The king, however, only said, " Asi
luto, loko ; hai-iko umlando gu-ee, Selous" (" That's nothing ;
there's no case against you, Selous"), and shaking hands, we
parted the best of friends.

I returned to my waggon, and was naturally very much
surprised when a few days later I was summoned by messengers
from the king to Bulawayo.   The messengers told me that
there was going to be a big row about the killing of the king's
hippopotami, and that M——, who had caused all the trouble,
and all the white men who had been in the veld, were
to be tried by a council of head men.   There were four of us
altogether, M——, Piet Ostenhuisen, Grant, and myself.   Piet
Ostenhuisen had shot a few hippos, but not many, during the
season, but Grant had not killed a single one.   The case lasted
three days, and during that time we had to sit in the rain all
day long, outside the king's quarters in the big kraal, listening
to the harangues of the head men whom the king had chosen
to try the case.   All the Griqua hunters and colonial boys who
had been in the hunting veld were also present, my own two

drivers amongst them. They asked me why I had shot the king's sea-cows ; to which I replied that I had not done so. "Well, then," they said, "you sent your man to shoot them ;" and to this I had no reply, for although in reality I had cautioned John against doing so, had I said as much, and disclaimed my responsibility in the matter, they would in all probability have killed him, and John Slaipstein was an old boy of mine, and a man I much liked. They overbore all argument with floods of vehement assertions, and heaped every description of insult upon M——— and Piet Ostenhuisen, and told Grant when he said that he had not killed a sea-cow, that they would make him pay for walking in the king's country and drinking the king's water. To me personally they said but little, except that I was the "witch, who had killed all the king's game," and that they would make me pay for the sea-cow that John Slaipstein had shot. At one point I was able to turn the laugh against Ma-kwaykwi, for when after saying, " It is you, Selous, who have finished the king's game," he went on, " But you are a witch, you mûst bring them all to life again. I want to see them—all, all. Let them all walk in at the kraal gate, the elephants and the buffaloes and the elands "—I stood up and called out, " All right ; but when the lions come in, will you, Ma-kwaykwi, remain where you are to count them ? " This caused a general laugh at Ma-kwaykwi's expense, and quite stopped his flow of eloquence.

On the third day the king came out to give judgment. His big chair was brought, in which he seated himself. He first called me to him and said, " Why did you kill my sea-cows ? " I of course denied having done so ; when he said, " Well ! you sent Moilo (John's native name) to shoot them." I replied that I had myself told him about the one hippo that John had shot, when he himself had assured me that it did not matter. To this he made no answer, but simply repeated that I had sent John to kill his sea-cows. I could not give poor John away, so I said, " John is my man ; he has shot a sea-cow ; if he has committed a fault, I will take it on myself." He at once said, " Do you say that because you are rich ? " and got very angry, as did all his endunas, when I told him that I did not say it because I was rich, but because I was one man

alone in his country, and saw that he wanted to " tumba," *i.e.*
to plunder me.   After remaining silent, drumming with his
foot, and looking very black for a few moments, he said, " You
say you will pay ; what will you pay ? "   I said I would give
him two heifers for the sea-cow John had shot, when he immediately said in a very angry tone of voice and holding up
and shaking both hands in the air with all the fingers extended,
" You shall pay ten."   I said, " You can take them ; you are
strong, and I am alone, but I won't give them."   I then walked
back to my companions in misfortune and sat down.   Being
now very angry, I fixed my eyes on one of the endunas who
attracted my attention by saying something, and stared him in
the face.   Seeing me look at him in a way that very likely suggested that I would like to put a bullet through him, he said
angrily, " What are you staring at me for ? " and as I kept my
gaze steadily fixed on him, jumped up excitedly, saying, " I
will tear those eyes out of your head, and throw them on the
ground, and stamp on them."   Presently the king again retired,
and finally we had to pay.   The business cost M—— about
£300, and myself over £60, of which sum I shall always consider that Lo Bengula robbed me.

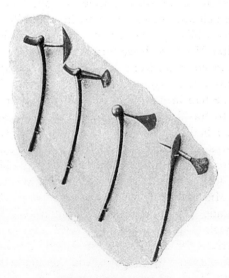

NATIVE BATTLE-AXES.

CHAPTER VII

As soon as the sea-cow case was settled I set out for the Transvaal, and reaching Klerksdorp in January 1884, at once commenced packing my collections for immediate transmission to Europe. At this time I felt so sore at the treatment I had received from Lo Bengula that I determined not to hunt in his country during the coming dry season, but to spend the year in the northern parts of Khama's territory, shooting and preserving specimens of those species of antelope for which I had orders, which are not to be found in Matabili or Mashunaland. It was whilst preparing for this expedition that the late Mr. Walter Montagu Kerr turned up one day in Klerksdorp. He had come up from Kimberley purposely to see me and to ask my advice concerning an expedition into the interior which he had in view, and as I liked him from the first, I asked him to travel up with my waggons as far as Bulawayo, for, although I had no intention of hunting in Lo Bengula's country, it was necessary for me to revisit Matabililand on business, before going westwards to the Mababi. On 5th March 1884 we set out on our travels northwards, but as my poor friend Mr. Kerr has given an account of this journey, which we made together as far as Bulawayo, in his very interesting book *The Far Interior*, I need say no more about it here. Arrived at Bulawayo we found Lo Bengula very friendly to all outward appearance, and he made no difficulty about allowing Mr. Kerr to set out upon his arduous journey

through Matabililand and Mashunaland to the Zambesi. I
was able to give my friend a few boys, whom I knew he could
rely on, to accompany him into the Zambesi valley as far as
one or other of the stations that are governed by one of the
native chiefs holding the official position of " Capitão Mor,"
under the Portuguese Government, from whom I knew he
would be able to obtain guides and porters to Tete. As my
friend was new to African travel, and his resources were very
slender, I advised him to limit his ambition to traversing the
then unknown country between Mashunaland and Tete, and
to give up his more ambitious project of extending his travels
from there through the Makanga country to Lake Nyassa ; but
Montagu Kerr was a true scion of the brave old Scottish
Border family whose name he bore, and he succeeded in carrying out his original programme in its entirety. Unfortunately
he suffered great hardships and privations in doing so, the
effect of which on his constitution no doubt had much to do
with hastening his untimely death whilst still in the prime of
life. Like poor Jameson, with whom he had much in common,
Montagu Kerr was a general favourite with all sorts and conditions of men in Africa, and by his death I lost a very dear
friend.

　　In the middle of May, after bidding adieu and God-speed to
my friend, I trekked away westwards towards the Mababi. I
was accompanied by my old driver Samuel and the Griqua
boy Laer. I shall give no detailed account of my travels
during 1884, as on looking over my diaries for that year I
find that they contain but little of any special interest.
Suffice it to say that I only took one waggon with me, and my
best span of bullocks, leaving my heavy buck waggon and the
greater portion of my live stock with Mr. Fairbairn at Bulawayo. I travelled right across country from Matabililand
to Koungyara (one of the permanent waters on the hunting
road from Bamangwato to the Mababi). The country was
perfectly level the whole way, and there was only one river to
cross in the entire distance—the Gwai. In certain parts, however, we had a good deal of chopping to do in order to prepare
a way for the waggon, as I followed no old track of any kind.
Luckily a very heavy rain-storm passed over the entire country

in the end of May which was most useful to me, as it filled all the vleys and pools with water on my line of march. I first made for Bukwela's town on the River Gwai, where I had been in 1873, and got some men from him as guides as far as the road which leads from Tati to the Zambesi. These men then turned back, but as water was plentiful, and the country pretty open on ahead, I had no difficulty in piloting my waggon myself, always travelling westwards. After reaching Koungyara I followed the waggon track to Sode Gara, and from thence to the Mababi. This is the same road I travelled over in 1879, but whereas in that year we found no water in any of the vleys along the roadside, in 1884 water was plentiful, rendering the journey easy for the oxen and pleasant for myself.

Towards the end of June I reached some large vleys that are situated near the northern end of the large open plain, known to hunters as the Mababi flat. Here I formed a camp, as it was a good spot from which to hunt eland and giraffe, and I was anxious to shoot some of these animals in order to secure a supply of good meat and fat before trekking down to the river. I soon had a lot of Bushmen and their families camped round my waggon all eager for meat ; and as I found them most anxious and willing to show me game, and they carried in all the meat I wanted for myself, I gave them a very liberal supply for themselves. However, though I could get fresh giraffe spoor every day, and shoot them when I wanted, I could not get hold of an eland bull, the animal I particularly wished for.

One day two Bushmen came up from the river saying that a lion had killed one of their people the day before, and two days previously, a Makuba Kafir. They begged me to try to shoot the animal for them, and I promised to do my best when I trekked down to the river with the waggon, which I intended to do in a few days' time. Three days later I started, and the same evening met a lot of Masubias coming from their towns on the river, who were carrying a good supply of mealies (maize), which they were anxious to sell to me, and which I was very glad to get for my horses. These men were accompanied by some Bushmen, who informed me that the same lion that had killed the two men a few days previously had since killed two more, the one again a Bushman, and the other a Makuba. All these four men had been killed in broad daylight, the two Makubas whilst digging up mice in the open plain, and the two Bushmen in the Mopani forest skirting the plain.

The next morning the men who had sold me their maize left the waggon early, in order to get home before nightfall. That evening I slept close to the top end of the reed bed in which the Mababi river disappears, and the following day trekked down to our camping-place of 1879, where some old buffalo heads still marked the spot. I had scarcely outspanned, when two Masubias, both of whom I knew well, as they had worked for me when I was last here, came up and told me that their companion had been killed that morning by a lion. On asking them how it happened, Ramakutzan replied : " Yesterday afternoon three of us, thinking your waggon was still far off, left home with mealies to sell to you, but had not travelled far when we met those of our people who first visited you returning. They told us that you were coming down to your old camp, and would be here that evening or the next day early, so we thought it useless to go any farther, and made a scherm for ourselves under those high trees yonder," pointing to some about two thousand yards distant, close to the edge of the reed bed. " Here we slept. A little before daylight, feeling very cold, I got up, and sitting by the fire, lit my ' dacha ' pipe, and commenced smoking. My comrades were lying under their skin blanket, and I was still smoking, when I saw an indistinct something coming rapidly along the ground towards them. 'Tauw, tauw! (Lion, lion),' I cried. ' Wake ! wake !' and as one of them threw the blanket off him and raised his head, the something, which even in the dim gray light I knew to be a lion, was on him, and seizing him by the head so that he never cried out, dragged him away from the fire. I seized my gun, which was standing in the back of the scherm, and fired after the lion ; but I am not a white man, that knows how to use a gun properly, and my bullet did nothing."

Upon hearing this tale of woe I got one of my horses up, and calling all the dogs, rode down to where the man had

been killed, to see if I could hunt up the lion. Under a tree
about fifty yards away from the fire from which he had
dragged him, we found where the brute had eaten his victim.
There was a lot of blood about, a broken string of beads, and
some odd portions of a man's inside. From here he had been
dragged into the reeds through some shallow water, and we
soon found his remains. The skull had been crushed when he
was first seized, and the intestines pulled out, and all the flesh
of the thighs and buttocks eaten off. The lion, I have no
doubt, was at this time somewhere not very far off in the reed
bed, but as the dogs either could not or would not take the
spoor in the wet ground, and it was a place where it was
impossible to see two yards in front of one, I could do
nothing.

As I had cows, calves, horses, and donkeys at the waggons,
I made sure I should have some trouble with this lion, and
determined, if I could not get a shot at him in the daytime,
to set guns for him at night. However, strange to say, he
never bothered me, nor did I hear of his killing any more
people during the month my waggon stood on our old camping-place. The first two nights he certainly prowled round,
but the moon was just at the full, and I had a very good lot
of dogs, so he did not venture very close, but I saw his spoor
both mornings on the footpath running along the reed bed.
After this my camp assumed the appearance of a market, as
crowds of Masubias came up from their towns every morning
with mealies, pumpkins, Kafir corn, etc., for sale, and as the
men always remained two or three days, and went out hunting
with me to get some meat, my waggon was soon surrounded
by several large camps. Perhaps all this bustle and noise
frightened and disconcerted this man-eating lion, and caused
him to move off to some other part of the country where he
could catch a Bushman every now and then and eat him
quietly, or else perhaps the last Kafir disagreed with him, and
he had resolved to change his diet.

The Mababi country used to be a very good district for
lions, and one sometimes found them far from the bush on the
open plain, where they had perhaps killed a wildebeest, and
were loath to leave the carcase. In October 1879 Mr. H. C.

Collison and myself, upon two occasions, saw lions right out in
the open—first two large males, and again two lionesses, one
of them with a small cub.   The two latter we shot, but, alack
and alas ! the two males got off untouched, and their skins are
not amongst our hunting trophies.   It happened in this wise.
My friend and I having ridden out, as we had to do every few
days, to shoot some Tsessebe and wildebeest to supply our
numerous native retinue as well as Khama's men with meat,
soon came in sight of several large herds of these animals and
galloped in pursuit.   They were very wild, and in order to kill
any without galloping our horses to death, we had to fire rather
long shots at about three hundred yards.   This day I killed five
animals—two wildebeest and three Tsessebe antelopes—with
my twenty cartridges, and heard Collison firing away to the right
though he was out of sight.   As soon as some of my boys
came up to where I stood by the last animal killed, I handed
one of them my now useless rifle and rode back to the first
wildebeest I had shot, where I could see Franz, my Basuto
boy, standing with a pack-horse.   I may say that the Mababi
plain was here as flat as a billiard table, without the smallest
bush, and free from holes and long grass, which had been burnt
off some months before.   It was impossible, however, to see
anything at a great distance upon it on account of the mirage.
As I came up to Franz I noticed two small objects close
together on the open plain, the best part of a mile off, looking
like two small ant-heaps.   As there were no such things about,
I could not make them out, and gazed fixedly at them for
some seconds ; but, as they remained motionless, I turned to
the wildebeest and helped Franz to skin it.   I soon looked up
again, however, and at once knew that what I had seen were
two lions' heads.   The animals had now got up and were
walking slowly over the open plain one behind the other.   I saw
at once that they were lions, from the length of their bodies
and the way they held their heads below the line of their
backs.   I could see, too, that they were males, from the
thick, humpy look of their necks caused by the mane.   Oh, for
a rifle and ten cartridges ! and then, as I was very well
mounted, in all probability I should have added two more lion
skins to my collection.   Thinking that as I could not shoot

"When within about one hundred yards, as they still stood defiant, and one of them, a very fine dark-skinned animal with a handsome mane, seemed particularly furious, I slightly turned my horse's head, so as to pass them at a distance of sixty or seventy yards."

them I would like to have a look at them, I mounted my good
horse Bob and galloped towards them.   They continued to
walk slowly along, until I was within four hundred yards of
them, when, after first turning to look at me, they went off
at a heavy canter, but soon commenced to trot, and when
I was about two hundred yards from them stopped, and facing
round stood side by side with their heads held low and their
mouths slightly open, and all the time twitching their tails and
growling savagely.   I continued to ride straight towards them,
thinking they would give way and run again ; but, when within
about one hundred yards, as they still stood defiant, and one
of them, a very fine dark-skinned animal with a handsome
mane, seemed particularly furious, I slightly turned my horse's
head, so as to pass them at a distance of sixty or seventy
yards.

Whilst executing this manœuvre, the dark-maned lion came
slowly towards me for a few steps, and then, bounding forward,
and growling loudly, charged out at his best speed.   As I had
to half turn my horse and get him into his stride, the lion got
to within some ten yards or so of his tail before he was
going at his best pace, and stuck close to him for some distance.
How far he chased me I am afraid to say, but a very considerable distance, and certainly twice as far as I have ever
been pursued by any other of his kind.   When at last he
pulled up, he trotted slowly back to his comrade, and they
then both lay down on the bare open ground, with their
massive paws outstretched, their heads held high, and their
mouths half open, with their tongues lolling out, for it was a
very hot day.   They lay almost exactly in the position of
Landseer's lions in Trafalgar Square, and it is quite a mistake
to say that that great artist has made an error in representing
lions lying with the fore-paws straight out like a dog.   When
on the alert, a lion always lies like this, and only bends his
paws inwards like a cat when resting thoroughly at his ease.

I now saw Collison in the distance, and riding back past
the lions—which, however, both stood up and growled at me
as I passed—I galloped up to him, hoping that he might
have some cartridges left.   He had still four cartridges, but,
having had a fall, had knocked his foresight off, so that his

rifle was practically useless.   However, we resolved to try what
we could do, and arranged to have two shots each, my friend
taking the first shot.   As soon as I left them, the lions had
resumed their way towards the forest skirting the plain, but
we got up to them again when they were still some distance
from it.   They made no attempt to run, but, as soon as they
saw us, faced round, and with lowered heads stood growling at
us.   How the black-maned one now chased us about is something I shall long remember, but it would be too tedious to
relate.   Once I believe that, but for a ruse, he would have
caught my friend's horse, which was not nearly so fast an
animal as mine.   The other lion, which was also a fine large
male, very light in colour, and with but little mane, only made
two short charges, both times in company with and alongside
of his irascible companion.   To make a long story short, suffice
it to say that, owing to there being no foresight on the rifle,
and the black-maned lion not allowing us to approach to within
one hundred and fifty yards of him without charging, we fired
our four shots away without effect, and then had to leave our
adversaries masters of the situation, and ride back with heavy
hearts to camp.

But this is a retrospect, and I will now resume my narrative.

I did not remain long in the Mababi, as there was not
much to be got there that I wanted, and so in August trekked
back to Sode Gara, where I remained for some time hunting
gemsbucks, and hartebeests, and ostriches ; then I travelled
slowly eastwards again, on my own waggon spoor.   One day
I camped at a small pool about a mile to the west of a deep
vley situated on the main road from Bamangwato to Pandamatenka, which is known as Horn's Vley, and here I remained
for some little time, as I found elands, giraffes, and gemsbucks
fairly plentiful in the neighbourhood.   One afternoon, as I was
thinking of moving forwards, I rode several miles along my old
waggon spoor to the eastward to see if the vleys which had
been filled by the great rain that had fallen in the preceding
May still held any water.   I rode seven or eight miles along
the now almost obliterated waggon track, and found that several
of them did.   I saw two small herds of giraffes on my way

HERD OF GEMSBUCK.

out, but did not molest them. On my way home, however, late in the evening, and when less than four miles from camp, I came across two more young bulls, one of which, after a short gallop, I shot. Early the following morning I returned with Laer, all my own Kafirs, and a lot of Bushmen, to cut up the meat, and found that nothing had touched the carcase during the night, but, as the animal was in a very low condition, I gave it to the Bushmen, and went away with my own boys to look for a fat cow. Though we made a long circuit we were, however, unsuccessful in meeting with any, or crossing fresh spoor until late in the afternoon. When nearing the place, however, where I had shot the giraffe the previous day, and whilst riding along an open glade in which were several pools of water, I suddenly saw a giraffe emerge not far ahead from the thick thorn bush which skirted and ran parallel with the open ground. The great size of the animal assured me it was an old bull, which was of no use to me, as the meat of a bull giraffe is not good, having often a very strong smell and taste. However, I reined up my horse behind a bush, and bade my boys crouch down. The first giraffe was soon followed by three others, only the last of which was a cow ; thus there were three big bulls and only one cow, a combination that I had never seen before, nor have witnessed since. They came right down to a large vley in which there was still a little water, and, as I have upon several occasions done before, I watched them drinking, straddling out their fore-legs by little jerks, until their feet were yards apart, before they could get their mouths down to the water. They sometimes stretch one foreleg in front of them, working the other-backwards until it touches their hind feet, and sometimes straddle both forelegs out sideways, one to either side. It was now growing late, and a tremendous storm, the first of the approaching rainy season, was coming up apace ; and the whole sky on one side of the heavens was as black as ink. However, I thought it might hold off for an hour or two, and give me time to shoot and cut up the cow giraffe, so I rode out from behind the bush and let my horse out as hard as he could go across the open, in the hope of cutting off the giraffes and getting a shot at the one I wanted before they reached the thick thorn bush.

I was mounted on Nelson, who had now become a first-rate shooting horse, and Laer was on the stallion that I had ridden the previous day.   The distance was, however, too short, and I only got up to the giraffes just as the cow, who was leading, entered the bush.   It was very dense, and it took me all my time to keep near the giraffes whilst going through it. Presently we emerged on another open space, and here I rode up to and shot the animal I wanted.   Laer and the boys were soon up, and to our joy we found that I had struck oil ; for the giraffe cow was in splendid order, and carried fat half an inch thick on her ribs.   The storm had now commenced, and was evidently fast approaching ; the thunder and lightning were simply terrific.   Some of my boys hastily collected wood and made a big fire, saying they would sleep at the carcase and make a night of it ; but I was anxious to get back to the waggon, so after cutting off all the choicest meat, and taking out the inside fat, Laer and I loaded up our horses and then started for home.   It was by this time growing dusk, and the rain was beginning to fall in heavy drops.   We just managed to get to the single waggon spoor, whilst there was still light enough to see it, and then one of the most awful storms I have ever been out in closed in on us.   In a very few minutes it was quite impossible to see anything of the waggon track, except by the lurid glare of the frequent flashes of lightning.   I put Laer in front on the stallion, and told him to give the old horse his head, for as he had been along the track with me the previous day I thought that was the best chance of getting home.   And now the rain came down solid, in such a way that, although the soil under foot was deep loose sand, the lightning showed a sheet of water, for the sand could not absorb the rain as fast as it fell.   Once before, in December 1879, did I see water lie like this, on the sands of the Kalahari.   Between the flashes of lightning, although my horse's nose was at the stallion's tail, I could see neither Laer nor the stallion, nor my own horse ; and the glare of the lightning was so intense, and the darkness that followed it so dense, that each lurid flash seemed to strike one blind.   And the rain and the thunder ! well, it was a fierce tropical storm, a grand but awful display of the dread powers of Nature; an open-air sermon on man's impotence and insignificance, preached in the grand old temple of Nature. But I was glad when the discourse was over, for it is a bit eerie riding on such a night through the African wilderness. Whether the stallion kept the waggon track I cannot say. Without the rain, of course, he could have done so easily enough, despite the darkness, for he would have smelt his own spoor of the previous day; but as it was, I do not know how he managed it. At any rate he kept pretty well on the line, for just as the storm was abating, and, the rain having ceased, the night grew lighter, we came into an open piece of ground, and soon afterwards struck the main waggon road near Horn's Vley, and on firing a shot to make sure of our whereabouts, were rejoiced to hear an answer from the waggon, from which we were less than a mile distant. Another ten minutes brought us home, and as Samuel had managed to keep a fire alight in the temporary hut he had made for himself, Laer and I soon got a cup of hot coffee to drink. The storm had now completely passed, and presently the moon coming up, the night became quite clear and bright. After drinking my coffee I turned in, and was lying reading in the waggon when Samuel called to me, and said in Dutch, "Sir, there are waggons coming along the big road from Bamangwato; I have twice heard a whip crack." As it was now nearly six months since I had left Matabililand, and as during all that time I had never seen a white man, or spoken a word of English, this was exciting news; however, though I sat up and listened for some time I heard nothing, and concluded that Samuel was mistaken. But the next morning I saddled up Nelson at daylight and rode over to Horn's Vley to examine the waggon track, and there to my great joy found two waggons outspanned, and the cattle feeding round the water. It turned out to be an old friend, Mr. Frank Watson, who was taking in two waggon-loads of goods to George Westbeech at the Zambesi. How inexpressibly delightful are such meetings in the wilderness, and how different the conduct of two Englishmen to one another on such occasions from the Continental idea, as expressed in caricatures! Watson offered to broach a case of brandy, in the old interior style, and the orthodox thing to

have done would have been for both of us to have remained at
Horn's Vley until the case was finished,—and a day or two
longer to recover from the effects of it.   However, as I am
practically a total abstainer, and knew, too, that poor George
Westbeech wanted all the brandy he could get to help him to
withstand the deadly climate of the Zambesi valley, I would
not consent to my friend's proposition ; so we only had a
friendly chat over numerous cups of tea and exchanged news.
The following day we parted, but before doing so I was able
to supply my friend with a good stock of meat, both fresh and
salted, sufficient to last him to Panda-ma-tenka.

I now resumed my journey eastwards, and early in
November reached the old waggon track leading from Tati
to Panda-ma-tenka, where Bukwela's guides had left me on
my way from Matabililand to the Mababi.   From this spot
I followed the old waggon spoor southwards, passing the
Makalaka kraals of Beri-Rima in the middle of November,
and reaching Tati by the end of the month.

BARTERING WITH NATIVES.

CHAPTER VIII

Ride to Bulawayo—Exposure to rain—Determine to hunt in Mashunaland again—
Make an early start for the hunting veld—The white rhinoceros—My best
shooting horse lamed—Cross the Umniati river—Reach the Umgezi—The
klipspringer antelope—Lioness shot on the Umgezi river—Reach the Zweswi
—Large herd of elephants—Hyæna shot—Zebra wounded—A day with the
elephants—Six elephants killed.

AFTER reaching Tati I had to go on to Bulawayo, both to look
after the property I had left there in Mr. Fairbairn's hands
and to get my letters, which had all been sent on there.
The distance between the two places is between one hundred
and twenty and one hundred and thirty miles, so I elected
to ride it on horseback, as I was anxious to get my letters.
I took my strongest horse, the old stallion. The first day
I rode right through to Mangwi, about sixty miles, as
a Boer friend was at this time living on what had once
been known as John Lee's farm, and I knew I should get
a kind welcome, a good supper, and a feed for my horse. Mr.

and Mrs. Greeffe received me with their usual kindness and
hospitality, and the next day I remained at Mangwi until late
in the afternoon, and then again resumed my journey, intending to ride on till late in the night, and to finish my journey
before mid-day on the following morning.   Latterly we had
been having intensely hot weather, but during the last few
days rain had been threatening, and of course it chose to set
in soon after I left Mynheer Greeffe's house.   I was soon soaked
through, and as I could not light a fire I passed a miserable
night, and got thoroughly chilled ; nor could I get a change of
clothes until I reached Fairbairn's house the following mid-day.
Returning to Tati I had much the same experience, as wet
weather had now set in ; and these chills, following upon the
great heat that had gone before, brought on a severe attack of
fever, which, though it never actually laid me up, hung about
me, and made me feel weak and ill for several months.   This
season I did not go down to the Transvaal, but remained in
Matabililand, and sent my specimens down country in a
trader's waggon.

As I still had a large number of unfulfilled orders for the
skins and skeletons of certain antelopes and other animals that
were more plentiful in Mashunaland than anywhere else, I
determined to spend another year collecting there, if I could
get leave from Lo Bengula to do so ; so in December I took
my waggon up to Bulawayo.   Lo Bengula demanded a salted
horse (worth say £60) for the right to hunt in Mashunaland.
This was a very long price to pay, as elephants were no longer
plentiful ; but as he would take nothing else I at last agreed
to give him a horse on my return to Bulawayo, provided I
might go into the hunting veld as soon as I liked, and remain
there till the end of the year.   I also got leave to shoot five
hippopotami if I wanted to do so.   When I told the king that
my heart was still sore at the way I had been treated in the
" sea-cow case," he said, " Houw ! that case is finished ! dead !
what is the use of thinking any more about it?   Go and hunt
nicely until your heart is white " (*i.e.* until you are in a good
temper).

After making everything right with the king, I trekked
over to Emhlangen, where I was the guest of my old friends

the Elliotts, from whom, as well as from all the other missionaries and their families in Matabililand, I have received the
most constant kindness.   I had intended to have waited here
for my friends, Mr. H. C. Collison and Cornelis van Rooyen,
and to have travelled to Mashunaland in company with them ;
but as I knew they would not return from the south before
April, I grew restless, and resolved to go on by myself, the
more especially as I thought that the change of air and scene
might be good for me, and help to shake off the feeling of
languor and weakness from which I was suffering.   It was
still early in February, therefore, when I left Matabililand, and
as it was so early in the year I had good hopes of finding
elephants outside the " fly " infested districts, and of having a
turn with them on horseback.

As the main object, however, of my expedition was to
collect the skins and skeletons of large mammalia for mounting
in museums, and as such things are very bulky, I took two
waggons with me, and thirty-two bullocks to pull them.   In
addition to these I had a good many loose cattle, amongst
which were a bull and ten milk cows, and I also had with
me five pack donkeys and four horses.   Of the latter, one was
Nelson, who had now served me well and faithfully for four
years.   A second was the stallion I had had with me in the
Mababi.   He was a big powerful animal and a wonderfully steady
shooting horse, but liable to become sulky and to refuse to run
at his best pace—a phase of temper recognised by the Transvaal
Boers, and described by them by the word " steeks,"—and when
in this mood spurring was simply wasted upon him.   Of the
other two, one was a horse that I had just bought from a
trader at Tati because of his good looks, and in spite of his
bad character.   He, however, turned out hopelessly bad, and
is the only really vicious horse I have ever had anything to
do with in South Africa.   I almost cured him of bucking by
riding him with an adze handle, and stunning him by a heavy
blow administered between the ears as soon as he commenced,
which he invariably did as soon as one touched the saddle ;
but I never could make a shooting horse of him, and
finally gave him to Lo Bengula in the hope that he would
present him to Ma-kwaykwi, or some other of his endunas,

against whom I had a personal grudge ; but, as I never heard
of any one being killed by him, I expect he was turned loose
amongst the large number of his horses that are never ridden,
and of which no use whatever is made.   My fourth horse was
a fairly good animal, but old, and in very low condition.

As it was now the latter end of the rainy season, and I
knew from experience that the whole country would be
covered with long grass, making it very difficult to see game,
I did not expect to shoot much along the road, though I
thought that after crossing the River Gwelo I should always
be able to keep my boys and dogs in meat.   However, it was
not till the fifth day after leaving Emhlangen, and when near
the River Se-whoi-whoi, that I saw a small herd of Tsessebe
antelopes, one of which I managed to kill.

It was within a mile of this spot that two years previously
I shot the last two white rhinoceroses (*R. simus*) which I have
killed, and they were probably the last of their kind that I
shall ever see.   They were male and female, and I preserved
the skin of the head and the skull of the former for the South
African Museum in Cape Town, where they now are.   I shall
never cease to regret that I did not preserve the entire skeleton
for our own splendid museum of natural history at South
Kensington, but, when I shot the animal, I made sure I should
get finer specimens later on in the season.   However, one
thing and another prevented my visiting the one district where
I knew that a few were still to be found, and now those few
have almost all been killed ; and, to the best of my belief, the
great white or square-mouthed rhinoceros, the largest of modern
terrestrial mammals after the elephant, will in the course of
the next few years become absolutely extinct ; and if in the
near future some student of natural history should wish to
know what this extinct beast really was like, he will find
nothing in all the museums of Europe and America to enlighten
him upon the subject but some half-dozen skulls and a
goodly number of the anterior horns.

In 1886 two Boer hunters, Karl Weyand and Jan Engelbrecht, got into the little tract of country where the few white
rhinoceroses were still left, and between them killed ten during
the season ; five more were killed during the same time by

some native hunters from the Matabili country. A few were still left, as in the following year (1887) I myself and some English sportsmen saw the tracks of two or three in the same district, but could not find the animals themselves. Some few white rhinoceroses no doubt still survive, but it is not too much to say that long before the close of this century the white rhinoceros will have vanished from the face of the earth. I hope my readers will pardon this long digression, but the subject of the extinction of this huge quadruped has a melancholy interest for me, when I remember that, twenty years ago, it was a common animal over an enormous extent of country in Central South Africa.

After shooting the Tsessebe antelope, as I have described, I had all the meat carried to the waggons, and then trekked on to the Bembisan river. Here I found that the banks had been washed away at the old ford by the heavy summer rains, and it was only after a couple of hours' work with all my Kafirs, and by putting the two spans of bullocks on to each waggon in turn that I managed to cross. However, by sundown I had got both my waggons standing on the farther side, and had chopped a small " kraal " for my loose cattle, milked the cows, and made everything snug for the night. That night a heavy misfortune befell me, for Moscow, my useless vicious brute of a horse, kicked my well-tried shooting nag Nelson on the inside of the hough, laming him completely ; indeed, so badly was he injured, that not until four months had elapsed from the date of the accident was I able, once more, to put a saddle on his back. Could he have had perfect rest from the commencement he would doubtless have recovered sooner ; but I was obliged to drive him, lame as he was, for more than one hundred and fifty miles to where I finally made my permanent camp on the Manyami river. After this my journey was an uneventful one till I reached Umfuli. I travelled very slowly as time was no object to me, and I wished to get a little stronger in health (as I was doing daily) before coming to the elephant country. As soon as I had got on to the high plateau of Mashunaland, although it was about the hottest season of the year, I found the heat by no means oppressive by day, and the nights cool and pleasant. Every day I saw

game of some kind or other, principally sable and roan antelope, Tsessebe, zebras, koodoos, water-bucks, and reed-bucks,
and was able to keep myself well supplied with fresh meat
without great exertion.

Late one evening, when near the Umniati river, having
pitched upon a suitable place for camp, and set all my boys
to work with the hatchets to make a kraal for the cattle, I
rode on ahead by myself, just to pass away the time till
sundown. I was about a mile from the waggons, perhaps,
when a reed-buck, with a fine head, jumped out of the long
grass in front of me, and bounded away. Dismounting hastily,
I took a quick shot through the long grass, my bullet striking
the animal just above the root of the tail, paralysing its hind
quarters, and bringing it instantly to the ground. I soon despatched it, and, as it had a fine pair of horns, cut off the head
with the skin of the neck, which I fastened, together with the
two hind legs, to the saddle, and then, dragging the remainder
of the carcase to a patch of timber near at hand, lifted it up
and placed it in the fork of a mopani tree, about six feet from
the ground, intending to return for it the following morning, if
it were not interfered with by lion, leopard, or hyæna during
the night. I then rode back to the waggons. I was up at
daylight the following morning, sitting over the fire drinking
a cup of coffee, when a lion commenced to roar loudly, the
sound coming from the direction of the spot where I had shot
the reed-buck the preceding evening, but seemingly not so far
off. I at once had the saddle put on the stallion, as now that
Nelson had been put *hors de combat* he was my best shooting
horse. Just as I was mounting the lion roared again, so, without waiting to have the dogs caught and led, I cantered off in
the direction from whence the sound appeared to come. This
was unfortunate, for had I taken the dogs with me they might
have hit upon his fresh spoor, in which case they would probably have followed it up and brought the lion to bay. As it
was I never saw him, which is not surprising, seeing that the
whole country was covered with long grass. When I reached
the spot where I had placed the reed-buck in the tree I found
that the carcase had been removed, and was lying on the ground
very considerably chewed up, and with very little meat left on

it. The lion, I think, must have been the marauder, and I fancy he must have roared just after finishing what, if he was hungry, must have been a very unsatisfactory meal for him. In the perfect stillness of the very early morning the loud roars had sounded much nearer than was really the case. Just beyond here were some low stony ridges, bordering the Umniati river, and thinking that the lion might possibly be lurking amongst the rocks and bushes, I rode all round them, and then along the bank of the river. However, I could see nothing of him, so gave up the search, and rode down to look at the ford. This I found to be quite impassable for waggons, as the heavy summer rains had washed the banks of the river completely away. I now rode up the river in search of another crossing place, and found a very good one about two miles off. Here I also saw much hippopotamus spoor only a day or two old, the animals all seemingly travelling up stream towards a range of hills named Taba Insimbi (the hill of iron). The whole country is over four thousand feet above the sea-level about here, and I myself was surprised to find hippopotami so high up the course of the river, but these animals wander very much when undisturbed in search of suitable food, especially during the rainy season.

Early in the afternoon I spanned in, and crossed the river with my waggons without difficulty, and then, having nothing particular to do, recrossed the river, and set a gun across our track, in the hope that the lion that had taken my reed-buck in the morning would follow my cattle spoor during the night, and cross the line attached to the trigger, with unpleasant results to himself. Just as I had arranged matters to my satisfaction, a small herd of Tsessebe antelopes came in sight, feeding over a neighbouring rise ; so, taking my rifle, I crept towards them, and succeeded in killing two, which both lay within a couple of hundred yards of our waggon track. I then sent for the donkeys, and had all the meat carried into the camp, removing the line attached to the trigger of the set gun from across the road until they had passed, and then resetting it. I now made sure that either the lion or a hyæna, attracted by the smell of blood, would follow up our tracks and come to an untimely end during the night, but was much afraid lest the latter should come first, and save the former's life. However, though I lay awake till late, hoping and expecting, no report broke the stillness of the night and I at last fell asleep, and found, on waking in the morning, that the set gun was still as I had left it on the preceding evening, neither lion nor hyæna having disturbed it.   After breakfast I trekked on, and in the afternoon reached the River Umgezi, where I slept.

This little river used to be a favourite resort of hippopotami, small herds of which animals were usually to be found in the deep black pools (some over a mile in length) that lie on either side of the Machabi hills.   Taking a ride along the course of the river, late in the afternoon, I came across much recent spoor, some of it not more than a day or two old, but the animals themselves seemed to have moved northwards, towards the deep pools which I knew lay beyond the hills.   Whilst riding down the river I saw a large herd of koodoos and a few water-bucks, but, as they were all females, did not interfere with them.   I also saw several agile wiry-haired little klipspringers. It is worthy of remark that in Northern Mashunaland these compactly-built, though active little antelopes are to be found along the courses of all the larger rivers, such as the Umgezi, Umniati, Umfuli, and Manyami, wherever they run (as they often do) amongst boulders and masses of rock.   Thus they may be shot by walking along the banks of the river, and without ever climbing a hill at all.   I say this because I have heard that in the Cape Colony, where these little antelopes are also to be found, they are only to be got at amongst the steepest and most rugged hills and mountains, amidst the highest portions of which they live.   This I have heard stated more than once, though I have had but little actual experience myself in that part of South Africa.   I once shot one years ago, in 1871, on the top of a high hill overlooking the Orange river, between Colesberg and Philipolis ; and in 1876, when snowed up for a week on the highest part of the Sneeuwberg range of mountains, between Graaf Reinet and Middleburg, I saw several of these hardy little beasts, but failed to bag any of them.   The snow then lay from one to two feet in depth on the mountains, and the air was bitterly raw and cold, especially at nights, yet the klipspringers managed to weather

GRANITE ROCK IN SOUTHERN MASHUNALAND, WITH THE WAGGONS OF THE PIONEER EXPEDITION IN THE FOREGROUND.

it out, finding food and warmth, no doubt, amongst the rocky ravines where the snow would not lie.   In Khama's country and in Matabililand klipspringers are found amongst hills of a very small elevation, and, indeed, may sometimes be shot from the level ground, when standing on the topmost rock of one of the little "kopjes" (composed of great blocks of granite poised one upon another, often in a most marvellous way) which form so prominent a feature in the scenery of Southern Matabililand ; but it is only in the Mashuna country that I have met with these little antelopes living amongst the rocks through which the rivers run, often at a considerable distance from any hills.

Whilst riding back to camp on the other side of the river I came across the remains of a koodoo bull that had evidently been killed very recently by a lion.   The horns were fairly large, though nothing remarkable, so I left them lying where I found them.   That night lions roared loudly not far off down the river, but did not approach my waggons.   In the course of my travels I have shot two lions on the banks of the River Umgezi, the one a male, and the other a female.   The former animal, when I first caught sight of him, was chasing some koodoos by broad daylight, which, I think, is a very unusual occurrence, as lions almost always do their hunting by night. However, it was a cold winter's morning, and the sky was cloudy and overcast, as it often is in Mashunaland during the coldest time of the year.

The shooting of the lioness was a very tame affair, and, owing to peculiar circumstances, was attended with as little danger to myself as would be the shooting of a lion in a menagerie through the bars of a cage.   It happened in this wise.   I was riding one day in May 1882 (without any attendants, as I had left all my Kafirs making camp) along the bank of a deep hippopotamus pool, nearly a hundred yards in breadth and half a mile or so in length, when I saw something move amongst the grass growing beneath a small bush on the opposite bank of the river, and some one hundred and twenty yards away from where I sat· on my horse.   The next instant the head and shoulders of a lioness appeared, looking towards me ; so, instantly dismounting, I fired at her across the river, and rolled

her over.   For some seconds I could see nothing of her, but I
knew she was rolling about, as she kept the grass in continual
motion, and, moreover, never ceased growling.   Suddenly she
appeared again, evidently in a dying condition, and, half falling,
half walking down the steep bank, lay all of a heap at the
water's edge, holding her jaws, now all besmirched with blood,
slightly open and growling softly.   I might have bombarded
her in perfect safety ; but, as I thought she was done for, and
did not want to spoil her skin, I refrained from doing so, and,
cantering up to the end of the pool, crossed the river and rode
down the bank close to the spot where the lioness lay.   She
was not quite so dead as I thought, for as soon as she saw me
she managed to raise her head and growl savagely, her eyes
gleaming with all the fierce fury of her unutterable though futile
rage.   I may here say that any one who has not seen at close
quarters the fierce light that scintillates from the eyes of a
wounded lion, or any other of the large Felidæ, can hardly
imagine its wondrous brilliancy and furious concentration.   In
the present instance the fury of the wounded lioness was impotent,
as she had not the strength to raise herself from the ground,
and, indeed, could do nothing more than lift her head and growl
savagely.   The small 450-bore expanding bullet had done its
murderous work, and the life that had so lately been strong
within her was fast ebbing away.   However, the sun was low,
my waggons were some distance off, and I was alone, with no
one to help me to skin the lioness ; so I killed her with a shot
through the brain, and at once set to work to remove her hide,
which I then fastened to the saddle and carried back to camp
—the first, but not the last, lion skin my good horse Nelson
ever carried for me.

   After leaving the River Umgezi an easy day's travelling
brought me to the Zweswi, and here I was obliged to delay for
five days in order to give Nelson a rest, as he had become so lame
that I was afraid he might knock up altogether.   I found that
about a fortnight before my arrival a large herd of elephants
(probably the big herd of Northern Mashunaland, in which there
were far over a hundred animals) had come up along the river,
through the Machabi hills, and then struck off in the direction of
the thick bush on the upper Umfuli.   The whole country near

where the waggon track crosses the Zweswi had been cut up by them ; they had trampled broad paths through the long grass which still covered all the open valleys.   In every patch of forest numerous trees had been stripped of their bark, or had had large branches broken off them, and in some cases had even been uprooted bodily ; whilst the ground had been dug up in all directions into deep holes in search of roots.   On seeing the spoor of this large herd of elephants that had passed here such a short time before my hopes were high of meeting them before very long, as they were well out of the "fly" country, and travelling still farther away from it ; and were, moreover, moving very slowly, feeding along quietly in perfect security.   Bitterly, indeed, did I repent my folly in buying the evil-tempered brute that had lamed my good horse Nelson.   Had he been sound I should have gone in search of this large herd of elephants forthwith, taking provisions enough for myself and Kafirs to last us four or five days, in order not to have had to shoot game, and run the risk of disturbing the more valuable animals before actually coming up with them.   As it was, I hoped that the stallion would prove himself to be a good elephant horse when the day came to test him, but I felt no confidence in him, and so resolved not to make any actual search for the great beasts before reaching the next river, the Umfuli.

On the second night of my sojourn on the banks of the Zweswi, I woke up suddenly about an hour or two after midnight, and for some reason unknown to myself got up and put my head out of the front of the waggon.   It was a brilliant moonlight night—and the moonlight of the tropics is very brilliant indeed.   My two waggons stood side by side, the four horses and the donkeys being tied between them.   On the other side of the buck waggon stood the cattle kraal, between which and the waggon my drivers and Kafirs were sleeping ; and, as it happened, my well-fed pack of dogs, all forgetful of their duty, were doing the same.   On the farther side of the waggon in which I was sleeping there was neither fire nor fence.   At the back of it hung half the meat of a sable antelope bull which I had shot the same morning.   As I have said above, I woke suddenly in the small hours of the morning, and, getting up, looked out of the waggon across the broad expanse

of veld that lay before me, and over which the brilliant moon
cast a pale soft light.   Then I turned my head and looked
round towards the back of the waggon, and there, not ten yards
off, stood a great hyæna, looming white in the strong moonlight.   He was standing gazing at the sable antelope meat that
hung within a few yards of him at the back of the waggon.
Cautiously withdrawing my head, I felt in the blankets for the
loaded rifle that always lay beside me, and then looked out
again.   The hyæna had advanced a yard or two nearer, and, as
I hastily took aim at him, either did not see me, or, at any rate,
paid no attention to me.   The next instant I fired, and, as he
was so near, it was not surprising that I hit him.   He fell to the
shot, but picked himself up again and made off into the bush
behind the waggon, closely pursued by all my dogs, which,
awakened by the shot, had rushed out *en masse* from behind
the buck waggon.   They soon brought him to bay, and when,
simultaneously with one of my drivers and some of the Kafirs,
I arrived barefooted at the spot where the worrying was going
on, I found the hyæna lying on the ground in the last agonies,
with a dog pulling at each ear, while Punch had him by the
throat and old Ruby was tearing at his flank.   A few minutes
later he was dead ; so, calling off the dogs, and bidding the
Kafirs drag the carcase up to the waggons, I again turned in
and slept till daylight.

      After having rested for a few days at the Zweswi, I again
moved on, and on 27th February slept within a few miles of the
Lundaza river, a tributary of the Umfuli.   Early the following
morning I saddled up the stallion and rode along the track
ahead of the waggons, not taking any of my Kafirs with me.
Presently I espied a small herd of zebras feeding in an open
glade in the forest, and, being in want of meat for my dogs and
Kafirs, resolved to try to shoot one.   As the animals had not
yet observed me, and as there was a large ant-heap standing
conveniently within shot of them, I dismounted, and, leaving
my horse standing amongst the bushes, which completely concealed him from view, crept cautiously forward towards the
unsuspecting herd.   I reached the ant-heap unobserved, and,
peering cautiously round the side of it, saw that I was well
within shot.   Picking out a big fat-looking mare, I at once

fired, and she fell to the shot, rolling over on her back with her legs in the air. She picked herself up again, however, almost immediately, and galloping off, soon caught up to her fast-retreating companions. As she regained her legs I saw where she had been struck, as the blood was running from a wound in the shoulder, too high to be mortal, but which showed me that my bullet had just grazed, without injuring, her backbone, causing her to fall to the ground suddenly. As I was anxious to secure her, I now ran to my horse, and, mounting quickly, galloped in pursuit. I was just getting within shot again when a freshly-broken tree, evidently the work of an elephant, caught my eye. I at once reined in, and, examining the ground, soon saw that a very large herd of these animals had passed during the night, and as the trees were broken in all directions, and many of them stripped of their bark, it was evident that they had been browsing along slowly without any suspicion of danger. What was to be done? To follow them up forthwith was out of the question, as I had only about half-a-dozen cartridges in my belt, all loaded with expanding bullets, which were perfectly useless for killing elephants. The first thing to do was to return to the waggons, so I cantered back along the road and soon met them. I then hurried them on to the head of the stream near where I had first seen the zebras, and outspanned. Knowing the Mashunaland elephants as well as I did, and their capabilities of travelling enormous distances in a very short time, I thought it very possible that I should have to sleep on their spoor, and not overtake them till the following day, so I resolved to have something to eat before starting.

Whilst this hasty meal was preparing, I got everything ready. I determined to mount my Griqua lad Laer on the old horse Charley, and to take up the spoor with him alone, leaving all the Kafirs at the waggons, so that we could follow up the elephants at a canter. As I was still very weak, I was afraid that the weight of my 10-bore rifle would be too much for me, and finally decided to see what I could do with my little 450-bore single Metford, by Gibbs of Bristol. Of course I used the military cartridges, loaded with 75 grains of powder and long-pointed, toughened 540-grain bullets. I had already killed giraffes, buffaloes, hippopotami, and a few rhinoceroses with one of these little rifles, and felt confident that I would be able to kill elephants too.   I fixed two strong leather pouches in front of my saddle, each containing twenty-five cartridges, and carried twenty more in my belt, being determined not to run out of ammunition whatever else might happen.   I also tied a warm coat over the pommel of the saddle, thinking it more than probable that we should have to sleep out for a night, and put a few pieces of dried meat in the pockets.   Laer carried a single 10-bore rifle and twenty cartridges, and tied a small kettle behind his saddle, together with a little tea and sugar in a handkerchief.   As he was still quite a lad, and had had no experience at all with elephants, I told him to keep close to me, and not to fire except at animals which I had first disabled.

It was still early when we took up the spoor, which there was no difficulty about following, as the herd was a very large one, and had trodden broad paths wherever they had crossed the open grassy glades intersecting the belts of forest ; whilst, in the forests themselves, so many trees had been broken and stripped of their bark that one could ride straight ahead without looking at the ground at all.   The elephants, I think, must have passed where I first saw their spoor in the early morning, not long before daylight, and had been moving very slowly, feeding quietly along, utterly unconscious of danger, otherwise we should not have overtaken them as soon as we did.   Cantering briskly along the spoor, we ere long crossed the Lundaza river, and upon emerging from a broad belt of forest, about a couple of miles beyond it, suddenly saw the elephants in front of us.   The herd was one of the largest it has ever been my fate to look upon, and as, when the animals first came into view, they were crossing a broad open grassy valley, between two patches of forest, I had an unusually good opportunity of observing them.   They were moving in masses across the valley, walking at that slow majestic step natural to the wild elephant when entirely unsuspicious of the presence of man.

As I reined in my horse on the border of the forest, and gazed over the valley across which stretched this great herd of mighty beasts, a thrill of excitement shot through my frame and braced my fever-weakened nerves ; for never can elephants be beheld by the South African hunter without feelings of intense excitement. When elephant-hunting, one seldom comes up with the animals without having followed them for several hours, and as a rule it is a pursuit which entails great hardships : fatigue, thirst, and exposure to the intense heat of the tropical sun. On the present occasion, however, I had come up with the elephants without having endured privation or hardship of any kind. It was a pure stroke of luck, and in many ways never had I had such a chance of doing a good day's work with these animals before. There was an immense herd of them before me—numbering probably nearer two hundred than one hundred—and for some miles all round the forests were fairly open. I had also a good little rifle and seventy cartridges. My bodily weakness, the result of fever, was certainly much against me, but what militated more against my success that day than anything else was the obstinacy of my horse, whose disposition I was soon to find out. Even to-day, as I think of this episode in my hunting career, I cannot but lament and rail at fate, when I think of what I did, and what I might have done that day had I but had my good horse Nelson between my knees. However, regret is vain ; the past is irrevocable, and I will now proceed to relate what happened to me.

As I looked eagerly over this great mass of elephants, the foremost amongst which were close upon the forest that skirted the farther side of the open valley, I could see but one bull, whose mighty form showed well above the backs of the cows that surrounded him. A fine pair of tusks showed out well beyond his trunk, but I could see that, though of fair length, they were not very thick. He was amongst the rearmost elephants, walking slowly forwards through the grass, which was some three or four feet high over the whole valley, and more resembled a field of wheat than an English meadow. Riding quickly down into the open with Laer following me, I was soon even with him, and about a hundred yards to his left. He then, in common with a lot of the rearmost elephants, seemed to become suspicious of danger, for, though none of them looked towards me, they all commenced to walk a great deal faster than they had been doing. I now dismounted, and taking a steady shot for his lungs, aiming rather high up behind his shoulder, fired.   I felt sure I had given him a good shot, but had no time to mark its effect, for at the very instant of the report a tuskless cow that was some distance beyond the bull I had just fired at, wheeled round with a loud scream, whirling her trunk at the same time high in the air, and then dropping it before her chest, came rushing towards me, accompanying the charge with shrill and oft-repeated screams.   At first, I suppose, she only heard the shot, and perhaps saw the smoke of the powder ; but, it being perfectly open, she must very soon have caught sight of me, as she came on in the most determined manner.   I was obliged to gallop away, and so take my eyes off the bull, but thought that I would be able to shake my pursuer off by galloping hard for a hundred yards or so, and could then circle round and get up to him again before he gained the shelter of the forest on the farther side of the valley.

I now plied my stallion hard with the spurs, but soon found that it was one of his sulky days, as I could not get him to gallop ; in fact, he was going considerably slower than the enraged elephant behind him, who kept up a constant succession of shrill screams, and who, seeing that she was gaining on the horse, pertinaciously kept up the chase, which she would have long ago abandoned had she been losing ground.   Nearer and nearer she came, till at last I saw that it was getting serious, and that if I did not manage to get into the bush and dodge her there, she would infallibly catch me.   Laer had wisely galloped straight back into the forest when she first screamed. I now made for a patch of rather thick machabel bush that projected into the valley, and, as I entered it, I do not think she was thirty yards behind me ; and when she first charged, she was at least one hundred and fifty yards away, probably considerably more.   Of course such an experience could only happen in a perfectly open piece of country devoid of trees. Once in the bush, I turned suddenly to the left, and, being no longer able to see me, and the wind being luckily in my favour, she lost me immediately.

As soon as I found that I had shaken off my pursuer I gave my sulky horse a good spurring, and then galloped

across the valley into the forest beyond, which now seemed
alive with elephants. I could not see my bull anywhere, however, and as I was looking for him, I saw a small lot of
elephants coming at a quick pace obliquely from behind me,
amongst which was a big bull, though his tusks were very
poor for his size. These elephants, I feel sure, were not in
the open when I first sighted the main herd, but must have
been still behind in the forest to my left. Thinking that if
I had hit the other bull through both lungs with my first shot
he must be dead, and that if not I had lost him irretrievably,
I now turned my attention to the next best animal I could see.
Just as I got up to him he turned and entered rather a thickish
piece of machabel bush, with two cows just in front of him.
He was not going very fast, so jumping off, I took a careful
aim for the ridge of bone which shows out so distinctly in an
elephant from above the root of the tail to the top of the
back. My bullet, a solid toughened 540-grain missile, propelled by only 75 grains of powder, struck him exactly in the
centre of the bone, and stopped him instantly. His hind
quarters seemed partially paralysed, as on mounting again and
riding in front of him he was unable to come towards me,
though he tried hard, poor brute, raising his great ears and
screaming fearfully. Though so near the elephant, and in spite
of the terrific trumpeting, my stallion paid no more attention
to the furious though disabled beast than if he had been a rock.
I quickly got on one side of him and gave him a shot through
both lungs, to which he succumbed very rapidly ; then, remounting, I was soon galloping on the tracks of a portion of
the retreating elephants, and presently got up to about thirty,
and could see another lot of about the same number to my right.

By this time I think that the whole of this great herd of
elephants had broken up into a number of smaller ones, each
diverging on its own line from the point where I had first disturbed them. One of these herds turned right back, recrossing
the Lundaza, and passing through the valley on the edge of
which my waggons were outspanned, in plain view of all my
people. Just as I was getting up to the elephants again, Laer
came up to me. As elephants, when running away, and when
there are a number of them together, go at a very different pace

from a single elephant when charging, I had no difficulty in getting alongside them, and gave one, apparently a cow with nice tusks, but which afterwards proved to be a young bull, a good lung shot. He hung behind almost directly after getting the shot, and very soon left his companions, and went off alone, going at a good pace, however, when I came near him. I gave him two more shots, and then seeing that he was very badly wounded, and fearing that the other elephants would scatter—as they nearly always do in Mashunaland—I called to Laer to try to finish him, and at any rate to watch him, and then again took up the spoor of the herd. I had followed it for some distance, and had got about a hundred yards beyond a sort of pass, between a rocky ridge on the one hand and a mass of large granite boulders on the other, when I came face to face with one of the elephants, a large cow, coming straight back towards me on the spoor of the herd she had left. The forest was very open about here, and she saw me as soon as I saw her, and, raising her head and spreading her ears, charged forthwith, screaming loudly. Turning my horse I galloped back for the rocks, but the stallion would not put out any pace, and I could tell from the screams that the elephant was gaining rapidly upon me.

Hastily turning my head I saw she was getting very near, and knew she would soon catch me ; so I resolved to dismount and run for the rocks. My stallion was, in some respects, a perfect shooting horse, and immediately I leant forward and seized his mane he stopped dead. I was off and in front of him in an instant, and running for the rocks, which were not twenty yards away. As I got round the first rock I turned, and this is what I saw. The horse was standing absolutely still, with his head up and his fore feet planted firmly in the ground, as if carved in stone, and the elephant, which had then ceased to scream, and was making a curious rumbling noise, was standing alongside of him, smelling about with her trunk. In front of my saddle was tied a leather coat, with a red flannel lining—a present the preceding year from my friend poor Montagu Kerr—and I suppose that the elephant must have touched the horse with her trunk, as he suddenly gave a jump round, throwing the red-lined coat into the air. He then walked slowly to the rocky ridge behind him, and again stood still about fifteen yards away from the elephant. All this time I had been afraid to fire, for fear of exasperating the elephant, and causing it to kill my horse. I now, however, determined to do so, and was thinking of firing for her brain, for she was very near me, when she raised her head and ears and came towards the rocks screaming like a railway engine. She must have got my wind, I fancy, suddenly. However, she could not get at me without going round the other rocks ; and as she did so, she gave me a splendid chance at a distance of not more than fifteen yards. I fired into the centre of her shoulder, and immediately the bullet struck her she stopped screaming, and, dropping her ears, swerved off. She only ran a hundred yards or so, and then fell over dead, shot through the large blood-vessels of the upper part of the heart. Directly she fell I ran to my horse and remounted. Prudence whispered to me to give up the hunt, but I could not make up my mind to do so just yet, though I resolved to be cautious and not go too near the elephants in future, as my stallion had evidently not the slightest fear of them, and had made up his mind that nothing should make him really gallop out this day. It was not that he could not do so ; he was simply sulky, as he had a very good turn of speed if he liked to exert himself.

I was soon hard on the spoor again, but had not followed it a mile before I found that the elephants had scattered, making it difficult to keep on their line, as they had no longer left a well-defined trail. However, by taking up the spoors of different animals, I got along at a good pace, and before long sighted a few of the hindmost animals. These were, however, with the exception of two, all scattered and diverging rapidly one from the other. The two were going off to the right, walking very quickly in single file, the hindmost animal being followed by a small calf. Riding out to one side of them through the open forest, which was just here quite free from underwood, I saw that they were two fine cows, both having long white tusks, and at once resolved to attack them. I did think of the poor little calf, but consoled myself with the thought that if I destroyed its mother it would follow up the herd and be adopted by another elephant. This is the case, I believe, if they are old enough to live without their mother's

milk.   These two elephants I ought to have killed very quickly
and easily, as the forest through which they first led me was very
open, and they kept close together.   I was now, however,
getting tired, being still very weak, and found it impossible to
shoot steadily.   Before long I had wounded both the elephants
severely, and the one with the calf especially seemed very hard
hit.   Presently they got into a patch of machabel scrub, the
soft fern-like leaves of which were, luckily for me, still very thick,
and one of them here charged savagely, screaming loudly.   I
thought I should have had to dismount and run for it again,
as I could not get the stallion out of a hand gallop, but by
making a quick turn round an immense ant-heap I managed
to give her the slip, but I saw that I had to be careful.   As
soon as she had lost me she rejoined her comrade, and they
continued their flight together, before long crossing a small
stream of running water.

As they were climbing the farther bank I came down
quite close to them and gave the cow with the calf a
dead shot, as she only just managed to reach the top
when she stopped, and, facing round, fell over backwards,
throwing her trunk high in the air as she did so.   I ought to
have killed the other one here too, as she stopped about a
hundred yards on ahead and stood broadside on, waiting
probably for her dead comrade.   I fired at her, but did not hit
her where I ought to have done.   She walked on again and
went right through a broad open valley covered with long
grass, like the place where I had first seen the herd of
elephants that morning.   As long as she was in the open I
dared not go near her, but as soon as she entered the machabel
bush on the farther side of the valley I followed as fast as I
could get my horse to go.   I was still a hundred yards away
from the bush, but could see the wounded elephant walking
slowly along, skirting just within its edge, when she must have
got my wind, for she suddenly swung round, and, raising her
head and ears, came out into the open, trumpeting loudly.   I had
already got my horse's tail towards her, and was doing my best
to get him into a gallop, but it was useless, and as it was at
least two hundred yards to the other side of the open valley I
knew she would catch me long before I reached the shelter of

the trees where I might have dodged her. Of course, directly she emerged from the bush she saw me plainly in the open before her and came on two yards to my one, screaming shrilly all the time.

I did not hesitate an instant what to do, but resolved to sacrifice the horse and try to get away myself in the grass. Catching him by the mane, when he instantly stopped dead, I jumped past him and ran forwards through the grass as hard as I could, which was not very hard, as I was now much exhausted. I had got some forty yards beyond him when the elephant suddenly stopped screaming and commenced making the rumbling noise I have spoken of as being made by the first elephant that came up to him. Turning my head I saw that she was standing exactly like the first one, alongside of the horse, who remained perfectly motionless, but that she had not yet touched him. I instantly ducked down in the grass and watched her. I was very much afraid lest she should get my wind and come on after me, and at the same time feared to fire at her, as I felt so terribly shaky after my run that I knew I should only give her a bad shot and let her know where I was. I was very much surprised at her leaving the horse alone. Had she been unwounded, like the first one that came up to him, I should have thought nothing of it, as there are many similar cases on record ; but, irritated as the poor brute must have been from the wounds she had received, I made sure she would have killed him instantly. She would most certainly have killed me had she caught me, and I think she showed more magnanimity than sagacity in sparing my horse, for, although he had taken no part in injuring her, he had, at any rate, been instrumental in bringing me within shot of her. However that may be, the fact remains that this wounded and furious elephant ran screaming up to my horse, and, finding his rider gone, stood alongside of him without touching him. After a space of half a minute, perhaps, she turned and walked back into the bush, and I then went back to my horse, who had never moved his feet since I placed my hand on his mane and sprang from the saddle. I mounted again at once, and riding into the bush soon caught sight of the wounded elephant walking very slowly forwards, and constantly stopping. At length she passed one of the enormous ant-heaps common in this part of Africa—ant-heaps twenty yards in circumference, and often with large trees growing on them—and, as soon as she was behind it, I left my horse and ran up to it. Peering round I saw her standing broadside on not fifty yards off, evidently listening and looking very suspicious. I now rested my rifle on the side of the ant-heap and fired into her shoulder. On receiving this shot she moved on for a very short distance and again stood, when I fired once more from the same spot. It was unnecessary, however, as the last bullet must have passed through her heart, I think, and she was just about to fall when I fired again.

I now resolved to give up any further pursuit of the elephants, as it was manifestly tempting fate to follow them up again, and could only end in getting caught myself, or, at any rate, in having my horse killed, who, in spite of his occasional obstinacy, was a valuable animal. Had I had Nelson I should certainly by this time have killed more elephants than I had done, without having tired myself very severely, and I should now have galloped hard round to the right until I had cut the spoor of another of the small herds into which the elephants had broken up, shot several of them before they scattered, and, if the horse had been equal to it, perhaps got round to a third herd. However, as it was, I was already much exhausted, and felt that it would be foolish to follow up the elephants again, and so, with large numbers of these animals still within my reach, in beautiful open forest country, entirely devoid of thick brush, and with my saddle-bags still full of cartridges, I had to give up the hunt. Still it might have been worse. Four animals I knew were dead ; the fifth that I had left badly wounded with Laer I hoped he had managed to kill ; and I still thought I might find the big bull I had first wounded, as I knew I had hit him about the right place. In going back to the waggons I visited the four elephants I had seen lying dead. The three cows were all pretty good ones, with tusks weighing from 10 lbs. to 14 lbs. ; but the bull, although a large animal, had very poor tusks, that proved to weigh only 25 lbs. and 23 lbs. respectively, both of them being slightly broken at the ends.

When I came to the cow that I had killed on the bank of the small stream, I found her little calf still standing beside the carcase. When I approached, the poor little beast, with the pluck always shown by elephant calves, raised its ears, and, screaming shrilly, charged right at me. I did not move, as the poor thing was hardly more than three feet high, and the old stallion never moved or paid the slightest attention to it. It came right up to the horse, but stopped without actually touching him, and, after standing there a few moments, returned to its dead mother. It would, perhaps, have been more merciful to have shot it at once through the brain and ended its troubles, but I had not the heart to do so, and thought it might perhaps escape lions and hyænas and follow up the spoor of its mother's relatives. At any rate, the next morning, when I returned to chop out the tusks, the calf was nowhere to be seen. On reaching the waggons I found Laer there before me, and an elephant's tail hanging from the side of the waggon showed me he had killed the animal I left in his charge. He told me that after I left him, as the wounded animal only walked very slowly forwards, he had dismounted and run round in front of it, and as it came past him had given it a shot in the shoulder with the 10-bore, to which it succumbed almost immediately. This made five elephants at any rate, and eventually I got the big bull too, which had been killed with a single bullet from the 450-bore Metford and had only gone a few hundred yards from where he had been hit. His tusks proved to weigh 41 lbs. and 43 lbs. respectively, and were a nice even pair, quite perfect at the points.

A KOPJE.

CHAPTER IX

Chop out the tusks of the dead elephants—Immense numbers of vultures—The
stallion lame—Resolve to proceed to the Manyami river— Form a main camp—
Game plentiful—Hyæna shot—My big cauldron—Trek to Golodaima's kraals—
Another hyæna shot—Hyæna killed at the Tchangani river—Find the big bull
elephant—Shoot another fine bull—Obtain specimens of Lichtenstein's hartebeest—Return to Matabililand—A sable antelope amongst the cattle—Several
of our best dogs are killed—Danger of approaching wounded antelopes.

ON the day following the elephant-hunt described in the last
chapter, I took all my boys and distributed them amongst the
carcases of the slain animals, in order to get the tusks chopped
out quickly.   I also took the pack donkeys to carry the hearts,
inside fat, upper parts of the trunks, and other choice portions
of the meat.   I thought I should have been able to have
finished this work early in the day, and intended to have
devoted the afternoon to looking for the big bull that I had
first wounded.   However, it was late before all the work was
done that required my personal superintendence, and the
enormous number of vultures that were either perched in the
trees or flying all round about in the neighbourhood of the
dead elephants, rendered it impossible to use them as a guide

to the exact whereabouts of any particular animal.   I was, too, feeling rather unwell and despondent after my disappointment at the way in which my horse had behaved on the previous day ; and finally I again returned to the waggon without looking for the big bull.   My stallion, too, was now dead lame, having trodden on a sharp stone and injured the frog of one of his fore feet during the hunt, and this annoyed and irritated me dreadfully ; for although I possessed four salted horses, two were now lame, one was useless for a shooting horse, and the fourth (old Charley) was in such low condition that he could not possibly do any hard work.   The following morning I resolved to bother no more about the wounded elephant bull, but to trek on across the Umfuli to the Manyami river, and there to form a strong permanent camp which should be my headquarters until the following rainy season.

As soon as I reached the Manyami I sent a messenger to Inyamwenda's people to tell them I had come, and at the same time let them know that I wanted to buy a good supply of mealies [1] for my horses.   The following day about forty of them came down to my camp, which I had pitched about a mile higher up the river ·than where my waggons had stood in 1883. With the assistance of the Mashunas I was able to make a fine strong camp in a couple of days, with fences that a lion could not very easily get through.   Game I found very plentiful in the district, and I had no difficulty in shooting a good supply of meat, without working old Charley very hard.   I used to ride out on him until I sighted game, and then get off and stalk it.

Before starting on this expedition from Matabililand, I had had an immense cauldron made of sheet iron by a very clever blacksmith, who was in the employment of the Gold Mining Company at Tati.   This cauldron I had made for the purpose of boiling down animals, in order to preserve their perfect skeletons.   The first night I got to the Manyami several hyænas came howling round the camp, so on the following evening I set a gun for them, with the result that I killed a fine old male tiger-wolf (*Hyæna crocuta*), and after skinning him and taking out his inside—there was a bit of a smell—I

[1] Maize.

put the whole carcase into the cauldron, which was about four feet deep and three in diameter. I made a fine skeleton of him—which has gone to America—but the Mashunas and my own boys thought I had defiled the pot by cooking the unclean beast in it ; and when the next day I boiled down a zebra, they actually would not drink the soup, as they said it would taste of hyæna. However, they had no scruples about the third and all subsequent animals, and they used to get the most glorious feeds out of my big pot, which became well known in the country-side, and was looked upon by the Mashunas as a sort of soup-kitchen, as there was almost always something in it ; for when I was not using it in the interests of science my boys used to get the benefit of it.

It was still very early in the season, and as I knew that I could not expect Collison and Van Rooyen for a month or six weeks to come, I resolved to cross the Manyami with my waggon, and trek along the eastern slope of the Umvukwi hills to Golodaima's kraals on the Gurumapudzi river. At these kraals I had heard from natives that I should be able to buy a good supply of maize ; for Inyamwenda's people did not seem to be very well supplied with that kind of grain. I expected to be away for about a fortnight, and by the end of that time I thought the stallion would be sound again, and also hoped that old Charley would have improved considerably in condition, as I was feeding him up with as much boiled maize, with a little salt sprinkled in it, as I could get him to eat.

On reaching a small stream, a tributary of the Gurumapudzi, not far from Golodaima's town, I sent word to the chief to let him know that I had come and wanted to buy a waggon load of maize. The next day he turned up with a lot of his people, and said the women would all come the following day with grain. He told me there was a large herd of elands in the neighbourhood, and asked me to go out and shoot some meat for him and his followers. He also informed me there was an old lion about that had lately killed several people. As I wanted to get hold of an eland bull for the sake of the fat, I saddled up old Charley after breakfast, and went out with the Mashunas. However, we were not lucky enough to see the elands or strike their fresh spoor, so coming across a small herd of zebras (Burchell's) on the way home, and when not far from camp, I shot two of them and had all the meat carried in. That night Golodaima and his followers remained at my waggon, and sat up eating and talking till a late hour. At last they all went to sleep, and I tried to follow their example.

I was lying on the "bed-plank" of the almost empty waggon, and in the back part of it, my rifle lying in front, with the barrel resting against the forechest. Suddenly I was awakened by hearing old Charley snort, and pull violently on the thong by which he was fastened to the hind wheel of the waggon. Starting up, and throwing the piece of sail-cloth that was hanging down behind my head to one side, I looked out into the night, which was dark, though clear and starlit. I at once saw what had frightened the horse; for a dark object was advancing rapidly along the ground from the direction of the stream near which we were camped. It was not coming towards the horse, however, but passing the waggon obliquely, towards where the oxen were tied to the yokes. I made sure it was the lion Golodaima had told me about, and fearing for my oxen, shouted out, "Hey! you brute!" and letting fall the sail-cloth, sprang to the front part of the waggon and seized my rifle. The creature, which I still thought was a lion, was now within a few yards of the oxen, none of which had moved or manifested the slightest alarm; so, looking at it, and levelling my rifle, though of course I could not see the sights, I fired, and rolled it over. Directly I fired I knew it was a hyæna, as it made a kind of cackling noise. The oxen had now all got up, but did not manifest any alarm, though the hyæna was rolling about on the ground. I now shouted to the Mashunas to bring torches of grass, and unfastening an Indian hog-spear, which was tied to the side of the waggon, I jumped to the ground and advanced on the wounded hyæna. When, however, I approached him, he clacked his powerful jaws so ominously that I waited until the Kafirs came up with wisps of blazing grass. Then I saw that the wretched creature was shot through the loins and his hind quarters paralysed, so I despatched him with the hog-spear.   He was, like the last one killed at the Manyami, an old dog hyæna.

Speaking of hyænas, I remember a curious fact in connection with one of these animals.   In December of this

CORNELIS VAN ROOYEN.

same year of which I am now writing — 1885 — I returned to Matabililand with Mr. Collison, Cornelis van Rooyen, and Mr. James Dawson of Bulawayo, who had come into Mashunaland, towards the end of the hunting season.   When we reached the Tchangani river, in the neighbourhood of which there are several Matabili kraals, we made a halt of a few days to rest our oxen. During this time Dawson and I rode into the mission station at Emhlangen to get our letters, returning to the waggons (about twenty-five miles) the following day.

On our arrival Van Rooyen told us that our dogs—we had a first-rate pack between us—had seized a hyæna the night before and held it fast, whilst the Kafirs assegaied it. He said it was a very large one, and that it was still lying less than a hundred yards away, on the bank of the river.   As it is very unusual for dogs to be able to hold one of these powerful beasts, Dawson and I went down to look at the carcase.   It was that of a huge old bitch hyæna (*Hyæna crocuta*) that had been the mother of many cubs, as her two suckling teats were quite an inch in length.   I soon noticed something that Van Rooyen had overlooked, namely, that the canine teeth of the lower jaw were missing, and examining more closely found that the ends of both lower jaw bones were gone.   It looked as if a bullet must have struck the animal in the mouth from one side, just behind the lower canine teeth, breaking both jaw bones, and the loose piece of bone left in the extremity of the animal's lower jaw must subsequently have rotted out.   However, this accident had evidently happened long prior to the date of the animal's death, as the wounds had long been healed.   Now the question is, how this hyæna had been able to feed with her jaws in this condition ; for one would think that the two lower jaw bones, being independent as it were, would be useless for crunching bones, and bones are what hyænas principally live on.   Yet this animal was excessively fat, and its coat in excellent condition.   As it was living in the near neighbourhood of several native villages I have no doubt it managed to unearth a corpse now and again, but it could hardly count upon an unfailing supply of such luxuries.   It has often puzzled me to imagine how this hyæna could have lived at all, let alone kept itself fat.   It was evidently unable to make use of its jaws to defend itself against the dogs.

As, on my return from Golodaima's to the main camp on the Manyami, I found that the wound in the stallion's foot was quite healed, and as the old horse Charley had by this time improved considerably in condition, I determined to take a round in search of elephants through the mahobo-hobo forests lying to the north-west of my camp.   I had made up my mind not to run any more risks with the stallion, so I rode old Charley, and mounted Laer on the stronger horse, but told him not to go near to elephants should we come across any of those animals.   On the evening of the first night we left camp I asked Laer if he had seen anything of the bull that I had wounded with my first shot at Umfuli, when the tuskless cow chased me away from the herd.   He told me that he had been some little distance behind me when I fired, and on seeing the cow coming towards my horse, had turned Charley round and galloped into the edge of the forest we had just left.   There he had reined in, and looked round, and had then seen the big bull, behind all the other elephants and still in the open.   He had then, he said, watched him walk slowly forwards, and gain the edge of the forest-covered slope beyond the valley in which we had first seen the herd.   " The last I saw of him, sir," he concluded, " he was standing still among the trees, holding his trunk straight up in the air ; then I heard you firing and galloped after you."   " Great Heavens ! " I said, on hearing this, " why on earth didn't you tell me so the day after the hunt ?   That elephant is dead.   He was dying when you saw him standing with his trunk in the air, and must have been shot through the big blood-vessels of the lungs." Laer pleaded that he was unused to the ways of elephants, and said that the fact of the animal's holding its trunk straight up in the air conveyed no particular meaning to him. But to me it was different ; I had seen many an elephant shot broadside through the lungs with a big-bore gun first run two or three hundred yards, as if there was nothing the matter with him, then walk slowly forwards a little farther, and then stand, throwing the blood in all directions from his upraised trunk, which usually he would stretch straight up in the air several times before falling dead ; and I felt sure that the remains of this particular elephant lay just where Laer had last seen the animal standing. My great fear was lest any Mashunas out hunting or looking for honey had been guided by the vultures to the carcases, and had found the remains of the big bull and gone off with the tusks.

I asked Laer if he thought he could find his way easily to where he had last seen the elephant standing, and he said he could. I did not doubt him, as he had Bushman blood in him, and I knew by experience that he could find his way back to any spot he had ever visited before with an unerring exactness to which no European or Kafir could ever hope to attain. I have already spoken of this faculty in my chapter on the Masarwas and Bushmen, and they are the only people I have met with in Africa who possess it in perfection.

The next morning I started straight away for the place where a month previously I had shot the five elephants, putting Laer in front. Late in the afternoon we crossed the Umfuli, and I soon saw that we were nearing the spot where the carcases lay, as we began to cross the broad trails made by the great herd through the grassy valleys between the patches of forest when the frightened animals first took to flight. Presently Laer said, " Sir, you shot the second bull just over there," pointing to a patch of machabel forest, " and the big bull was standing out in that direction," pointing on ahead, " when I last saw him." " Very well, then go straight to the place," I replied ; and Laer rode on. Soon we came to the sole of an elephant's foot, which had rotted off, and had probably been dragged away from the carcase by a hyæna or jackal. Immediately afterwards, Laer cried out joyfully, "There he lies!" and the Kafirs, catching sight of the remains of the carcase, at the same time rushed forwards with a shout.   I galloped up, and was mightily pleased to see that the tusks were still in the skull.   They proved to be a fine even pair, not very large, but at the same time by no means to be despised, as they proved to weigh a little over 40 lbs. each, and were worth

HEAD OF AN AFRICAN ELEPHANT.

therefore at least £20 apiece.   Thus at last, more than a month after having shot it, did I find the remains of the big bull I had first fired at on the day of the elephant-hunt.   One bullet through the lungs had killed it—a 540-grain bullet propelled by only 75 grains of powder.   The bullet was, of course, solid and toughened, and was fired from a 450-bore Metford rifle by Gibbs of Bristol.

Before returning to the Manyami I made a round in search of elephants through the thick scrubby forests which grow on both banks of the Upper Umfuli, and was one day lucky enough to come on a small herd. I heard one of them trumpet at a great distance early one morning, and riding in the direction of the sound at last cut their fresh spoor. Before I came up with them, however, the keen-scented animals winded me, and decamped, and almost immediately began to scatter. Galloping after them, first on the spoor of one, then on that of another, I soon came up with some young and worthless animals. Old Charley behaved well and showed no fear. At last I caught sight of a fine cow, with long white tusks, and not having seen a bull, and concluding there were none, I resolved to kill her. I had given her three shots, and sustained a pretty smart chase, as the scrubby forest was very awkward to get through with a horse, when I suddenly saw three big bulls, walking one behind the other through the bush not far to my left. I thought no more about the cow, but at once rode towards the more valuable animals. One bull had a fine pair of tusks standing out well beyond his trunk. A second had very short tusks, protruding less than a foot beyond the lip ; whilst the third was a tuskless male, a great big brute, but without a pound of ivory in his head. I soon got a chance, and fired at the bull with the best tusks, upon which each one of the three at once took a line of his own. I of course followed the one I had wounded. The bush was excessively dense, and awkward to work in, and once I nearly lost my elephant, which suddenly doubled back in a very thick bit. However, I just saw him passing. After giving him seven or eight shots he stopped, and facing round stood with his ears extended in a manner that showed me he meant to charge if he could see me or scent me. The bush was here so thick that I could not get a good view of him from where I sat on my horse ; so dismounting I walked away from old Charley, always facing towards the wounded elephant, and trying to get a clear space to fire through into his chest. I was about twenty yards from my horse and was still moving away from him, when the elephant must have smelt one or other of us, for he suddenly came rushing on, crashing down the small trees, and trumpeting shrilly. Old Charley thought it was not worth while waiting for me, and galloped off directly the elephant screamed. However, I think that I must have

walked out until a breath of wind had enabled him to scent
me.   At any rate he came straight for me with ears outspread,
trumpeting out the shrill short screams of rage with which a
wounded elephant usually accompanies a charge.   I only had
my little single Metford, and I must say I had grave doubts as
to whether the small 450-bore bullet would stop the angry
monster.   I aimed carefully, however, and put the bullet, when
he was about fifteen yards from me, just under his tusk, and
past the side of his trunk into his chest ; for his trunk was
hanging down in front of him, as it always is, I fancy, when
an elephant really charges through bush ; though they will
often rush out at the start and scream, with their trunks held
up in the air.   When they settle down to a regular charge,
however, they drop the proboscis in front of them, turning the
end in towards their forelegs.   Directly the bullet struck him,
this big bull elephant at once stopped screaming and swerved
off, almost at right angles to the way he had been coming.   I
believe my bullet must have gone through his heart, for he
almost immediately settled down to a slow walk, and soon
stopped and stood still again ; I then gave him another bullet,
aiming once more for his heart,•and soon afterwards his limbs
began to quiver and I saw he was done for.   Just then Laer
came up with the Kafirs, and they were just in time to see
the elephant fall.   Old Charley had not gone very far away,
and the boys soon tracked him up and brought him back
to me.   This elephant was a fine big bull, and his tusks
were quite perfect, and weighed a little more than those of
the other I had so fortunately recovered, as together they
turned the scale at 88 lbs.

I will here record my belief that the tuskless bull I
saw this day was the same animal that seven years previously, in 1878, had torn one of our Matabili Kafirs[1]
into three pieces.   This I say, because, although tuskless
cow elephants are comparatively common in Africa, and one
or more may be seen in every herd, tuskless bulls are very
exceptional, and the only two I have ever heard of or seen in
Mashunaland are the one that killed Quabeet, and the one I
have mentioned above ; and I believe they were one and the

[1] See *A Hunter's Wanderings*, p. 334.

same animal, as it was close to the spot where Quabeet was killed in 1878 that I saw the tuskless bull again in 1885. He must be still at large, for I have not heard of his being killed since.   The other bull with the short tusks, however, was killed about a month later by Collison, Van Rooyen, and myself. Though so short, his tusks were very thick and weighed nearly 40 lbs. apiece.

As to give any detailed account of my various journeys in search of game during the remaining months of 1885 would not only in all probability prove tedious to my readers, but would certainly oblige me to curtail other portions of my narrative of more general interest, I will content myself by saying that in the course of the season I again made a journey to the River Sabi in search of Lichtenstein's hartebeests, and on this occasion succeeded in shooting and preserving five fine specimens of those animals.   One pair of these are now in our national collection at South Kensington, whilst the second are in the collection of the South African Museum at Cape Town, the odd one having gone to a foreign museum.

In December I returned to Matabililand in company with Mr. H. C. Collison, Cornelis van Rooyen, and Mr. James Dawson of Bulawayo, who had come into Mashunaland with an empty waggon in order to help me out with the large number of natural history specimens I had collected, which amounted altogether to more than a load for one waggon. I remember one incident of our return journey, which I think is worth relating.

One night we had outspanned at the head of a lovely grassy glade, between the Umniati and Sebakwi rivers, down the centre of which ran a nice little stream of water.   Just at daylight the next morning the cattle were all unloosed to get a bit of a feed before being inspanned for the morning's trek, and soon spread out over the open valley which lay in front of our bivouac.   I was drinking a cup of coffee, seated in the front part of my own waggon, when I saw a fine sable antelope bull come out of the forest that skirted the open ground and advance towards the cattle, which he kept examining inquiringly, standing still for a few seconds at a time, and then coming slowly forwards again.   Before long he had come quite close up to some of the foremost oxen, and was then not more than one hundred and fifty yards or so from Van Rooyen's waggon, which was some distance in advance of mine. My friend had all this time been watching the sable antelope as well as I, and at this juncture he fired at and wounded it, shooting from the inside of his waggon. Directly the shot was fired every dog rushed out from beneath the particular waggon to which he or she belonged, and the whole motley pack, about twenty in number, were soon streaming out down the valley. The foremost dogs soon caught sight of the sable antelope, which, badly wounded by Van Rooyen's bullet, was making off slowly towards the stream which ran down the centre of the open ground. As it disappeared down the steep bank the foremost dogs were almost up to it. Van Rooyen, Dawson, and myself were now running as hard as we could to call the pack off and despatch the wounded antelope before any of our valuable dogs were killed ; for we knew from experience what havoc a wounded sable antelope can make amongst a pack with its long curved horns. Just as we were nearing the water two of my own dogs came howling up the bank, both badly wounded, and the loud barking of the rest of the pack, coupled with the defiant snorts of the sable antelope, which proceeded from the bed of the stream, let us know that the brave beast was still making a gallant fight and doing his utmost to sell his life dearly. A moment later we despatched him with two bullets through the head and neck, and not a moment too soon. Four of our best dogs lay dead around their quarry, one of which, a kind of mongrel deer-hound, Van Rooyen would not have parted with at any price. Besides the four that were killed outright, four more were badly wounded, one of which subsequently died. My old bitch Ruby had one more very narrow escape. She had been struck right through the throat by the sharp horn of the sable antelope, which, however, had only pierced through between the skin and the windpipe. She must, I fancy, have been swung up into the air, and then twisted off with such violence that the skin had torn ; so that a great piece of it as large as the palm of my hand hung down under her jaw. This piece of loose skin, however, I sewed in its place again, and the wound soon healed up.

I have mentioned this instance of the able manner in which a sable antelope can use its horns when beset by dogs to show that these animals are often very savage when wounded, and I would caution young sportsmen against approaching either a sable or roan antelope, a gemsbuck or a wildebeest, when any of these animals are standing at bay.   Individuals of all these species will often make a short rush if approached too closely, and are very quick with their horns.   Not long ago one of Lo Bengula's men, belonging to the village of Churchin, was killed by a wounded sable antelope cow, which drove one of its horns right through his kidneys.

NATIVE HOUSEHOLD UTENSILS.

CAVE OF SINOIA (UNDERGROUND LAKE).

CHAPTER X

I HAVE now brought my narrative down to the end of 1885,
and shall pass briefly over the next two years.

During 1886, though I twice visited Matabililand, I did
but little shooting or collecting, and between those two visits
took a quick run home to England, where I spent six weeks
during August and September, getting back to Bulawayo
again by the end of November. In 1887 I made another
hunting expedition to Mashunaland, in company with three
English sportsmen, Messrs. J. A. Jameson, A. C. Fountaine,
and F. Cooper. Space will not permit of my giving any
detailed account of our various peregrinations during this year,
though I shall relate certain incidents of our sport in a later
chapter. Suffice it to say that we travelled over much country,
and on the whole enjoyed good sport, the bag including
amongst other items twelve lions. It was during this year
that we discovered the limestone caves of Sinoia, and the sub-
terranean lake in the principal cave. The colour of the water
in this cave is most remarkable, being of the deepest cobalt
blue, like that in the celebrated grotto of Capri. I wrote an
account of the caves of Sinoia at the time of our first visit,
which was published in the Proceedings of the Royal Geographical Society of London for May 1888.

We established our main camp on the Upper Manyami, and from this central point made hunting expeditions of from a fortnight to six weeks' duration to all points of the compass. In this way we went northwards between the Angwa and Manyami rivers as far as the conspicuous mountain called by the natives Techenena ; and on another occasion reached the Sanyati, as the river is called below the confluence of the Umniati and Umfuli. Between these two journeys, too, we travelled south-eastwards to the Manica country, reaching a point on the Odzi river just below the mouth of the Umtali, and not more than twelve miles from the spot where the township of Umtali has now sprung up. Later on in the year we broke up our camp and, crossing the Manyami, trekked over to the Gwibi river near Mount Hampden. From here we cut a road direct to the source of the Umgezi river (the spot where Fort Charter was established by the pioneer expedition of the British South Africa Company in 1890), and trekked right over the ground where the town of Salisbury now stands. In 1890 the spoor made by our six waggons was still plainly visible in the sandy soil near Fort Charter, but had entirely disappeared in the firmer ground near Salisbury. From the head of the Umgezi river we made a road for ourselves to Matabililand, and then returned to the Transvaal. My friends then set out for England, and I returned once more to the interior.

On 9th April 1888 I left Bamangwato for the Zambesi, with two waggons, five salted horses, sixteen donkeys, etc. My intention was to have crossed the river with everything I possessed and to have journeyed up to Lialui, in the Barotsi valley, the residence of Lewanika, the ruling chief, and there to have taken up my abode for at least a year ; my principal object being the collection of specimens of natural history, combined with a little elephant-hunting and trading. I may here mention that Mr. Coillard, the chief of the French Protestant Mission now established in that country, had already taken several waggons across the Zambesi, and it was he who made the waggon track which now exists right up to Lialui. The journey to Panda-ma-tenka may be dismissed in a few words. The country is well known, most monotonous and uninteresting, and game at this time of year very scarce. I managed, however, always to keep my Kafirs and dogs in meat, and, amongst other things, shot five ostriches (two beautiful cocks and three hens, all at this time of year in splendid plumage) and seven gemsbucks. I only once saw giraffe, and shot a fine fat cow.

On 16th May I reached Panda-ma-tenka, with all my live stock in good condition. Here I had hoped to meet my old friend, Mr. George Westbeech, the well-known Zambesi trader, but I found that he was still at the river, some seventy miles distant. I found, however, my old acquaintances, John Weyers, a colonial Dutchman, and all the half-caste elephant-hunters in Mr. Westbeech's employ. From them I heard all the news, and, to my intense chagrin, learned that the country across the Zambesi was in a very unsettled condition, and that there was no chance of my getting through the river. I heard, too, that Marancinyan, a rival claimant to the Barotsi chieftainship, had lately made a raid on Sesheki, burning down the town and killing some of the inhabitants, that Lewanika with all his people was away, with the double object of following up and exterminating the raiders, and also of capturing cattle from the Mashukulumbwi, and that I might have to wait months before being able to cross the river.

To a man of my impatient, restless temperament this was crushing news, and the next morning I saddled up one of my horses, determined to ride on and get correct information from George Westbeech. I met him a few miles beyond Gazuma, and spent a day discussing the situation with him. He confirmed all that I had heard at Panda-ma-tenka, and put things in a worse light still, saying that a revolution was on the point of breaking out in favour of Marancinyan, in which case it would be months before the country became settled again, and that at present, at any rate, it was impossible to cross the river with my waggons, as all the people were away, and there was no one to work the canoes. Mr. Westbeech then showed me a letter which he had received from Mr. Frederick Arnot, a young missionary and a worthy countryman of Dr. Livingstone, who had once travelled with me, and had now established himself in Central

Africa. In this letter, which was dated from "Moshidi's Town, Garanganzi country, about ten days' journey west of Lake Bangweolo," and had been carried by Mambari traders first to the west coast, then to the Barotsi valley, and finally down the Zambesi, Mr. Arnot said that he was in a fine country under a powerful chief, and that elephants were in astonishing numbers. " If you should meet our mutual friend, Mr. F. Selous," he wrote, " tell him how delighted I should be to receive a visit from him." By Jove, thought I, the very thing ; as I cannot get up to the Barotsi with my waggons, I will accept Mr. Arnot's invitation, and try to make my way to the Garanganzi country. I at once set about making prepara- tions, and arranged packs for the sixteen donkeys, and loads for about fifteen boys, containing ample supplies of everything— provisions, ammunition, and goods—for a year; for my intention was to make my way to Mr. Arnot, and remain there hunting and collecting during the following rainy season, and to return to Panda-ma-tenka the next winter.

Consulting my maps, I determined to cross the Zambesi at Wankie's Town, and after following the river down to its junction with the Kafukwi—my old route of eleven years before—to cross the latter river, and then strike away to the north until I got into about the right latitude, by which time I thought I should be sure to hear something of the whereabouts of the chief Moshidi. I now stored all my surplus goods at Panda-ma-tenka, and on 5th June started on my journey, John Weyers accompanying me as far as Wankie's, from whom he hoped to buy some ivory. I had with me three men who spoke Dutch—Daniel, a Hottentot, who had driven one of my waggons in from Bamangwato ; Paul, a Natal Zulu, who had married and been living amongst Wankie's people for some years ; and Charley, a lad who had been brought up by one of Westbeech's hunters, and was an excellent interpreter and a good shot. I also had two of Khama's people with me, each of whom carried a double 10-bore rifle (two splendid weapons, one by Rigby and one by Purdey), whilst Paul carried a single 10, all three taking one cartridge, and Charley and myself had two 450-bore Metfords by George Gibbs of Bristol. I also had four Mashunas with me who belonged to me—two

WAGGON TEAM STARTING FOR INTERIOR.

young men and two boys. All the other boys were hired at Panda-ma-tenka, and no dependence was to be placed on their sticking to me ; but I trusted to my own people and the donkeys.

We took eight days getting to Wankie's on the Zambesi, as the road is a most difficult one for donkeys, especially along the banks of the Matietsi river. One of them was jostled, pack and all, off a high bank right into a deep pool, everything of course getting wet, and the donkey being all but drowned before we could loosen the pack, and even then we had the greatest difficulty in getting the unfortunate animal out of the water. As we neared the Zambesi the country became more and more rugged and barren, the stony, desolate hills being nevertheless sparsely covered with stunted, leafless trees. In the way of game there is little else in these hills beyond a few koodoos and impala antelopes, and we saw nothing at all to fire at. It took us a whole day, from early morning till nearly sunset, to get the donkeys and all the goods through the river, working with two canoes, one a pretty good one, the other very rickety. The river here is about four hundred yards broad, and the stream strong. The donkeys were towed across, one by one, at the tail of the big canoe. At length everything was safely landed on the other side, and we camped beneath an immense baobab-tree, close to Wankie's Town. Early the following morning the old fellow came down to our camp. He must then have been a very old man, but he still managed to get about, and seemed in the full possession of all his faculties. I had to pay him for bringing me through the river, and found him much more grasping and difficult to deal with than when I crossed here eleven years previously. However, at last I satisfied him, and at once made ready to start. My boy Daniel had complained during the morning of severe pains in the head and back of the neck, and I now found that he had a bad attack of fever. He evidently could not go on with me, so I left him in charge of John Weyers, who was going to remain a few days at Wankie's. I subsequently learned that the poor fellow only lived three days, dying on the fourth after he was taken sick, so dangerous is this disease in the Zambesi valley to unacclimatised men, whether white, black, or yellow. Striking an average, I think the yellow has the least power of resistance, the black the greatest.

By mid-day I had everything once more ready for a start, and with a hearty handshake bade adieu to John Weyers, not expecting to see a white man's face again for some time to come. The following day my troubles commenced. In the morning, when I wanted to get under way, the boys I had hired at Panda-ma-tenka said that one of their number was ill. " Very well," I said, " then he had better go back to Wankie's, and then home to his kraal." If one went home, they replied, they must all go. Seeing that it was what the Americans call a " put-up job," I at once told them to go, and bade them get out of my camp forthwith. Ten of them at once tied up their traps, and with their sick comrade moved off to a tree at some distance. Only a fortnight before these fellows had protested most solemnly that they would stick to me through thick and thin, and return with me to Panda-ma-tenka. Before hiring them I had explained to them most minutely where I wanted to get to, and the route I wished to take, so that they had entered my service under no delusion in this respect. Although this desertion was most annoying, I was too well used to native character to feel surprised at it. They doubtless thought they had me in a fix, but, if so, I soon showed them their mistake by packing all their loads on the donkeys and proceeding on my journey.

The humble donkey is proverbially the poor man's friend, but nowhere more so than in the interior of Africa. Hardy and enduring, he can carry as much as five ordinary Kafirs, and makes no complaints. In countries where the tse-tse fly is in excessive numbers, the donkey, strong as he is, will not live long ; but he resists the poison far better than any other domestic animal, and will pass through belts of " fly " country without taking much harm, his constitution being so strong that he will recover from the effects of the poison if not kept too long in the infected district, whereas an ox or a horse, if once impregnated, will almost to a certainty pine away and die. I say almost to a certainty, because I have heard of cases of oxen and horses recovering after having been bitten ; but such cases are very exceptional. The younger the animal, whether horse, ox, or donkey, the better will he resist the " fly " poison.

But I must get on with my narrative. A couple of days' journey through barren stony hills and dreary leafless forests, in which we found water very scarce, brought us once more to the banks of the Zambesi at the village of Shampondo, a Batonga headman.   During these two days I had recruited several fresh boys at the small Mashapatan villages by which we passed, and the donkeys were now no longer overloaded.   We had heard that there was at present a scare amongst the Batongas about a Matabili " impi," which was said to be camped on the southern bank of the river, and on reaching Shampondo's found that there were really some Matabili camped there.   They wished to cross the river, and a large force of Batongas had been collected to prevent their doing so ; but as the latter had all the canoes on their side it was difficult to see how the Matabili could have crossed, even if the Batonga army had not been there.   However, they were in a great state of excitement, and had sent all the women and children and goats away into the bush.   That evening we camped just below Shampondo's village, the Batonga army of observation being about a couple of miles farther up the river.   Old Shampondo came down to my camp.   I made him a present, received a goat in return from him, told him my plans, and that I wished to start again early the following morning, and everything seemed friendly and pleasant.   At daylight the next day, however, he came down again, accompanied by a lot of men, all armed with barbed spears, and intimated that he was not satisfied with my present, and that he wanted this, that, and the other.   His men at the same time assumed a threatening attitude, standing round in a semicircle, talking and gesticulating violently.   My two Mangwato men, alarmed at the warlike aspect of affairs, now caught up their rifles and commenced putting cartridges in, whereupon the Batongas seized their assegais, and stood, every man of them, with a long throwing spear, poised and quivering, in the right hand, and half-a-dozen more in the left, their language at the same time becoming very threatening.

These Batonga throwing spears, I may here say, are all horribly barbed, and altogether most indigestible-looking weapons. The situation began to be unpleasant ; however, upon my advancing unarmed, and asking the Batongas what they meant by raising their assegais to my people, they laid them down and sat down themselves. We were utterly in their power, and they knew it, for with a dozen men, most of them boys in fact as well as in name, one cannot fight a hostile tribe. The most I could have done would have been to have shot some natives, and then escaped, leaving all my property in the enemy's hands and giving up my enterprise.

I now called Paul, and with him walked to where old Shampondo was sitting, and discussed matters with him. After a great deal of talking, and when I had given him a piece of black calico, a tin of powder, and two rings of brass wire, only producing each article after a vast deal of argument, the old fellow professed himself satisfied, and said that the road was open for me. We had just got the donkeys loaded when a long string of Batongas appeared, emerging from the village, and advancing towards us. This proved to be the army of observation, about one hundred and fifty in number, many armed with guns, the rest with spears and shields. Upon coming up they all squatted down, and their headman informed us that the Matabili had left their camp, and were in full retreat to their own country. He now also demanded payment from me, on the ground that he and his men had driven the Matabili away, and that if they had not done so, and the Matabili had crossed the river, they would have taken my goods and killed me and all my people. Old Shampondo now also made fresh demands, and all the trouble commenced anew. Suffice it to say that before they had done with me, and would let me proceed on my journey, they had got about £10 worth of goods out of me.

It is such experiences as this, when, one's heart almost bursting with rage and indignation, it is necessary to pre-serve an outward appearance of equanimity, talk, argue, and pay calmly, that turn the hair of the poor African adven-turer gray before his time. The leader of an expedition fitted out regardless of expense, and with a small army at his back, is, of course, free from such annoyances, but he who, on the one hand, has sufficient goods to excite native cupidity, and, on the other, not sufficient strength to resist extortion, will have a fine opportunity of studying the most unamiable points in the negro character.

At last we were free, and once more got under way. I pushed on hard for the rest of the day, passing one or two small villages, and at sundown reached Shamedza's, another Batonga headman of some importance. There were a lot of small villages about here, and the natives flocked round us in great numbers, the women examining myself and the donkeys with great interest. Early the following morning Shamedza himself came to see me, telling me that he was the chief of the district. I knew what he meant, and my prophetic soul told me that I should have to submit to fresh extortion. However, I made him the customary small present with a little speech, and told him that I wished to proceed at once on my way. He took his present and retired with it to where a knot of elderly men were sitting, with whom he held a consultation. Presently he sent one of them to me, to inform me that I must give him something more. I now saw plainly that I must abandon my intention of following the Zambesi any farther, or the extortions of the Batongas would ruin me before I reached the Kafukwi. About ten miles farther on I should have to pass Mwemba, the biggest man and the biggest scoundrel amongst them, besides several more of bad repute, and I therefore determined to alter my route if possible, and try to get away from the Zambesi to the Kafukwi. With this object I now offered Shamedza a good present if he would give me guides through the mountains which lie between the high country and the Zambesi valley. He at once, to my joy, agreed to do so, and gave me as guides one of his sons and two other men as far as the Zongwi river, where, he said, we would be able to get fresh guides on to the plateau.

Before proceeding farther, I will here say a few words about the astonishing change that had taken place in the character of the Batongas since I first travelled among them in 1877. I was then very well received, had presents of goats and food made me at every village, and nowhere met with the slightest attempt at extortion. The reason was this. They were afraid of me. No white man had been through their country since

Drs. Livingstone, Kirk, and Charles Livingstone had passed up the Zambesi on their way to Linyanti, many years before, and they had a superstitious dread of the white stranger who, with his breech-loading rifle, killed game afar off, and travelled among them without fear that they could harm him. Since then numbers of them had been to the diamond fields, and found out that white men are mortals like themselves. Many, too, had been to the Matabili country, and worked with white men there, and had seen with how little respect Europeans, whether missionaries, traders, Government envoys, or any other class, are there treated by Lo Bengula and his people. In fact they had found out that a white man is not a god to be worshipped at a distance, but only a mortal like themselves.

In 1880, acting, I am sorry to say, at my suggestion, a party of Jesuits visited Mwemba with the intention of founding a mission station there. My Zulu man Paul was with them, and from him I have learnt full particulars of their cruel experiences. They crossed the Zambesi at Chichilaba's, a Batonga living— fortunately for me—on the southern bank of the river between Shampondo's and Shamedza's. This rascal would not take them through the river at all until he had extorted an enormous payment, and after at last agreeing to do so, landed them and their goods on an island, and would take them no farther until he had received a second payment. At last they got across the river, and proceeded to Mwemba's, with seventy loads of goods. Here they all fell ill with fever, and in a few days' time Father Teroede, the head of the party, died, believing that he had been poisoned. Mwemba now demanded an enormous payment because the white man had died in his country, and the remaining members of the party being too ill to attend to his demands or to anything else, he seized their entire outfit— viz. seventy loads of goods—leaving the unfortunate expounders of the Gospel to the heathen to get back to Panda-ma-tenka the best way they could. The survivors, like Father Teroede, thought that they had been poisoned as well as robbed ; but John Weyers and other old hands, who saw them on their arrival at Panda-ma-tenka, say that they were simply suffering from fever, which on the Lower and Central Zambesi is most deadly to white men freshly arrived from Europe. This stroke of business was followed by no unpleasant consequences, and must have been most encouraging to the Batongas.

Three years before my last visit to the Central Zambesi in 1888, Mr. David Thomas, a son of one of the first missionaries to the Matabili country, had formed a station on an island in the Zambesi, near the mouth of the River Lufua, from whence to hunt and trade to the north. Here he was murdered in the night by the Batongas, and all his property seized, amongst it two breech-loading elephant guns which I had lent him, poor fellow. Lastly, only two months before my own arrival, as I afterwards learned, a white Portuguese trader was murdered with a lot of his people farther down the river. Altogether, I feel sure now that, had I persisted in following the Zambesi to the mouth of the Kafukwi, myself and party would have been robbed and murdered by the Batongas sooner or later. On the other hand, on the route which I now wished to take, I was well aware that I might get into trouble with the Mashukulumbwi living along the Kafukwi, who two years previously had looted Dr. Holub's camp, and killed Oswald Zoldner, one of his subordinates. However, I hoped for the best, and breathed a sigh of relief as we turned our backs on the Zambesi and followed our guides along a good footpath leading to the north. I also chuckled at the thought of what a sell it would be for Mwemba, who, of course, had heard that I was coming down the river, and would pass his town, when he learnt that I had changed my route.

In the evening we reached the River Muga, after having crossed a range of hills, amongst which we saw a great deal of buffalo spoor, but none of the animals themselves. On the Muga we found several small villages, but the people, never having seen a white man before, were frightened and friendly. The following day I remained where I was, for the double purpose of buying food and giving the donkeys a rest, as my guides said it would take us three days to reach the nearest villages on ahead. The next morning, striking towards the north, we crossed the Kachomba river and got into a country in which buffaloes were evidently numerous. We did not run across any, however, but saw several herds of impala antelopes, one of which I shot in the afternoon, and Charley another in

the evening.   Tse-tse fly were also pretty numerous, and must
be very much so later on during the hot months.

As our guides had said, we reached on the third day some
small Batonga villages at the junction of the little river Mwedzia
with the Zongwi (or Morongo Mineni, as it is called here).   In
the evening, whilst my men were making camp, I took a stroll
through the hills, and shot a zebra whilst returning and when
close to camp, so that we got in all the meat.   This was the
fourth shot I had fired since leaving Panda-ma-tenka, the result
being a duiker, impala, and zebra killed, and a koodoo wounded
but lost ; four shots in over two hundred miles of country, the
latter part of which was almost virgin ground to Europeans.
However, even in quite unexplored parts of Africa one must
not expect to find game everywhere plentiful.

At this camp I hired several Batongas, who had followed
me from the Zambesi, in the hope of entering my service.
They were a good set—strong, active young fellows, and always
willing and cheerful.   They agreed to go right through with
me, and I believe they would have done so, for had I got them
across the Kafukwi they would scarcely have dared to leave
me and go home by themselves, but, as will be seen later
on, I was not destined to cross the Kafukwi.   I here also got
two men who said they would act as guides through the
mountains to the north, and show me a path that would take
me right on to the high country.   Shamedza's men here left
me and returned home.   Besides the men I had hired, several
others accompanied me in the hope that I would shoot game
and give them some meat.

MASHUKULUMBWI VILLAGE.

CHAPTER XI

DURING the two following days our route lay through what I think must be about the roughest country to walk over in the whole world, a chaotic mass of detached conical hills of from five hundred to one thousand feet in height. These hills are stony and barren in the extreme, and have a fearfully dry parched-up appearance. Water is excessively scarce and there is little or no game ; indeed, no animal with legs to take him anywhere else could be expected to live in such a miserable country. Our guides, however, evidently knew it well, and followed a path, or rather what once had been a path, but which at the time of our visit was in many places quite invisible. These two days' journeys were terribly trying to the donkeys, and I was surprised to see what break-neck places these sure-footed animals climbed up and down ; let him take his own time, and a donkey will clamber up and down almost anywhere, no matter how steep it may be. Without competent guides it would be, owing to the scarcity of water and the broken nature of the country, a very difficult matter to get through these hills.

On the afternoon of the day we left the Zongwi, one of the Batongas who had followed me for meat, a strong, active-looking young man, was seized with acute dysentery, and on the following morning about six o'clock he died—pretty quick work. His friends remained with the body, which I afterwards learned they did not take the trouble to bury, but simply threw into the water-hole below our camp. I was afraid that this sudden death might cause a scare amongst my own boys, but they did not appear to think anything of it, and some of them imitated the spasmodic twitching of the poor wretch's fingers, the turning up of his eyes, and the protrusion of the tongue as he was dying; laughing all the while and saying that they saw it was all up with him. Paul told me that his friends attributed his sudden illness to the machinations of an enemy at his own kraal, by whose spells he had been bewitched and done to death.

On the third day after leaving the Zongwi the character of the country began to change very much for the better, the hills becoming more rounded in appearance, and being covered with forests of machabel and mahobo-hobo trees in full foliage; beneath the shade of which grew a plentiful supply of grass. I spent a couple of hours during the middle of the day in catching butterflies, and took several good ones, amongst them some of the handsome *Achræa acrita*. I found them to be identical with those met with on the northern and eastern slopes of the Mashuna country south of the Zambesi, at an ˏelevation of between three thousand and four thousand feet, and the same was the case with the vegetation.

On the evening of the following day we camped at a small Batonga village, situated in a fertile valley beneath the shadow of a range of hills, the main range, which, I think, runs all the way from the Victoria Falls to the Kafukwi. Here I got another guide (though the two men from Zongwi still remained with me) to take me to Monzi's, a Batonga chief living on the high plateau over which I knew from Mr. Ravenstein's map that Dr. Livingstone had passed more than thirty-five years before, on his journey from the Makololo country to the Lower Zambesi. Our new guide told us that we now had only to climb this one range of hills and we would then be fairly upon this plateau, and that once there I would see plenty of game, and find the travelling easy for the donkeys. I was delighted indeed to hear it, and the next morning we made an early start, and ascended the steep face of the hill by a winding footpath. After reaching the summit, an hour's walk through undulating forest-clad country brought us to a stream of water, beyond which lay open grassy downs. Here I shot a roan antelope bull, and so halted for breakfast by the carcase. Shortly after we came upon a large herd of blue wildebeests, which on seeing the donkeys came running towards us to have a look at them ; but as I knew that we should see more game farther on and nearer to our camping-place, I did not fire at them. In the evening I shot another roan antelope bull, and the following morning a fine wart-hog boar. From here to Monzi's we travelled very pleasantly through an uninhabited country of alternate forest and open downs, well watered and full of game. The climate, too, on this high land and at this time of year was delightful, the days being quite cool even in the sun, and the nights very cold. Every day I shot whatever game I wanted, Lichtenstein's hartebeests, Burchell's zebras, and elands being the most plentiful. At length we reached Monzi's.

When Dr. Livingstone was here in 1853 this chief was living close to the little hill U-Kesa-Kesa (marked Kesi-Kesi in Mr. Ravenstein's map). Since then he had probably changed the site of his village more than once, and at the time of my visit he was living about eight miles to the north-east of U-Kesa-Kesa. I found Monzi to be a little wizened old man, bleareyed, and getting very infirm, but very chatty and friendly ; he remembered Dr. Livingstone's visit quite well, and did not speak of it as though a long time had since elapsed. In fact, leading the lives they do, these savages have really no idea of time, and five years or fifty is much the same to them. He told me that since Dr. Livingstone's visit, more than thirty-five years prior to my own, no other white man had ever passed through his country, from which I concluded that European enterprise was not making much headway in this part of Africa. Poor old Monzi at the time of my visit was bewailing the loss of his cattle, which had all been carried off about two months previously by that section of Lewanika's forces which had followed up Marancinyan, who, as I have mentioned, was an aspirant to the Barotsi chieftainship, and had not long before made a raid upon Sesheki, in the very heart of Lewanika's country. Marancinyan, Sikabenga, or Makunguru, for he rejoiced in three names, was then living, with a considerable following, near the Nyandabanji hills, some fifteen miles south of Monzi's, and it would appear that Lewanika's men were afraid to attack him, since they turned back when within a few miles of his town, sweeping off, however (not to return empty-handed), all the cattle they could seize from the small Batonga villages where they were not likely to meet with resistance.

I stopped over a day at Monzi's, and we were on very friendly terms with the people. I gave them the best part of an eland and a zebra, and my boys revelled in sweet potatoes and ground nuts, besides any amount of good meat—in fact, they were enjoying themselves thoroughly, and were perfectly happy and contented, and ready to follow me anywhere.

Many of the men about here were perfectly naked. We also saw some with their hair dressed in the Mashukulumbwi fashion, that is, plastered up into a lump at the back of the head, the rest of the head being shaved. I found it impossible to get any precise information about the country on ahead. No one in the village ever seemed to have been more than twenty miles north of where he was born and reared. At last I got two men, who said they would guide me to the Kafukwi; but I am convinced they had never been there, and knew nothing of the character of the people on ahead. After leaving Monzi's we travelled over open treeless downs, much of the country being covered with grass from six feet to seven feet high. However, we followed good native footpaths leading from village to village, breakfasting near one village and sleeping near another. At the second of these two villages the people were all Mashukulumbwi, and the men were without exception stark naked, and wore their hair dressed in the fashion I have described, which is peculiar to that tribe. At the village where we slept we could get no bush to make a "scherm," nor wood for cooking, the surrounding country being an open grassy plain. We were therefore obliged to do the best we could with corn-stalks,[1] which we planted in the ground, and we bought firewood from the Mashukulumbwi, who had carried it from a distance.

After dark one of our guides, who had been in the village, came and reported that a lot of Sikabenga's men had arrived, and that they had come after me. They did not, however, come down to our camp that night ; but early the following morning they paid me a visit. There were about fifteen of them, all Barotsi, and all carrying guns, and they came accompanied not only by the Mashukulumbwi men belonging to the village, but by a lot more, whom they must have collected from other villages during the night. Every Mashu-kulumbwi carried a large bundle of finely-tapered throwing spears, about seven feet long, all villainously barbed. I put on my cartridge belt and took care to have my rifle in my hands. However, the Barotsi were apparently friendly. They said that the news of my having passed by Monzi's had been communicated to their chief Sikabenga by the Batongas, and that he had thereupon sent them after me with two tusks of ivory, to buy ammunition. I told them that I had no powder to sell, and indeed, none at all, with the exception of what was in the cartridges that I was carrying for my breech-loading rifles. These cartridges I informed them I could not afford to part with, as my journey was to a far country, where I should require all I had for my own use. They did not, however, believe what I said, and insisted that some biscuit tins, in which were packed some medicines, books, and other miscellaneous articles, contained powder.

They then wanted me to return with them to Sikabenga, saying that the Mashukulumbwi would be sure to murder me and my people before we reached the Kafukwi. I asked them why they had collected the Mashukulumbwi in the night ; to which they replied that they were Sikabenga's people, and had come to pay homage to them as his representatives. They then again tried to persuade me to return with them to their own town, and when I once more refused to do so asked me if I

---

[1] The stalks of maize and Kafir corn grow to six or eight feet in height, and in the Zambesi valley those of the latter grain (*holcus sorghum*) attain a length of fifteen feet.

had never heard how Dr. Holub's camp had been attacked and plundered two years previously by the Mashukulumbwi, and told me that I would never cross the Kafukwi. "You will live two days more," they said, "but on the third day your head will lie in a different place from your body." However, I paid no heed to their threats, and finally gave them a blanket for Sikabenga, and a few yards of calico for themselves. They and the Mashukulumbwi then left us to pack the donkeys and proceed on our journey.

A couple of hours' walk brought us to the banks of the Magoi-ee river, which rises a little to the south of U-Kesa-Kesa, and runs north into the Kafukwi. Here I shot a zebra, and as there was water close at hand and the day was already far advanced, I decided to proceed no farther, but to camp for the night. Moreover I wished to question our guides closely about the country on ahead, as I did not exactly like the appearance of the Mashukulumbwi, and had no wish to get into the middle of their country, knowing what had happened to Dr. Holub amongst these same savages not long before. My idea was that it would be wise to change our course, and instead of continuing due north direct to the Kafukwi, to strike to the eastward, and cross it lower down at Semalembui's, where Dr. Livingstone had crossed it years before, by which means we would avoid all but the small outlying villages of the Mashukulumbwi. Paul and Charley agreed with me, but we unfortunately allowed ourselves to be dissuaded and led into the jaws of death by our ignorant guides, who said that they did not know the country to the eastward, or where we should get water (which was doubtless true enough), and that by the route we were taking we should pass no large Mashukulumbwi towns, but only small isolated villages, where the people were friendly. Thus we were deterred from taking a route by which we might have got through to the Kafukwi.

Early the next morning we passed another small village, where the people were evidently frightened of us. After leaving this we followed a path leading due north, parallel with the course of the Magoi-ee. This river is marked Makoe in Mr. Ravenstein's map. During the day we travelled through a country teeming with elands, zebras, and other game, and passed through a strip of forest where tse-tse fly were also numerous, and in the afternoon reached the River Ungwesi. Here we found more Mashukulumbwi villages, and as it was already late determined to camp on the farther bank of the river. At first the people were shy, standing watching us from a distance, every naked warrior, however, with his bundle of dangerous-looking, long barbed javelins. Soon the head-man came up to us with a few of his followers, and, becoming assured we had no evil intentions towards him or his people, was apparently very friendly, pointing out a good place to pitch our camp, and telling my men where to collect wood, cut grass for the donkeys, etc. I think that this man really was kindly disposed, as he had a friendly, good-natured face. I made him a small present, at which he seemed mightily pleased, and, after going back to his village, he presently returned with a basket of meal, with which he presented me. This time he was accompanied by about thirty men, who were all absolutely naked, unless a porcupine quill stuck through the lobe of the ear may be considered an article of clothing. Every one of them carried a bundle of spears over the left shoulder, and at the same time held one or two in the right hand. I confess I did not like the appearance of these warlike-looking savages, for in all my travels I had never before met with a tribe whose members apparently never stirred from their huts unless fully prepared for battle. I learnt from the head-man that the River Ungwesi is the same which Dr. Livingstone crossed near its source, between Monzi's and Semalembui. On Mr. Ravenstein's map it is marked as running into the Kafukwi., This is a mistake, however, as it runs into the Magoi-ee, only a few miles from here.

The next morning the headman again paid us a visit, and gave me a man to take me to Minenga, the headman of the district, whose village is situated on the River Magoi-ee, about six miles to the north from here, and not far from the Kafukwi. Minenga, he told me, owned canoes on the latter river, and would be able to ferry my goods and donkeys across. Shortly after starting I came upon a herd of Lichtenstein's hartebeests grazing along the Ungwesi river ; and, as I knew that Minenga was only a short half-day ahead, and that I would not be able to get beyond his kraal that day, I thought it would be wise to shoot one or two if possible, and take a supply of meat with me. I shot three of them, and so halted for breakfast while my boys were cutting them up. I also sent one of my guides back to the village we had just left, with a message to the headman that if he would send a couple of men to me I would give them some meat. The old fellow came himself with a good many of his people, bringing meal and ground nuts for me. I gave him and his men a lot of meat, and he appeared to be, and I think really was, immensely delighted.

After breakfast we followed the Ungwesi till close to its junction with the Magoi-ee, when we left it and cut across to the latter river. We soon found ourselves amongst a number of small Mashukulumbwi villages, and I saw that we had suddenly got into the midst of a thickly-populated district. The landscape was now, too, dotted with herds of cattle of a very small breed. We were soon completely surrounded by crowds of naked men, every one carrying his bundle of barbed javelins. The crowd seemed, however, a good-natured one, and the men appeared to be thoroughly enjoying themselves as they walked alongside of the donkeys, laughing, shouting, and gesticulating violently. At length we reached Minenga's village, which, like all the others, we found to be a very small one. It was situated close to the bank of the Magoi-ee, in the middle of a space cleared of the long grass with which most of the country is here covered, and dug into irregular ridges and furrows, ready to be sown with maize later on. Minenga was at another little village, a few hundred yards away from his own, when we arrived there ; but a man was instantly despatched to call him, and he now appeared—a tall spare savage, with neither a particularly good nor a particularly bad expression of face. Upon my asking him where we were to camp, he replied that we must do so right alongside of his village, and when I objected that there was no bush near with which to make a " scherm " and nowhere to tie the donkeys, he replied that this was not a country where travellers could sleep safely in the bush, and that we could make a scherm of cornstalks, and plant poles to which we could secure the donkeys. So, seeing that we were now, if anything should be wrong, in the lion's den, and must brave it out, I gave orders to off-load the donkeys, and to make a scherm of cornstalks, as he had suggested.

Now, the only spot of level ground to be found was immediately alongside the village ; thus the back of our camp was within ten yards of the chief's hut, and on one side of the cattle kraal. The village therefore lay just at the back of our scherm, and between it and the river, which was about two hundred yards distant. In front of us lay an open space of cleared ground dug into uneven ridges and furrows, bounded at about sixty yards' distance by a large patch of long grass. Minenga now sent me a pot of beer, and shortly afterwards I went with Paul to his hut, and, making him a present of a blanket and some fancy-coloured calico, told him that I wanted him to put me through the Kafukwi, and that I should like to cross the river the following day. He replied that the road was open for me, and that his own children should take me through in his own canoe. He then said that he would like me to remain with him the following day and drink beer, or I could go out hunting and shoot some game for him, as there were lots of elands, zebras, etc., to be found close to his town. He also said that his large canoe was some distance off, but that if I would remain with him the following day he would send and have it brought down to the nearest crossing-place, so that the next day I could get through the Kafukwi without any delay. This statement induced me to comply with his wish, and stop a day over, and I told him that I would do so, and that if he would give me men to show me where the game was I would go out early the next morning and try to shoot something for him. He thanked me, and gave me some more beer, and I left him with the impression that he was a very good fellow, and that I should get through the Kafukwi without any trouble. By sundown my boys had made a pretty good scherm of cornstalks and put the donkeys in the kraal with Minenga's cattle. After dark the entire population of the village came to our camp, and the women and girls sat round the fires eating meat with my boys and giving them ground nuts and sweet potatoes in return. The young men, now without their spears, went in for a dance with my Batongas, and a fellow with a musical instrument, formed of flat bits of hard wood laid across the open mouths of large calabashes—which, when struck with a stick, emitted a good deal of noise and no music—made such a din that at last I was glad to bribe him to silence with a small piece of calico. Altogether, as I lay and viewed the whole scene, I thought that we had thoroughly gained the goodwill of the people, who, though wild and savage, I decided were easy to deal with if properly treated.

It was about nine o'clock, I think, when Minenga sent his son to ask Paul, Charley, and myself to come and drink beer with him. I was already undressed and under the blankets, or I probably should have gone, but I did not care about dressing again, and so sent word to say that it was now too late, and that I had turned in, as I wanted to go out hunting at daylight the next morning. Nor would Charley go either, but Paul, being, like most Zulus, very fond of native beer, could not resist the temptation, and so went up alone. When he came back he said that Minenga had asked him a lot of questions why I had come there, where I was going to, what was the object of my journey, what I intended doing with my goods, etc. etc., and had told him that the natives on the other side of the Kafukwi were a dangerous people to travel amongst, but that he would give me one of his own sons to take me through the unsafe district. Judged by the light of after events, I now believe that, had I gone that night to drink beer accompanied by Charley and Paul, all three of us unarmed, as of course we should have been, we should certainly have been murdered then and there ; and I feel convinced that the fellow with the musical instrument was simply sent down with the young men to get up a dance and make such a noise as would drown any disturbance we might make whilst being assassinated. We three disposed of, they knew they had no one else to fear, as they could see for themselves that my two Mangwato men, and the two Mashunas who carried guns, were in an abject state of terror. However, they wanted to get us all together, and as Paul went up alone they did not molest him.

At length the dancers went away, and I went to sleep, never dreaming that anything was wrong, but flattering myself that we were on excellent terms with the people. The next

morning I went up to Minenga's hut with some of my own
boys, and asked him for the men he had promised to give me
to show me where the game was.   I was rather surprised to
find that he seemed all at sea, and had no one ready to go
with me, although on the previous evening he had been so
eager that I should shoot some game for him.   However, after
a slight delay he sent his son and two more men with me.
Crossing the river by a ford just behind the village, where the
water was about waist-deep and very cold, we followed a footpath leading south, which soon brought us to some ground
where the long grass had been burnt off.   Here we soon espied
some zebras and hartebeests.   The zebras allowed me to walk
up to within one hundred and fifty yards of them, and I killed
two with my first two shots.   I might have shot more of them,
but I wanted a hartebeest for meat for myself.   Firing at
something over two hundred yards, I missed, but with my
fourth shot I killed one.   I now gave Minenga's men the one
zebra and half the hartebeest, keeping the other half and the
second zebra for myself and my own people, and then returned
to camp, which was not more than two miles off.

On my telling Minenga that I had given his men a whole
zebra and half a hartebeest, he thanked me profusely, as did his
wives, and gave me a pot of beer.   The rest of the day I passed
reading and writing at the scherm, where we were constantly
surrounded by crowds of Mashukulumbwi, who had flocked in
from all sides to see the white man.   Some of them wore a few
strings of beads round the waist ; otherwise all were naked.
This nakedness does not arise from poverty, for these people,
having large herds of cattle, are well off for hides ; but it is the
fashion in this part of the world to go naked.   Many of the
men had a small cat-skin made into a bag, in which they
carried tobacco, dacha, etc.   These small skins, however, were
always hung either round the neck or over the shoulder, or on
the hip, or behind, but never where, with European ideas, one
might have expected them to be placed.   Some of the men
had their hair worked up into a cone like a strawberry pottle,
quite two and a half feet in height.   The base of these cones
was always fixed on the back of the head, but they were made
to curve upwards and forwards, so that the point of the cone

MASHUKULUMBWI WARRIOR.

was pretty well straight above the head, and in the apex of these conical head-dresses was fixed a long thin strip of sable antelope horn, looking like a piece of whalebone, which, though strong enough to stand upright, yet waved with every movement of the head. The extreme point of these curious head-dresses was certainly over five feet above the skull of the wearer. These people must necessarily live in a very open country, for with such head-dresses they could never get through bush. During the day some hundreds of Mashukulumbwi must have visited our camp, and I had a good opportunity of observing them. They are a fine, sturdy-looking race of men; very many of them have rather aquiline features, and are at the same time lighter in colour than their fellows; and it appears to me that amongst them there is a strong admixture of some other blood than the negro— perhaps Arab or some other North African race.

At length the sun went down, and our visitors all left us. Just before sunset I went up again to Minenga with Paul, and told him that I wanted to make an early start in the morning, and he replied that the road was open for me, that I could start as early as I liked, and that his own son should take me through the Kafukwi, and not leave me until we were three days' journey on the other side of the river. His wife asked me for a small piece of brass wire, and I went and cut off a ring and brought it up to her. She was most profuse in her thanks, and said I must come and drink some beer with her before starting in the morning. I went back to camp still thinking that Minenga was a very good fellow, and his wife a friendly, good-natured woman. This evening we again put the donkeys in the cattle kraal. My boys were trading meat for meal, ground nuts, etc., until after sundown ; but when it got dark there was not a single stranger in camp. After a good supper—which I discussed with a light heart, for on the morrow I hoped to cross the Kafukwi—I turned in. It was the 8th of July, the last day of the old moon, and a dark though starlight night.

Although on the previous evening our camp had been thronged with a crowd of men, women, and children, who had danced and sung and kept up a constant chatter till after midnight, it did not escape my notice that this day there was not a single stranger in our camp when it grew dark ; nor, with the exception of a little conversation carried on in a low tone of voice, did there appear to be any life or movement in the village behind us. I must confess that I felt uneasy, for I could not help contrasting the quiet and constraint with the noise and revelry of the first night of our arrival in the village. My boys too seemed uneasy, and sat in groups round their respective fires, whispering to one another, and all holding their assegais in their hands. As it grew later, however, they lay down one by one, and as the fires burnt lower and lower an absolute quiet and stillness took possession of the night.

I could not sleep, however, and was lying under my blanket, thinking of many things, and revolving various plans in my head, when about nine o'clock I observed a man come cautiously round the end of our scherm and pass quickly down the line of smouldering fires. As he stopped beside the fire, near the

foot of Paul and Charley's blankets, I saw that he was one of
the two men who had accompanied us as guides from Monzi's.
I saw him kneel down and shake Paul by the leg, and then
heard him whispering to him hurriedly and excitedly. Then I
heard Paul say to Charley, "Tell our master the news ; wake
him up." I at once said, "What is it, Charley? I am awake."
"The man says, sir, that all the women have left the village,
and he thinks that something is wrong," he answered. I thought
so too, and hastily pulled on my shoes, and then put on my
coat and cartridge-belt, in which, however, there were only four
cartridges. As I did so I gave orders to my boys to extinguish
all the fires, which they instantly did by throwing sand on the
embers, so that an intense darkness at once hid everything
within our scherm.

Paul and Charley were now sitting on their blankets,
with their rifles in their hands, and I went and held a whispered conversation with them, proposing to Paul that he and
I should creep round the village and reconnoitre, and listen
if possible to what the inhabitants were talking about. "Wait
a second," I said, "whilst I get out a few more cartridges," and
I was just leaning across my blankets to get at the bag containing them, when three guns went off almost in my face, and
several more at different points round the scherm. The muzzles
of all these guns were within our scherm when they were discharged, so that our assailants must have crawled right up to
the back of our camp and fired through the interstices between
the cornstalks. The three shots that were let off just in front
of me were doubtless intended for Paul, Charley, and myself,
but by great good luck none of us were hit. As I stooped to
pick up my rifle, which was lying on the blankets beside me,
Paul and Charley jumped up and sprang past me. "Into the
grass!" I called to them in Dutch, and prepared to follow.
The discharge of the guns was immediately followed by a
perfect shower of barbed javelins, which I could hear pattering
on the large leathern bags in which most of our goods were
packed, and then a number of Mashukulumbwi rushed in
amongst us.

I can fairly say that I retained my presence of mind perfectly at this juncture. My rifle, when I picked it up, was

unloaded ; for, in case of accident, I never kept it loaded in
camp, and I therefore had first to push in a cartridge.   As I
have said before, between our camp and the long grass lay a
short space of cleared ground, dug into irregular ridges and
furrows.   Across this I retreated backwards, amidst a mixed
crowd of my own boys and Mashukulumbwi.

I did my best to get a shot into one of our treacherous
assailants, but in the darkness it was impossible to distinguish
friend from foe.   Three times I had my rifle to my shoulder to
fire at a Mashukulumbwi, and as often some one who I thought
was one of my own boys came between.   I was within ten
yards of the long grass, but with my back to it, when, with a
yell, another detachment of Mashukulumbwi rushed out of it
to cut off our retreat.   At this juncture I fell backwards over
one of the ridges, and two men, rushing out of the grass, fell
right over me, one of them kicking me in the ribs and falling
over my body, whilst another fell over my legs.   I was on my
feet again in an instant, and then made a rush for the long
grass, which I reached without mishap, and in which I felt
comparatively safe.   I presently crept forwards for about
twenty yards, and then sat still listening.   Standing up again,
I saw that the Mashukulumbwi were moving about in our
camp.   It was, however, impossible to see any one with
sufficient distinctness to get a shot, for whenever one of the
partially-extinguished fires commenced to burn up again it was
at once put out by having more sand thrown over it.

But I now thought no more of firing at them.   I had had
time to realise the full horror of my position.   A solitary
Englishman, alone in Central Africa, in the middle of a hostile
country, without blankets or anything else but what he stood
in, and a rifle with four cartridges.   I doubt whether Mark
Tapley himself would have seen anything cheerful in the
situation.   Could I only have found Paul or Charley, or even
one of my own Kafirs, I thought my chance of getting back to
Panda-ma-tenka would be much increased, for I should then
have an interpreter, I myself knowing but little of the languages
spoken north of the Zambesi.   I now began to quarter the
grass cautiously backwards and forwards, whistling softly, in
hopes that some of my own boys might be lying in hiding near

me ; but I could find no one, and at length came to the conclusion that all those of my people who had escaped death
would make the most of the darkness and get as far as possible
from Minenga's before day-dawn, and I decided that I had
better do the same.   I knew that such of my boys as had
escaped and who were most probably in ones and twos, would
now make their way south through the veld, and would be
afraid either to use the native footpaths or to approach any of
the villages, which would make the chance of my falling in
with one of them very small indeed.   The first village, I thought,
where they would dare to show themselves would be Monzi's,
where the people were not Mashukulumbwi, and where we had
been so friendly with them.   Therefore I determined that my
best plan would be to make for Monzi's, also travelling through
the veld, and to endeavour to get there before my boys, and
to wait for them there.

In my belt I had a knife, a box of matches, and a watch.
I looked at it, and by the light of the stars saw that it was
now eleven o'clock.   First of all I had to cross the Magoi-ee
river, and I now made a half-circle round the village, always
keeping in the long grass, until I reached its bank, and then
made my way cautiously up to the ford.   I found, however,
that a party of men were watching here, as one of them spoke
in a low voice to his companions, just as I was approaching, and so luckily gave me notice of his whereabouts.
After standing still listening for a few seconds, I cautiously
retreated, but when I had got about three hundred yards off
I thought I was far enough, and resolved to take it as it
came, and cross the river at all hazards.   The bank, I found,
was guarded by a dense bed of reeds, and when I got through
this I found there was a high perpendicular bank between me
and the black sluggish-looking stream, which I knew to be full
of crocodiles.   As the water looked deep, I stripped so as not
to get my clothes wet.   These, together with my shoes, I tied
into a bundle and left on the bank, and then, holding my rifle
and the two belts in my left hand, I slipped down into the
river.   The water, I found, was out of my depth, but, being
an expert swimmer, I had no difficulty in getting across,
holding my rifle well out of water.   I had some trouble

in getting up the steep muddy bank on the farther side, but at length succeeded, and, depositing my rifle amongst the reeds, once more slipped into the water, recrossed the river, and returned again with my clothes in safety. The water was bitterly cold, and I was shivering as I climbed up the bank. I now re-dressed in the long grass, and, climbing an ant-hill, took a last look towards my scherm. The Mashukulumbwi I saw had now made up the fires, upon which they were throwing bundles of grass, by the light of which I suppose they were dividing my property. I turned my back upon this most melancholy spectacle, and, taking the Southern Cross for my guide, which was now almost down, commenced my lonely journey.

CHAPTER XII

THE night was very cold, and my whole clothing consisted of a thin coat, a light shirt, and a pair of trousers cut short off above the knee, my legs being bare. I now walked steadily to the south until 4 A.M. by my watch, always in long tangled grass, through which it was most fatiguing to force my way. I then felt so cold that, coming to a small patch of forest, I lit a fire and sat by it till sunrise. I heard no lions during the night, though there are plenty of them in this country, but hyænas howled dismally the whole night through. Soon after sunrise I continued my flight, reaching the hill Karunduga-gongoma about mid-day. This hill was about two miles from our first camp on the Magoi-ee river, and was near the spot where I had shot the zebra, on the evening of the day on which I had parted with Sikabenga's men. I thought it very likely that Paul or Charley or some of my boys who had escaped from Minenga's might visit this camp, so I crossed the river on a ledge of rocks, and walked up the footpath which led to our old scherm. I could not find, however, any sign of footprints made by the boots that Paul and Charley were wearing, nor indeed any tracks whatever coming from the north, so I recrossed the river, and finding a large tree that cast a good shadow over a patch of grass beneath the

ALONE IN AFRICA.

"Luckily I restrained myself, and lay quite still with my loaded rifle in my hands. Very soon two heads appeared above the grass, on the farther bank of the river, and the shaven crowns and cone-shaped head-dresses at once assured me that none of my own men were near me, as I had hoped, but only two of the natives of the country."

steep bank, lay down in the shade, and determined to remain
there until the evening, watching the ford, in the hope that
some of my boys would presently come along the footpath.
I had seen plenty of game during the morning, but had been
afraid to fire, thinking that I was still too near to Minenga's ;
but as I was now getting hungry I resolved to shoot something as soon as I got another chance.   I had been lying in
the shade cast by the tree on the top of the river's bank for
some hours, when at last I heard voices and was on the point
of jumping up and shouting out, as at first I thought that
some of my own people were approaching.   Luckily I
restrained myself, and lay quite still with my loaded rifle in
my hands.   Very soon two heads appeared above the grass,
on the farther bank of the river, and the shaven crowns and
cone-shaped head-dresses at once assured me that none of my
own men were near me, as I had hoped, but only two of the
natives of the country.   Each man carried the usual bundle
of long throwing spears over his left shoulder, and each of
them held one of these weapons ready for use in his right hand.
They were evidently discussing the imprints left by my shoes
in the soft sand of the path which led from our old camp to
the river.   When they reached the bank they were at fault,
for I had crossed the river by a ledge of rocks, on which of
course there was no trace of my footsteps.   With my rifle and
four cartridges, I was of course safe from these men, but, had
they seen me, I should have been obliged to have shot them
both in self-defence ; for if they had run away after having
seen me, they would have alarmed the country-side, and I
should then in all probability have been waylaid and assegaied
in the long grass.   I could see them so plainly from where I
lay that I thought every moment they would have seen me.
However they did not, and after talking together a little
longer they turned round and went back the way they had
come.   I then got up and moved away to a tree a couple of
hundred yards from the river, where I again lay down and
watched the ford until late in the afternoon.   Having had
nothing to eat for nearly twenty-four hours, I was now getting
hungry, and on resuming my journey made up my mind to
try to shoot an animal off which I could dine.   I had not

gone far when I espied a single wildebeest feeding in the distance.

There was no bush about and the grass was short all round him, but I was by this time very hungry and determined to try to shoot him. With a great deal of care I reached a single small bush something more than two hundred yards from him, and nearer it was impossible to get. Having only four cartridges to keep me in food all the way to Panda-ma-tenka, more than three hundred miles distant, I hesitated to risk a shot at this distance, and had made up my mind rather to go another day without food when the wildebeest turned and came walking straight towards me. There was a small stream of water a short distance behind where I was lying, and I think he was coming down to drink. He came on steadily without stopping until he was level with the bush behind which I was sitting, and not more than thirty yards from me, when I gave him a bullet through the shoulders, killing him on the spot. I at once cut off meat enough to last me for three days, and, carrying it down to the water, lighted a fire and roasted some on the ashes forthwith.

By the time I had satisfied my hunger the sun was low, so, shouldering my rifle and load of meat, I resumed my journey. I determined to walk through the night and, if possible, pass all the remaining Mashukulumbwi villages between here and Monzi's before daylight, and lie and sleep there the following day, waiting until some of my own boys should turn up. I also determined to take the footpaths by which we had come, as the labour of forcing one's way through the long grass was too severe. Early in the night I passed by the village where Sikabenga's men had come up with us. From here it was two and a half hours' hard walking, by the watch, to the village where we had breakfasted after leaving Monzi's. I was now on a high open plain, the night was bitterly cold, and I was tired, sleepy, and thirsty. After an hour's walk, coming to a few thorn-trees, I collected some small dry sticks, and, lighting a fire, cowered over it until there was no fire left. Then I had to go on again and try to keep out the cold by fast walking. At length I reached the last Mashukulumbwi village, a little over two hours' walk from Monzi's. I was

perished with cold, and tired and thirsty besides. It was now
long after midnight, and the inhabitants of the village were all
wrapped in slumber.   Going close up I could see that there
was a fire burning outside one of the huts, beside which some
one was lying. The village only contained half-a-dozen huts
in all, and, being near Monzi's and far from Minenga's, I thought
the inhabitants might be friendly.   At any rate I determined
to chance it, and warm myself, so I walked in and sat down by
the fire.   There was a boy lying on the ground on the other
side of it, fast asleep. Presently I woke him up and asked him
for water, but he said there was none.   The talking must have
awakened a man in one of the huts behind me, as he came up
to the fire and spoke to me.   I saw at a glance that he was
unarmed, and when he sat down beside me I tried to explain
to him what had happened to me since I had passed his village
about a week before with my boys and donkeys.   He could
not understand me very well, nor were his answers very
intelligible to me, as I spoke to him in Sintabili with only a
small leaven of Satonga, and he replied in pure Satonga.
However, when I told him I was thirsty and asked him for
water, he got up, and going to his hut soon brought me a
calabash full.   I had just finished drinking when I heard some
whispering going on in a hut just opposite to where I was
sitting, and presently I saw a man emerge from it, and move
stealthily away in the darkness. After a short interval he
returned, and as he re-entered his hut I saw that he had a gun
in his hand.   Presently I heard the sound of a bullet being
tapped with a ramrod, and knew that the owner of the gun was
either loading his weapon or making sure that it was already
properly charged.

   All this was not very reassuring, but I felt so comfortable
alongside the fire that I determined to rest there for an hour
or so, and then leave the village and continue my journey to
Monzi's.   Everything soon became perfectly quiet again, and
every one in the village was apparently asleep.   At any rate
the boy was who was lying on the other side of the fire.
Presently I too lay down with my back to the warmth and my
head resting on one of the logs that protruded from the fire.   I
held the butt of my rifle between my thighs, and had my hands

clasped on the barrel. I had no intention of going to sleep, but thought that I would rest and get warm for an hour or two and then leave the village again without wishing any one good-bye. However, I was tired and sleepy, and must presently have dozed off and fallen fast asleep.

How long I slept I do not know, but I awoke suddenly with a feeling that some one was near me, and starting up, found that two men were just approaching the fire. Seeing that they had no weapons in their hands, I sat down again and laid my rifle alongside of me, with the barrel resting on one of the fire-logs. The two men now sat down beside me, and commenced to question me as to what had caused my return, alone and in the middle of the night, and I endeavoured to tell them something about the disaster that had happened to myself and my people at Minenga's. I only partially understood what they said, and was not able to explain myself very well to them. In endeavouring to do so to the best of my ability I kept gradu-ally turning more towards them, till presently my rifle lay almost behind me. It was whilst I was in this position that I heard some one behind me. I turned quickly round to clutch my rifle, but was too late, for the man whom I had heard just stooped and seized it before my own hand touched it, and, never pausing, rushed off with it and disappeared in the darkness. I sprang up, and at the same moment one of the two men who had engaged me in conversation did so too, and, in the act of rising, dropped some dry grass which he had hitherto concealed beneath his large ox-hide rug on to the fire. There was at once a blaze of light which lit up the whole of the open space around the fire. My eyes instinctively looked towards the hut which I had seen the man with the gun enter, and there sure enough he sat in the doorway taking aim at me not ten yards from where I stood. There was no time to remonstrate. I sprang out into the darkness, seizing one of the pieces of wildebeest meat as I did so ; and, as the village was surrounded with long grass, pursuit would have been hopeless, and was not attempted. My would-be assassin never got off his shot.

I now got on to the footpath leading to Monzi's, and

walked along it rapidly to keep out the cold. My thoughts were gloomy indeed. My position had not been a particularly enviable one before the loss of my rifle, but now it was ten times worse. I could no longer procure myself food, and was at the mercy of any one of the cruel savages amongst whom I was, who might choose to make a target of me for his barbed spears. My only hope was that Monzi would prove friendly, and that there I should fall in with Paul or Charley and some of the boys. Just before daylight I reached Monzi's, and sat by a fire until the people turned out of their huts. Monzi and his men—one of the latter could speak a little Sintabili, and I was able to tell my story—were friendly, I could see, but the old man was in a great state of alarm when he heard how my rifle had been stolen and my life attempted at the next village. " You must leave my village immediately," he exclaimed ; " they will follow you up and kill you. Be off! be off instantly ! " He filled my pockets with ground nuts, and sent me out of his town, with three of his men, at once. The man who spoke Sintabili told me most emphatically not to trust the Batongas, but to hide during the daytime and travel at night, and make my way to the Zambesi as quickly as possible. After walking a mile or so with me they returned home, telling me again not to trust myself in the Batonga villages, or I would certainly be murdered. This was pleasant.

As soon as Monzi's men had left me I turned into a patch of forest, and, lighting a fire, cooked myself a piece of wildebeest meat and roasted a few ground nuts. From where I sat I commanded a good view of the Nyanda Banji hills, about ten miles to the south-east, and, as I looked towards them, a thought struck me. Why not try to make my way to Marancinyan, whose town I knew was somewhere about those hills, and put myself under his protection. I knew that he was a friend of George Westbeech, was well acquainted with white men and their ways, and that he would, therefore, know that I would be able to pay him well for any assistance he might give me in getting back to Panda-ma-tenka. To find his town was the difficulty. However, I thought that if I made my way to the hills I would be sure to find footpaths leading there, and I determined to spend that day, at any rate, in the attempt, and if unsuccessful to strike westward again on the morrow till I struck our trail coming from the Zambesi.   Here I hoped to find some of my men, and if I did not do so I should have to make my way as best I could to the river.

A tiring walk through long tangled grass brought me to the foot of the hills, where I struck a footpath. This I followed, and it soon brought me in sight of a few Batonga huts, which I saw were inhabited.   I did not much like trusting myself amongst these people ; still it was necessary to ask the way to Marancinyan's, so I determined to run the risk. Advancing cautiously I reconnoitred the village, and saw that all the huts with the exception of one were placed amongst some trees at the farther end of a large cleared piece of ground that had been prepared for planting maize and corn.   One hut was much nearer than all the others to where I was standing, and on the farther side of it I saw a man scraping the dry skin of some large antelope, which he no doubt intended to prepare for a blanket.   His bundle of long throwing spears were standing against the eaves of the hut.   I walked round the edge of the clearing, in the shelter of the long grass, until I got the hut between myself and him, and then advanced rapidly across the open ground until I reached it ; then walking round it I appeared suddenly in front of the astonished savage, standing close to his bundle of assegais.   As I was the first European he had ever seen he was no doubt much startled, and at any rate he looked as if he was.   " Zila-ā-Sikabenga ankai ? " I said, which is good Satonga for " Where is the footpath to Sikabenga's ? " This question I repeated several times before I could get any reply at all ; and when the man I was speaking to at last re-covered from his surprise sufficiently to answer me he would say nothing but " No ziba " (" I don't know "). I did not half like the appearance of this savage, and began to regret having shown myself at all ; and I thought that if I could only get back to the long grass without the remaining inhabitants of the village noticing me I would try to avoid being seen by any one else.   I therefore said to the man by whose side I was standing, " Where is the path to the water?" when he at once pointed to

one running down the clearing.   I then turned and walked
down this path as quickly as possible, hoping that I should
reach the end of the clearing and gain the shelter of the long
grass before the rest of the Batongas saw me.

However, the man I had been talking to must have
rushed off and called his friends immediately I left him ;
for before I had got very far I heard shouts behind me,
and, looking round, saw about a dozen naked men running
towards me, all carrying their bundles of long throwing
spears.   I could not tell their intentions, and I thought
it as likely as not that they would murder me forthwith.
But I knew that to run would be the very worst policy,
for it would be sure to increase their hostility should they
be unfriendly, whereas a bold front might tend to overawe
them.   I must say that as I stood thus unarmed and helpless,
whilst these savage-looking men came running up to me, I
did not feel at all happy, and bitterly regretted the loss of my
good little rifle.   However, when they came up to me, talking
and gesticulating violently, I found them not unfriendly.   They
asked me a lot of questions, some of which I understood more
or less, as to why I was alone ? where were my people ? and
where was my rifle ? but I pretended I did not understand
them, and only asked them to show me the footpath leading
to Sikabenga's (Marancinyan).   They told me that I was
on the path, which ran past their village, and one of them
accompanied me a considerable distance, until we were through
the hills, and then pointed out to me a small hill in the distance,
and gave me to understand that Sikabenga was living not far
beyond it, and that the footpath to his town passed close
beneath it.   I gave him the empty cartridge case with which I
had shot the wildebeest as a reward for his friendliness, and he
left me highly pleased.   I passed several more small Batonga
villages, and inquired my way of the people, of whom I now
had little fear, as I did not think that they would dare to harm
me so near to where Marancinyan was living.   At last, late
in the afternoon, I reached the town, having been walking
almost continually during the previous twenty-four hours.

Marancinyan, or Sikabenga, as he was called by the
Batongas, I found to be a young man, tall and well built, but

with a rather weak-looking face.   As he spoke Sintabili fairly
well, I was able to converse with him without difficulty.
He did not treat me with any excessive hospitality, as he
neither gave me enough to eat nor lent me a blanket to
keep out the cold at night ; yet had it not been for him I
should in all probability have been murdered by the orders of
his uncle.   This, however, I only learnt some time afterwards,
and though for three days I must have lived constantly in
the very shadow of death, I had no idea at the time that
my life was in any danger.   On the morning after my arrival
I tried to get Sikabenga to send a party to try to recover the
Metford rifle that had been stolen from me, and offered to give
him four muskets for doing so if he would send men with me
to Panda-ma-tenka to get them.   He told me an hour or two
later that he had sent off a party of men on this errand.   I
then asked him if he would give me men to attack the
Mashukulumbwi who had looted my camp and killed my
people, and he said he would if I would supply them with
powder.   During the afternoon a sort of council of war was
held, at which most of his principal men attended.   I tried to
get them to give me a sufficient number of men to accompany
me to Panda-ma-tenka to bring back a good supply of powder,
and offered also to get Mr. Westbeech's elephant-hunters to
help me.   In addition to this I told them that I would bring
all my five horses with me to assist in the attack.   However, I
could not get them to promise anything, and on the following
day Sikabenga told me he was afraid to send men to Panda-
ma-tenka, as they might meet some of Lewanika's partisans
on the way.   Shortly afterwards he told me that the men he
had sent to try to recover the rifle that had been taken from
me in the little village beyond Monzi's had returned, and that
they had been unsuccessful.

Late in the afternoon of this same day he came up
to where I was sitting in the courtyard attached to his
own hut and said, "You cannot remain any longer in my
town.   The Mashukulumbwi have followed you, and are
now close at hand ; they demand your life, and I cannot
protect you.   You must go at once to a small Batonga
village near here, whose headman is my close friend (umligan).

At sundown this evening I will come to you, and bring guides with me who will take you to Panda-ma-tenka." I could see that Sikabenga was anxious and disturbed, but I felt convinced he was lying, as I knew very well that the Mashukulumbwi, who have very few guns, would never dare to threaten the Barotsi, who are all well armed with guns and rifles. However, I could not understand what was the matter, though I saw that something was wrong; and when Sikabenga urged me to go away at once with his friend the Batonga, and reiterated his promise to bring me the guides that evening, I thought it best to comply with his wish. The man in whose charge I now was was an elderly Batonga with a rather pleasant face, and I found that his village was situated on a small hill not two miles from the Barotsi town. Arrived there, I sat down on a rock waiting for Sikabenga. I felt angry and suspicious. Presently the sun went down and it began to grow dusk, but Sikabenga did not come. I then began to suspect some treachery, and determined to return to his town and upbraid him.

Without saying a word to the Batonga into whose charge I had been given, I got up and walked quickly along the footpath by which I had come to his village. He at once ran after me and commenced to expostulate, but I walked on without answering. Finding that I paid no attention to him, he simply followed behind me, but as he carried a large assegai I made him go on in front. It was dark when we reached Sikabenga's kraal. I walked straight into his courtyard, where I found him sitting with only a few of his wives and servants about him. Addressing him in Sintabili I said, "What do you mean, Marancinyan, who say that you are George Westbeech's friend, and the friend of all white men, by sending me to sleep amongst your dogs? Have you given them orders to murder me in the night? If you want to kill me, you can do so here in your own town." He was evidently much put about at my reappearance in his town, but beat his breast and swore by Beetjee, the daughter of Umziligazi, that he was truly a friend of white men, and had no intention of doing me any injury. However, he again told me that I was in great danger in his town, and urged me to return and sleep in the village of his

friend the Batonga. " To-morrow morning," he said, " I will
come and see you, and bring two men with me who will guide
you to Panda-ma-tenka." Something in his manner told me
that he was really trying to do his best to help me, and although
I could not understand exactly where the danger lay, I felt
that it was nearer to me in Sikabenga's town than in the
Batonga village I had left ; so I once more went back with the
headman. That night I slept in a hut with several young
men, and all sense of immediate danger having passed, got a
good night's rest alongside the fire that burnt in the centre of
the hut. I lay, of course, on the ground and without a blanket.

On the following morning Sikabenga came to see me, and
brought three men, who, as I understood him, were to go with
me to Panda-ma-tenka. I started at once, and late on the
following day we reached a Batonga village, under one Shoma.
Farther than this Marancinyan's men would not go, but I here
found a friend in an old blacksmith, who had been to Penda-
ma-tenka years before, and there seen waggons and horses, and
who also spoke a little Sintabili. He gave me four boys to go
with me to Panda-ma-tenka, on condition that I paid them
certain articles on my arrival there, and also sent him a tin of
powder and a blanket. To these conditions I gladly agreed.
Here, too, I heard news of some of my people. A man told
me that ten of them had slept at a village not far off on the
previous night, and left again that morning, and that they were
making for Shankopi's, a Batonga headman living in the hills
about thirty miles on this side of Wankie's. I therefore asked
my friend the old blacksmith to let his boys take me also past
Shankopi's. The following morning we made an early start,
and, to make a long story short, in five days reached Shankopi's,
on the same day and almost at the same time as the remnant
of my people.

They were mightily glad to see me, as they had given me
up as dead long ago, and patted me on the breast and kissed
my hands. I now learned the extent of our losses on the
night of the attack on our camp. Twelve men had been killed,
and six more wounded out of twenty-five. Amongst the
killed was one of Khama's men, who carried my double 10-
bore Rigby rifle. The other, who carried the double Purdey,

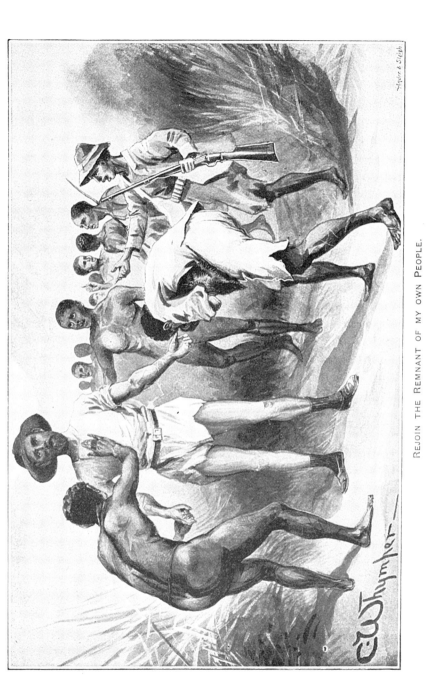

REJOIN THE REMNANT OF MY OWN PEOPLE.

"They were mightily glad to see me, as they had given me up as dead long ago, and patted me on the breast and kissed my hands."

had had his cheek grazed by a bullet, and had left his rifle behind him. Every one had had his escapes. Paul, the Zulu, got through the first rush of our assailants unhurt, but was nearly drowned in crossing the river, where he lost my single 10-bore rifle. Charley also got out of the scherm unwounded, and, making his way to the river, there fell in with two of our boys, and with their assistance crossed safely with rifle, cartridge belt, and clothes. I found that we had all done the same thing, namely, held to the south through the night, across country. Charley said he was close to me when I shot the wildebeest ; he heard the shot, and ran with the two boys in the direction, but never saw me. I fancy he must have passed me whilst I was cooking the meat, as I was then in a deep hollow. He too had been seen and pursued in the day-time near the village where my rifle was captured, but again escaped in the long grass. This had also happened to the survivor of the two Mangwato men, who, being likewise alone and unarmed, had incautiously approached a village. He said that one man got close up to him and threw three assegais at him, one of which cut his right hand. At last, however, he outran him and escaped. Neither Paul, Charley, nor the rest had gone near Monzi's or any other village, being afraid of the inhabitants, but had kept through the veld, and only cut into our trail beyond the hill U-Kesa-Kesa. Here Charley shot a zebra, and was shortly afterwards joined by Paul, who had then been three days without food. Farther on Charley shot another zebra, and here he and Paul remained for three days more, hoping that I would turn up, and collecting all the other survivors of our party. Our hardships were now over, except that we had still to sleep without blankets. Shankopi gave me a sheep, to be paid for at Panda-ma-tenka, and on the following day we reached the village where Paul's wife lived. Here we got a supply of meal and another sheep to take us to Panda-ma-tenka, and next day reached Wankie's and recrossed the Zambesi.

From here we walked to Panda-ma-tenka in three days, about the shortest time on record, I think, five days being con-sidered good time. On the third day we did exactly ten hours' actual walking (by my watch) at a great pace, and Paul,

Charley, and myself, with three of the Kafirs, got in just at sundown, the remainder not arriving till mid-day the following day. I do not know exactly what the date was, and there was no one who could tell me, John Weyers being away at the river ; but, judging by the moon, it must have been just about three weeks after the night of the attack on my camp near the Kafukwi. All that time I had slept on the bare ground without a blanket, and had suffered much from the cold, and had also undergone much hunger and fatigue, but I did not appear to be any the worse for it, and felt very well. I had, however, lost so many things that I could not do without—all my medicines, books, maps, compass, etc., besides four breech-loading rifles with their ammunition—that I was obliged to return to the Transvaal again at the end of the year, instead of spending the summer beyond the Zambesi, as I had intended to do.

In order that my readers may comprehend some incidents in my narrative, to which I had no clue at the time they occurred, I shall now put them in possession of certain information in connection with the attack upon my camp of which I myself was ignorant for some months after I wrote the first account of that event.

In August 1888 a large Matabili war party crossed the Zambesi near Mwemba's, with the assistance of the Batongas, and made their way on to the plateau to the north. Their allies guided them to Sikabenga's villages, which they surrounded one night and attacked at daylight next morning. The Barotsi were taken completely by surprise, and Sikabenga (or Sitwala, as he was called by the Matabili) was killed, together with the greater portion of his people. A few, however, escaped, and subsequently made their way back to their own country. In the following October one of these men told my boy Charley many circumstances connected with the attack that was made upon my camp, which left no doubt that Sikabenga's men had been the instigators and organisers of the whole business. When I passed by Monzi's, so Charley's informant said, Sikabenga himself was away at the Zambesi, but his uncle sent a party of men after me, with orders to get powder from me at all costs, even if they had to murder me in order to secure it. These were the men who came up to me on the evening of the day I left Monzi's. Instead, however, of returning home, as I thought they had done after saying good-bye to me, it appears that they followed me up and collected the Mashukulumbwi together and persuaded them to assist in the attack upon my camp. One of the Barotsi who was sent after me fell ill on the way, and remained behind his companions in the first little village beyond Monzi's. This was the man who tried to shoot me, as I have described in the course of my narrative. It appears that he first asked Monzi's sister to order her people to assegai me, which the old lady refused to do, saying that the white stranger had treated her well, and that therefore she did not wish his blood to run in her village. Sikabenga's man then said he would shoot me himself, and got a certain amount of assistance from some of the villagers, who, however, could not have been very keen about killing me, or they might have assegaied me twenty times over without difficulty.

There remains one point more, which I must explain, and that is Sikabenga's behaviour to me when I arrived at his village. As he could talk the Sintabili language I was able to converse with him freely, and he at once saw that I did not suspect his people of having been in any way concerned in the attack on my camp, and being a man of a kindly nature, and moreover having been a great friend of Mr. George Westbeech, the well-known Zambesi trader, he made up his mind to protect me, and did so. What made him tell me that I must leave his town on the third day after my arrival was the return of his people with my donkeys and part of the loot that had been taken after the attack on my camp. Sikabenga was, I think, afraid that had I seen any of my own property, and so become aware that his people had been the ringleaders in the treacherous attack that had been made upon my camp, he would have been obliged to have had me killed, on the principle that " dead men tell no tales."

CHAPTER XIII

UPON my return to Panda-ma-tenka from the disastrous journey to the Mashukulumbwi country I took a few days' rest, during which I wrote a hurried account of what had occurred, and at once sent it, together with many letters, by special messengers to Bamangwato. By that time I had quite recovered from the fatigue and hardships I had so lately undergone, and the restlessness of my disposition—which I think must be nearly equal to that of the Wandering Jew—urged me to set out upon another journey across the Zambesi. This time I determined to visit the Barotsi valley, in the hope of selling some of my horses to the chief Lewanika. At the same time too I hoped to obtain from him permission to travel and hunt next year in the unknown country to the north of the Kabompo river (one of the main affluents of the Upper Zambesi).

I had first to visit my cattle post at Gazuma, in order to shoot some game and leave a supply of meat for the herd boys. In this matter fortune favoured me, as the day after my arrival there I found a herd of elands, which I drove to within a short distance of my camp. I then shot five of them, and had every scrap of the meat carried in and cut up the same day. The following afternoon I started for the river, where I arrived with three horses on the night of 11th August. Here I met my old friend Mr. Harry Ware, whom I had known since both of us were little more than boys, and who is now one of the most experienced of the traders and travellers in the interior of South Africa. My friend was conducting a shooting party, which included a plucky young Englishwoman (Mrs. Thomas), who had accompanied her husband to this distant part of the world. They had all just returned from a trip to the Majili river, near Sesheki, and were now about to visit the Victoria Falls. Mr. Percy Reid, who was of the party, very kindly gave me a compass, to replace the one I had lost in the Mashukulumbwi country.

The following afternoon I crossed the Zambesi, towing my horses through the river at the tail of a canoe without difficulty, and that night I slept at the village of Mambova. We left Mambova early the following morning, and after travelling eight miles or so to the north-west reached the River Ungwesi, where I saw three roan antelopes and a few pookoos (*Cobus vardoni*). They were, however, excessively wild, and as the ground was full of holes and sun-cracks, and altogether very unfavourable to ride over, I did not go after them. I found that the River Ungwesi flows into the Zambesi some eight or ten miles west of Mambova, and not to the east of the junction of the Zambesi and Chobi, as it used to be represented to do in the best maps.

In the afternoon I continued my journey, and that night passed through an extensive mopani forest, to the east of the Kasaia river, in which the tse-tse fly still lingers, though in no great numbers. After crossing the Kasaia we kept on for another two or three miles, and slept on the edge of the plain through which the waters of the Majili river find their way to the Kasaia. In the rainy season the whole of this plain is under water ; but during the winter the Majili, though a large river on its upper course, containing reed beds, in which hippopotami are plentiful, is only connected with the Kasaia by a chain of small pools, at a considerable distance from one another.

On awaking the following morning and looking across the plain on the edge of which we had slept, we saw herd upon herd of wildebeests and zebras, all feeding slowly up wind. Altogether there must have been many hundreds of these animals in sight at once. As we were out of meat I saddled up one of my horses and shot a wildebeest, and we then continued our journey, the path turning to the south-west. An hour's walk, during which we were continually in sight of herds of wildebeests and zebras, brought us to a small vley,[1] and here I called a halt for breakfast. Whilst preparing this meal a herd of zebras approached the water, and seeing the horses, came towards them, upon which the latter apparently took fright, and went off at a gallop in the direction from which we had come, the herd of zebras galloping close behind them. I at once sent all my boys after them, hoping that they would not go far; but in about two hours' time some natives turned up, travelling to Sesheki, and from them I learned that the horses had turned into the footpath near our last night's camp, and gone right into the fly-infested forest, which we had been at such pains to pass through during the night. I now fully expected that the horses would go right back to Mambova before my boys would be able to overtake and turn them, and made up my mind that I should be detained for at least two days waiting for them. However, late in the evening Charley turned up with them, having managed to catch them about half-way between the Kasaia and Mambova. The horses had twice passed through the fly-infested forest beyond the Kasaia, but as it was a cloudy day and a high wind was blowing, and the flies there are few and far between at this time of year, I do not think they were " stuck," and at any rate they never showed the slightest sign of being in any way affected.

Whilst waiting for the horses I took a stroll along the footpath towards Sesheki with my butterfly net, and as I was walking slowly along, saw, sitting on a patch of bare ground beneath a thorn-tree, and not ten yards from me, a very small species of owl, which I know well, though I am unacquainted with its Latin name. Surprised at its tameness, I walked towards it, but it did not move until I was quite close to it,

1 Pool of water.

VIEW ON THE ZAMBESI BELOW THE VICTORIA FALLS.

(From a Photograph by Mr. W. Ellerton Fry.)

when it opened its wings and flew for two or three yards.   As
it did so I saw that there was something attached to one of its
legs, and on catching it found that a large chameleon was fast
secured to it, having its tail firmly twisted two or three times
round one of the owl's legs.   How they had got into this
position I cannot say, but I fancy that the little owl must first
have attacked the chameleon, though upon detaching it I could
find no wounds or scratches of any kind upon it.   Neither
was there anything amiss with the owl, which, as soon as I had
released it, flew away and perched in a neighbouring thorn-
tree.

Early the following morning I rode on ahead of my boys
to Sesheki, which I reached in an hour and a half.   I was here
very kindly received by Messrs. Jeanmairet and Jalla and their
wives—missionaries belonging to Mr. Coillard's mission to the
Zambesi, which is an offshoot, I believe, of the French Protestant Mission so long established in Basutoland.

Mr. Jeanmairet informed me that the crocodiles were a
great nuisance to him, having devoured all his pigs, all his dogs,
and nearly all his goats.   These reptiles are very savage and
voracious at Sesheki, as in Sepopo's time they became accustomed to eating human flesh, a practice they are loath to discon-
tinue ; so that for a man to fall into the water near Sesheki is
a very dangerous matter.   In Sepopo's time many people were
executed for witchcraft and other offences, and their bodies
thrown to the crocodiles, as in the Matabili country they
are given to the hyænas.   I will here relate a story I had
from the mouth of an eye-witness, and which I think is true,
which shows that Sepopo had a strong sense of humour.   In
October 1874, when returning to my waggons from a hunting
trip up the Chobi, I met Mr. T., a trader, who had just returned
from Sesheki.   In the course of conversation he told me that
one day, as he was drinking beer with Sepopo, a very old man
crept up and begged for food.   The king, turning to some of
his men, asked who he was, and learned that he belonged to
one of the slave tribes.   He then said, " He's a very old man ;
can he do any work ? " and was informed that the old man was
quite past work, and dependent upon charity—a very, very
scarce article in the interior of Africa.   Then said the king,

" Take him down to the river and hold his head under water,"
and the old man was forthwith led down to the river.   Presently
the executioners returned.   " Is the old man dead ? " said Sepopo.
" Dead he is," they answered.   " Then give him to the crocodiles," said the king, and went on drinking beer and chatting to
my friend T.

I left Sesheki on 16th August, and followed Mr. Coillard's
waggon road to the north, sleeping that evening on the bank
of the Loanja river, or rather swamp.   The road from here
follows the western bank of the Loanja for about forty miles, the
whole of which distance is infested with " fly," and has therefore
to be traversed at night by both oxen and horses.   It can be
done in two nights by ox waggons, but is usually done in three,
and there are two islands in the swamp free from " fly," to
which the oxen can be driven to feed and rest during the day-
time.   These islands are, too, conveniently situated so as to
divide the journey into three easy nights' work.   With my
horses, and walking with the boys by bright moonlight, I passed
this " fly " infested district in two nights, making my halt at
Kalangu's, where I had an attack of fever and had to delay a
day in consequence.   From the spoor which I saw in the moonlight there must be a great many buffaloes on the Loanja, as
well as other game ;   indeed, we saw a herd of the former
animals and several herds of antelopes as we were walking
along by the brilliant moonlight.

After leaving the Loanja we entered upon a forest country,
with fine white sand under foot, very similar to the country
south of the Zambesi on the road to Bamangwato ; and the
character of the country never altered all the way to the Barotsi
valley.   In fact I found the journey by land from Sesheki to
the Barotsi inconceivably monotonous, and utterly devoid of
interest of any kind.   Game was exceedingly scarce, far more
so than it is south of the Zambesi.   At some large vleys
between the Loanja and the N'joko rivers I saw a few wildebeests and zebras, and also a small herd of Lichtenstein's hartebeests.   I tried, and failed, to shoot one of the latter animals,
but managed to kill a wildebeest.   Near the N'joko I shot three
elands, and managed to get a little fat for cooking purposes.
Before reaching the N'joko we left Mr. Coillard's waggon track,

and, travelling more to the westward, did not re-enter the road till we were near the Mutondo river. On 25th August we reached the Lumbi, the largest of the affluents of the Zambesi between Sesheki and the Barotsi valley. Here we saw a great many Leechwe antelopes, but as I did not care about wading through the swamp after them, I gave my rifle to my boy Charley, who is a very good shot, and he managed to kill two —a fine ram and a ewe. Where we struck the Lumbi it was not more than twenty yards broad, though very deep, and running with a strong current. The water was as clear as crystal, so that in spite of the depth we could see the bottom quite plainly. We crossed everything—goods, boys, and horses —by the help of a canoe which my guides obtained from a neighbouring village.

After crossing the Lumbi the country became, if anything, more uninteresting than it had been, and almost destitute of game. I managed to shoot a solitary wildebeest near the Mutondo, the only animal I saw between the Lumbi and the chief's village of Lialui. We passed many large lagoons that seemed to be exactly suited for wildfowl ; but as I saw none, I suppose there was something wanting. Suffice it to say that on 2nd September I reached Mr. Coillard's mission station at Sefula. Here I was very kindly received by Mr. and Mrs. Coillard, who, together with a young Scotch artisan (Mr. Wardell), are living here alone in Central Africa, far indeed from the busy hum of civilised life. As Mr. Coillard himself said to me, nothing but a very strong sense of duty could induce a European to live in such a country, so utterly out of the world, and cut off so entirely from all communication with his kind. The mission station stands upon the top of the wooded sand-ridge which bounds the Barotsi valley on the east, and is, I suppose, one hundred feet or so above the level of the poisonous valley itself. The chief's town, Lialui, is about fifteen miles distant, situated in the middle of the Barotsi valley, which I think is about as unhealthy a spot as could be found in all Africa. Although Mr. Coillard had not yet been two years at Sefula he had built a comfortable dwelling-house, and several outhouses and store-rooms, the whole being fenced in. Mr. Wardell at the time of my visit was hard at work building a church, which was already approaching completion. Whilst I was at Sefula the thermometer registered from 98° to 105° daily, although it was protected by an artificial shade, and hung under a thick-foliaged tree.

After spending three days beneath the hospitable roof of the Sefula mission station, I went on to Lialui to see Lewanika, Mr. Coillard accompanying me, and taking his photographic apparatus with him, as he intended to spend a few days at the chief's. Mr. Coillard, I may here say, has already taken a great many most interesting photographs representing different phases of native life and customs, and others of the scenery of the Upper Zambesi.

On reaching Lialui we were very kindly received by Lewanika, and Mr. Coillard welcomed as an old friend. To him was assigned a large hut within the royal enclosure, whilst another was given to me outside for the use of myself and my people. In appearance my hut was clean enough, the floor being even, and plastered with mud ; however, I found it to be infested with " tampans," a kind of ground-bug, whose bite is very irritating, and whose attentions effectually banished sleep. The following day Lewanika made me a present of an ox, and later on of a large tusk of ivory. On my part I presented him with a very good hammerless shot gun and some rugs. He also bought my three horses with ivory, and undertook to give me canoes to enable me to return by river to Kazungula. He always dressed in European clothes, and seemed desirous of acquiring civilised habits. He had given up drinking beer, and taken to tea and coffee instead. Mr. Coillard has a good deal of influence over him, I think, and has, too, I believe, gained the confidence of those of his people with whom he has come in contact. Having been for many years in Basutoland before coming to the Zambesi he understands and speaks Sakalolo—the court language of the Barotsi, and which is a corrupted Sasuto—perfectly, and is a man of so kindly a nature that I think he is sure to gain the goodwill of the people.

The Barotsi valley itself is a most miserable place to live in. During the rainy season it is inundated by the overflow of the Zambesi, and is entirely under water, with

XIII UNHEALTHINESS OF THE BAROTSI VALLEY 253

the exception of the sandy mounds on which the villages are built, which are just above the water level. When the floods recede, the grass, which has been months under water, is rotten, and then the hot sun beats down upon it more fiercely every day until the following rainy season. If one walks outside Lialui after sundown the smell from the rotting vegetation is very strong and disagreeable. Under such conditions the Barotsi valley must be very unhealthy, and it is in fact a hotbed of malarial fever. But Lialui has other drawbacks besides its unhealthiness. There is no wood within five or six miles, and the people burn a kind of little bush which grows amongst the grass, and which it takes a long time to collect. In the dry season when the floods have receded there is no water to be got within a couple of miles, and it is very bad water when you have got it. Food of all kinds is very scarce and difficult to obtain. The people keep neither goats nor fowls ; and if you cannot get an odd fish you must go without animal food as a rule. During my stay at Lialui the chief almost daily sent me some fish, always all ready broiled in the ashes ; and Mr. Coillard most kindly supplied me with corn for my people from his store at Sefula, so that, with the meat of the ox that had been given me and some eland biltong, I managed to rub along *tant bien que mal.*

I did not see any interesting ceremonies during my stay in the Barotsi country. One evening there was a dance in honour of the new moon, but it was of no interest whatever. Every morning and evening the chief sat for two or three hours in his " kotla " or courtyard, and was occupied whilst I was there almost exclusively in distributing the cattle, lately taken from the Mashukulumbwi, amongst his own people. When strangers came in they saluted the chief most ceremoniously. First they would kneel down in a row, and after clapping their hands bend their heads forward until their foreheads touched the ground, when the head was moved slowly from side to side ; then, raising their heads again, they would look towards the chief, and throwing their arms quickly and wildly into the air would shout twice in unison, and in slow measured tones, the words " So-yo, so-yo." This ceremony would be twice repeated, when, after clapping their hands again, they would get up and retire.

Sometimes, whilst the chief sat in the "kotla," a man appeared dressed in—or, rather, covered with—the skin of a hyæna. He imitated the animal in a most realistic manner, and must often have watched hyæŋas prowling about on moonlight nights to have obtained so minute a knowledge of their habits. Lewanika, like the lady in the fairy tale, "has music wherever he goes," being always accompanied to and from the "kotla" by two drums and another barbarous instrument made of flat pieces of wood laid over the mouths of calabashes. The drums are beaten the whole night through by relays of drummers, so that whenever Lewanika awakes he may hear them, and know that his people are keeping guard. Before leaving the Barotsi I had a sharp attack of fever, as had also both my Dutch-speaking boys, Paul and Charley, and several of my Mananzas and Batongas, from below Wankie's, all of whom ought to have been acclimatised ; but, as I have said before, the Barotsi valley is, I believe, a perfect hotbed of fever, and a most dangerous place for Europeans. At last the chief informed me that the canoes, paddles, and paddlers were all ready, and on the morning of 21st September I bade him good-bye and walked to the place of embarkation, which is in an arm of the Zambesi, and about four miles distant from Lialui. The following day we reached the main stream of the Zambesi, and slept at Nalolo, the chief town of the king's sister Moqui, whom I had seen at Lialui. Three days later we reached the end of the Barotsi valley at a place called Sinanga. Here the forest comes down to the water's edge, and we were able once more to get wood to cook with, a luxury we had not known for some time, having had to do all our cooking lately with dry weeds and odds and ends of that nature.

The river scenery in the Barotsi valley is very poor, as the river flows through a perfectly flat country like Holland, but is without the windmills, farmsteads, and orchards with which that country is studded. We saw a few Leechwe antelopes and every day a few hippopotami and crocodiles. The bird life was very interesting. Pelicans and various

VIEW ON THE ZAMBESI ABOVE THE VICTORIA FALLS.

(From a Photograph by Mr. W. Ellerton Fry.)

species of cranes and storks were very numerous, as were avocets, spoonbills, herons, bitterns, and egrets. I also noticed wattled plovers, spur-winged plovers, and stilted plovers, besides dotterel and a few curlew, which latter seemed identical with the European bird. Two species of ducks, and both spur-winged, and Egyptian geese, were also in considerable numbers. The day we reached Sinanga I left the canoes about mid-day and accompanied some of my men to the grave of a former Barotsi chief named Nonambing, as our headman wished to pray to him for a prosperous journey, and also for success in hunting. Arrived at the little village where the deceased chief lay buried, he placed about sixpennyworth of calico on the grave and offered up his prayers. The ceremony was concluded by the headman of the little village—who is the hereditary keeper of the grave—spitting upon all the guns of the party, mine included. After this we had a long walk across the open plain and under a burning sun to the canoes, which we did not reach till sundown.

Below Sinanga the scenery of the Zambesi becomes very pleasing, as the forest comes down to the river's brink on both banks, and the river itself is studded with wooded islands. On the morning of the 28th I left the canoes, and walked for more than three hours along the western bank of the river. This is a great country for elephants and buffaloes ; indeed, there are said to be more of the former animals here than in any other part of Lewanika's dominions, and he will not allow any one but his own hunters to shoot in this part of the country. Walking along the bank, I crossed the spoor of two herds of elephants that had drunk in the river during the previous night, and must have been feeding for hours amongst the trees on the water's edge. The one herd was composed entirely of big bulls, the other of cows and calves. The whole country had been trampled by large herds of buffaloes, which, however, had left the river and retired into the bush for the day. All other game had done the same, and I saw nothing but a small herd of impala antelopes. Tse-tse flies now swarmed on both banks of the river, which about here is very broad, certainly quite a mile from bank to bank, and full of wooded islands, many of them of very considerable extent. Both banks of the river are wooded, and the scenery often reminded me of portions of the Upper Thames between Maidenhead and Pangbourne. The Zambesi itself, however, is a magnificent river, its waters being of a deep blue and very clear and pure. As an old friend of mine used to say, " There's life in a draught of Zambesi water."

On 29th September we reached Sioma, a town about a mile above the Falls of Gonyi, the river continuing very broad, and studded with islands all the way. Here we were delayed three days, as the canoes had to be dragged overland for about three miles to a point some distance below the falls.

The day after our arrival at Sioma I went to have a look at the falls, but found that they were in the centre of the river, so that I could not get a good view of them from the eastern bank. On the following morning I again visited them, and, by the help of a ledge of rocks, waded across the two hundred yards of river between the eastern bank and the chasm into which the main river discharges itself. I was well rewarded for my pains, for the Falls of Gonyi, seen thus at close quarters, are well worth taking some trouble to get at. They are of course a small matter compared with the stupendous and incomparable Victoria Falls ; but they are, nevertheless, very beautiful, and were they situated in Scotland, or any accessible part of Europe, I have no doubt would attract crowds of visitors. The height of these falls is not more than thirty feet, I should say, but in the central portion an immense mass of water rushes into a rocky chasm—a seething torrent of fleecy foam, very beautiful to look upon. This central fall is flanked by others, where the mass of water is not so great. As I have said before, these falls can scarcely be seen from the bank, as they fall into a chasm in the centre of the river. However, it is not a difficult matter to wade out to them, and their beauty will well repay the trouble.

On 2nd October we again got under way, but did not get very far, as my boatmen discovered a sort of backwater with a bar across the entrance, full of fish, and we spent nearly the whole day spearing fish. Altogether we must have killed considerably over a hundredweight, many of them very fine fish—a sort of perch—and very good eating.   The following day we reached the rapid of Kali, where we had to partially unload the canoes and drag them over and amongst rocks for several hundred yards.   Here I saw a small herd of pookoo antelopes, and after a long stalk got within shot of them, and broke the shoulder of the ram whose head I coveted.   There was a great deal of blood on the spoor at first, but after a time it ceased, and we then lost it, and I had to return to the canoes without the buck.   In the evening, however, I shot another ram close to our camp at the mouth of the little river Nangombi.   During the day the boatmen killed a rodent, a kind of huge reed-rat, like an immense guinea-pig, but of a uniform brown colour and with very coarse bristly hair.   It had four toes on each foot armed with strong nails, small eyes, and small rounded ears, and a tail about eight inches long. It must have weighed quite 10 lbs.   This animal is, I believe, known to naturalists, but it is the first of its kind that I have ever seen.

The next day I walked along the bank in the early morning for a couple of hours, and shot two impala antelopes —a ram and a ewe.   I had one boy with me, whom I left with the ram to wait for the canoes, and was alone when I shot the second antelope.   After a time three of the canoes came in sight, and I heard that the fourth—my canoe—was behind, getting the impala ram on board ; so I put the ewe into one of the others and got in myself, intending to go a little distance farther and then make a halt for breakfast. However, we had scarcely paddled three hundred yards, and had just rounded a small island, when we were stopped by yells and shouts behind us, and soon one of the paddlers belonging to my canoe came running along the bank, calling out, " The canoe is dead ! the canoe is dead ! a hippopotamus has killed the canoe ! "   We at once paddled back, and soon met various articles floating down the stream, amongst them my cooking pot, which, having the lid on, was full of air, and the waterproof bag containing my blankets ; and I realised that I had met with one of those accidents to which one is liable on African rivers.   My canoe had been attacked and sunk in about twelve feet of water, and now lay at the bottom of the river, with several tusks of ivory, all my provisions, cartridges, trading goods, and, in fact, everything I had with me but the cooking pot and my bag of blankets.

The first thing to be done was to try to shoot the hippopotamus that had played me such a sorry trick. The animal was in a not unfavourable place for the purpose, being in a large pool between an island and the mainland, with shallow water at each end, so that it could not get into the main river without exposing itself. The pool was about four hundred yards long and two hundred broad, and, as the animal had shown itself to be so vicious, I hoped it would be also fearless, and give me a few good chances, but I soon found that I had to do with a very cunning beast. It just raised its head for an instant of time above the surface of the water, but gave no time to get a sight on it. At last I fired, but just too late, and for a long time after this the cunning animal never showed its head at all, but only its great snout, which it just pushed out of the water to take breath. I only fired now at long intervals, as the animal really gave me but a very slight chance of hitting it in the head. I think that I hit it three times altogether, twice in the snout and once in the neck just behind the head, none of which shots can have done it much harm. At three o'clock the troubled beast disappeared altogether, and never showed itself again until half-past five. During all that time it must have been lying somewhere close under the bank, with nothing but its nose out of water. I remained trying to get a shot until it was almost dark, but did not fire again, and then left the hippopotamus master of the situation, and retired to where the boys had made camp.

During more than an hour I took the times with my watch that this hippopotamus remained under water. The shortest was forty seconds, and the longest four minutes and twenty seconds: the usual time being from two to two and a half minutes. It always remained under water for a long time after being fired at. I have little doubt that as soon as it grew dark the animal left the pool, in which, in spite of its success in sinking the canoe, it must certainly have spent a most uncomfortable day.

The following morning, as soon as it got a little warm, we

went with the three remaining canoes to look for the one that
had been sunk, accompanied by two very small canoes, in which
were four natives whom my headman had collected the previous
day, and who were expert divers.   It took us a long time to
find the lost canoe, as the water was very deep, from twelve to
fourteen feet ; however, after prodding about for a couple of
hours with their long paddles, my men at last found it, and one
of the divers immediately went down to make sure, and came
up with the good news that it was indeed the canoe.   Another
now dived down with a rope and attached it to the projecting
prow, and our two largest canoes then towed the sunken one
into shallow water.   All that remained in it, however, was the
impala antelope, two small tusks of ivory, and two muskets belonging to the paddlers.   A large tusk of ivory weighing about
60 lbs., two bags containing my cartridges, besides all my trading
goods, provisions, plates, cups, fork, spoon, etc., and all my little
necessary odds and ends, together with a third musket belonging
to one of the boys, were all gone.   How on earth the large tusk
of ivory and my cartridges got out of the canoe I cannot understand.   However, they were gone, and, as it would have been next
to impossible to recover them, I had the canoe bailed out at once,
and we then paddled round to camp, and got ready to proceed
on our journey.   The canoe, I may here say, was not injured
in any way.   The hippopotamus, my boys said, first came up
underneath it, throwing one end of it out of water, at the same
time dipping the other end, and half filling the heavy craft with
water.   Two of the paddlers either fell or jumped out at this
first attack, the one swimming to the island, the other to the
bank of the river, and the two who remained in the canoe were
paddling as hard as they could towards the island when the
hippopotamus made a second attack.   This time, they said, the
animal raised its head out of the water, and laying it over the
canoe, simply pressed it down under water, when of course it
filled and sank to the bottom, and the two boys swam ashore
without being followed—very luckily, as in these accidents the
enraged hippopotamus often kills one or more of the occupants
of the canoe, biting them with its formidable tusks.

Before mid-day we resumed our journey, and in the afternoon
reached the mouth of the River N'joko, where we slept.   There

used to be a great deal of small game about here, and elephants
and buffaloes as well ; in fact, we found game plentiful from
here to within a day's journey of Sesheki, and on both banks
of the river.   The tse-tse flies, too, were in swarms about this
part of the Zambesi, and were an intolerable nuisance whenever
I left the canoe and walked along the bank.   The loss of all
my cartridges just as I was getting amongst the game was most
annoying.   I still had four in my belt, but subsequently lost
one of them.   The lid of my cooking pot now had to serve me
for a plate, and my fingers and knife for fork and spoon.

CAPE BUFFALO.

On 6th October we passed the rapids of Lusu, and reached
the Nambwi rapids the same afternoon.   Here the canoes had
again to be dragged a short distance overland, and whilst this
was being done I took a walk and shot a pookoo ram.   Below
Nambwi the Zambesi becomes very shallow, running continually
amongst rocks and stones.   At the same time the river is broad
and full of little wooded islands, amongst which the small
channels find their way.   The scenery about these rapids, with
their wooded islands, is very pleasing, but not in any way
grand.

On the following day we passed three more rapids, and
reached Sekkosi's, or Katongo, in the afternoon.   Here the

country again becomes perfectly flat and uninteresting on both banks of the river, closely resembling the Barotsi valley in its general features. Sandbanks, too, once more appear, and the bird life again becomes very varied and interesting. Just below Sekkosi's we found hippopotami in very great numbers, and passed several large herds in the distance of a couple of miles.

From Sekkosi's another day's good paddling brought us to Sesheki, where I spent a day with the hospitable missionaries and then hurried on to Kazungula, where my waggon was standing on the southern bank of the Zambesi. I arrived there on 12th October, and so ended my second journey across the Zambesi in the year 1888.

As the weather was now very hot, and I knew that water would be very scarce in the desert country between Panda-ma-tenka and Bamangwato, I remained in the neighbourhood of the Zambesi for a couple of months, hoping that rain would at length fall and fill some of the vleys along the road. The greater part of this time I spent on the banks of the Zambesi, shooting and collecting specimens of natural history, and during the month of November paid what will probably prove to be the last of the many visits I have made to the incomparable Victoria Falls.

At last I got so tired of waiting that I resolved to push through the thirst-land at any hazard ; and on 10th December, although as yet no rain had fallen but a few light showers, I made a start. The journey was a most arduous one, but at length I reached Bamangwato early in January 1889, and not many days afterwards the long-delayed rainy season set in.

RUINS ON THE LOWER MAZOE RIVER.

(From a Photograph by Mr. FRANCEYS, of Salisbury, Mashunaland.)

CHAPTER XIV

Arrange for journey to the Upper Mazoe—Mr. Edward Burnett—Mr. Thomas—A
trip home to England—Take passage for Quillimani—Description of town—
Portuguese custom-house—Boat journey up the Quaqua river—Reach the
Zambesi—Start for Tete—Pass Shupanga—And Sena—Scarcity of animal life
—Bush-buck shot—Lions heard—The Lupata gorge—Pass the mouth of the
Ruenya—Reach Tete—Portuguese system of government on the Zambesi—
Secure a good interpreter—Difficulty of obtaining carriers—Rumours of war—
Abandon the idea of following the course of the Mazoe river.

ON my arrival in Mangwato in January 1889 I met Mr.
Frank Johnson, and was asked by him to conduct a gold-
prospecting party to the head of the Mazoe river in Eastern
Mashunaland by way of the Portuguese possessions on the
Zambesi. This route was to be adopted owing to the impos-
sibility of reaching that country through Matabililand, Lo
Bengula having definitely closed all roads passing through his
territory. The party as proposed by Mr. Johnson was to have
consisted of one mining expert, two practical miners, Mr. Edward
Burnett, and myself, and my duty was simply to have been to
guide the expedition to the gold regions on the Upper Mazoe.

Ultimately the party consisted of Mr. Burnett, Mr. Thomas, a miner of considerable experience, and myself.

In Mr. Edward Burnett I had a very pleasant companion. He was an old acquaintance, as I had met him in Matabililand in 1887. Besides being a good shot, and a strong active young fellow, he was possessed of the happy disposition which enables a man to bear with equanimity the little troubles and annoyances which are seldom entirely absent from the life of an African traveller, and which are perhaps more disturbing to the temper than trials and hardships of a far more serious nature. Mr. Thomas I had also known as a very good miner and hard-working man in the " blue jacket " shaft at Tati.

Having suffered such heavy losses the previous year, I decided to accept Mr. Johnson's offer rather than go to the expense of fitting out another expedition to the Barotsi country ; but, as it was not advisable to proceed to the Lower Zambesi until the rainy season was at an end, I took a trip home to England, which I reached in the end of February, returning to South Africa in May, in time to catch the Union S.S. *Courland*, which was advertised to leave Cape Town on 10th June for Mozambique, and the intermediate Portuguese settlements on the east coast of Africa.

On 16th July we were landed at Quillimani, which is situated on the eastern bank of the Quaqua river, and about fifteen miles from its mouth. Quillimani is, as is well known, one of the oldest of the Portuguese military posts and trading stations in South-Eastern Africa, having been established about three centuries ago. It is still quite a small place, but the houses of which the town consists are well built, and their red-tiled roofs look very pretty and picturesque amongst the palm trees and banana groves by which they are surrounded. The one street is lighted on moonless nights by oil lamps.

It took us some time to get our goods through the custom - house, as a large mission party, going up to the Scotch mission station at Blantyre, had been fellow-passengers with ourselves on the *Courland*, and had of course a large amount of stores with them, which together with our own belongings almost filled the custom-house. Thinking to do the authorities a good turn, Burnett, Steve Thomas, and myself,

and two of the Scotch missionaries pulled off our coats, and
with sleeves tucked up in South African fashion commenced
sorting out the boxes ; but I believe our conduct was taken in
bad part by the custom-house officers, who thought it most
disrespectful on our part to appear before them without coats,
and with bare arms.   Certainly no offence was meant, and the
climate of Quillimani is not one to encourage the wearing of
coats and collars.   Mr. Ross, the vice-consul, was most kind
and obliging, and did everything he could do to assist us, and
without his help we should have had far more difficulty than
we experienced as it was.   At length we got everything
arranged, and our goods packed in bundles suitable for
carriage by natives, and none of them weighing over 50 lbs.

We arranged with Mr. Teixeira to provide a boat as far as
Lokoloko on the Quaqua, from which place we were to get
carriers over to the Zambesi, which is about forty miles distant.
We also hired two personal servants in Quillimani.   One of
these, who rejoiced in the name of Rebecca, was being boarded
and lodged at the Government expense at the time of our
visit, but we were able to buy him out for a small sum.   Mr.
Ross recommended him to us, as he thought he could speak
English, and would be therefore useful to us as an interpreter.
As Rebecca had once been a mission boy at Blantyre I
suppose he had once known a little English, but he must have
forgotten it, and learned Portuguese instead, as he certainly
knew a good many words in the latter language.   When he
was first introduced I said to him, " Well, Rebecca, can you
speak English ? " to which he at once replied with great
alacrity and a perfect accent, " Yes, sir ! " and I thought we
had got a treasure.   Before many days, however, we found out
that " Yes, sir ! " were the only two words in the English
language that Rebecca knew, and that he trotted them out
with perfect satisfaction to himself on every possible occasion.
Although sodden with the vile drink with which the Portuguese are destroying the natives of South-Eastern Africa, poor
Rebecca was naturally a good-tempered, harmless creature, and
stuck to us throughout the journey, as did his companion, our
other servant, a boy named Rocky, who had also been much
demoralised by bad drink.

At last, after hours of delay, caused by the drunkenness of our crew, we managed to get away from Quillimani late in the afternoon of 19th July.   A second rainy season seemed to have set in, for showers had been falling continually, day and night, during the previous three days.   After getting under way we made very slow progress, merely drifting up the river with the tide, as our crew were too drunk to row, so that by seven o'clock we were not more than five miles from Quillimani.   Although the tide was still running strongly our boatmen now dropped the anchor, near high-water mark, and went to sleep, and as it was getting dark, and we knew nothing about the navigation of the river ourselves, we judged it best to allow them to sleep off the effects of their last drinking bout.   Several heavy showers had fallen during the afternoon, and as darkness set in the dull leaden sky, shot with black rain-charged clouds, portended a dirty night.   Nor was the promise falsified, for again heavy showers commenced to fall, and continued to do so, with slight intermissions, all night through.   We had a slight shelter from the sun at the back of the boat, but nothing capable of keeping out even a light shower of rain ; so as we lay on our goods at the bottom of the boat we of course got very wet.

As day broke on the following morning we found that the tide had left us stranded high and dry, or rather high and damp, on an oozy, slimy mudbank.   Rain was still falling, we were wet and chilly, and the dull leaden sky looked very cheerless.   There were a few huts on the bank, just above our boat, and an old, deserted, tumble-down house that might once have been owned and inhabited by a Portuguese trader.   In this house we at last managed to get a fire lit, and then made a kettle of coffee, and cooked some food.   We were much delayed in effecting this by our still lingering belief in Rebecca's knowledge of English, for as, in order to get to shore, it was necessary to wade for some distance through deep soft mud, we at first remained in the boat, and sent Rebecca on shore with Rocky to light the fire and make the coffee. We gave the former the kettle, together with a tin of coffee and a large spoon, explaining to him at the same time how many spoonfuls of coffee he was to put in when the water boiled, and as he answered "Yes, sir!" with a beautiful accent to everything we told him we thought he had understood what was required of him.   After waiting some time, old Thomas called out, "Rebecca, have you cooked that there kettle?" and at once the ready answer came back, "Yes, sir!" After a pause, Thomas asked again, "Rebecca, have you made that there coffee?" and again the answer was "Yes, sir!" "Then why, etc. etc., don't you bring it?" said the old man, losing patience.   Once more the answer was "Yes, sir!" but still the coffee did not come.   Then we began to suspect that something was wrong, and, pulling off our boots and socks and trousers, waded ashore, when, lo and behold! there stood Rebecca, smiling all over his face, and warming himself at the fire, and there stood the kettle, full of water indeed, but not even on the fire.   Burnett and I grasped the situation at once, and burst out laughing, but our old miner said,—well, I will not tell you what he said; but when you reflect that as a young man he had been twenty years at sea, and then twenty years a miner in Australia and elsewhere, and that his ordinary language was an impartial blend of that of a sailor and a miner, I think that if you are imaginative you may perhaps guess the character of his remarks.   After this Rebecca was voted a failure as an English scholar, and was never taken into favour again by old Thomas, who invariably referred to him as that —— ——.

It was not until the tide was nearly at the flood that we were enabled to float our boat, and we were then only able to proceed for an hour or so before it again turned, so that we did not make much headway, although our crew were by this time sober, and worked hard.   With the next tide we made better progress, and kept it up till about 10 P.M.   During the day several showers of rain had fallen, and the night was again damp and drizzly, but, as we had made our thatch roof a little more watertight, we managed to sleep through it.

The following morning we got off just at daylight, and kept on with the tide, but against a head wind, until two o'clock, when we anchored, as we could make no farther headway.   Just before halting we saw two large iguanas and five good-sized crocodiles lying on the slimy mud at the water's edge. We went on shore whilst waiting for the turn of the tide, and tried to take a walk round with our rifles, but found it almost impossible to do so, as the ground was muddy and soft, and covered with a dense growth of coarse grass and reeds, and in places with thick scrub. The mosquitoes, too, rose from the mud and attacked us in clouds, and fairly drove us back again to our boat, and even there did not leave us in peace. A little before sundown a large crocodile came up close to the boat, offering a strong temptation for a shot, so I fired at and hit him about the head, the ball telling loudly. The ugly reptile gave one lash with his tail and disappeared, but I think he was well hit, and if killed he must have sunk at once to the bottom. With the next tide the missionary party, bound to Blantyre, caught us up and slept alongside of us. They had left Quillimani a day later than we did, but probably with a sober crew, and having three light boats, were able to travel much quicker than our heavy lighter.

From this point the Quaqua began to narrow very rapidly, and soon became a mere ditch, with banks of slimy, unhealthy-looking mud. There is very little life along this river. After it narrowed we saw no more crocodiles, nor any sign of hippo-potami. A few birds alone enlivened the otherwise dreary and uninteresting landscape. Of these the most conspicuous were the large, handsome, white-headed fish eagles so common on the Central and Upper Zambesi. Kingfishers were also numer-ous. I noticed three varieties—the black and white (*Ceryle rudis*), the tiny blue (*Corythornis cyanostigma*), and the large blue (*Alcedo semitorquata*). During the day we passed several small clearings along the banks of the river, where a few natives were living. Their huts were all raised on platforms about six feet above the level of the ground, doubtless on account of the inundations, to which the whole of this perfectly level country must be liable.

Late at night on 22nd July we reached Lokoloko, the terminus of our boat voyage on the Quaqua, from whence we were to proceed overland on foot with carriers to the Zambesi. We found it to be eleven hours' fast walking from Lokoloko to Mazaro on the Zambesi, which we reached about mid-day on the second day. The country between the rivers is a dead

level, and very sparsely inhabited, but the natives seemed very
well off for food ; and the soil, I should imagine, must be very
rich and fertile.   At Mazaro I once more stood on the eastern
bank of the mighty Zambesi, a river whose course I have
followed for many hundreds of miles in the interior of this
vast continent.   Here the great river runs in several channels
through an immense valley, and altogether does not impress
the mind by its grandeur and the beauty of the scenery on its
banks, as it never fails to do in the interior, whether near
Zumbo, or in the neighbourhood of the Victoria Falls, or about
Sinanga, or near the far-off and little-known Falls of Gonyi.
Its waters appeared to me dull-coloured compared with the
deep blue of the waters of the Central and Upper Zambesi.
From Mazaro a walk of five miles brought us to Vicenti, where
the African Lakes Company have a station, and where Mr.
Peter Moore, the Company's agent, did all he could to make
us comfortable.   The *James Stevenson* was lying at anchor
by the bank, ready to start for Namalindi, on the Shiri river,
as soon as the mission party for Blantyre had arrived ; for,
as they had proceeded up the Quaqua by boat to Mopea,
a station only three miles distant from Vicenti, we had
reached that place before them by travelling overland from
Lokoloko.

I now hired a light boat and a native canoe from the African
Lakes Company to convey our goods and ourselves up the
Zambesi to Tete.   Burnett, Thomas, and myself found sitting
room in the back part of the boat, where we were sheltered
from sun and rain by a light framework of reeds thatched with
grass.   There was some little delay about getting crews, but
on the afternoon of 27th July we once more got under way.
We did not travel very rapidly, as the current of the Lower
Zambesi is strong, and the channels amongst the sand islands
intricate, but our men were a good-tempered, willing lot, and
gave us no trouble.   On the day after leaving Vicenti we passed
Shupanga, where lies the neglected and well-nigh forgotten
grave of Mrs. Livingstone, who, poor woman, in the endeavour
to be near her famous husband, made her way to this far-off
spot only to fall a victim to the pestilential climate of the Lower
Zambesi.

The day after passing Shupanga we passed the mouth of
the Shiri river, and on 31st July reached a trading station on
the eastern bank of the Zambesi, just opposite Sena. This
station belongs, I believe, to the French House in Quillimani.
We found a very dilapidated-looking, fever-stricken Frenchman
in charge, and also a representative of the Portuguese Government (a Goanese), whose business it was to collect taxes from
the natives. Although we endeavoured to visit Sena we were
unable to do so owing to the depth of water being insufficient
to float our boat up the channel which, our boatmen said, was
the one that led to the settlement. I may here say that during
this boat trip from the mouth of the Shiri to Tete, and again
on my return journey in the following November, I formed a
very unfavourable opinion of the facilities for navigation afforded
by the Lower Zambesi during the dry season. The river is in
most parts, below the Lupata gorge, enormously broad—quite
two miles, I should think, in certain places—being spread out
over a bed of constantly shifting white sand. It is cut into
numerous channels by sand islands, many of them of large
extent, and some of them no doubt permanent ; but the greater
part probably changing with every flood. Whether, if one only
knew where to find it, there is always one channel with a fair
depth of water, I cannot say, but I know that there was not
one single day that our boat, which only drew about a foot of
water, did not stick, and we often had to drag it for long distances over sandbanks only just submerged.

Travel on the Lower Zambesi is monotonous, as there is but
little animal or bird life to interest one. Egyptian geese were
not uncommon, and we shot a few for the pot. Crocodiles
were not nearly so numerous as I had been led to suppose
they would be, and all we saw of any size were very wary.
Burnett shot a small one, which our boatmen ate, and evidently
looked upon as a dainty. We saw a few hippopotami, but not
many, and one night one came grunting and splashing in the
shallow water, close to where we were sleeping on a sandbank,
but it was so dark we could not see him.

Owing to the breadth of the river, and the fact that our
boatmen always insisted that the best channels were out
amongst the sand islands, we seldom got a chance to land ; but

one morning, getting in under the eastern bank, which was well
wooded, Burnett and I landed to look for game. We saw a
good deal of koodoo and water-buck spoor, though none of the
animals themselves, but came across several bush-bucks, one of
which I killed.   This was a full-grown ram, and was interesting
to me, as I found him to be intermediate in colour and markings
between the bush-bucks found farther south, and those I have
seen farther north, along the rivers running into the Zambesi
from Mashunaland.   I preserved his skin for mounting, and it
is now in the collection of the Natural History Museum at
South Kensington.

After waiting for our boat to come up, we breakfasted on
the liver of the buck, and then Burnett and I walked on again
along the bank with a couple of the boys. We followed a
native footpath and saw a great deal of game spoor, including
that of elands, Burchell's zebras, koodoos, water-bucks, and
impala antelopes.   We also saw three wart-hogs, and some
water-bucks, but could not get a shot at them.   Whilst we had
been walking along at a good pace, expecting to see game
every moment, our canoe and boat had made very poor progress
amongst the sandbanks and islands ; so, late in the afternoon,
after waiting some time and seeing no signs of their approach,
we retraced our steps, and did not get back to the boat till
some time after dark.   We then put off from shore and slept
on a very wet sandbank, only a few inches above the level of
the river.   During the night some lions roared grandly several
times, not far away, on the eastern bank.

On 7th August the day broke cool and cloudy, and the air
being clear we saw in the distance a range of hills running
across the course of the river, through which it makes its way
by the narrow gorge of Lupata.   By mid-day we were not more
than five or six miles from these hills, but could not make out
the gap through which the Zambesi flows.   In the afternoon
we reached Bandari Cliff, which is a bold precipitous mass of
rock, at the foot of which the Zambesi runs in a deep narrow
channel.   Bandari forms the southern or eastern entrance to
the gorge of Lupata, during its passage through which the
Zambesi is compressed into a channel from two hundred to three
hundred yards in width.   At Bandari itself the river was not

more than two hundred yards broad, though it would be broader during the rainy season.

On the afternoon of the following day we reached the northern or western extremity of the Lupata gorge, and here the scenery is wild and striking. In the centre of the river stands a small island, called the Isle of Mozambique, whilst the entrance to the gorge is guarded on both sides by high rugged cliffs of dark red rock, whose precipitous sides fall sheer into the deep water of the river as it rushes through these mighty gates. The cliff on the western bank is called Tipwi, that on the eastern Kalumanuman. A few miles beyond the Lupata gorge we came to a place called Sungwi, on the eastern bank. Here there was a Portuguese fort or stockade, with four small cannons, one mounted at each corner. There were a few black soldiers about, armed with breech-loading rifles and bayonets, and a white man who was possibly the commandant, though I think not, for he wore no uniform, but was dressed very much like the drivers of the bullock sledges one sees in Madeira—in coarse whity-brown trousers and coat, with a large home-made straw hat. He looked very sickly and fever-stricken.

On the following day we passed the mouth of the great river Ruenya, called on its upper course the In-yang-ombi (Yankombi of Mauch), which drains the whole of Eastern Mashunaland, from the Umvukwi hills in the north to the sources of the Pungwi in the south. It has, however, but little surface water left when it reaches the Zambesi in the dry season, though during the rains it must become an immense river, bringing down with it enormous masses of sand, which it has already spread over the country to the width of a mile. Such vast quantities of sand, indeed, have been poured into the Zambesi at this point as to have narrowed its channel to little more than one hundred yards in width.

Soon after passing the mouth of the Ruenya we sighted the hill of Caroera, behind which, our boatmen told us, lay the town of Tete, or In-yung-wi, as the natives call it; and on Sunday, 11th August, we reached the goal of our boat journey at about ten o'clock in the morning.

Tete is too well known to need much description. It is one of the oldest of the Portuguese stations on the Zambesi,

having been founded in 1632. At the time of our visit
there were about twenty Europeans in the town, the major
portion of whom were either officers of the black troops
stationed there, or civil officials of the Portuguese Government. The Messrs. Teixeira de Mattos, who are partly Dutch
and partly Portuguese, had a house of business there,
and some Portuguese were also engaged in trade. We also
met Father Courtois of the Society of Jesus, from whom we
received much kindness. Another Father was at Baroma,
about twelve miles distant, where he was establishing a school
for the education of children. The altitude of Tete is officially
given as one hundred and sixty-three metres, or about five
hundred and twenty feet.

The Zambesi just opposite the town is not more than four
hundred yards broad. There are about twenty European
houses in the town, including a well-built church and the
residence of the Governor, which is a very substantial structure,
built purposely with very thick walls to keep out the heat and
cool lofty rooms. All the buildings are in the Portuguese
style, with roofs of red tile, which give them a picturesque
effect. The European quarter stands in the foreground near
the river, and the native town, composed of the ordinary
thatched huts, is built in a semicircle behind it.

The country about Tete is excessively dry and parched,
being all rock and stone, with little or no soil. At the time of
our visit there was not a blade of grass or vegetation of any kind
to be seen in the immediate vicinity of the town. The crops
grown in this part of the country, Father Courtois informed us,
are always poor, and often fail altogether, and there appears to
be more or less of a famine at the end of nearly every dry
season. There are a good many cattle in the town, all, I think,
owned by Europeans, that were originally brought from
Mashunaland; though how they passed the "fly" infested
district between Tete and that country is a mystery to me.
These cattle had to be driven a long distance every day to
pasture, but were in good condition. The inhabitants of Tete,
both white and black, also keep great numbers of pigs, which
animals play the part of scavengers, and no doubt do much for
the sanitation of the place. The trade of Tete is in ivory and

gold dust. The latter is brought from the Mazoe river in the west, and from the Makanga country in the east, but not in very large quantities. The ivory is obtained for the most part in the Angoni country to the west of Lake Nyassa or brought down from Zumbo.

Just before we reached Tete Burnett got a sharp attack of fever, which made him very weak, but he soon shook it off, and began to gain strength again, and was almost well when at last we were ready to start ; for we were delayed a whole week collecting carriers, without whom it was impossible for us to proceed on our journey.

Although the native population of the Portuguese posses- sions on the banks of the Lower Zambesi may not be slaves, they certainly do not seem to be free men in the English sense of the word. The country is divided into praços, or districts, each praço being let by Government to some person, usually a European or a Goanese, for a certain annual rental. The person who rents such a praço naturally tries to make the best of his bargain, and get as much as he can out of the people ; and the inhabitants practically become his serfs, and cannot leave the praço without his consent. There may be laws in force in the more civilised districts which tend to mitigate the abuses to which such a system is open, but that the powers derived from Government are shamefully abused in the outlying dis- tricts I can myself bear witness.

The Governor of Tete, at the time of my visit, Senhor Alfredo Alpuina, neither assisted me nor stood in my way in the matter of getting carriers. I do not think he quite liked the idea of our journey to the sources of the Mazoe, as there was already a little friction between the British and Portuguese Governments regarding jurisdiction in that part of the country ; but I fancy he consoled himself with the thought that we would not get any carriers from Tete to accompany us so far. Certainly neither he nor any of the traders in Tete knew where the Mazoe really took its rise. They all said that it rose in Motoko's country, as indeed it was represented to do in all maps published prior to 1890. I may here say that I had left Cape Town with instructions from my employers to mark out mining areas, in accordance with the Portuguese mining law, if

Mr. Thomas found what he considered to be payable gold in Portuguese territory, and I had a letter of introduction from the Portuguese Consul in Cape Town to the Governors of Quillimani and Tete. It is possible that without this letter Senhor Alpuina would not have allowed me to pass, but surely he ought not to have imagined that because I had such a letter it was incumbent upon me, an Englishman, to acquiesce in the claim of Portugal to any part of Mashunaland. I say this because, on my return to Tete some months later, Senhor Alpuina was very angry with me because I had obtained a mining concession from native chiefs far beyond the Portuguese boundary.

Whilst we were at Tete Rebecca picked up a Quillimani boy, whom we engaged on the same terms as himself, and we were also fortunate in securing the services of a very good interpreter. This man, the son of a Goanese by a native woman, rejoiced in the name of Augusto Melitão de Souza, and was a well-educated intelligent fellow. He had been four years in Bombay, and there learned to speak English fluently ; and as he also spoke several native dialects and Portuguese (which latter language he could also read and write), he was most useful as an interpreter. He was, too, a good-tempered, willing servant, and during our whole journey I never had any fault to find with him, though he played us a bit of a trick on our return to Tete. He also brought with him two serfs from his father's praço who dared not leave him, so that besides Augusto we had five men who were bound to stick to us.

After a week of weary waiting we succeeded in getting forty-two carriers from Senhor Martins, the Capitão Mor of Tete, a very kind-hearted, hospitable man, who, I am sure, did all he could to assist us. He harangued them all before starting, and told them that they were to go with us wherever we wanted them to go, and not to return to Tete without us ; but I could see that their hearts were not in it from the beginning, and that they had been impressed for the service against their wills. In accordance with the pernicious Portuguese system, these men were all paid a large portion of their wages in advance.

My original plan had been to strike straight from Tete to

the Mazoe, and then follow the river up to its source, but this
I found to be impossible, as there was a rumour that Colonel
Paiva d'Andrada and Manoel Antonio de Souza were making
war on Motoko, a powerful chief living to the south of the
Mazoe, whose territory extends to the junction of that river
with the Ruenya, and nothing would induce the cowardly
Shakundas from Tete to travel anywhere near the scene of
the "guerra de Motoko" (war with Motoko). Under these
circumstances I determined to first work up to somewhere near
the head of the Luia, one of the principal tributaries of the
Mazoe.

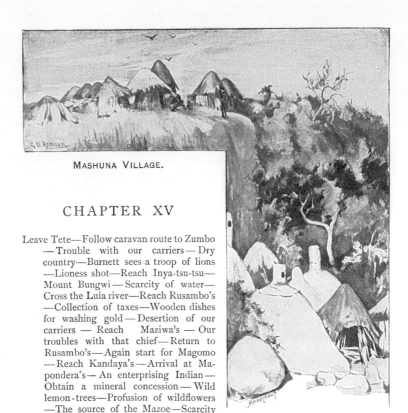

MASHUNA VILLAGE.

CHAPTER XV

IT was on the afternoon of Sunday the 18th of August that
we at last left Tete, and as it was a rainy day we had great
difficulty in getting our carriers to move. They grumbled
about their loads, about their food, and about anything and
everything they could think of.

For the first few days we followed one of the caravan routes
to Zumbo, along the course of the River Mufa. We had an
infinity of trouble with our carriers, and I think there is no
doubt that they did all they could to delay us and annoy us,
hoping that one of us would lose his temper and strike one of
them, when, as Augusto informed us, they would have at once
returned to Tete and accused us of having ill-used them, and
we should have got no more carriers. Knowing this dodge,
we were very careful not to strike one, though we exhausted

the English language in order to find epithets expressive of our
feelings towards them.   The country we travelled through was
exceedingly dry and short of water, which we only found in
holes that had to be dug in the sandy beds of small streams,
often at long distances from one another.   We saw no game
along the footpath, and had not time to go out hunting.

On 24th August we crossed the River Kangudzi in the
morning, and after mid-day reached the little river Kansawa,
where we found a little water in a hole in the sand.   Late in
the afternoon Burnett went out with his rifle and a couple of
boys to look for game, and came upon a lot of lions lying in
the river's bed, scarcely three hundred yards from our camp.
At first he only saw one, a lioness, standing in the river's bed,
and firing at her, shot her through the back, paralysing her in
the hind quarters.   Directly he fired a whole lot of lions that
had been lying on the sand, but out of sight, under the bank,
jumped up and scuttled across the open sandy bed of the
river.   Burnett thought there were about ten of them altogether ;
but probably more than half of them were big cubs.   A fine
old full-grown male brought up the rear, walking slowly across
the sand.   Burnett fired two shots at him, the first of which
struck beneath him, on which he stopped and looked round.
Burnett then fired again, but again missed, when, with a growl
and a whisk of his tail, the lion sprang up the bank and
disappeared.   Burnett then returned to camp, and I took my
rifle and went back with him to the lioness.   We found her
still in the river's bed, but she had dragged herself about
fifteen yards away from where she was first hit.   With her
was a cub about two years old, and Burnett caught sight of
another lion under the bank to her right.   We did not fire at
the cub, which bounded away as soon as it saw us, but at once
finished off the lioness.   We then crossed the river and walked
about a mile in the direction taken by the other lions, but as
the ground was hard and dry, so that their footprints had left
no mark, and the cover soon became thick, we never saw anything more of them, and so returned and skinned the lioness.
I expected that her friends would have come and smelt about
round our camp in the night and roared, but we heard nothing
more of them.

On the following morning we continued our journey, and on 26th August reached Inya-tsu-tsu, a native town situated about three miles to the north of a range of hills called Vunga. I am persuaded that this town is the place marked Vunge on Dr. Livingstone's map, through which he passed on his first journey across Africa, from the west to the east coast, and that the Umrenji river, which passes close to it, is Dr. Livingstone's Molinji. The Makololo escort naturally changed the Um into Mo, and the "r" into "l," and the Doctor adopted their pronunciation. From Inya-tsu-tsu we could see Mount Bungwi, a large hill near the Zambesi, quite plainly ; it lay a little to the east of north by compass, and looked about twenty-five miles distant.

Up to this point we had followed one of the Portuguese trade routes, between Tete and Zumbo, but as we were getting too far north I determined to leave it and strike back towards the Mazoe ; so I now endeavoured to obtain guides direct to the country of Magomo, Eastern Mashunaland, or at any rate to some place in that direction.

Ever since leaving Tete we had travelled through a very dry, burnt-up country, almost destitute of inhabitants, owing principally, I think, to the great scarcity of water, and possibly also to the presence of tse-tse fly, which precludes the possibility of keeping cattle. We had been rising steadily but gradually through an undulating and more or less hilly country always covered with open forest, till, at Inya-tsu-tsu, my aneroids registered one thousand seven hundred feet. The whole country is intersected by numerous dry watercourses, which look exceedingly well on a map, but they were all dry, and it was only here and there that we were enabled to obtain a little water by digging in the sand.

We were delayed a day at Inya-tsu-tsu buying a supply of native meal for our carriers, and during that time we managed to secure a guide to a native chief named Rusambo, living between the Luia and Mazoe rivers. From Inya-tsu-tsu to the source of the Mazoe we travelled through country which, having never before been traversed by a European, we found to be not at all in accordance with the maps published previous to 1890.

Early in the morning of 30th August we crossed the Luia, the main tributary of the Mazoe, from the north, and here a river with a sandy bed about one hundred yards in breadth. There was no running water in it, but plenty of small pools at frequent intervals. We had a lot of trouble to get our carriers beyond this river, as the guides said it was a long way to the nearest water. Finally we started on with our guides without having breakfasted, leaving the Shakundas to follow. After an uphill walk through broken country for nearly five hours under an intensely hot sun we reached Rusambo's town.

It was already late in the afternoon when we arrived at the village, as we had rested several times during the day, Mr. Thomas being ill and weak from fever. Luckily we got a little water by digging in the bed of a creek about half-way, or we should have suffered much more from thirst. As it was, having had nothing to eat since the previous evening, we were very hungry on our arrival at Rusambo's. Borrowing some of the calico which we had paid in advance to our chief guide, and which he had with him, we soon bought a few ground nuts and a couple of fowls, and before dark had a good dinner. About 8 P.M. our carriers all turned up very footsore and sulky. I found that we had ascended one thousand feet in the course of the day after crossing the Luia river.

On the following day we remained at Rusambo's buying provisions. I found on inquiry that three white Portuguese had visited this part of the country within the memory of Rusambo, but I met no chief beyond him who had ever seen a Portuguese. When I asked him if he had given his country to the Portuguese he said that he had submitted to Ignacio Jesus de Xavier, the black Capitão Mor of Baroma, in order to live, and that he now paid him an annual tribute in corn and gold dust. This year, 1889, was the third in which he had paid tribute. Augusto told us that Rusambo's country had been given to Ignacio Jesus de Xavier as a praço by the Portuguese Government, on the usual terms ; that is to say, in consideration of the payment of an annual rental, and no questions asked as to the amount of taxes he exacted from the natives. I asked Augusto what would happen should Rusambo, or any native chief in a similar position, refuse to pay up ; and he replied that Colonel Ignacio, as he called him, was able to enforce payment, as he had a strong force of well-armed men in his service, who would either get the corn and gold dust required, or in default take women and children.   This year Rusambo's people had had an abundant harvest, and the old chief had a fine lot of fat fowls.   He is the only African native I have ever seen who fed his fowls.   Every night they were all driven into a large wattle and daub hutch, and morning and evening they received an allowance of grain.

Hanging up in the kraal, one to each hut, were the wooden dishes in which the women wash alluvial gold.   These dishes were all square with rounded corners, and as all the other wooden pans I saw for gold washing in many other kraals in the Mazoe valley were of exactly the same pattern, and as all their other household utensils are round, these wooden pans may possibly retain the form of the original pans for gold washing introduced into South-Eastern Africa by the gold-seeking nations of the ancient world in very remote times.

On 1st September we found that twenty-nine of our forty-two carriers from Tete had decamped during the night.   Fear of punishment by the Portuguese authorities had alone restrained the others ; but I did not expect they would go many days farther with us, as they were such a miserable lot that although there was no earthly cause for alarm, I felt pretty sure that their fear of the unknown country and unknown people on ahead would soon outweigh their fear of deserting us and running the risk of punishment at Tete.   We at once set to work collecting porters from the surrounding villages, and by the evening had enlisted twenty-two to carry twenty-two loads for liberal payment as far as Maziwa's, a chief whose town is three days' journey (for men carrying loads) from here.   The remaining loads we left in charge of Rusambo.

On 5th September, after having travelled through a very dry stony country, and passed the villages of two miserable famine-stricken chiefs, Chibonga and Matopi, we reached Maziwa's.

During the last few days we had shot a little game and seen fresh rhinoceros tracks, and near Maziwa's village we saw much spoor of elands, Burchell's zebras, sable antelopes, koo-

doos, etc. We camped at the foot of the hill on which Maziwa's
village was situated, but there were two or three more villages
about, all subject to the same chief and all perched on the
summits of high rocky hills. The people here had very little
food to sell, and appeared very poor and famine-stricken.
Maziwa is an independent chief on a very small scale, being
beyond Portuguese influence, either direct or indirect. Yet
this is scarcely a correct statement, as he has been raided upon
by one of the black Capitão Mors from the north, who are
supposed to be subject to the Portuguese.

At this place we had a lot of trouble. In the first place
Rusambo's men, having fulfilled their bargain, returned home,
and we were left with twenty-two loads for which we wanted
carriers, whom I thought we should have obtained from Maziwa
without difficulty. However, Maziwa turned out to be singularly
avaricious and grasping, even for a Kafir, and I never knew a
Kafir yet, whose mind has been uninfluenced by contact with
Europeans, who, when the opportunity presented itself, failed
to make a large profit out of another man's necessity.
Believing he had got us in a fix, Maziwa thought he would be
able not only to skin us, but to pick the flesh from our bones,
figuratively speaking. He demanded ten yards of calico per
man for carrying our loads a distance of less than twenty
miles, and wanted a large present for himself into the bargain.
It was impossible to comply with this exorbitant demand, as,
had we done so, the next petty chief, when he learned what
Maziwa had screwed out of us, would have wanted at least as
much to put us a short distance farther on our journey, and in
this way in a very short time we should have been left without
any goods at all. During the day I did a lot of talking to
Maziwa ; but he remained obdurate, and was deaf to all argument, persuasion, sarcasm, invective, and insult, for he thought
we were in his power and would have to agree to his terms,
however exorbitant. One of his remarks was, that an elephant
had come and died in his country, and he and his people
would fatten on the carcase.

In the evening, our thrice-accursed Shakundas from Tete,
who were probably in communication with Maziwa, thinking
that now we were in a mess they would be able to make

capital out of our misfortunes, came up in a body and demanded ten yards of calico per man to carry their loads two days' journey farther, threatening to leave in the night if we did not comply with their request. Though boiling over with indignation we were obliged to talk quietly with them, and argue and temporise, for if these fourteen men had left us, *plantés là*, with only Augusto and five boys, we could never have removed the greater part of our thirty-seven loads, and the expedition would have come to an end. After much discussion we gave the Shakundas each a common shirt, and they then promised to carry our goods as far as we wanted to go.

The next morning Maziwa came down to our camp with a good many of his tribe, but we found him even more unreasonable than he had been the previous day, and after a short and stormy interview he again retired to his kraal. I now resolved to destroy a portion of our goods, and to push on without Maziwa's aid. With the fourteen Shakundas and our five boys (three from Quillimani and Augusto's two), we had nineteen carriers for thirty-seven loads. I now went through everything and made up nineteen loads of what we most required, and then collected the remaining things, principally trading goods and provisions, about seven hundredweights altogether, into an immense heap. We then collected large quantities of fuel and set the pyre alight. It seemed a pity to sacrifice goods that had been carried so far, but it was much better than submitting to the extortions of a miserable savage. During this operation Maziwa and his greedy clansmen stood looking on from the hill, and the old chief, as he saw the calico and blankets which he coveted being licked up and destroyed by the flames, lost all his self-possession, and declaimed loudly against us from his coign of vantage. I did not understand him, but Augusto told us that he said we were his enemies, and that every one was his enemy who came from Tete ; that if he had men enough he would kill us and seize our goods, and finally threatened that if we went on he would follow and raise the country on us. As we had four good breech-loading rifles, and all our Shakundas were armed with muskets belonging to Senhor Martins, we knew we could afford to laugh at Maziwa's threats, especially as the moon was just at the full ; but our craven crew of Shakundas were actually so frightened, that they began to get their things together, declaring their intention of going off in the night.   I now saw that it would be impossible to get these men any farther, and so resolved to return with them as far as Rusambo's, and there dismiss them from my service, and then endeavour to obtain men again from Rusambo, and take a different route up the valley of the Luia, passing to the north of Maziwa's.   As the Shakundas were delighted at the idea of going back to Rusambo's, and thought I would then return to Tete with them, I easily persuaded them to wait until the following morning, pointing out to them Maziwa's weakness and evident fear of us.   We, however, kept watch all night to see that they did not bolt and leave us alone with the remaining goods, and at daylight we started on the return journey to Rusambo's, which we reached on 10th September.

On the following morning I told our Shakundas to return to their Portuguese masters on the Zambesi, as I had had enough of them, and all but one were only too glad to avail themselves of the opportunity. This one boy, as he begged to be allowed to remain with us, and as he had always been the most willing of the lot, I re-engaged ; he accompanied us throughout the trip, and I have never had a better boy in my service than he proved himself to be.

I do not think that the natives of South-East Africa who have been accustomed to the Portuguese like working for Englishmen ; we are too energetic for them.   Many of my countrymen believe that the natives despise the Portuguese, and admire the superior strength and energy of North Europeans, but I think there is a good deal of misconception in this matter.   Doubtless the descendants of the brave and warlike tribes of Zulu stock despise effeminacy and admire manliness, but it is my opinion that the more mean-spirited and cowardly tribes reverence nothing but wealth, and when they see an Englishman, Scotsman, German, or Swede—for all North Europeans I have observed have the same pride of a dominant race, that forbids them to show any sign of effeminacy before an inferior people—walking in the hot sun, bare-armed and often bare-legged, carrying his own rifle and running after game, they think he only does so because he is poor and cannot afford to pay men to hunt for him, and porters to carry him in a palanquin, sheltered from the heat of the sun by an awning or an umbrella ; and they despise him accordingly and contrast him unfavourably with the more effeminate and luxurious Portuguese, whom they respect more than the Englishman, because they think he is rich enough to afford comforts which the latter cannot command.

On making careful inquiries I found that I could take another route to " Magomo " by the kraals of Dombo Chena, and Kandaya, and after reducing the number of loads as much as possible—leaving the remaining goods in Rusambo's charge until our return — I was able to hire porters as far as Kandaya's.

On the 14th of September we again started, and leaving Maziwa's to the south-west, reached Dombo Chena's, on the little river Umkaradzi, on the 18th. We saw a great many quartz reefs on the upper course of the Umkaradzi, some of which Mr. Thomas liked the look of very much. The natives of the little village of Dombo Chena had done a great deal of work along the river washing for alluvial gold, but Mr. Thomas did not think it would prove payable for white men. Besides these recent workings we also found traces of much work having been done in ancient times in search of gold, which shows that this little river must have been known as a gold-producing stream for a very long time.

Near the head of the Umkaradzi valley stands a lofty mountain, a splendid landmark for many miles round. The range of hills from which this peak rises is called Fura by the natives, but as we were now in a country in dispute between the British and Portuguese, and as I could not discover from the natives that any white subject of Portugal had ever travelled in this district, I had what some people will call the impertinence to name it Mount Darwin, after that illustrious Englishman whose far-reaching theories—logical conclusions based upon an enormous mass of incontrovertible facts—have revolutionised modern thought, and destroyed for ever many old beliefs that had held men's minds in thrall for centuries.

About five miles beyond Dombo Chena's we crossed the Umfuri river, a tributary of the Luia. The Umfuri had plenty of water in it, and was the first river we had seen for some time that was a river in anything but the name. About seven miles beyond the Umfuri we reached a miserable little native village, and were surprised to find that this was the abode of the chief Kandaya. On examination we found that the village consisted of nine very small and villainously ill-constructed huts, placed on the side of a small hill, and unenclosed by any kind of fence. These miserable savages seemed to have very little food of any kind, and neither cattle nor goats, their sole riches in the way of live stock being represented by a few fowls, and one gaunt hungry-looking dog. Kandaya, the wretched starveling chief, said he would try to get his people to carry our loads on to Mapondera's, but protested that he did not know their hearts. I gave him a present of a shirt and four yards of calico, and also some meat of a reed-buck I had shot in the morning. He did not seem at all thankful, retaining the same gloomy, discontented expression of countenance that he had worn when he first put in an appearance. He evidently looked upon life as a very poor business.

A few hundred yards from Kandaya's village stood a high and conspicuous cone-shaped hill, called by the natives Tchakari. This name I altered to Mount Thackeray, as a tribute to the memory of the immortal novelist, whose genius has so often enabled me to escape, for the time being, from my surroundings ; to forget the filthy, soulless, sordid, mean, and vermin-swarming savages amongst whom I actually was, and to live again, in spirit at least, amongst the dwellers in Vanity Fair.

On the evening of our arrival at Kandaya's town all the villagers came down to our camp, bringing a drum with them, and got up a dance, our own men joining in. They made a most diabolical noise, shouting and beating on the drum, and kept it up till nearly midnight, when I thought it time to stop the entertainment. The dancing itself was monotonous and uninteresting in the extreme. The mass of the performers stood in a ring, shouting and clapping their hands, and two or three kept continually advancing slowly into the ring and then retiring. There seemed to be no step, and there was no graceful movement of the arms.   Noise appeared to be the great end and aim of the whole performance, and the drum was beaten with great vigour and without the least cessation. The entire population of the village assisted at this dance—men, women, and children ; and many of the women had children slung on their backs.

On the following morning we got away with seven women carriers and four men, besides a few children, and after this had no further difficulty.   As we were now on the eastern slopes of Mashunaland, the country became better watered as we proceeded, and that night we slept amongst the old familiar mahobo-hobo forests at the head of one of the tributaries of the Umfuri, and at an elevation of over four thousand feet above sea-level.

On 22nd September we reached the village of Temaringa, who is a brother of Mapondera, the chief of the Makori-kori tribe, living between the Mazoe and Luia rivers.   After explaining our business to him he agreed to accompany us to Inyota, his brother's residence.

On 25th September we reached Inyota, where all the people knew me by name, and many of them personally, as in former years I had often shot elands and other game within sight of Mount Inyota.   We here found an enterprising Indian, Vallji Mussagi by name, trading gold dust.   He had his wife with him, a native woman, and had built a little shanty for himself in Mapondera's kraal.   He had a Portuguese flag with him, which Augusto said had been given him by the Governor of Tete to carry about with him.   From this man we learned that Colonel Paiva d'Andrada, and Manoel Antonio de Souza, had established a military post of black soldiers at Mangwendi's town, from whence they would proceed across the high plateau to Inyamwenda's and Lo Magondi's, where they would meet Lieutenant Cordon from the Zambesi, who in his turn had established military posts on the Lower Sanyati.   All the chiefs in Mashunaland, he told us, had given in their submission to Colonel d'Andrada, and hoisted the flag of Portugal in their kraals. He also told us that he had heard that Lieutenant Cordon had been attacked by the Matabili, whom he had driven off with great slaughter.   In this report there was, however, no truth.

MAPONDERA, A CHIEF OF THE MAKORI-KORI.

(Drawn from a Photograph by Mr. FRANCEYS, of Salisbury, Mashunaland.)

After hearing all this news I called Mapondera and Temaringa into Mussagi's house, and had no difficulty in obtaining
a mineral concession from them, and I also got them to sign a
paper in his presence, to the effect that they were entirely
independent and had never paid tribute either directly to the
Portuguese Government, or indirectly to any Capitão Mor holding office under the Portuguese Government ; and further, that
they had never yet seen a white Portuguese, the only white
men they had ever seen being Englishmen coming from the
west—Mr. Walter Montagu Kerr in 1884, and Mr. Cherry, a
short time before my visit, in 1889.   Our interpreter, Augusto
Melitão de Souza, attached his signature as witness to these
documents.   Vallji Mussagi left on the following day for Tete,
and of course informed the Governor of what I had done
immediately on his arrival.

Having now satisfactorily concluded my business, I determined to settle definitely the actual source of the Mazoe,
which I knew was very inaccurately laid down on all previously
published maps.   Mr. Thomas being very weak from repeated
attacks of fever, I left him with Augusto at Mapondera's, and
with Burnett started on 26th September for the Mazoe.   We
first crossed the Umrodzi at its junction with the Wainji, from
where a walk of about two miles brought us to the banks of the
Mazoe.   The river is here very narrow, but the water is deep,
running with a slow sluggish current.

We found a great many lemon-trees growing just on the
water's edge, many of them loaded with fruit.   These lemons
were large and thick-skinned, and not so sour as the lemons
one gets in England, and they seemed to me quite as good as
any lemons I have seen growing in the Transvaal, even on
farms where the trees are carefully tended and manured every
year ; and, as the lemon-trees on the Mazoe have grown wild
and untended in the wilderness for ages and ages, they ought
to improve with cultivation.   The natives have no tradition
as to how the lemon-trees were introduced, but that there is a
connection between them and the ancient gold-workings seems
certain, for wherever lemon-trees grow, old gold-workings will
invariably be found in the neighbourhood.   They may have
been introduced by the Portuguese two or three centuries ago,

or they may date back to much more ancient times, when South-Eastern Africa was visited by the trading peoples of Asia and Arabia in search of gold.

On the following morning we walked on along the Mazoe, and in two hours reached its junction with the Tataguru. Here the Mazoe runs from the south through a gap in a high range of hills. The country near the junction of the Mazoe and Tataguru rivers we found to be literally carpeted[1] with a profusion of wildflowers, all of the most exquisitely delicate shades of colour, pale mauve, pink, and lilac predominating, though yellow and white flowers were scattered amongst them too, and there was one little gem of a rich deep red. These flowers, though many of them were very beautiful, had nothing tropical in their appearance, but all looked as if they might grow in the open air in an English garden ; as indeed no doubt they would, for this country, though by its geographical position it is well within the tropics, is really by reason of its altitude a temperate country, with the climate of Southern Europe.

Shortly after getting through a gap in the hills we came to another small tributary stream running into the Mazoe, and made a halt for breakfast. As we were now entirely out of food for ourselves and boys, and as we could see a native town on the side of a hill at no great distance, we sent a couple of our Kafirs to try to buy some meal and rice. The Mazoe had now become very small, little more than a deep ditch, in fact, and it was evident that its source could not be at any very great distance, so Burnett and I decided to leave the remainder of our Kafirs, who were all bad walkers, or pretended to be so, and push on to the head of the river by ourselves. Three hours later we stood at the actual source of the Mazoe. We found that as a river the Mazoe took its rise in two deep black pools, surrounded and overshadowed by thick-foliaged trees, the water being twelve or fifteen feet below the level of the banks. But above these pools there is a swamp, extending for about a mile, at the head of which stands a cluster of dark-leaved evergreen trees, and amongst these trees the actual spring of the Mazoe may be said to be.

[1] End of September 1889.

Into one of the deep pools I have spoken of as being the commencement of the actual river, a small rill of water, draining out of the marsh, falls, forming a tiny waterfall of twelve or fifteen feet in height. The Mazoe does not take its rise on the top of the high open downs of Mashunaland like the Manyami, the Sabi, the Sanyati, etc., but in a marsh just below the high level, its source being enclosed in low ridges, through which the water must percolate from the higher ground. After a rest we started back for camp, which we reached just before sundown, having done over eight hours' very fast walking during the day. We found that our boys had bought a little rice and pogo meal, but having no meat we did not sit down to a very sumptuous repast. Since leaving Mapondera's we had seen no game, with the exception of a few reed-bucks, which were very wild and unapproachable.

GRANITE BOULDER, MASHUNALAND.
(From a Photograph by Mr. E. A. MAUND.)

CHAPTER XVI

HAVING traced the Mazoe to its source (in the neighbourhood
of which I had often been in former years, without, however,
knowing its exact position), I determined to revisit Mount
Hampden on the Gwibi, in order to complete my compass
surveys from the east and the west.

Ascending the little river Dasuru, we reached the Gwibi,
after a walk of about three and a half hours. Leaving Burnett
and the Kafirs there, I then climbed Mount Hampden and
took some compass bearings from trees, as the hill itself being
rich in ironstone, no readings could be relied upon that were
taken near the ground. Mount Hampden, which has now
become a household word in Mashunaland, and which in
1890 was named as the goal of the British South Africa
Company's expedition to that country, had been familiar to me
ever since 1878, and many a time in 1883, 1885, and 1887
had I climbed its sides in order to look for ostriches, elands,
and other game on the plains by which it is surrounded. The
hill itself is about five hundred feet in height ; but, standing as
it does on the eastern edge of the Mashuna plateau, and being
all by itself in the midst of open downs, it forms an excellent
landmark, and from its summit, which must once have been
the site of a native town (as it is surrounded by a stone wall
about four feet in height), a splendid view is obtainable, extend-

ing to the Umvukwi hills to the north-west, and over the whole of the Mazoe valley as far as Mount Inyota to the north-east. Most of the Kafirs know no name for this hill, though Inyamwenda's people call it Si-kwi, so in 1880, in a sketch map which I sent to the Royal Geographical Society, I called it Mount Hampden, naming it after that good Englishman, John Hampden, who struggled so manfully for, and eventually gave his life in defence of, the liberties of his countrymen in those evil days when the second prince of the House of Stuart reigned in England.

After leaving Mount Hampden we made for the head of the Umrodzi, which river we followed down to its junction with the Gurumapudzi ; and then passing close beneath the hill from which Wata and his people were driven by the Matabili in 1868, and crossing the Wainji and the Sawi, two fair-sized rivers, and several other strong running streams, got back to Inyota on 1st October.

In the valley of the Umrodzi, as in the valley of the Mazoe, I noticed a wonderful profusion of wildflowers, one a very lovely species that I had never seen before, and which I only saw along the Umrodzi for a space of about two miles, where, however, it was plentiful. It was not large or imposing, but singularly beautiful. From each little plant half-a-dozen long trumpet-shaped flowers about three inches in length, and of a delicate creamy-white colour, shot up, and from each of these flowers two or three long club-headed pistils of a dark magenta protruded, rearing themselves in their turn a couple of inches above the flowers. These had a most sweet and delicate scent, which is wanting in most flowers growing on the ground in South Africa.

As I was anxious to follow the course of the Mazoe as much as possible on our return journey to Tete, and at the same time wished to get some specimens of quartz from the reefs on the Umkaradzi, I sent Mr. Thomas back with Augusto and three of our six boys by the route by which we had come, passing Dombo Chena, whilst Burnett and I, with the other three boys, struck down to the Mazoe from Temaringa's kraal. Thomas and Augusto were to wait for us at Rusambo's. On the 5th of October we parted company.

Where Burnett and I struck the Mazoe we found it a good-sized river with large deep pools of water, and a strong running stream between the pools. We then followed the Mazoe for four days, and found its general course to be east and west. We did not see much game along its banks, but sufficient to enable us to keep ourselves in meat.

On 7th October we crossed the Inyagui, a large river flowing from the south, which at its junction with the Mazoe is the bigger river of the two. The Inyagui, or Inyagurukadzi, as it is sometimes called, rises near Mangwendi's village, fifty miles south-east of Mount Hampden, and drains a large extent of country. Even at the end of the dry season it carries to the Mazoe a large body of swiftly-running water, which rushes over a pebbly bed amongst great boulders of rock, and in the rainy season it must become a formidable torrent, impossible to cross. Just below the junction of the Mazoe and the Inyagui we shot a very large old hippopotamus bull. We were here accompanied by a lot of natives, who indeed had guided us to the pool where we found the hippo. Burnett and I were both shooting with Gibb's Metford 450-bore rifles, and between us had only one solid bullet, all the others being expanding. Burnett first fired at the hippo, and hit him in the back of the head, but the hollow bullet must have expanded in the muscles of the neck, and did not penetrate the skull. After this the old bull became wary, and it was some time before he gave another chance ; but presently, having crossed the river below the pool, and gone round to the other bank, I got a good shot at the side of his head, and hit him with my one long solid 540-grain bullet somewhere about the ear. This shot partially stunned him, but it could not have touched his brain, or of course it would have killed him instantly. However, it gave him a very severe shock, as for some minutes after being hit he rolled about on the top of the water, often opening his huge jaws to their fullest extent, and dyeing the waves, into which he lashed the pool, with the blood which he blew from his mouth and nostrils. We thought he was dying, and did not fire at him again, but presently he began to recover from the effects of the wound, and went under water, reappearing almost immediately, however, but soon going down again and not showing himself for some time. At last he reappeared near Burnett, and he got a good steady shot, and put an expanding bullet just under his ear, and I saw by the way he just sank away that the bullet had reached his brain and killed him on the spot. It was then late in the day, so that he did not come up till the night, but we found him floating the next morning. As he was, however, as lean as a crow, and quite uneatable for us, we gave him to the natives just as he was, and continued our journey. On the following day we left the Mazoe and made for Chibonga's, which we reached on 10th October, having travelled through a very dry, dreary, and uninteresting country. The next morning we walked over to Rusambo's, where we rejoined Mr. Thomas and Augusto.

I now determined to return to the Mazoe and follow that river down to its junction with the Ruenya, which point I knew was not very far distant from Tete ; so, obtaining a guide from Rusambo to a village called Diwa or Zongoro, we started on the afternoon of 14th October, but did not reach the village that evening. On the following day we reached Zongoro early, and had breakfast there. We here met a black man named João (pronounced Jwong), who was a nephew of the Capitão Mor of this district. This man had been educated at Tete and spoke Portuguese fluently. As he was just starting for his own town near the junction of the Luia and Mazoe rivers, and asked us to accompany him, we gladly did so, and on the following day about noon arrived there. All this part of the country, lying in the angle between the Luia and Mazoe rivers, is broken and hilly, very dry and barren, water being very scarce and bad.

João's town was well built and very strongly stockaded. He gave us a large roomy shed in which to sleep and put our things. On our way here we passed the pit where his people obtained water. It was a well quite thirty feet in depth, dug in the bed of a dry creek, and it took us exactly fifty minutes to walk from this well to the village. Even at the bottom of the well there was very little water, and it had to be ladled out in cupfuls. Altogether it must have been a four or five hours' job for the women every day to walk to the well, get their pots full of water, and carry them home again. The name of João's village was Maramba. From this village we got guides to Sanyara's, who is a sister of João, and after a six hours' walk, the greater part of which we did by moonlight, because of the absence of water, and in order to escape the mid-day heat, which was now intense, reached the Mazoe on the morning of 18th October.   The Mazoe had now become a large sand river with a bed fully three hundred yards in breadth, down which meandered a tiny stream in a vast expanse of sand—a mere dribblet of water only a few yards broad and a few inches in depth. The thirsty sand had swallowed almost the whole of the generous stream which fills the bed of the river from bank to bank some fifty miles higher up its course.   In Cape Town I had been gravely informed that the Mazoe was navigable for a distance of eighty miles above its junction with the Ruenya, but in no part of its lower course, after it has become a broad sand river, could the smallest of Rob Roy canoes ever built be floated during the dry season.   In the evening we reached Sanyara's village, having had to walk during the last three hours (as the banks of the river were covered with dense jungle and there was no footpath) down the bed of the river, in soft yielding sand, and under a terrifically hot sun during the first hour.   Sanyara received us very kindly and gave us a nice clean hut, and mats to sleep on.   She had once been married to a Portuguese, by whom she had two children who were living with her at the time of our visit : two pretty little girls with fine dark eyes, about eight and ten years of age respectively.

The following morning we started early and crossed the Luia almost immediately, just at its junction with the Mazoe, which here runs to the north-east—still an immense sand river, with a small thread of water running above the sand.   The bed of the Luia was also about three hundred yards broad, but perfectly dry.   From this point until we reached the Ruenya we had to walk all down the soft sandy bed of the Mazoe, and very trying it was in the intense heat, especially to poor Mr. Thomas, who was weak from repeated attacks of fever.   We saw a great deal of lion spoor in the bed of the river, usually the spoors of several together, so there was doubtless a good deal of game about.   Indeed every living animal in the surrounding country must of necessity have been in the vicinity of the river in order to get water.

The day before reaching the Ruenya, and just at a time when I had left the bed of the river and gone into the bush to look for a bush-buck, Burnett and Thomas came upon five lions lying on the hot sand near the water. There was a fine male amongst them, but they saw the string of men a long way off, on the open sand, and, getting up, retreated slowly into the reeds and bush growing on the river's bank. Burnett fired a couple of long shots at them, but without effect. They had killed a monkey and were lying round it on the sand, but had not commenced to eat it. By the spoors, Burnett said, they had apparently chased the monkey, and rushed upon it from different directions, perhaps just for a bit of sport, as they were coming down to drink.

On the following morning we reached the Ruenya, down whose bed even at this season of the year a fine stream of water, sixty to eighty yards broad and three feet in depth, rushes swiftly along, in a channel which it has cut for itself through a mass of hard rock. In the rainy season this river Ruenya must bring down a very large body of water, as it ultimately receives the whole of the waters of the countless perennial streams which drain Eastern Mashunaland. About a mile below the junction of the Mazoe and Ruenya we came upon five hippopotami in a deep narrow pool. Here there were a lot of natives camped who had killed a young hippo the previous day, or rather found it dead, as they said they had wounded it in the night some time ago, and found it dead on the day before our visit. As we still had some of João's and Sanyara's men with us, who had been sent by their master and mistress to show us the hippos in the Ruenya, and as the large number of natives who had secured the one animal were clamorous for more, Burnett and I set to and killed the four big animals in the pool whilst our breakfast was being prepared. There was then only a small calf left, which we were anxious to kill for meat for ourselves. However, the little animal was very wary, and it was not until after breakfast that I managed to kill it. Such wholesale destruction seems cruel, but all the meat was really required, as the people in this district were very short of food at the time of our visit. It would have been useless to spare the calf, as it was too young to shift for itself.

One of these hippos, an immense bull, was very cunning, and would not show his head at all, but only just raised his great broad snout above the surface to breathe. I got upon a mass of rocks well above the water, and when he next executed this manœuvre put a bullet into his nose, which, as we afterwards found out, went right into his nostril. On this he withdrew his nose very quickly, and by the commotion he made beneath the water it was evident that he was very much disturbed ; and he must have been in a fury, for he very soon appeared on the surface, showing his whole head and shoulders, and dragging up from the bottom one of his dead fellows, which he held firmly in his jaws by the hind leg. Burnett and I at once saluted him with two bullets, which both hit him, and caused him to disappear. He almost immediately came up again, however, still holding the dead hippo firmly by the hind leg. Again we gave him two bullets in the head, quickly followed by two more, as he was floundering about in his death struggles, when both animals sank together, the one as dead as the other. Presently from the top of a rock we could see two dark objects lying together at the bottom of the beautifully clear water, which, although the Kafirs said they were two rocks, ultimately turned out to be the two dead hippos. After about three and a half hours one of the animals first shot came to the surface, and as none of the Kafirs would go in to fetch it ashore, I swam in myself, and climbing on to the carcase, paddled it ashore with my hands. I think it is very foolish doing this sort of thing in a river full of crocodiles, especially in hot weather, when the water is warm, but one cannot help it, if only to show the natives that a white man will do what they dare not attempt.

Soon after this a portion of the smaller of the two animals that were lying together, and which turned out to be a young bull, appeared, and I again swam in and attached a strong bark rope to one of its legs. This time some of the Kafirs followed me. On hauling on the rope we found, however, that its one hind leg was still fast in the jaws of the big bull, and it was only after a considerable amount of pulling that we got the two animals separated. This story sounds like a traveller's tale, but it is nevertheless true, and the incident was witnessed, and

WOUNDED HIPPOPOTAMUS ATTACKING THE CARCASE OF ONE PREVIOUSLY SHOT.

"And he must have been in a fury, for he very soon appeared on the surface, showing his whole head and shoulders, and dragging up from the bottom one of his dead fellows, which he held firmly in his jaws by the hind leg."

can be attested to by my companions.   In his rage and fury
the old bull must have attacked the first thing he came across,
which happened to be the body of his former friend and
companion.   Strange to relate, although the four hippos all
came up within four hours of the time they were shot, the
carcase of the little calf did not float until the next day, fully
twenty-four hours after it was shot.   I cannot account for this,
unless it had got jammed under a rock, which prevented its
rising until it became very buoyant.

In the afternoon I walked up to the junction of the
Ruenya and Mazoe rivers to take some compass bearings.
Just at the junction of the rivers the bed of the Ruenya is
about one hundred and fifty yards broad, that of the Mazoe at
least three hundred.   But whereas the Ruenya, even at the
time of year when I saw it, which was towards the end of
a very dry season, brought down a fine stream of water about
sixty yards wide and several feet in depth, rushing like an
Alpine torrent amongst great masses of rock, in the Mazoe
there was only a very meagre stream of water a few yards in
breadth and a few inches in depth.   Just at the junction of
the two rivers there is a small fall in the Ruenya, and below
this fall the river is narrowed into a deep channel only a few
yards in breadth, which it has cut for itself through a solid
mass of rock, and through which the water rushes at a terrific
pace.   The place reminded me of Kariba Gorge, on the Upper
Zambesi, though, of course, everything is here on a much
smaller scale.   The Ruenya soon opens out again into a
channel sixty to eighty yards wide, always running very swiftly
between terraces of rock.   It was in a deep reach of the river,
about a mile below the mouth of the Mazoe, that we found and
shot the hippo.

Just before going up the river to take my compass bearings,
I had been standing alongside of Burnett, who was fishing,
when he caught a fine tiger-fish.   He was playing this fish,
when it was seized and bitten in two just behind the gills by a
large flat-headed fish, which in the water looked like a South
African barbel, except that it was much more active.   It bit
the tiger-fish clean in two just behind the gills without pulling
on the line at all, and I left Burnett preparing a bait to catch

the robber.   When I came back, he said to me, " Oh, I say, I
caught that fish, and Steve Thomas says it's a shark."   I
asked where it was, and was told that the Kafirs had got it,
but that Thomas had secured the liver.   However, the head
was still intact, and it certainly looked like that of a small
shark, with a semicircular mouth underneath and about three
inches from the end of the broad flat head.   As far as I
remember, this mouth was armed with only one row of small
sharp teeth.   Thomas said that as a young man he had served
in whaling ships in the southern seas, and that this fish was
nothing else but a small shark, with a forked tail and back fin
complete.   We ate the liver, which certainly was good.   This
fish was about three and a half feet long.   Augusto said he
knew it well, and that the species is common in the Zambesi
at Tete.   I daresay this fish is known to science, but if not, I
see no reason why a race of sharks should not have become
gradually suited to live in the tidal waters of the Lower
Zambesi, and ultimately in the fresh water of the upper river,
only modified in size to suit their surroundings.   From
the sea to the Kuroa Basa rapids on the Zambesi, and
to that part of the Lower Ruenya where we shot the hippopotami, there is no barrier of any kind that would prevent a
fish from swimming up from the ocean.   I never heard of
these shark-like fish in the Zambesi above the Victoria Falls,
and do not believe that they exist there.

From the junction of the Mazoe and Ruenya rivers it took us
ten hours' actual walking, following the course of the latter river,
to the Zambesi, which we reached on 23rd October, and on the
following day we got into Tete in time for breakfast with Father
Courtois, by whom I was informed that I would meet with a bad
reception from Senhor Alpuina, the Governor ; and indeed I expected nothing else, as I knew that Vallji Mussagi must have informed him of the interview I had had with the Makori-kori chiefs,
and their repudiation of Portuguese jurisdiction in their territory.

On 25th October I called upon the Governor of Tete, Mr.
Teixeira accompanying me as interpreter.   Our interview was
a very stormy one, but too long to relate in detail.   He accused
me of being an agent of the British Government, and I do not
think he ever fully believed my assertion that I could lay no

claim to that honour.   He then said, " You have a document
signed by a native chief, saying that he is independent of the
Portuguese Government, and that the only white men who have
ever been in his country are Englishmen.   I demand that
document."   To this I replied that I had obtained a mineral
concession and a declaration of independence from certain
native chiefs, but that as the country in question was a long way
beyond Portuguese territory he had no right to ask me for the
document, and that I would not surrender it to him.   On this
he said he would have me arrested and sent to Mozambique,
and when Mr. Teixeira assured him that the document in
question was a mineral and not a territorial concession, he not
unnaturally asked to be allowed to see it.   However, I did not
care about putting my concession in the hands of a Portuguese
official, especially as the door was guarded by black soldiers, so
I said that I would let him have a copy, which should be made
out in the presence of Father Courtois, the French priest, who
would be able to certify that it was a true copy, and to this the
Governor agreed.   In the course of this interview, when I
stated that both Mapondera and Temaringa had in the presence
of Vallji Mussagi and Augusto denied the Portuguese claim to
jurisdiction in their country, Senhor Alpuina said very angrily,
" In twelve days' time (from 25th October) they will have
taken the Portuguese flag," meaning that, as I had already
heard, an expedition under a Portuguese officer, and supported
by Ignacio Jesus de Xavier, had already started for Inyota, in
order to coerce the Makori-kori chiefs into accepting the
Portuguese flag.   Such annexations are, however, unworthy of
serious consideration.   For some reason or other this expedition does not appear to have reached Inyota.

As soon as my interview with the Governor of Tete was
over, I at once made out a copy of the mineral concession I
had obtained from Mapondera in the presence of Father
Courtois, inserting the obnoxious clause relative to the independence of that chief at the end.   With this document I
returned to the Residency in the afternoon, but was informed
by the Governor's secretary that I could not see Senhor
Alpuina, as he was down with bilious fever.   I then handed
in the paper, and heard nothing more about the matter, as

the Governor remained confined to his bed until after I had
left Tete.

I will here put it on record that personally I have never
experienced anything but kindness at the hands of the Portuguese traders and others whom I have met with on the Zambesi.
Of course it is impossible for Englishmen and Portuguese
officials to regard certain questions now arising in South-East
Africa from the same point of view, yet I cannot complain of
any injustice or ill-treatment at their hands.

We remained in Tete until 29th October, and were on very
friendly terms with the principal residents.   Senhor Martins,
the Capitão Mor, expressed great indignation when I told him
how our carriers had behaved, and was, I am sure, perfectly
sincere.   He succeeded in making several of them restore the
calico they had received as wages in advance before leaving
Tete, and said that he would have some of them flogged if I
liked ; but having succeeded in my object in spite of them, my
resentment had cooled, and I begged him to do nothing further
in the matter.

One day Burnett and I went to breakfast with this most
hospitable Lusitanian, who is a right good fellow, though bitterly
opposed to the acquisition of any territory by the British in
South-East Africa.   It being Sunday, Senhor Martins thought
it would be the correct thing to make the two Englishmen
drunk.   He first plied us with wine, and then ordered a case
of beer and several flasks of Hollands gin.   Several of the
inhabitants of Tete dropped in, and every one drank as much as
he liked, and they all liked to drink a good deal.   Although
not a teetotaler, I am by habit a very abstemious man, and
practically a total abstainer.   I drank as little as possible, as
did also Burnett, but for the honour of our country we were
obliged to drink a good deal more than we wanted.   About
eleven o'clock a coloured gentleman who had formerly been
the schoolmaster of Tete was carried home crying drunk, and
soon afterwards our hospitable entertainer, who had lately lost
his wife, got into a very lachrymose condition.   We thought
this a good opportunity to get away, but he then rallied and
insisted upon going with us to the house we had hired, and
here of course we had to do our best to return his hospitality.

Presently, to our dismay, the schoolmaster again rolled up, now intensely polite, and constantly bowing and saying "Tank you." He was a weak-headed man, however, and soon again became melancholy, and at last fell backwards over the little parapet that surrounded our house, and a recumbent position just at that time suiting him better than any other, he lay where he fell until some friends presently removed him.   Altogether, although no rain fell, this was a very wet Sunday, though I think the two Englishmen came very well through the ordeal.

On 29th October we bade adieu to Tete, and in the afternoon passed the mouth of the Ruenya.   Before leaving I called upon Senhor Alpuina, the Governor, but, as I have said before, was unable to see him.   For this return journey down the Zambesi we hired a boat and crew from Senhor Anakulete Nunes, who had boarded us during our stay in Tete.

On 4th November we passed Sena, keeping, however, near to the opposite bank of the Zambesi to that on which the town is situated.   Here were encamped a portion of the black levies with which Colonel Serpa Pinto soon afterwards attacked the Makololo beyond the river Ruo in a country which Consul Johnston had proclaimed to be British territory.

Two days later we passed the mouth of the Shiri.   Soon afterwards heavy rain began to fall, and a strong head wind lashed the river into waves that threatened to swamp our boat, so that on reaching Missongwi, where the Dutch East African trading company have a station, we took advantage of the hospitality of their agent, Mr. Van Yssom, and spent the rest of the day with him.

On 7th November we reached Vicenti at about 1 P.M., where we found Mr. Baird in charge.   This young Scotsman, who had been a fellow-passenger of ours on board the *Courland*, had shortly before our arrival been shamefully assaulted and ill-used by a Portuguese officer, backed by a rabble, for complaining of the theft of some of the African Lakes Company's property by black soldiers.   Had there been a few Britishers about there would assuredly have been a row on the spot.   It was very evident from many things that Mr. Baird told us that relations between the British and Portuguese were now getting very strained in South-East Africa.

From Vicenti we walked over to Mopea on the Quaqua, where we were hospitably entertained by Mr. and Mrs. Henderson. Mr. Henderson was managing an opium plantation, which I think has since been abandoned.

On 8th November we started for Quillimani in two small boats belonging to the African Lakes Company, but as the river was very low, and the boats had to be continually pulled over shoals, our progress was very slow.

Knowing that the steamer for Cape Town was due in Quillimani from Mozambique on 13th November, and that she was advertised to leave on the 15th, we dropped down to the anchorage on the 14th, and ran our boat alongside of the *Courland*; and although the Portuguese guard on the gangway made some demur, I went on board and deposited all my papers, diaries, and map with the purser, as I thought I might have to undergo another inquisition at Quillimani. Then we went on shore, but no one asked us any questions. That evening we spent very pleasantly with Mr. and Mrs. Ross, and the next morning, after settling off with Rebecca and Rocky, went on board the *Courland* again, and getting away with the afternoon's tide, reached Cape Town early in December.

LUNTI RIVER, LOOKING EAST.

CHAPTER XVII

Portuguese claim to Mashunaland—Lord Salisbury's proclamation—Expeditions of
Colonel d'Andrada and Lieutenant Cordon—Letter to the Selous syndicate—
Interview with Mr. Rhodes—Scheme for the occupation of Mashunaland—
Letter to the *Times*.

FROM observations made during the progress of the expedition,
an account of which I have just brought to a close, I imagined,
rightly or wrongly, that the Portuguese were making strenuous
efforts to establish a claim to Mashunaland, and saw that if
my surmises were correct it was absolutely necessary for the
British to take possession of the country during the coming
year. The Portuguese had for a long time laid claim to the
country now called Mashunaland, but without any just title, I
think. In 1888 Lord Salisbury proclaimed this same country
to be within the sphere of British influence, and declared that
he would not recognise the Portuguese claim unless they could
show occupation. Now I thought that it was in order to be
able to prove occupation that the expeditions of Colonel
d'Andrada and Lieutenant Cordon were undertaken in 1889, for

not only were chiefs interviewed and Portuguese flags distributed, but stations and forts were established in which small
bodies of black soldiers were left in charge of Portuguese
Government property.   This, I thought, should the points in
dispute be brought to arbitration, might be held to constitute
occupation, and the verdict given against England, for, although
on other grounds we had a far better title to the country than
the Portuguese, yet as far as occupation was concerned there
was not at the close of 1889 one single British subject living
nearer to Mashunaland than the English missionaries and
traders in Matabililand on the west (more than two hundred
and fifty miles as the crow flies from Mount Hampden) and the
Scotch settlement at Blantyre on the east.

TEAM CROSSING LUNTI RIVER.

Now to one who like myself had an intimate acquaintance
with the high plateau of Mashunaland, with its fine climate,
great abundance of water, and probable great mineral wealth,
and who believed it to be, as I did, the finest portion of all
South Africa, it was an intolerable thought that we should lose
it and the Portuguese get possession of it.   I saw that immediate action was necessary, or else the Portuguese might have
it assigned to them by arbitration, or the Boers of the Northern
Transvaal might move into the country, in spite of Lord Salisbury's proclamation or the opposition of the Matabili.   I
knew that Mr. Rhodes had a scheme for the occupation of the
country, but I did not know on what scale, and feared that
time might be wasted in trying to negotiate for the occupation
of Mashunaland through Matabililand.

Full of these ideas, I wrote in a letter to the "Selous
syndicate" in Cape Town, dated Tete, 28th October
1889: ". . . If the block still continues, as no doubt it

does in Matabililand, a road must be made from Khama's
new town (Palapye) all along the Limpopo to near the
eastern bend, which then, after crossing the Nwanetsi
and the Lunti rivers, must strike north, and passing near
the head of the Devuli river and south of Umtigeza's
town, must cross the Sabi a little to the south of Wedza, and
from there take my old track to the head of the Manyami, and
from thence to the neighbourhood of the source of the Mazoe.
This road will not pass within the territory of a single chief
who owns allegiance or pays tribute to Lo Bengula.   Should
Mr. Cecil Rhodes have got the charter, then this is his true
policy : to open up a southern route from the British Protectorate to Mashunaland (which only requires to be made, and
which will be quite as good a road as the northern one passing
through Matabililand), and then first to develop the eastern
slopes of Mashunaland, and not only to exploit and work the
gold there, but to send in emigrants and settle up and occupy
the country.

   " It is folly to promulgate wild schemes for the colonisation
of Central Africa, and to leave a country with the glorious
climate and great natural resources of Mashunaland out in the
cold.   In Mashunaland Europeans can live and thrive and rear
strong healthy children.   In Central Africa they cannot.   Once
get a footing in Eastern Mashunaland, and the country will
quickly be settled up westwards, and before very long the
Matabili question will settle itself.   Now or never is the time
to act.   Make a southern road to Eastern Mashunaland, have
the country thoroughly prospected and reported upon this
coming year ; and if the reports are favourable pour in men
and machinery, and at the same time establish cattle and
agricultural farms.   In a word, work the gold, and open up
and occupy the country.   If Mashunaland is not worth this
experiment, then there is no country in the interior of Africa
that it will pay any company to spend money upon."

   Upon reaching Cape Town, I proceeded to Kimberley and
saw Mr. Rhodes, and was delighted to find that that far-seeing
statesman was fully alive to the absolute necessity, in British
interests, for the immediate occupation of Mashunaland, and
was determined that the country should be taken possession of,

in the name of the British South Africa Company, during the
coming year, 1890.   I then laid before him the plan for the
occupation of the country by a new road, passing to the south
and east of the country actually ruled over by the Matabili.
This plan Mr. Rhodes did not at first approve of, but it was
finally accepted as the only means of effecting the immediate
occupation of Mashunaland, with the minimum of risk of
collision with the Matabili.

It is due to Mr. Cecil Rhodes alone, I cannot too often
repeat, that to-day our country's flag flies over Mashunaland.
He alone of all Englishmen possessed at the same time the
prescience and breadth of mind to appreciate the ultimate value
of the country, combined with the strong will which in spite of
all obstacles compelled the means and the power successfully
to carry out the scheme for its immediate occupation.   What
the acquisition of this vast country means is as yet scarcely
apparent to the great majority of Englishmen, perhaps to none
who are not acquainted with the history of South Africa during
the present century, or who have not watched the giant strides
which have taken place in its development during the last
twenty years.   But, in the not distant future, when quick and
easy communications with Mashunaland have been established,
and the many difficulties which now hamper the development
of this the youngest of British colonies have been overcome,
then I think Englishmen will be able to appreciate what they
owe to Mr. Rhodes for inaugurating a new departure in South
African history, and securing for his countrymen the first
"show in" in a country which must ultimately become a very
valuable possession.

Before the end of 1889 a scheme for the occupation of
Mashunaland during the ensuing year was elaborated by
Mr. Rhodes, and approved of by Sir Henry Loch, the High
Commissioner for South Africa, in concurrence with Sir
Francis de Winton, Sir Sidney Shippard, and Colonel Sir
Frederick Carrington.   The guidance of the expedition was
left entirely in my hands, and, as is well known, the original
route laid down was followed as far as the head of the Devuli
river ; but being then in a country with which I had a most
intimate knowledge, gained during many hunting expeditions,

and as the cattle were getting in low condition, I slightly changed the original plan and took the expedition along the top of the watershed to the head of the Umgezi (Fort Charter). From this point, as it was necessary for me to accompany Mr. Colquhoun to Manica in order to interview the chief Umtasa, my lieutenants, Mr. Edward Burnett, and Mr. Nicholson of Zoutpansberg, acting under my instructions, guided the expedition to a spot on the Makubisi river, about ten miles south-east of Mount Hampden, where on 11th September the British flag was hoisted, and the country taken possession of in the name of the Queen ; and here the township of Salisbury was soon afterwards laid out.

After seeing Mr. Rhodes in Kimberley I returned to Cape Town, and about this time sent a letter home, which was published in the *Times* of 4th January 1890. As this letter is an Englishman's vindication of the justice of the occupation of Mashunaland, in spite of the indignant protests of Portuguese statesmen, I will here reproduce it.

To the Editor of the "Times"

SIR—Before this letter reaches England news will doubtless have been received from Mr. Ross, the British Vice-Consul at Quillimani, concerning the serious complications that have lately arisen on the Shiri owing to the invasion by Colonel Serpa Pinto's band of Zulu mercenaries of the Makololo country, a territory which was last August proclaimed to be under British protection by Consul H. H. Johnston. The Makololo chiefs unanimously placed themselves under British protection, and were informed by Her Majesty's Consul that they might rest assured that the Portuguese expedition under Colonel Serpa Pinto, then encamped on the Lower Shiri, would never dare to cross the River Ruo and invade their country. What has been the result ? The Ruo river has been crossed by some portion of Colonel Serpa Pinto's force, some Makololo have been killed, and some villages have been burnt. The Makololo have now, not unnaturally, to use a homely phrase, "rounded" on the British. "What sort of people are you English ?" they say.

"One of your headmen (Consul H. H. Johnston) came to us, telling us he bore the words of your great Queen's chief adviser from across the seas. We listened to him, and we believed what he told us; we accepted the British flag, and put ourselves under the protection of Great Britain, and thought that, as your Consul told us, we had no longer any reason to fear invasion. And what has happened? Your Consul has left us, and the Portuguese have invaded our territory, killed our people, and burnt our villages. You have played with us. You boast of a power you do not possess. We now believe you to be at heart our enemies as much as the Portuguese." This is their line of argument, and just the day before I left Quillimani Mr. Ross received a letter from Mr. Peter Moore, one of the African Lakes Company's agents, informing them that the Makololo had seized the *Lady of the Lake*, one of the Company's steamers, looted her, and, report said, sunk her, though Mr. Moore doubted the truth of this report. There was no doubt, however, that the steamer had been completely gutted, and what had become of Messrs. Morrison and Lindsay, the two Scotsmen who were in charge of her, no one knew. What has happened subsequently I cannot say, though before this news has very likely been cabled from Quillimani. It is to be hoped that further complications may not arise, though there already appear to be the makings of a good deal of trouble.

However, it is not of the rival claims of the British and Portuguese to the territories bordering on Lake Nyassa and the Upper Shiri that I propose to write, as I know little about that part of Africa, but I wish to bring to the notice of the British Government and the British people the claims which are now being put forward by Portugal to the rich and fertile country lately proclaimed to be within the British Sphere of Influence, which has come to be known as Mashunaland, and the steps which they are now taking to coerce the independent native chiefs into an unwilling submission to the Portuguese Government. Having just returned from Eastern Mashunaland through the Portuguese possessions on the Zambesi, and having kept my eyes and ears open, I have seen what is going on, and I trust that the following notes, written in a boat on the Zambesi in November last, may prove of some interest to all those who are interested in British expansion in South Africa.

It is, perhaps, not very generally known that during the last few years the Portuguese Government has been making the most strenuous efforts to overrun and annex the territories of the various independent native chiefs living to the south of the Zambesi within the line which they claim as their western boundary in this part of Africa. Gungunyan, the son of Umzila, and the present chief of the powerful tribe of Gaza Zulus, it is asserted by Portuguese officials, has already voluntarily given in his allegiance to their Government, and a Goanese named Manoel Antonio de Souza has, during the last few years, coerced many of the Muzizuru chiefs living between the Ruenya and the Mazoe rivers into an unwilling submission to the same Government. This Manoel Antonio is a Goanese, and must be a man of great force of character. Many years ago he came from India to seek his fortune in Africa, where his talents were soon recognised and taken advantage of by the Portuguese Government. About 1868 or 1869 he was sent in command of a large force of Landeens (Zulus) to compel Makombi, then the independent chief of the Barui country, to pay taxes to the Portuguese Government, the said chief having hitherto successfully resisted all attempts to make him do so. Manoel Antonio, with his Landeens, however, overcame his resistance, thoroughly subdued his tribe, and persuaded him to pay. After this he seems to have obtained great power and influence amongst the people with whom he was living, and finally became their chief, and, as the ruler of a numerous and warlike tribe, at once became an object of the highest interest and consideration in the eyes of the Portuguese Government. Two years ago he was taken to Lisbon, where he met with quite an ovation, and where no pains were spared to flatter his vanity and to ensure his loyalty to the Portuguese Crown. He was very highly honoured, I believe, and his two sons are now being educated at the expense of the State in Lisbon, where they also remain as hostages for their father's loyalty, which, it is whispered, has more than once been doubted. On his return to Africa his services were called for almost immediately, and he and his men played the leading part last year (1888) in the capture of Bonga's stockade at Masangano and the dispersal of his people.

But besides the country to the south of the Mazoe and to the east of the Sabi, which the Portuguese have been quietly engaged in absorbing during the last few years, there remains a large tract of country, ruled over by independent native chiefs, lying to the north of the Mazoe and to the east of the Upper Manyami, which also comes within the line which they wish to have assigned to them, by arbitration or otherwise, as the western boundary of their East African possessions—a country about which they know absolutely nothing, except what they have learnt of late years from the writings and maps of English hunters and travellers. In order to establish a claim to this part of Africa, two expeditions were fitted out early this present year to traverse this country and to conciliate or frighten the native chiefs into accepting the Portuguese flag. Captain Cordon was sent up as Governor of Zumbo, with orders to take Kanyemba, Matakania, and other powerful chiefs holding official positions under the Portuguese Government, with all their men, to proceed up the Zambesi to the mouth of the River Sanyati, and from thence to the junction of the Umfuli with the latter river, and there to form a stockade, and await the arrival of Colonel Paiva d'Andrada and General Manoel Antonio from the south. The two latter officers were apparently ordered to first overcome Motoko, an independent chief living near the headwaters of the River Inyadiri, one of the chief southern tributaries of the Mazoe, and from thence to proceed to the Upper Manyami, and then, passing by Lo Magondi's town, to effect a union with Captain Cordon at the junction of the Umfuli and Sanyati rivers. Whether this programme has been fully carried out or not I have not been able to ascertain with certainty. When Mr. Burnett and myself were at the source of the Mazoe in the end of September last either Colonel Paiva d'Andrada or General Manoel Antonio, coming from the direction of Mangwendi's town, near the head of the Inyagui river, passed Inyamwenda's town, on the Manyami, and proceeded to Lo Magondi's. An Indian trader from the Zambesi, a Mahom-

medan named Vallji Mussagi, whom we found at Inyota
buying gold, told us that Captain Cordon had built a strong
stockade at the junction of the Sanyati and Umfuli rivers,
and that he had been attacked by a war party of Matabili,
whom he had repulsed with great slaughter, killing thirty of
them, and capturing the cattle which they brought with them
for food ; that Lo Bengula had then sent a stronger force
against him, which Captain Cordon had again beaten off. This
Indian trader also informed me that Lo Magondi had given in
his allegiance to the Portuguese Government, and accepted the
Portuguese flag, and that Mapondera, the most influential of
the Makori-kori chiefs, was ready to do the same. These
stories I did not for an instant believe, as I could see that
Vallji Mussagi was thoroughly Portuguese and anti-English in
his feelings, but I took steps to ascertain if they had any
foundation in fact by at once despatching messengers—men
whom I knew, and who had worked at my waggons on the
Manyami in former years—to Inyamwenda's, who, after an
absence of a week, returned with the news that Colonel Paiva
d'Andrada had passed on his way to Lo Magondi's, but told me
that they could hear nothing of Captain Cordon, and that
there had most certainly been no fighting between him and the
Matabili ; as for Mapondera being desirous of taking the
Portuguese flag, he and his brother, Temaringa, repeatedly
assured me that they had no intention of putting themselves
under Portuguese protection. However, Vallji Mussagi will
certainly circulate these reports in Tete, where they will be
accepted as true, and from whence they will spread to Quillimani and Mozambique, and very likely to Lisbon.

These expeditions of 1889 into a country that has been
proclaimed to be within the " British Sphere of Influence "
will shortly be followed by others—nay, have probably been
already so followed, for on my return to Tete, in the end of
October, I heard that Colonel Ignacio de Jesus Xavier, a full-
blooded native chief in the service and pay of the Portuguese
Government (who can raise a considerable force), accompanied
by a Portuguese officer, was already on his way up country
with a view probably to persuading Mapondera to accept the
Portuguese flag. The result of these expeditions will very

likely be that several independent native chiefs, who are too
weak to resist even a small armed force, will be temporarily
compelled to profess an unwilling allegiance to the Portuguese
Government.   But what I wish to point out is that the validity
of the Portuguese claim to the high plateau of Eastern
Mashunaland, between the Upper Manyami and Mazoe rivers,
rests entirely upon the question as to the legality or illegality
of the semi-military expeditions of the present year, and
whether the fact of a European Government having sent an
armed force of subsidised natives, accompanied by one European
officer, through the territories of independent native chiefs,
gives that Government the right to claim such countries as
subject to its jurisdiction in direct opposition to the wishes of
the inhabitants.   Now, on the 6th of June last, Senhor de
Serpa Pimental, leader of the Conservative party in the Portuguese Chamber of Peers, brought forward a resolution declaring
that the Chamber once more affirmed the rights of Portugal
in Eastern and Central Africa, they being based upon discovery,
conquest, effective occupation, or permanent commercial enterprise, and the political influence of Portugal during centuries
past.   Well, no one will dispute the well-known fact that for
a period of over three centuries the Portuguese have possessed
settlements at various points along the south-east coast of
Africa, and that they have formed and still hold several forts
and trading stations along the course of the great River
Zambesi as far as Zumbo, and those who have visited
these settlements know how far the political influence of
Portugal extends beyond these forts, and the vastness of the
commercial enterprises undertaken by Portuguese subjects in
this part of the world ; and they also know how much Portugal
has done during those three centuries in the cause of civilisation
and material progress.   These are matters which, however, I
will not discuss here, and I am prepared to grant without cavil
that the Portuguese have a certain amount of political influence
along the south-east coast of Africa, north of Delagoa Bay
(an influence which they have strained every nerve to extend
inland during the last five years), and along the course of the
Zambesi, from its mouth as far as Zumbo, or even as far as
the mouth of the River Kafukwi.   South of the Zambesi,

between Tete and Zumbo, this influence three years ago nowhere extended beyond the low country, which may be called
the Zambesi valley.   But the last three years, owing to jealousy
of British expansion, have been a period of unprecedented
activity with the Portuguese Government in South-Eastern
Africa ; and by the judicious employment of such men as
Manoel Antonio and Ignacio de Jesus Xavier, and other influential native chiefs, that Government has very rapidly
extended, and is still extending, its influence all over South-
Eastern Africa.   Still, I say decisively that on 1st October
last Portuguese influence, even of the most indirect kind, north
of Tete and on the southern bank of the Zambesi, nowhere extended to any point distant over one hundred miles in a direct
line from that river, or to any country lying at a general elevation of over three thousand feet above sea-level.   Rusambo and
Chibonga are the last two chiefs west of Tete and north of the
Mazoe who can be considered within Portuguese influence, and
that of a very indirect kind.   Rusambo this year, for the third
time, paid taxes to the native chief, Ignacio de Jesus Xavier,
and not to any representative of the Portuguese Government,
whilst Chibonga's people paid very unwillingly for the second
time, under threats of having their women seized if they refused
to do so.   I was at Rusambo's and Chibonga's kraals whilst
Xavier's men were collecting the taxes, and so know what I
am writing about.   West of Chibonga's all the native chiefs
are entirely independent.   As to the country on the eastern,
southern, and northern slopes of what has come to be known
as Mashunaland—the rich and fertile country in the development of which I am particularly interested,—with all due
deference to Senhor Serpa Pimental, I maintain that it is a
country with which Portugal has no historic associations whatever, and one to which the Portuguese can lay no claim, either
upon the score of conquest, discovery, effective occupation,
permanent commercial enterprise, or the political influence of
Portugal at any time up to the present day.

   I am not altogether unacquainted with the early records
of Portuguese conquest and discovery in South-Eastern Africa
in the sixteenth, seventeenth, and eighteenth centuries, nor
of the enterprises undertaken in the same region during that

period by the zealous and self-denying disciples of Francis
Xavier and Ignatius Loyola.   In those records will be found
accounts of numerous expeditions, military, diplomatic, and
philanthropic, both along the course of the Zambesi as far as
Zumbo, and into the interior of the country lying between the
Lower Zambesi and the River Sabi.   The latter were almost
always undertaken either from Sofala or from Sena on the
Lower Zambesi.   The barbaric chief, grandiloquently termed
by the early Portuguese writers " The Emperor of Monomotapa,"
was converted with many of his people to Roman Catholicism ;
and at one time there were as many as nine Jesuit priests
in the Manica country, where they established churches and
schools, and where there was also a Portuguese military post.
On the Zambesi too the silver mines of Chicova were visited,
churches were built, and military posts established at various
points as far as Zumbo.   Neither the military genius, however,
nor the religious enthusiasm expended upon these expeditions
was able to render them of any permanent value to the cause
of civilisation.   Savage potentates were conquered, and their
territories nominally became part of the Portuguese East African
possessions ; but their descendants long ago shook off the yoke
of their conquerors.   Heathens were converted and baptized
by the Jesuit priests in very large numbers ; yet the descendants of these Christianised barbarians reverted ages ago to the
heathenism of their remote ancestors.   In fact, from a variety
of causes, the power and influence of the Portuguese, which
two hundred years ago was very great in South-Eastern Africa,
gradually declined, till not very long ago the political influence
of that country was entirely confined to the immediate neighbourhood of a few forts on the coast, and along the course of
the Zambesi as far as Zumbo ; notwithstanding which the
natives in the immediate vicinity of Tete (which was established
as a military post as far back as 1632) were in continual
insurrection.   Still no one can deny the historic associations
of Portugal with the Zambesi from its mouth as far as Zumbo,
nor with the immense tract of country between the Lower
Zambesi and the Sabi, and if Englishmen are inclined to laugh
or sneer at the tenacity with which a country that is often
stated to have lost all its ancient vigour clings to mere historic

associations, at any rate they ought to admire the energy and enterprise (unaccompanied by any loud talking) which the Portuguese are now displaying in South-Eastern Africa in order to make good their claims and re-establish their ancient supremacy.   As an Englishman I wish to see Portuguese enterprise in Eastern Africa met and checked by British expansion from the West, though I would not have Portugal jockeyed or bullied out of a single inch of territory to which she can prove any real claim.   But to the northern, eastern, and southern slopes of what has come to be known as Mashunaland they have no claim.   This is a country with which their records fail to prove any historic association whatever, nor has it ever been visited by any white man of Portuguese blood until the present year, 1889, when Colonel Paiva d'Andrada passed through it during the time of my visit to the source of the Mazoe.

On the other hand it is only necessary to compare the best maps of South-Eastern Africa, published either in Portugal, Germany, or England twenty years ago, with those of the same country that have appeared during the last few years to prove that not only Mashunaland, but other territories also lying nearer the Zambesi, and over which I will admit that the Portuguese exert a certain amount of indirect political influence, but of the topographical features of which they have no exact knowledge—a fact which their own maps prove beyond dispute —have been traversed in every direction and very thoroughly explored by various Englishmen, amongst whom I may mention the names of Thomas Baines, W. Montagu Kerr, and Dr. Knight Bruce.   The German explorer, Carl Mauch, also travelled extensively in the southern portion of Mashunaland ; and besides these well-known names I could give a long list of the English, Scotch, and Dutch hunters who have traversed Mashunaland in every direction ; yet previous to the journey undertaken during the present year by Colonel Paiva d'Andrada, to which I have already alluded, no Portuguese subject, either in ancient or modern times, has added one iota to our knowledge of this region ; in fact, on his journey from Inyamwenda's to Lo Magondi's kraal, Colonel d'Andrada must have travelled the whole way on the waggon road which an Englishman chopped through the dense mahobo-hobo groves bordering the Manyami river. At any rate, it is a fact that will admit of no dispute that, during the last twenty-five years, English hunters and travellers have explored every nook and corner of Mashunaland. They have chopped waggon roads through the forests and made practicable fords across all the large rivers ; they have established the most friendly relations with the natives, by whom the advent of the hunters' waggons is anxiously looked forward to and expected every year ; and, as I have said before, some of them have made very careful and accurate route maps of their various journeys, and published accounts of the capabilities and natural resources of the country. Many Englishmen, indeed, have spent years of their lives in the Mashuna country, whilst not a few have left their bones there. In fine, the associations of England with this portion of South Africa are most intimate, and I maintain that, through the work done by her sons, England, in the general partition of Africa which is now taking place, has a better claim to administer that country than any other European nation. Englishmen, at any rate, amongst all other Europeans, hold the first place, I will not say in the affections, for Africans are not affectionate as a rule, but in the esteem of the natives ; and the implicit trust that the Mashunas now have in the honour, truth, and justice of the white man is the outcome of their dealings with Englishmen and South Africans, for it would not be fair to omit mentioning the fact that the few Dutch hunters who have visited Mashunaland have always treated the natives honourably and fairly, and no man is more respected by them than my old friend and companion in many a hunt, Cornelis van Rooyen.

These surely are strong points. But, say that England is frightened into a resignation of its just claims to administer Mashunaland, and that the Portuguese Government, more bold, resolute, and persevering, secures that country nominally—for it will never be anything more than nominally—what will Portugal do with it? The Portuguese are not a colonising nation at the present day, as Englishmen understand the word, and even if they were it would be almost impossible to send immigrants into Mashunaland from the Zambesi, for between

that river and the high plateau lies one of the most inhospitable
countries in Africa.   Rough and mountainous, infested with
tse-tse fly, and during half the year almost destitute of water,
this tract of country is so sparsely inhabited and the inhabitants
are usually so badly off for food that any large expedition of
Europeans would have the greatest difficulty in traversing the
country.   I speak here of the country between Tete on the
Zambesi and the high plateau.   I am aware that Mashunaland
is easier of access from the south-east coast through the Manica
country, but even there a railway must first be made through
the " fly " infested district, between the Pungwi river and Massi
Kessi, before anything can be done on an extended scale.   Such
a railway, it is true, is spoken of, but before it can be made I
hope and believe that Mashunaland will be occupied by a large
population of British and South Africans, under the government of the Chartered Company.   Portugal can never do anything with this, the fairest portion of all South Africa, but
farm it out in districts to men of the stamp of Manoel Antonio
(a Goanese) or Ignacio de Jesus Xavier (a full-blooded African).
I say men of this stamp, for there are many other full-blooded
native chiefs with long Portuguese names besides those I have
mentioned, and it is these men who virtually rule South-Eastern
Africa for the Portuguese, and there is not one of them whose
treatment of the natives would commend itself to the Aborigines
Protection Society.   Yet it is by such men that Mashunaland
will be governed, if the Portuguese can make good their claim
to the country.   A certain rental will be paid to the Government for the administration of each district, the renter being
then left at liberty to squeeze as much as he can out of the
natives under his jurisdiction.   This at any rate is what has
been done with the countries I have spoken of as being indirectly under Portuguese influence, and judging the future by
the past, as I think one is justified in doing, it is not too much
to say that, under Portuguese administration, in two hundred
years' time the natural resources of the Mashuna country would
remain in the same undeveloped condition as they are at the
present day, or in the same condition as the whole of South-
Eastern Africa between the Lower Zambesi and the River Sabi,
the country to which, in the words of Senhor Serpa Pimental,

Portugal possesses rights based upon discovery, conquest, effective occupation, permanent commercial enterprise, and political influence during centuries past.   More than this I cannot say in condemnation of Portuguese rule.

But, as I have said above, Portugal can never become anything more than the nominal possessor of Mashunaland, for it will infallibly be settled up and occupied before many years have passed by men from the British and Dutch States in South Africa.   The geographical position, combined with the high altitude of the Mashuna plateau, which gives it a cool and temperate climate, thoroughly suited to North Europeans, and the natural capabilities of the country, which, both for stock farming and agriculture, are equal to any in South Africa, seal its fate as the heritage of the British and Dutch colonists in South Africa, and such men and their descendants will laugh at the Portuguese pretensions, even should they be ratified by every Government in Europe.   And should "the good old rule, the simple plan," have to be resorted to, "that they should take who have the power, and they should keep who can," it is not too much to assert that on the open plateau of Mashunaland two hundred mounted South Africans would disperse all the native levies that the Portuguese could muster in South-Eastern Africa ; and native levies are all that can be employed, for the military strength of Portugal in this part of the world consists of a few Portuguese and Goanese officers, a few black soldiers from Angola, and the native levies of Manoel Antonio, Ignacio de Jesus Xavier, Matakania, Kanyemba, and other native chiefs at present friendly to the Portuguese.   Should white troops be sent from Portugal they would be decimated by fever on the coast or on the Lower Zambesi, as happened during the prosecution of the first Bonga war in 1868.

Of late the Portuguese have talked much about British arrogance and presumption, but surely it can be retorted that they themselves have shown overmuch pretension in the claims which they have lately put forward to Mashunaland.   The South Africa Company claims the right to govern that country, to protect its people, and to develop its natural resources, under the charter lately granted by the Queen.   But, before the charter was granted, the promoters of that great enterprise had gained an intimate knowledge of Mashunaland and its people, and that not from old Portuguese records, but from the writings, maps, and conversation of modern Englishmen ; and they know that the native Mashunas would welcome the advent of British settlers in their country, as a protection not alone against the bloodthirsty Matabili, but also against the cruel and brutal slave-dealers from the Zambesi, such as Kanyemba, Matakania, Perizengi, Lobo, Chimbango, etc., all of whom have long Portuguese names, and all of whom hold the official position of " Capitão Mor " in their districts, and govern the countries they live in for the Portuguese, without the assistance or sur- veillance of a magistrate or any kind of Portuguese official. Or it may be asserted that they do not govern for the Portuguese ; then I say that Portugal has no jurisdiction in any of the countries over which these men rule—a supposition which would reduce Portuguese territory in South-Eastern Africa to very small dimensions.   For my part I always speak of countries governed by these native " Capitãos Mors " as being indirectly under Portuguese rule.   But give Portugal all the territory ruled over by these men (surely she cannot claim anything more), and not an acre of Mashunaland will come under her jurisdiction.

In the future, should trouble come between the servants of the British Company and the Portuguese, the latter will be responsible and must bear the blame.   For British subjects have been the first to explore Mashunaland and to find out its value, and under the auspices of the Chartered Company let us hope that British subjects will develop it, and make it one of the richest and most prosperous states in the South African Dominion of the future.   This may be a dream that is never to be fulfilled, but, at any rate, I feel sure that it is not the Portuguese who will prevent its realisation.

CHAPTER XVIII

Mashunaland—Its topographical features—Ancient inhabitants, industries, and antiquities

SALISBURY, MASHUNALAND.

I HAVE now brought my narrative down to the close of the year 1889, at which time active preparations were already being made by the British South Africa Company for the occupation of Mashunaland during the following year.

Before, however, proceeding to give any account of the cutting of the pioneer road from the Macloutsie river to Fort Salisbury—for a distance of four hundred and sixty miles through what was then a trackless wilderness—I will first say something concerning the country it was proposed to open up to European enterprise.

In this part of Africa I have spent the greater portion of eight years, and as during that period I have been constantly engaged in travelling over every part of the plateau of Mashunaland, I have gained an intimate knowledge of the geographical features of the country; for I have climbed

almost every hill, in order to take compass bearings, and have
sketched in the courses of the rivers and streams from the
tops of the hills.   In the course of my many journeys I have
learned, too, something of the history of the native races by
whom the country is inhabited, and have visited the ancient
temple of Zimbabwi, and carefully examined many of the
walled towns in the territories of Makoni and Mangwendi.   I
have, too, formed opinions as to the suitability of the climate
of Mashunaland for Europeans, the general capabilities of the
country, and its future possibilities ; and I shall now therefore
devote a few pages to the discussion of these subjects.

To begin with, the name Mashunaland is a coined word,
and how it became current I have never been able to discover.
The native inhabitants of this part of Africa belong to many
different clans, some of which are probably the remnants of
once powerful tribes.   Each sept has its own tribal name and
tribal marks, and the territory of each is fairly well defined.
Thus, Motoko's people are Mabuja ; Makoni's tribe, Ma-ongwi ;
Umtasa's, Mabocha ; Mangwendi's, Muzizuru, etc.   I have never,
however, met with any clan whose members called themselves
Mashunas ; and the name is altogether unknown amongst the
natives of this part of Africa, except to a few who have learnt
the word from Europeans.   As a generic term, however, the
word is useful, and may be taken to designate all the tribes
of South-Eastern Africa that are not of Zulu blood.   These
tribes, it may be remarked, all speak dialects differing very
slightly one from another, and all of them quite comprehensible
to the Makalakas living to the west and south-west of Matabililand.

There being a considerable amount of uncertainty as to
the number of tribes that may legitimately be classed under
the generic term of Mashunas, there is naturally some doubt
as to the actual extent of the territory that ought to be called
Mashunaland.   In former days we used to speak of the whole
of the plateau to the east, north-east, and south-east of Matabililand as Mashunaland ; but a name is wanted which will
include Matabililand and Manicaland, and in fact take in
the whole of the British South Africa Company's territories.
Zambesia and Rhodesia are the only two names that I have

heard suggested, and the latter, which has been given out of compliment to Mr. Cecil Rhodes, to whom alone it is due that what may soon become a rich and prosperous territory has been added to the British dominions (practically I think it is so), seems to be steadily gaining ground in popular favour, as the principal paper published in Mashunaland is called the *Rhodesia Herald.*

People who scurry through the country, and especially those who do not go beyond Salisbury, have but little idea of the extent of the high plateau of Mashunaland. Stretching away to the east and south-east of the main road between Salisbury and Umtali there is a very fine tract of country which is but very little known. In this direction I have travelled a good deal, and made a careful survey, a glance at which will show how magnificently watered is this part of the country. Portions of this district, especially in the neighbourhood of the sources of the Rusapi river and its numerous tributaries, are remarkable for the abundance of huge naked masses of granite which rise abruptly from the grassy downs. Some of these, though formed of a single block of stone, are worthy to be called hills, notably the huge cone named Dombo, which, standing as it does on the extreme eastern edge of Mashunaland, commands a truly magnificent panoramic view over an immense extent of country; for the plateau itself, on the edge of which Dombo stands, here attains a height of six thousand feet; and whoever climbs this naked crag will stand six thousand seven hundred feet above the sea, perhaps the highest point in South-Eastern Africa; for I doubt much whether the loftiest hills in Manica attain a height of seven thousand feet.

It was in February 1891, during the height of the rainy season, that after two attempts, rendered unsuccessful by blinding storms of rain (during one of which my companion, Mr. W. L. Armstrong, was nearly washed down a fissure in the mountain side), we stood at last, compass in hand, on the summit of Dombo. Well indeed were we repaid for our perseverance. The air, freed by months of rain from the smoke of the winter grass fires, was extraordinarily clear, and enabled us to see, at one and the same time, several of the most

conspicuous hills in Mashunaland : the peaks of Wedza far in
the west ; the great table mountain of Inyarugwi, away down
in Maranka's country, near the Sabi river ; the granite cone
of Temwa, which stands far to the north-east, near Motoko's
stronghold ; besides Mount Anwa, beyond the sources of the
Masheki, and many another well-known hill.   Stretching away
to the north-east lay the great mountain range of Inyama,
culminating in a conspicuous peak, which may, possibly, be
the Mount Bismarck of Mauch ; while to the south lay a
wilderness of rugged mountains, which form a portion of the
wild and beautiful land of Manica.   Amidst the gorges of
these mountains two important rivers take their rise : the swift
and impetuous Odzi, one of the main tributaries of the Sabi,
and the equally swift and much more important river, the
Ruenya, loved of hippopotami, which, after receiving the waters
of almost every river in Eastern Mashunaland south of the
Umvukwi range of hills, pours the impetuous waters of a
mountain torrent, clear and cool to the very end of its career,
into the giant Zambesi.   The upper course of the Ruenya is
called the Imyang-ombi (Yankombe of Mauch), and from the
top of Dombo it may be seen for many miles, winding like a
silver thread (by the bye, I think I have heard that simile
before) down the valley running parallel with the Inyama
Mountains.

Although Dombo, viewed from a distance, looks like a uni-
formly smooth, rounded cone of granite seven hundred feet in
height, a close inspection shows that in places deep furrows have
been worn in its sides by the action of rain.   This phenomenon
may be seen in many of the higher granite crags of Mashunaland, but nowhere to such perfection as on the western face of
a large isolated hill called Zomba, which stands near the head
waters of the little river Inyazuri.   This hill stands within
half a mile of the main road, between Fort Salisbury and
Manica, and cannot fail to attract the attention of any passers-
by for whom the operations of nature have any interest.   The
centre of the western face of the solid granite rock has been
scored and furrowed in such a way that it presents the appearance of a water-worn glacier, and the depth of the furrows
must be measured not by inches, but by feet and yards.   Now

imagine what this means. This hill is a bare granite crag, perfectly isolated, and the only possible agency that can have scored its sides is rain. Yet the effect produced by the showers which actually fall upon it during ten years, or even a century's wet seasons, must be so infinitely small that countless eons of time must have elapsed since this old rock first bared its face to wind and storm.

Judging by our calculation of time, what a very old world this planet must be, for all this erosion of hard rock by rain must have occurred subsequently to the last elevation of this portion of the earth's crust, as, except on the supposition that all this part of Africa was once submerged, I cannot understand how the curious kopjes of wonderfully-balanced granite stones, which are so remarkable a feature in the landscapes of many portions of South-Eastern Africa, can have been formed. As the land slowly rose, I take it that the soil was washed by the water from amongst the huge loose boulders which had previously drifted together, leaving them at last high and dry and piled one upon another in the most fantastic confusion. Other single blocks weighing hundreds of tons may be seen standing singly on the slope of a granite hill, and can only have been brought there by water, just as blocks of stone have been left stranded in various parts of Europe by ancient glaciers which have long since disappeared. I think I have read somewhere that Africa is geologically a very old continent, and I think that the rain-worn furrows in the granite rocks I have above alluded to are a proof that it is so ; and what is more, the hippopotamus paths worn deep into the solid rock along the Lower Umfuli river, formed in the hard stone, with the central ridge plainly shown, as in a hippopotamus path made but yesterday in muddy ground, prove that the mammals existing in it at the present day have roamed the land for countless ages.

As regards the native races inhabiting Mashunaland at the present day, they seem to be much the same as they were in the time of Dos Santos three centuries ago. They belong to the Bantu family, which is spread over the whole of South-Eastern and South-Central Africa ; but what the Bantus are ethnologically who can say ? They are certainly not a pure race, though the negro blood predominates in them. The infusion of foreign blood which undoubtedly runs in their veins must have come from a lighter-skinned people, I fancy, for I have noticed that in all the tribes of Kafirs amongst whom I have travelled, good features, thin lips, and well-shaped heads are almost invariably correlated with a light-coloured skin. Now I will here hazard a theory which may or may not have any foundation in fact. I will first, however, assume that Mr. Bent is correct in the supposition that the original builders of Zimbabwi came from Southern Arabia. Dr. Schlichter, in a criticism upon Mr. Bent's lately-published book, *The Ruined Cities of Mashunaland*, proves conclusively that during the six centuries which elapsed between the founding of the Christian religion and the birth of Mohammed there was no intercourse between the natives of Southern Arabia and South-Eastern Africa, so that we must put back to a very remote period the first incursion of the worshippers of Baal into the country we now call Mashunaland. That the builders of Zimbabwi were a very rude people, possessing no written characters and doing all their building by eye and without measurement, was the impression left upon my mind after two short visits to the ruins. Mr. Swan, however, who assisted Mr. Bent in his researches and excavations, is of opinion, I believe, that the builders of the temple of Zimbabwi were a highly-civilised race. It is to be hoped that further researches will throw new light upon this most interesting subject. In the meantime I will theorise.

Let us suppose, then, that two or perhaps three thousand years ago a commercial people penetrated from Southern Arabia to Mashunaland. They were acquainted with the requirements of the civilised nations of Asia at that period and understood the value of gold. This metal they discovered amongst the hills and in the streams of Mashunaland. In time these Arabian merchants gained a footing in the land and taught the black aborigines to mine for them. Their principal station was at Zimbabwi, where they built, with the forced labour of the aborigines, a temple for the worship of Baal, and a strongly-built and well-situated fortress. But I take it that, like the Arabs in Central Africa at the present day, these ancient Arabians brought few or no women with them, but took a very handsome allowance of wives from amongst the aboriginal blacks. For a long period intercourse was kept up with Arabia, and during this period the gold-seekers spread over the whole of South-Eastern Africa from the Zambesi to the Limpopo, everywhere mixing with the people, and teaching them their own rude arts of wall-building and gold-mining. In course of time we will suppose that events happened in Arabia which put an

PORTION OF WALL OF THE ANCIENT TEMPLE OF ZIMBABWI.

end to all intercourse with the distant colony in Mashunaland, and as time went on, as the alien race were still in small numbers compared with the aboriginal blacks, and as they had none of their own women with them, they gradually became completely fused, and nationally lost amongst the aborigines. The mixed race called the Bantu had been formed, which spread in course of time northwards as far as the Congo, and southwards as far as the Cape Colony, or the migrations may first have been northwards and then again southwards down the east coast, with an admixture of other tribes, such as the Zends,

spoken of by El Massoudi.   At any rate I am absolutely convinced that the blood of the ancient builders of Zimbabwi still
runs (in a very diluted form, if you like) in the veins of the
Bantu races, and more especially so amongst the remnants of
the tribes still living in Mashunaland, and the Barotsi of the
Upper Zambesi, who are, there is little doubt, a branch of the
Barotsi tribe who were destroyed by the Matabili in Mashunaland, though the separation took place long prior to this event.
      I make this suggestion after much thought, a close study
of the relics unearthed at Zimbabwi, and a knowledge of the
natives of South-Eastern Africa gained during many years of
travel.   Between the builders of Zimbabwi and the people living
in Mashunaland at the present day it appears to me that there
is no impassable gulf dividing a highly-civilised race from an
utterly savage one, as some people would have us believe.
Many things tend to prove that the ancient builders of
Zimbabwi were a rude people.   They had a religion, and
possessed sufficient energy and concentration of purpose to
carry to an end the immense work of building the temple of
Zimbabwi.   But the work itself, though very wonderful, appears
to me to be rude and unsymmetrical.   Nowhere is the wall
absolutely plumb, and on the top it varies in different parts
considerably in breadth.   The fact that no written characters
have been found on any of the flat granite or soapstone beams
imbedded in the walls, or the large flat stones standing upright
like tombstones in the floor of the Zimbabwi, seems to me to
prove that the people who built this temple were unacquainted
with writing of any kind.   The only carvings on the sides of
the soapstone beams are lozenge-shaped and herring-bone
patterns (badly carved, not a single line being quite straight),
agreeing exactly in some cases with the ornamentation on the
outside of the temple, and more curious still, not alone with the
patterns carved on the wooden knife-sheaths and scored on the
pottery of the natives all over Mashunaland at the present day,
but also with the patterns used in ornamenting the household
utensils of all kinds in the Barotsi valley hundreds of miles
away.
      The most curious relics that have been found at Zimbabwi
are, undoubtedly, the birds carved sitting on the tops of the

soapstone beams ; these bear no resemblance to anything now seen amongst the Bantu people, and were doubtless connected with the ancient worship.   Not so, however, the carvings on the soapstone bowls.   These are very rude—so much so, that the animals that have been taken by Mr. Bent to represent hippopotami I take to be meant for baboons, as they have long tails.   But the curious thing about these bas-reliefs is the close resemblance they bear to the wooden carvings of animals to be seen amongst the Bantu people at the present day.   The genius of the ancient artists still lives amongst them.

Mr. Bent speaks of the ruined cities of Mashunaland. What trace of them is there, I would ask.   I have seen the temple of Zimbabwi and some smaller ones, the fortress on the hill near the large temple, and further, many hundreds or thousands of stone walls in various parts of South-Eastern Africa, but never a trace of a city built of stone.   There is strong presumptive evidence that the structures in which the people lived, near the great temple, were huts plastered with mud.   For this reason : at the foot of the hill on which stands the fortress are two immense holes dug in the ground.   I have heard the theory advanced that these holes were used as reservoirs for water ; but I take them to be merely the holes excavated by the people living on the hill to obtain clay for their pottery, and with which to daub their huts.   The native population was large and endured for a long period of time ; therefore the excavations are larger than those found at the side of any Bantu village at the present day, but wherever there is a village, or the site of a deserted village, a similar hole, larger or smaller in proportion to the size of the town and the length of its duration, will always be found.

As to the relations of the ancient builders of the temple of Zimbabwi to the present inhabitants of the country, on my theory the blood of the ancient worshippers of Baal still runs in their veins ; very much diluted, no doubt, but still in sufficient strength to occasionally produce amongst them men with light-brown skins and high features, and sometimes of great intellectual power.   After a certain lapse of time, when the higher race had become entirely fused and practically lost amongst the lower and more numerous aboriginal people, the

worship of Baal died out, and was superseded by the old
religion of ancestor-worship which still prevails ; but it appears
to me that the wall-building and gold-mining, originally learnt
from the ancient Arabians, were carried on continuously from
their first inception up to the middle of the present century.   It
is the Zulu migrations northwards through Mashunaland, which
have taken place during the present century—invasions that
have absolutely depopulated large areas of country,—that
finally obliged the Mashunas to cease working in the shafts
which their ancestors had, centuries before, commenced to sink
on the quartz reefs which abound in the country.   As the
mining had been carried on for a long period of time, naturally
an enormous amount of work has been done in the aggregate,
some of the shafts recently discovered in Mashunaland being
as much as one hundred and twenty feet in depth.

Many people seem to imagine that a highly-civilised race once
existed in Mashunaland, who built temples and cities and did an
immense amount of work in the way of gold-mining, and were
finally destroyed by the ancestors of the present inhabitants of
the country.   The destruction of this people put an end, it is
said, to the gold industry until the advent of the Portuguese,
by whom it was again revived.   It is this idea which I wish
to combat.   When the Portuguese arrived in South-Eastern
Africa at the close of the fifteenth century they found Arab
settlements on the coast, and first learned from the Arabs of
the gold mines in the interior of the country.   These gold
mines were being worked by the natives of the country, who
used the gold as a medium of exchange to buy the goods
brought to them by the Arabs, and for centuries before this
time their ancestors had, in all probability, made use of gold,
whose value had been first taught them by the ancient builders
of the temple of Zimbabwi, to trade with the commercial peoples
of the East who, from time to time, penetrated to Mashunaland.   Thus when the Arabs were driven from South-Eastern
Africa by the Portuguése the mining did not cease, as the
native miners simply sold their gold to the new-comers, whom
they probably found even more anxious to obtain the precious
metal than the Arab merchants had been.

After this period Portuguese records abundantly prove that

the gold-mining went on without interruption till early in the present century, and the old men amongst the Matabili, who took part in the first raids made amongst the Mashunas by Umziligazi's warriors, state positively that they found the Amaholi working for gold in the "Amaguti," *i.e.* "in the deep holes," between the Zweswi and Umfuli rivers. An interesting confirmation of this statement lies in the fact that at the bottom of an old shaft, one hundred and twenty feet deep, at Concession Hill, near the Zweswi river, Mr. Cock, in 1891, found a bucket and rope made of machabel bark, besides some iron implements. Now this bucket and rope, evidently intended to haul quartz up from the bottom of the shaft, being made of such perishable material as bark, could not possibly have been of any great antiquity, whilst the iron implements, axes, etc., were absolutely the same as those in present use amongst the Mashunas, and showed no signs of age. Mr. Rolker, the American mining expert, lately in Mashunaland, also told me that, from the condition of the heaps of débris at the mouths of some of the shafts, he was convinced they had not been long abandoned. If my readers will turn to Mr. Baines's well-known book on the gold regions of South-Eastern Africa they will find that the Mashunas were still, little more than twenty years ago, getting quartz from the reefs, which they roasted in great fires, and then pounded up with round stones in order to extract the gold. The passage I refer to reads as follows :—

"G. Wood took me to a place in which he had seen a heap of quartz burned, and another heap, piled with wood among it, ready for burning. The crushing stones, like a painter's slab and muller, had also been lying in a hut near, but at the time of my visit these were removed, and the calcined quartz also ; but the other heap had been fired, and now lay mingled with the charcoal ready for crushing."

The Mr. George Wood here referred to was my constant companion for two years, and he often used to tell me how he had seen the Mashunas extracting gold from quartz ; and he further told me that, after crushing the roasted quartz, they used to melt the gold into little ingots in small crucibles made for the purpose. There is nothing to be surprised at in this, as both the Mashunas and Makalakas still extract copper from the ore and run it into moulds, whilst in Katanga the form of the mould into which the natives run their copper is almost identical in shape with the soapstone mould found by Mr. Bent at Zimbabwi.

Before quitting the subject of the ancient mining, there is

FIRST ENGINE-HOUSE AND BATTERY ERECTED ON THE TATI GOLD-FIELDS.

one other fact which I will adduce as evidence that gold-mining was carried on by the natives up to a comparatively recent date in South-Eastern Africa. I was at Tati, in South-Western Matabililand, some years ago, when Mr. S. H. Edwards discovered an old shaft, and I examined it carefully in his company. At the mouth of the shaft was a heap of débris, on which a small tree was growing, about four inches in diameter, and, just beyond, a stack of roasted quartz, ready for crushing, and several peculiar round stones, of a kind that we had never seen in the district, intended to be used in grinding the quartz. The quartz vein itself had been about five feet broad on the surface of the ground, and dipped at an angle of about forty-five degrees, going down in the shape of a wedge, and becoming thinner and thinner, until at the lowest point where the work had stopped it was not more than eighteen inches thick, and the quartz at this depth could only have been extracted most laboriously by a man lying head downwards and picking at it. The *modus operandi* had probably been to first light fires against the face of the quartz in order to soften it before picking it out, as, where the work had been abandoned, the quartz was burnt black by fire.   But the most remarkable thing about this shaft was the fact that, at its upper end, the roof was supported by about ten logs of mopani [1] wood.   At the time I had never seen a gold mine ; but lately I have seen mines in Johannesburg with portions of the roof supported in precisely the same manner as in the old shaft at Tati.   We knocked all these supports out, and Mr. Edwards and I examined them one and all very carefully.   They had all been chopped with the same kind of narrow-edged axes used by the natives at the present day, whilst all of them were still covered with bark, and, in fact, were in such good condition that they could not have been very ancient.   I imagine that this shaft was abandoned, together with others in the district, at the time when Umziligazi first took possession of Matabililand, in about 1840.   So much for the gold-mining in Mashunaland ; now for the wall-building.

It appears to me that, so far from there having been an abrupt transition from a people who built the temple of Zimbabwi to a race who never put one stone upon another, the inhabitants of Makoni's and Mangwendi's countries in South-Eastern Mashunaland only ceased to surround their towns with well-built stone walls during the last generation, when they found that these walls offered but an inefficient protection against the Zulu hordes of Manikos, and his son, Umzila, by whom their country has been continually ravaged during the present century.   The more ancient the towns

---

[1] This is the common wood of the district.

appear to be, however, the better, speaking generally, they
have been built ; and in Makoni's country, at any rate, there is
clear evidence that there has been a gradual deterioration from
a people who were capable of building walls which will compare with any part of the great Zimbabwi to the very inferior
hut-building barbarians of the present day.   Makoni's [1] town
as it now stands is a monument of filth and uncleanliness, and
is undefended by anything but a small fence.   His old town,
which I also visited, and from which I believe he was driven
by Umtasa, was surrounded by a moat and a loopholed mud
wall ; whilst the town, which it is said was built by his ancestor,
Chipadzi, is surrounded by a well-built loopholed stone wall.
This is one of the best old walled towns I have seen.   I
visited it for the first time in October 1890, and again last
year.   There are many other walled towns in the district, some
of them reminding one strongly of the fortress on the hill at
Zimbabwi.

Let me here make an extract from my diary, bearing date
19th October 1890.   "On that day I left Makoni's and
passed some very curious old ruins.   First, there was a hill on
which were built several concentric walls and the stone foundations of round huts, the whole being surrounded by a moat.
A little farther on there was a small kopje composed of a few
large blocks of granite, some of which were piled up in the
centre in the form of a tower.   The whole of this kopje was
enclosed by a very well-built wall about two hundred yards
in circumference, eight feet in thickness, and ten feet in height.
The stones composing this wall had the appearance of having
been cemented together with mud, which is the first time I
have ever noticed anything of the kind in South-Eastern
Africa.   Through this wall there were four entrances, apertures
about four feet in height and two and a half feet in breadth.
These apertures were let into the base of the wall, and were
roofed over with large flat slabs of granite.   Inside this wall were
the foundations of numerous round buildings.   These foundations were all very well built of closely-fitted pieces of squared
granite, and were about eighteen inches in depth.   The huts
that were built upon them must have been at least four times

[1] Father of the present chief.

the size of the huts used by the natives at the present day.
Whilst speaking of these carefully-fitted stone foundations on
which to build huts, I may mention that in the centre of
Umtasa's deserted town on the Chodzani river—a town which
he built himself, and from which he was driven a few years
ago by the Abagaza—will be found a similar hut foundation,
very carefully built of small slabs of granite, beautifully fitted
without mortar or cement, which proves that the art of building walls of carefully-fitted granite stones is not even yet
dead amongst the Mashunas."

However, to return to the walled town of Makoni's
ancestor.   Besides the four entrances into the stronghold,
there were numerous small holes let into the wall, some of
which may have served as loopholes through which archers
discharged arrows, but others, from their position, I judge to
have been intended for drains to carry off water.   This stronghold is said to have been built by Chipadzi, the ancient chief
of all this part of the country, and an ancestor of Makoni.
The name of the walled town is Chitiketi.

About half a mile from this old walled town was the
burial-place of Chipadzi, one side of which was enclosed by
a beautifully-built wall about ten feet high, of evenly-laid and
squared granite stones, most carefully fitted together without
mortar or cement of any kind.   This wall was an exact facsimile of the best-built portions of the great Zimbabwi, and
no one who has examined carefully both these relics of a
bygone age can doubt for an instant that they were both
built by the same race of people.   This place is the Zimbabwi
or temple of Makoni's people, and is spoken of by them as
" The Zimbabwi."   Here in time of national trouble the chief
slaughters cattle, and makes propitiatory offerings to the spirit
of Chipadzi, and private individuals make offerings of goats,
fowls, or pots of beer.   Now there is no tower or indeed
anything to make one believe that this Zimbabwi was ever
connected with Phallic worship.   It was probably built long
after the great temple, when the Arabian element had become
lost amongst the more numerous aboriginal race, and when the
people had replaced the worship of Baal by the still older
form of ancestor-worship.

The enclosure is probably simply the burial - place of Chipadzi, but the wall could not have been better built had it been the work of the actual builders of the great temple. I may here say that the word Zimbabwi[1] is in all probability derived from the words "umba" or "imba," a building, plural "zimba," and "mābgi," stones, these words being used at the present day in Mashunaland. Thus Zimbabwi means the "buildings of stones," and, as there were no other buildings except grass-thatched huts, came to have a special significance, and may be best translated by the English word "temple."

In the foregoing pages I have endeavoured to show that there is no evidence that any high form of ancient civilisation ever existed in South-Eastern Africa at all, whilst many facts go to prove that the two industries, or arts, which are supposed by many to separate the ancient inhabitants of the country from the Bantu people living there at the present day, namely, gold-mining and wall-building, have only been abandoned very recently. The evidences of Phallic worship which have been discovered at the temple of Zimbabwi give one a fair right to suppose that the original builders of this structure came from a country where that form of worship is known to have been practised in very ancient times ; but I do not believe that this foreign race, in its pure state, spread over the whole country between the Zambesi and the Limpopo, and did all the gold-mining and wall-building that has been done in that vast territory, and was then utterly destroyed and supplanted by a more barbarous people. The evidence available seems to me to be far stronger in favour of the theory which I have advanced of the gradual fusion of a numerically small number of a race of traders and merchants, who were themselves in a low state of civilisation, with the aboriginal inhabitants of the country. Thus alone can I account for many things : the long continuance and the gradual deterioration noticeable in the wall-building in Mashunaland ; the in-grained inherited impulse which causes the Barotsi of the Upper Zambesi, who are an offshoot of the Barotsi of Mashunaland, to still carve the same chevron patterns on their pottery,

[1] This word is pronounced in some parts of the country Zim-bāb-gĭ, and in others Zim-bāb-wĭ.

on their knife-sheaths, and on their wooden pots and bowls, that the ancient worshippers of Baal represented in stone-work round the temple of Zimbabwi, and carved in soapstone hundreds or thousands of years ago. Add to this, that the wooden bowls themselves still retain the same form as the ancient ones carved in soapstone, that the wooden carvings of animals made at the present day and the rude bas-reliefs on the soapstone bowls are the products of the same school of art, and the fact that the Bantu races inhabiting Mashunaland and adjoining countries to-day are subject to atavism or reversion to a type of man which is Asiatic or Semitic rather than negroid, and it seems to me that only one theory is possible, which is, that the ancient builders of Zimbabwi were not first destroyed and then supplanted by an inferior race, but that they became gradually fused with a lower race, which still bears traces of its admixture with the more intelligent people.

FIRST HOUSES IN UMTALI.

CHAPTER XIX

Mashunaland (*continued*)—History of, in modern times—Occupation of the country
by Europeans—Climatic and sanitary conditions—Material progress since 1890
—The gold industry, ancient and modern—Dr. Jameson, the Administrator.

I WILL now say a few words concerning the history of
Mashunaland in modern times, which I think will show that
it is not to be wondered at that the native races inhabiting
that country should have abandoned some of their arts and
industries, and become the timid and broken-spirited race
which they now are.

As far as we can learn, the country we now call Mashunaland was in the early part of the present century ruled over
by the ancestors of the petty chiefs Makoni, Mangwendi,
Motoko, Sosi, Umtasa, etc., who were the rulers of large and
prosperous tribes living in huts, the foundations of which,
where they still exist, show them to have been at least three
times the size of the miserable tenements which satisfy their
degenerate descendants, and whose towns were, for the most
part, surrounded by well-built and loopholed stone walls,
many of which still remain in perfect preservation to-day,

especially in the country of Makoni, the chief of the Ma-ongwi. Hundreds of thousands of acres that now lie fallow must then have been under cultivation, as is proved by the traces of rice and maize fields which can still be discerned in almost every valley, whilst the sites of ancient villages, long ago crumbled to decay, and now only marked by a few deep pits, from which the natives obtained the clay used by them in plastering their huts, are very numerous all over the open downs, where no stones were procurable with which to build walls round the towns. On almost every hill traces of the stone walls will be found which once encircled and protected ancient villages. At that time the inhabitants of this part of Africa must have been rich and prosperous, possessing large flocks of sheep and goats and numerous herds of a small but beautiful breed of cattle.

This state of things was not, however, destined to continue, for some twelve or fifteen years after the Cape of Good Hope became a British Colony, in 1806, some of the outlying Zulu clans broke away from the harsh and cruel rule of Chaka and commenced their migrations northwards ; and wherever these ferocious warriors went their track was marked by the flight of the vultures which feasted upon the corpses of the men, women, and children they had slain, and the flames of the villages they had set fire to. Manikos, the grandfather of Gungunyan, the present chief of the Abagaza, was the leader of one of these bands, whilst the ancestor of Pezen, the principal chief of the Angoni, who are now settled to the west of Lake Nyassa, led another horde. These two Zulu chiefs, after devastating a great portion of what is now called Mashunaland, both settled near the head waters of the Sabi, where they soon came into collision with one another. A great battle was fought, lasting—so Lo Bengula told me he had heard from old men of the Abagaza—for three days, at the end of which time the Angoni were defeated and driven from their settlements. They retreated northwards, devastating the whole country through which they passed, and crossing the Zambesi to the east of Zumbo, made their way on to the high plateau which lies to the west of Lake Nyassa, where they are living at the present day, a scourge to all the surrounding tribes.

After the battle with the Angoni, the Abagaza retreated

southwards and settled on an elevated and fertile tract of country to the east of the Central Sabi, and from that date, until a few years ago, they never ceased to devastate the southern and eastern portions of Mashunaland, their principal raiding grounds being in the countries of Motoko, Mangwendi, Makoni, Sosi, and Makwirimba. In spite, however, of the devastations committed by the Angoni and the Abagaza, large portions of Northern and Western Mashunaland remained untroubled by the Zulu raids until about 1840. About this time the Amandibili, under their warlike chief, Umziligazi, being unable to hold their own against the Dutch Boers, who were then commencing to settle in the Transvaal, crossed the Limpopo, and travelling northwards, destroying as they went, finally halted, and built permanent kraals in the country now known as Matabililand ; and soon well-disciplined bands of desperate savages, men born and bred amidst the ceaseless slaughter of Chaka's never-ending wars, overran every portion of Mashunaland which had up till then escaped the blood-stained assegais of the Angoni and the Abagaza.

These oft-recurring raids upon the unwarlike inhabitants of Mashunaland—raids carried out with all the ruthless ferocity of savage warfare—almost completely depopulated large tracts of country, and, as may be easily understood, at once put an end to the gold-mining industry, which, there is no doubt, was still being carried on in the early part of this century, and also put a stop to the wall-building, as the Mashunas found out that the walls with which they had been accustomed to encircle their towns, and which were probably very often an effective means of defence against other tribes of their own race, were of but little avail against the braver and better-organised Zulus. Thus the high plateau of Mashunaland, which at no very distant date must have supported a large native population, once more became an almost uninhabited wilderness, as the remnants of the aboriginal tribes who escaped destruction at the hands of the Zulu invaders retreated into the broken country which encircles the plateau to the south and east. Had it not been for the constant destruction of the native races that has been going on in Mashunaland during the last seventy or eighty years, there would be no room for European immigration to-day. As it is, not only has the occupation of the country by the British South Africa Company been effected without wronging the native races, but it has very likely saved some of them from absolute destruction at the hands of the Matabili.

I have now brought the history of Mashunaland up to the time of the recent occupation of the country by Europeans, and I must, before leaving the subject, say a few words about the country itself. Almost the whole of Mashunaland and Manica lies at an elevation of over three thousand feet above the sea, whilst much of the plateau (especially that portion of it lying to the south - east of the main road from Salisbury to Umtali) reaches an altitude of from five thousand to six thousand feet. The higher portions of the country, though lying well within the tropics, possess a thoroughly temperate climate, which is primarily due no doubt to their altitude above sea-level, but also in a minor degree, I think, to the fact that it is the highest land in South-Eastern Africa, and therefore catches directly the cool winds coming from the Indian Ocean. At any rate, during the hottest months of the year the heat of the sun is almost always tempered by the breeze which constantly blows from the south-east—a breeze which, during the winter months, is apt to become so keen and cold that an Englishman suddenly transplanted from home, and deposited, without knowing where he was, on some portion of the Mashuna uplands, would never dream that he was in tropical Africa, but would rather be inclined to believe that he stood on some wild moorland in Northern Europe ; and the sight of a bed of bracken, looking identical with what one sees at home, would only lend colour to this belief. The nights are cool the whole year round and during the winter months bitterly cold, whilst the excessive heat of the sun during the spring and autumn is always tempered, as I have said above, by the south-east breeze. An ounce of fact is worth any amount of theory and assertion, and a table of temperatures kept daily for two years by Major Forbes at Salisbury, in Mashunaland, which is now in the possession of Mr. E. G. Ravenstein, and from which the following table has been compiled, will, I feel sure, satisfy any one

who cares to examine it that the climate of this part of Africa
is an exceptionally fine one for North Europeans.

FORT SALISBURY.

METEOROLOGICAL OBSERVATIONS made by Major P. W. FORBES
during the years 1891 and 1892.

	Atmospheric Pressure.	Mean Temperatures. (Degrees F.)			Rainfall.		Prevailing Winds.
	Inches.	Maxima.	Minima.	Mean.	Inches.	Days.	
January .	25.301	79°	62°	70.5°	7.20	17	N.E.
February .	.301	79°	58°	68.5°	6.74	14	E.
March . .	.342	81°	58°	69.5°	7.32	12	E.,N.E.
April . .	.398	79°	53°	66°	1.19	4	E.
May . .	.441	77°	48°	62.5°	.18	1	E.
June . .	.436	75°	42°	58.5°	...	...	E.
July . .	.480	72°	43°	57.5°	...	...	E.
August .	.472	77°	47°	62°	...	...	N.E.
September	.433	84°	52°	68°	...	...	N.E.
October .	.392	82°	55°	63.5°	.81	4	E.
November	.389	82°	59°	70.5°	3.51	7	E.
December	.344	79°	60°	68.5°	6.89	16	E.
Mean yearly average from two years' observations	25.394	78°	53°	65.5°	33.84	75	E.

EXTREMES OF TEMPERATURE OBSERVED :—

93 in October 1891.
34 in June 1892.

It has already been conclusively proved that European
women and children enjoy excellent health all over the plateau of
South-Eastern Africa—whether in Matabililand, Mashunaland,
or Manica. In fact these are emphatically countries that will rear
a strong and hardy race of men—such men as are the descendants of the English and Scottish colonists of the Cape Colony,
or the burly Boers of the Transvaal. During eight months of
the year the whole country is very healthy, but during the

remaining four, from the middle to the end of the rainy season,[1] fever is very prevalent in the lower parts of the country, and will almost certainly be contracted by any one who is unduly exposed to cold and wet in any part of the country.

The same may probably be said concerning many other portions of the world, in which large communities of Europeans are now living; and it has already been thoroughly proved, alike in Mashunaland, Manica, and Matabililand, at Salisbury, Umtali, and Bulawayo, that, given the most ordinary conditions of comfort, and freedom from excessive exposure, white men, women, and children enjoy as good health in these countries as in any other part of South Africa.

The development of Mashunaland is now going on so rapidly that, were I to give a detailed account of its present condition, my remarks would be out of date before this book is through the press. However, before I left the country in August 1892 Salisbury had already been in telegraphic communication with the rest of the world for some months. Three

---

[1] As a rule, the rainy season may be said to last from the beginning of November till the end of March. That is to say that during any one of these months a heavy rainfall may be expected; but in no single season does heavy rain prevail during all these months. In some years a great deal of rain falls in November, followed by a month or two months of fine weather, heavy rain again falling in February or March. In other years but little rain falls before the end of the year, in which case heavy rains may be expected after the new year. Sometimes the rainfall is evenly distributed over the five months; but, as a rule, there is a fair allowance of fine weather during the period called the rainy season. On the other hand, during the first and last months of the dry season, in April and October, heavy thunderstorms usually occur, and a year seldom passes without a few light showers of rain falling during the cold months, either in June, July, or August; more especially in the south-eastern portions of the country. On the plateau, during May, June, and July, the sun has little heat, and the nights are very cold. After August the sun gets hotter and hotter, but the nights continue very cold until October. The month which immediately precedes the commencement of the rainy season is always the hottest. During the rainy season itself the heat is seldom oppressive, as the sky is usually overcast and the sun obscured. The nights are always cool, and in April again become very cold. From the 1st of May till the end of December the climate is wonderfully healthy, and fever is very seldom contracted during this period; but great care must be taken to guard against exposure to wet during the months of January, February, March, and April, at which time the vegetation is rank, and malaria prevalent. To reach the plateau of Mashunaland either from the east coast or from the Transvaal it is necessary to cross a low-lying belt of country in which malarial fever is very prevalent from the end of November to the beginning of June; and as it is all-important to any one intending to take up his residence in Mashunaland to arrive in the country with no fever poison in his system, I strongly advise all intending immigrants to that country to make their way to the plateau between the months of June and November. Experience has shown that people arriving in Mashunaland in good health and with no fever poison in their systems enjoy perfect health in that country, unless exposed to unhealthy conditions; whilst others who have contracted fever in the hot low-lying country on the east coast, or between the Limpopo and Victoria, suffer from continual relapses, when exposed to the cold rarified air of the plateau, and in some cases are never able to regain their health.

FACSIMILE (¼ SIZE) OF THE TWO FIRST SHEETS OF THE FIRST NEWSPAPER EVER PUBLISHED IN MASHUNALAND.

townships had been laid out, in which building sites, sold by auction July 1892, realised the sum of £10,000[1]; a respectable figure when it is understood that these plots of ground were all bought, not by speculators, but by residents in the country. In two of these townships, Salisbury and Victoria, many substantial brick buildings had already been put up, and I hear that building is now going on in Umtali as well. In Salisbury and Victoria good weekly newspapers were being printed.[2] Much of the land had been taken up by farmers, and it had already been proved that wheat, oats, barley, and all kinds of vegetables, such as potatoes, onions, cauliflowers, cabbages, carrots, etc., could be grown with great facility. Whilst on the subject of agriculture I will quote a few lines from a private letter I have received from Salisbury, dated 16th March 1893. "Farmers have already done a good deal of ploughing in the several districts during this past wet season—vegetables are a drug in the market, and already a good many loads of forage have come in. B—— on our farm has one stack cut, and reckons on getting three thousand bundles altogether this year. The small patch of wheat he tried during the rains has ripened well."

In fact, it can no longer be said of Mashunaland that an interesting experiment is being tried, etc. etc. The experiment has been tried and has succeeded, and Mashunaland is now a British colony in which it has been proved that European men, women, and children can live and thrive, and when the railway, now in course of construction, from the east coast has been carried into the heart of the country, enabling capitalists to introduce the heavy machinery necessary for quartz-crushing on a large scale, then will reefs innumerable in all parts of the country be worked to advantage. Each gold district will then support a large population connected with the gold industry, and in each of these centres of population farmers will find a market for the produce of their fields and dairies. The future of the vast gold-fields of Mashunaland and

[1] A further sale of building sites held in July 1893 realised £19,500.
[2] A facsimile (reduced in size) of two pages of the first number of the first paper ever produced in Mashunaland has been reproduced as an illustration. This sheet was produced by the cyclostyle process, but has long since been superseded by a well-printed newspaper, which in its general get-up will bear comparison with the newspapers of much older communities in other parts of South Africa.

Manica seems now so absolutely assured that it appears odd that doubts should ever have been entertained as to their value. And yet there have been doubters who were credited by the faint-hearted with a wisdom which it has now been proved they never possessed.

From time immemorial Mashunaland has been one of the gold-fields of the world.   Mr. Bent believes that the people who first discovered the sacred metal were of Semitic race ; and, however that may be, it is an undoubted fact that at the present day, wherever there is a gold-field in Southern Africa, men of another branch of the Semitic family are not uncommon.   Probably the gold-belts existing all over South-Eastern Africa were worked continuously from the date of their first discovery up to the early part of the present century. In all that time dynamite was unknown, but slowly and laboriously shafts were sunk and cuttings made in the gold-bearing quartz reefs, which in the course of ages in many instances reached a depth of over a hundred feet.   The aggregate of all the work done in all parts of Mashunaland is something stupendous, and must, considering the nature of the work, and the rudeness of the tools available, have required a long period of time for its accomplishment.   In the early part of this century Mashunaland and Manica were overrun by various Zulu hordes, immense numbers of the aboriginal inhabitants were put to the assegai, and the working of the gold reefs almost, though not entirely, put a stop to (for I have shown that Mr. Thomas Baines, as late as in the year 1870, found the Mashunas extracting gold from quartz near Lo Magondi's kraals).   At this time nothing was known in Western Europe of the ancient history of Mashunaland, or the existence of gold reefs in that country.   Portuguese archives, it is true, showed that large quantities of gold had been brought to Europe from South-Eastern Africa during the sixteenth, seventeenth, and eighteenth centuries, but the great mass of Englishmen were not interested in Portuguese archives, and the Portuguese themselves, after they were driven from Manica in 1832 by Manikos and his Zulus, were only just able to retain their hold on the coast-line and the shores of the Zambesi, and so the gold industry very nearly came to an end in Mashunaland.   Then Thomas

Baines and Karl Mauch revisited the ancient gold-fields, and the accounts they wrote as to their probable richness caused such an excitement in South Africa that it spread to Australia, and a party of miners came from that country in 1870 to try their luck on the gold-fields of Mashunaland. They reached Tati in South-Western Matabililand, where they found some good reefs, but did not go any farther. For at that time Mashunaland was a very distant and inaccessible country, whose southern and western borders were inhabited by jealous and warlike Zulu tribes, who looked upon it as a raiding ground and a slave preserve that they were anxious to keep for themselves as long as possible.

And so twenty years went by, and though during all that time Mashunaland was spoken about and written of as a rich gold country, prospectors were unable to make their way into it owing to the jealousy of the Matabili. From time to time hunters like myself bought quills full of alluvial gold washed from the sands of the Mazoe river, from the Mashunas, and by showing them to friends in Kimberley and Cape Town kept up the belief in the richness of the country. Then came the expedition to Mashunaland, which was carried out with such singular success. Hundreds of men were turned loose in the country to look for gold who knew no more of the theory and practice of gold-mining than I do of the fourth dimension of space. Most of them thought they were going to peg out claims on rich reefs within a week or two of their disbandment, whilst many of them believed they would be able to pick up lumps of gold, or wash cupfuls of the precious metal out of the river's sands. They were disappointed, and many of them soon became disheartened.

Then came a very heavy rainy season, which, owing to the utter want of accommodation or comfort, and the scarcity of all kinds of provisions, was a time of misery to the greater part of the settlers. Though there were very few deaths, almost every one suffered more or less from fever, the result of exposure to wet and poor food. After this first rainy season a great many of the men who had come up to Mashunaland with the pioneer expedition left the country with hearts full of bitterness. They gave the country a bad name, of course, and declared there was no gold there, or that the ore was of such low grade that it would not pay to work it. The accounts that had been written by Baines and Mauch twenty years before were declared to be absolutely mythical. The parrot cry was taken up and echoed and re-echoed throughout South Africa and England. There was no payable gold in Mashunaland it was said. There had been once, perhaps, but if the Jews had been there in King Solomon's time, it was not likely they would have left the country until they had worked out all the good reefs. However, all this time a residuum of hard-working men remained in Mashunaland. They found what they thought to be good reefs in every district—in Victoria, Manica, Hartley Hills, Mazoe, Angwa, and Mount Darwin. Through good report and evil report they worked away, developing their properties, buoyed up by the faith that was in them, and the conviction that truth would at last prevail. And so indeed it has ; for I believe that in the financial world at the present time the future of the gold-fields of Mashunaland is considered, as I have said already, to be absolutely assured. Payable reefs have now been proved to a considerable depth in every district. All that is required is the capital necessary to erect quartz-crushing machinery and carry on the development. The introduction of heavy machinery into the country is now not only very difficult but very expensive. When the railway, however, has been completed from the east coast into the heart of Mashunaland, its gold mines will be worked at a reasonable cost ; and every mail now brings the most encouraging reports from the different mining centres.

As the work of development has gone on, so have the prospects improved in every district, till now it can, I think, no longer be doubted that before the end of this century Mashunaland will take a high place amongst the gold-producing countries of the world. Capital, however, must first be put into the country before the gold can be got out of it.

I have not yet said anything concerning the administration of the country, but I will conclude this chapter by saying that I consider that it was a veritable inspiration that prompted Mr. Rhodes to ask his old friend Dr. Jameson to take over the arduous and difficult duties of Administrator of Mashunaland.

Dr. Jameson has endeared himself to all classes of the community by his tact and good temper, and has managed all the diverse details connected with the administration of a new country with a correctness of judgment which amounts to nothing less than genius—and genius of a most rare and versatile order.   He was *the* man for the position.   No other, taken all round, could have been quite what Dr. Jameson has been as Administrator of Mashunaland in its early days.

CHAPTER XX

The Expedition to Mashunaland (*continued*)

As soon as Mr. Cecil Rhodes recognised the fact that, if Mashunaland were to become a British province, it would have to be occupied and taken possession of without delay by a British force, he at once set about organising an expedition for the purpose of cutting a road from Khama's country to Mount Hampden, which would skirt round the southern border of Matabililand. Such a road would not pass within a hundred miles of any Matabili village, nor through any territory over which Lo Bengula had any real jurisdiction; although he claimed the whole country right down to the Limpopo river, on the ground that he had sent raiding parties in that direction as far as the northern border of the Transvaal. As, however, he claims the whole of Khama's country on the same ground—a claim which the British Government has refused to recognise, having long ago proclaimed Khama's country to be within the British protectorate—I think that the British South Africa Company showed him every reasonable consideration by cutting the road to Mashunaland at a distance of more than a hundred miles from the country actually occupied by his tribe. Of course it was not to be expected that Lo Bengula or his people would regard the occupation of Mashunaland by Europeans with any peculiar satisfaction. To begin with, it would mean a curtailment of their raiding grounds, and would, besides, be likely to affect their power and prestige amongst the tribes they had conquered to a very considerable extent.

Many experienced people thought that the Matabili would

resist the occupation of Mashunaland to the last, and declared that such an occupation could never take place until they had been conquered and destroyed.   In fact the Boers of Zoutpansberg considered that such an expedition ought not to be undertaken with a force of less than two thousand men.   I myself was of the opinion that it was quite possible the Matabili would attack our expedition ; but at the same time I thought that if we had a good strong mounted force, and kept well away beyond the radius of their outside kraals, they were just as likely to let us alone.   What I think had as much, or more, to do with keeping them quiet than anything else, was the placing of several companies of that most serviceable corps, the Bechwanaland Border Police, on their western border just before the expedition started.   Had the Matabili attacked the pioneer force on its way to Mashunaland, they knew very well that Major Grey, who was then in command at Macloutsie camp, would have ridden in at once with his troopers and made things lively for their king in the neighbourhood of Bulawayo.   I do not know whose idea it was to advance the Bechwanaland Border Police from Elibi camp to the western border of Matabililand, but I am sure that it had a very salutary effect on Lo Bengula and his people.

About the end of the year 1889 and early in 1890 the agents of the British South Africa Company at Bulawayo were on very good terms with Lo Bengula ; and Dr. Jameson, who was an especial favourite with him, not only obtained his consent to the plan of cutting a new road to Mashunaland, but also promises of assistance in the way of men to chop the trees down and prepare the track.   However, I think it is probable that Lo Bengula, when he gave these assurances, had no idea that an expedition was already in preparation with this object in view, and either thought that he would never be called upon to make good his promises, or trusted that he would be able to evade them when the time came, in his usual fashion.

In March 1890 I was sent up to Palapye.   My instructions were to get men from Khama and chop a waggon road to the eastern border of his country.   There I was to meet

Mr. Johan Colenbrander from Bulawayo with a hundred of
Lo Bengula's men, with whom I was to go on with the road-
making towards Mashunaland.   On this road the force then
being equipped for the occupation of the country was to
follow.   On my arrival at Palapye I was, however, to have
found a letter from Mr. Denis Doyle, at that time the
Company's agent at Bulawayo, with further instructions as
to where I was to meet Mr. Colenbrander.   I found no letter,
and knowing Lo Bengula's shifty, procrastinating ways, and
having very strong doubts in my mind as to the sincerity of
his professions of friendship, or promises of assistance in
making the new road, I resolved to ride in to Bulawayo and
find out for myself if he was really prepared to co-operate
with the British Company that was bent on undermining his
power, and taking possession of a
country over a portion of which he
claimed jurisdiction.   From Palapye
I rode to Tati on the western border
of Matabililand, and from there Mr.
S. H. Edwards drove me in to Bulawayo, in three days, in his light mule
waggon.

MR. S. H. EDWARDS.

Mr. S. H. Edwards, better known
to his friends as " Far Interior Sam "
or " Dear Old Sam," is one of the old
landmarks still left standing in the
interior of Southern Africa.   The son of one of the first
missionaries who settled amongst the Bechwana tribes on
the western border of the Transvaal, Mr. S. H. Edwards is
the contemporary of Gordon-Cumming, Oswell, and Livingstone, all of whom he knew personally.   Of Mr. Oswell he is
never tired of talking, and he regards him as the beau ideal
of what a roving British gentleman should be—kindly and
generous in disposition, and a most daring and successful
hunter.   As Mr. Edwards was born on his father's mission
station, he grew up amongst the natives and learned to speak
Sechwana like one of themselves, and he has a better knowledge of that language and of native manners and customs
and modes of thought than any other white man.   In 1854

he accompanied the venerable Scotch missionary, the Rev. Mr. Moffat, on his visit to Lo Bengula's father, Umziligazi, and was thus one of the first two Europeans who ever visited Matabililand. Little did young Sam Edwards think at that time that he would live to see a thriving British colony grow up in the country *beyond* Matabililand. As may be imagined, Mr. Edwards is a perfect walking dictionary concerning all matters connected with sport and travel in the interior of South Africa during the last fifty years. He accompanied Fred Green on some of his hunting expeditions long long ago, between Lake Ngami and the Chobi river, and knew personally Chapman, and the two Swedish naturalist-hunters, C. J. Andersen and Professor Wahlberg, the latter of whom was killed by an elephant. Of late years Mr. S. H. Edwards has acted as Managing Director of the Tati Gold-Mining Company, and his great knowledge of native character, and the tact he has displayed in his dealings with both Khama and Lo Bengula, have been invaluable to his employers. Both Khama and Lo Bengula have the most implicit trust in " Samo," for they both know by long experience that he is an upright, honourable English gentleman, on whose word they can thoroughly rely. Like the natives, all white men in the interior, whether Boer hunters or European traders and travellers, love "old Sam," and will be pleased to read what I have said about him, so that I hope my dear old friend will not be angry with me for introducing him to the British public.

When, in company with Mr. Edwards, I presented myself before Lo Bengula, he received me in the most friendly manner, and was evidently pleased to see me again, for it was more than two years since I had last been in his country. But when I told him that I had been sent by Mr. Rhodes to make the road round the outskirts of his country to Mashunaland, and wanted him to give me men to open up a waggon track, as he had promised Dr. Jameson he would do, he denied ever having given any such promises, and then said plainly that he would not allow such a road to be made. When Mr. Doyle reminded him of his promises to Dr. Jameson he avoided any discussion of that question, and only said, " There is only one road to Mashunaland, and that goes through my country

and past Bulawayo"; and he further said, "If Rhodes wants to
send his men round my country let him send them by sea
to beyond the Sabi river." At last he said to Mr. Doyle,
"Rhodes has sent me many emissaries, and amongst them
Dr. Jameson, whom I like, and whom I am told is Rhodes's
mouth; but I am Lo Bengula, and I want to see the big
white chief himself; I am tired of talking with Rhodes's
messengers and the bearers of his words : their stories don't
all agree. Now, therefore, let Selous go back once more to
the Diamond Fields, and let him take Rhodes by the hand
and come back here with him, that I may speak with him
face to face. I will then settle my business with him very
quickly." Mr. Doyle pointed out that Mr. Rhodes was a
very busy man, and would hardly be likely to be able to
spare the time for so long a journey ; and he further reminded
Lo Bengula of his own dilatory ways, and finally asked him
whether, if Mr. Rhodes really did come to see him, he would
come to a definite understanding with him at once and without
any delay. "Tell him," said Lo Bengula, "that on the day
that follows the one on which I see him all the questions at
issue between us shall be settled, and on the third day he
will be able to start back to his own country."

As the making of the projected road was now at a stand-
still, Mr. Doyle asked me to take this message down to Mr.
Rhodes, though no one thought that the Cape Premier would
be able to spare the time necessary for a journey to Matabililand, however much he might desire to accept Lo Bengula's
invitation. My idea is that Lo Bengula now for the first time
realised that a determined attempt to open up Mashunaland was
really about to be made. As he had signed treaties with the
British South Africa Company, and had not only taken large
presents from them, but had also for some time past been
receiving a subsidy in money, paid monthly by the Company's
agent in Bulawayo, he saw that he had committed himself to
more than he dared perform ; for I think he feared that, should
the white men persist in endeavouring to cut a road round his
country to Mashunaland, he might not be able to restrain his
young men from attacking them, and he was wise enough to
know that if once a war were to break out between his people

and the whites, no matter how successful the former might be in the beginning, in the end they would be vanquished and he himself probably killed. Now at this time Lo Bengula had some white advisers who were doing all they could to undermine the work of the Chartered Company, and it is my impression that, acting under their advice, had Mr. Rhodes visited him he would have returned him all the money and presents he had received from his agents and then refused to have any further negotiations with him. At the same time, he would have sent messengers to the High Commissioner for South Africa to protest against what he called the violation of his territory. This, however, is only a suspicion, for which there may be no foundation.

I now hurried back to Kimberley, which I reached in eleven days from Bulawayo. This was of course before the railway was built from Kimberley to Vryburg. I rode the one hundred miles between Tati and Palapye on my old shooting-pony Mars, in a little under twenty-seven hours. Mr. Rhodes, although he would have liked to have accepted Lo Bengula's invitation, could not possibly spare the time for such a journey, but Dr. Jameson, his *alter ego*, returned with me forthwith to Matabililand. To me it seems that matters were now on a much more satisfactory basis than before my visit to Bulawayo. We knew exactly where we were, and realised fully that the new road to Mashunaland would have to be made not only without the assistance of Lo Bengula, but in despite of him and all his tribe.

Every effort was now made to equip and muster a sufficient force on the banks of the Macloutsie to occupy Mashunaland whether the Matabili liked it or not. As it turned out, the expeditionary force of about four hundred white men, together with the Bechwanaland Border Police, who remained at Macloutsie, and two companies of the British South Africa Company's Police that protected our base at Tuli, proved sufficient to overawe the Matabili and to keep them quiet ; but had they made a determined attack with eight or ten thousand men on the expeditionary force, they might possibly have annihilated us, and would most certainly have retarded the occupation of Mashunaland for a year or two. As it turned out, they made no attack, and it is a matter of history that in two and a half months from the time it left Tuli, the British South Africa Company's expedition planted the British flag near Mount Hampden, after having found and cut a road through four hundred miles of wild country.

So much has been written concerning the march up to Mashunaland, and the composition of the force that took part in it, that it would be mere repetition were I to say very much on the subject. The whole force of police and pioneers was commanded by Lieutenant-Colonel Pennefather of the 6th (Inniskilling) Dragoons ; but the pioneers, one company of whom were always in advance to prepare the road, were commanded by Mr. Frank Johnson. Every one in South Africa has heard of Frank Johnson and Co.—the Co. being Messrs. Heany and Borrow. All three names are household words in Mashunaland. Johnson and Borrow are two fine young Englishmen, and Heany is an American, and all three are brimming over with enthusiasm and energy, and are possessed of that dogged perseverance and untiring patience which has already won half the world for the Anglo-Saxon race. They are the men who raised and equipped the pioneer corps, with an admirable attention to every detail of outfit ; and ever since the occupation of Mashunaland they have been the life and soul of the country. In 1891 they tried to open up a transport road to the east coast. Owing to the tse-tse fly this enterprise was a failure, and cost the firm a large portion of the money they had won by the successful conduct of the pioneer force. All honour to them for the valiant attempt they made to overcome what proved to be insuperable difficulties. " It is not in mortals to command success." During the hard times experienced by the pioneers, during the first rainy season after the occupation of Mashunaland, Heany and Borrow (Johnson had gone down to Cape Town to prepare for the opening up of the east coast route from Beira) endeared themselves to all classes of the community by their kindness to all who were in distress ; and I think all old pioneers will join me in wishing luck to Johnson, Borrow, and Heany, and hoping they will live to reap the reward their pluck and perseverance so richly deserve.

I accompanied Dr. Jameson on his journey to Bulawayo as far as Tati. Farther than this the Doctor would not allow me to proceed, and as he was my superior officer I was bound to obey him. He was afraid that Lo Bengula, who knew that the projected expedition depended on my services as guide to the promised land, might make me a prisoner and detain me at Bulawayo. My orders were to go down to the camp of the Bechwanaland Border Police, on the Macloutsie river, and examine the country thoroughly to the eastward as far as the Shashi and Tuli rivers, in order to be able to pick out a good line for a waggon road ; for it was very important that the expedition should make a good start, and keep as far as possible from the Matabili kraals. I therefore first rejoined my waggon at Palapye, and then trekked to the police camp on the Macloutsie, and from thence to a spot about twenty miles lower down the river. I here formed a camp, and during the month of May 1890 examined the whole country between the lower courses of the Macloutsie, Shashi, and Tuli rivers, and finally selected a good line of country for a waggon road, that would be fairly well supplied with water all the year round, would cross the Tuli at a point about six miles below its junction with the Shashi, close to a flat-topped hill which I saw at once could be easily turned into a very strong strategic position. On this hill Fort Tuli was built some weeks later.

Towards the end of May I had occasion to visit the police camp twenty miles up the Macloutsie, and late on the afternoon of 23rd May started on my return journey to my own waggon. I was about half-way, and it was just getting dusk, when I saw some koodoo cows standing in the mopani bush to the left of the old waggon track along which I was riding. Turning my head to look at them, but without checking my horse, I saw the head and horns of a big bull showing above the bushes beyond them, and perhaps two hundred and fifty yards from the road. I wanted a good koodoo's head, so instantly checking my horse, I jumped off, and putting up the second sight prepared for a shot. I could only see the head and neck of the koodoo above the bushes, and had to judge whereabouts his shoulder ought to be, and there was so little light left that had I not had a white sight of hippopotamus ivory I could not have seen to shoot at all. As I fired I heard my bullet tell distinctly, but saw the koodoo dash away through the scrub and vanish.   I now remounted and rode out to about the place where the koodoo had been standing when I fired.   I soon found the spoor of the wounded animal, and had no difficulty in following it, as the hoof marks had cut deep into the ground; it was, however, too dusk to distinguish any traces of blood.   After following the hoof marks for about a hundred yards they brought me to the edge of a steep thickly-wooded ravine, into which I thought that the wounded koodoo must have plunged.   By this time I had come to the conclusion that my bullet must have struck too high and had not inflicted a mortal wound, so, as I had still ten miles to ride by moonlight before I could get supper at my waggon, I decided to give up the pursuit for the present, but resolved to return and again take up the spoor on the following morning. An hour and a half's riding took me to my camp, where I found that my boys had a substantial meal awaiting me, to which I at once proceeded to do full justice.

Before turning in I gave orders that my horse should be fed as soon as it was daylight in the morning, and told three of my boys to be ready to accompany me to where I had wounded the koodoo.   By the time it was broad daylight the next day we were ready to start, and the sun was not very high above the trees when we reached the spot in the road from which I had fired on the preceding evening.   We were soon once more on the tracks of the wounded animal, and I now saw that blood was sprinkled plentifully along the trail. On reaching the edge of the ravine we found that the koodoo had not plunged into it, but had made a sudden turn, and rushed into a patch of bush to our left ; and here we found him lying dead, not twenty yards from where I had stood the day before.   When I had first seen him standing in the bush in the dusk of the evening I had thought he was a fine bull, but nothing more.   My joy may therefore be imagined when I saw that the most superb specimen of a koodoo bull that my eyes had ever looked upon lay dead before me.   His horns were perfectly symmetrical, very long, and beautifully twisted. I preserved this koodoo's head most carefully, and it eventually

"My joy may therefore be imagined when I saw that the most superb specimen of a koodoo bull that my eyes had ever looked upon lay dead before me."

reached England in safety, and is, I think, the gem of gems amongst my large collection of hunting trophies.

The measurements of these horns are given in Mr. Rowland Ward's most useful book on *Horn Measurements of Great Game* as, measured in a straight line from base to tip, forty-five and three-eighth inches ; round curve of horn, sixty and five-eighth inches ; circumference at base, eleven and a half inches ; spread between tips, thirty-three inches. At the time when Mr. Ward's book was published no other koodoo head was known to exist in England which equalled this in length of horn, and it therefore stands first on his list ; but lately I have heard of one in South Africa that is longer ; however, I am well contented with mine, and feel sure that, no matter how many more koodoos I kill, I shall never get another with a head to equal it. After cutting off the koodoo's head I carried it up to the police camp, where I at once skinned and preserved it, and left it in charge of a friend. That evening I received a note from Dr. Jameson, who had returned from Matabililand, telling me he was on his way to Palapye to meet Colonel Pennefather, and asking me to join him as soon as possible ; so I at once saddled up and overtook him near Fort Elibi. On 27th May we reached Palapye, and on the following day Colonel Penne-father arrived there from Kimberley.

Mr. Frank Johnson was now at Camp Cecil, on the Limpopo, with his pioneers, and the British South Africa Company's Police had all reached the Macloutsie, where they were camped alongside of the Bechwanaland Border Police force. Lieutenant-General the Honourable Paul Methuen (now General Lord Methuen) was expected up shortly to review the whole of the expeditionary force, and report on its efficiency ; and should this report be favourable the advance was to be made at once.

At this time there was not a yard of road made beyond the Macloutsie, and no one but myself had any idea as to what route the expedition was to take when it did at last make a move. It appeared to me that some of the authorities at Cape Town did not realise that between Macloutsie camp and Mount Hampden there lay a trackless wilderness of four hundred and sixty miles in extent, over which a road would have to be found and prepared in advance of the expedition.   The idea seemed to be, that when everything was ready a trumpet would be blown, and the advance would then be made along known roads, as had been the case from Mafeking to Macloutsie. However, after a conference between Dr. Jameson and Colonel Pennefather, at which I expressed my views, I got leave to at once set about cutting the first piece of new road from Macloutsie camp to the Tuli, a distance of about fifty miles.   Khama with his usual courtesy and kindness gave me twenty picked men to open up the track, and sent with them one of his most trusted headmen, an old friend of mine named Makamana.   I was also accompanied by Lieutenant Capper of the British South Africa Company's Police, whose business it was to examine all the hills on the line of route with a view to the establishment of heliograph stations between Macloutsie and Tuli.   By the 10th of June we had opened up a waggon track to the Tuli, and the first section of the new road to Mashunaland lay ready, waiting for the advance of the expedition.

Before returning to Macloutsie camp I collected all the information possible from Khama's Makalaka subjects living on the lower course of the Tuli concerning the country on ahead, and planned out the next section of the road to Matipi's, passing to the south of Sitoutsi's.   With Makamana's assistance I obtained what proved to be a very accurate description of this part of the route, and from Matipi's to Chibi's I knew there would be no difficulty, as the Boer hunters from Zoutpansberg had in former years made a regular hunting road between these two places, the line of which, as well as the fords through the rivers, were well known to the natives, from whom I felt sure there would be no difficulty in getting a guide.   The only piece of the route about which I had any misgivings was the section beyond Chibi's, where I knew there would be a sharp ascent to the plateau.   Once on the table-land I had no further fears, as I was familiar with the whole country along the line we would have to take.

CHAPTER XXI

The Expedition to Mashunaland (*continued*)

AT length, in the end of June, the forces were inspected by General Methuen, and the inspection having proved satisfactory, Major Johnson's pioneers, and four troops of the British South Africa Company's Police, advanced simultaneously along the new track to the Tuli river. Here we were met by a small party of Matabili, bearing a letter to the chief of the white men. The purport of this letter was that there was no road round Lo Bengula's country, and that he would not have one made, and it was also intimated that should the white impi (army) cross the Tuli and try to make a road they might expect trouble. To this letter Colonel Pennefather, as commander of the forces, and Dr. Jameson, as political agent and Mr. Rhodes's *alter ego*, sent fitting replies. At this period all the coloured boys attached to the expedition, the drivers and leaders of the waggons, the cattle-herds and horse-boys, etc., were in a state of the most abject terror at the thought of crossing the Tuli river and invading the country of the Matabili king ; great numbers deserted, and it is my belief that, had not Khama come to our assistance at this juncture, not a coloured boy would have crossed the Tuli, and the expedition in that case would have been most lamentably crippled. I have never yet seen Khama's aid acknowledged or even referred to, and I therefore take this opportunity of stating that, in my opinion, he, by his hearty co-operation in every way, and whenever called upon, with the leaders of the expedition to Mashunaland, not only rendered inestimable services to the British South Africa Company, but earned the gratitude of all Englishmen who are interested in British expansion in South Africa.   Just when we reached the Tuli, and the panic amongst the coloured boys was becoming acute, Khama sent a contingent of two hundred men under the command of his favourite brother, Radi - Kladi,   to assist us in whatever way they were required.   Thirty-seven of these men were mounted, and these I divided into five   parties,   each under the command of   a   white   man

KHAMA.

(always a picked frontiersman), and used as scouts—for I may here say, that besides being the guide of the expedition I was

also at the head of the Intelligence Department, and had
to plan out and arrange all the far-out scouting. My five
scouting parties followed one another in rotation, day by day
each party riding first twenty miles or so along our back track
and then circling round the advancing expedition at a distance of
from ten to twenty miles towards the Matabili border. Each
party slept out three nights and on the fourth picked up the
expedition again. No Matabili army attacked us, but it is my
firm belief that, had it done so, one or other of my parties of
circling scouts would have crossed their track, and brought in
news of their approach when they were still some miles distant,
and thus given time for everything to have been got ready to
resist an attack. Many people who took part in the expedition
were probably never aware that any outside scouting was going
on at all : the system I have described was, however, constantly
carried out during the progress of the expedition. Besides the
mounted men sent by Khama, there were more than fifty
men armed with breech-loading rifles, and these I employed
in assisting the pioneers to make the waggon road. All
the remainder were required as leaders, horse - boys, and
cattle-herds. None of course dared to desert and leave the
expedition as long as Radi-Kladi, the brother of their chief,
remained with it.

As soon as ever Lo Bengula's messengers had started on
their return journey to Bulawayo with the answers sent by
Colonel Pennefather and Dr. Jameson respectively, I obtained
leave from General Methuen (who was still with us), and
Colonel Pennefather, to cross the Tuli and commence the road
eastwards with one troop of the pioneers. It seemed to me a
most important matter to get on with the road at this juncture
with as little delay as possible ; for I knew that Lo Bengula's
messengers would take ten days to reach Bulawayo, and, should
war be decided upon, that it would take some days more to
muster an army, and at least another ten days for that army to
get down to where we were ; so that I calculated that we had
at least twenty-five days during which we could work on un-
molested, and get through all the low country, which, being the
most thickly wooded, would be the worst in which to sustain an
attack from the Matabili.

Dr. Jameson, Mr. Colquhoun, Colonel Pennefather, and General Methuen all concurring in the soundness of these views, I was allowed to commence the road beyond the Tuli on the day after the arrival of the expedition there. This first section of the road beyond Tuli was cut by "B" troop of the pioneers, under Captain Hoste. The whole expedition was to follow on our track as soon as a fort had been constructed on the flat-topped hill, overlooking the river, of which I have before spoken. Dr. Jameson accompanied us, though I think he ought to have remained behind with the main expedition ; but he is a man of so generous a nature that, because he thought there was more danger with the small advance party of forty men than with the main column, he must needs come on ahead with us. Here's your health, and good luck to you, Doctor !

The men were all full of enthusiasm, and we got on well the first few days, and on 9th July reached the river Umzingwan. Beyond the Umzingwan we had about the heaviest piece of chopping to do on the whole road, seventeen miles of thick forest with no water on the line of march. It took us a little over two days to do it, and on the second evening, our water cart having run dry, the men suffered somewhat from thirst. Early on the morning of 13th July, however, we reached the Umshabetsi river, where we all had a most refreshing bathe. A herd of elephants had been drinking in the river just before us, and were shortly afterwards sighted by our scouts ; but as strict orders had been given that no shots were to be fired at game, they were not molested. There were about twenty elephants in this herd, but no good tuskers.

Since leaving Fort Tuli we had heard nothing of the main column, nor did we bother much about it. Our small advance party was perfectly fitted out in every way, the men were a first-rate, willing lot, mostly young colonists, and we were all well mounted. As we were in the enemy's country, we took every precaution to guard against surprise. Scouting parties were always out, and whilst one half of the men walked, and cleared a road through the bush with their axes, they were closely attended by their mounted comrades, who led their friends' horses, ready saddled and bridled, and carried their rifles and bandoliers; so that any sudden attack would have been met by the whole troop ready mounted. Every night we surrounded our camp with a strong "zeriba" of thorn-trees, the pickets mounting guard outside. We made up our minds that if we heard nothing from the main column we would work away, and never stop until we had cut a road right through to our destination and planted the Union Jack we carried with us on the top of Mount Hampden. As the men were, however, much fatigued by the heavy work they had done in opening up a track through the seventeen miles of forest country between the Umzingwan and the Umshabetsi, we took a day's rest after reaching the latter river.

That night a hyæna made the most unearthly noise round our camp that I have ever heard. No one, I feel sure, who belonged to "B" troop of the pioneers will have forgotten it. To me it sounded most ominous, for only once before had I heard anything like it, and that was on the night of the day following that on which poor French got lost beyond the Chobi, when one of these foul brutes rushed backwards and forwards several times round the little scherm, where Miller and I lay wondering, all the time howling and laughing and shrieking, like a fiend alternately wailing and rejoicing. As we afterwards learned, it was on this very night, and about the same time that the hyæna was howling round us, that our poor friend, worn out with thirst and fatigue, must have breathed his last.[1] I have never forgotten it, and the hideous serenade with which we were entertained on the banks of the Umshabetsi stirred sad memories within me, and almost made me think that an African banshee was wailing and crying round us, and forewarning us of woe and disaster to come. My superstitious fears, however, proved to be without foundation, as nothing went wrong with the expedition, nor were we ever assailed by any danger.

On the 14th July we were just busy cutting down the steep banks of the river and preparing a ford across its sandy bed, when a mounted trooper rode up from the main column with a letter from Colonel Pennefather, which proved to be an order not to continue our advance, but to wait where we were

---

[1] For an account of this sad experience see *A Hunter's Wanderings*, pp. 392-401.

until the column had come up with us, as we were getting too
far ahead.   On the receipt of this letter Dr. Jameson and I at
once saddled up and rode back to the main column, which we
found about thirty-five miles distant.

On 18th July the whole column reached the Umshabetsi
early in the morning, and on the following day I again went
on ahead, this time with "A" troop of the pioneers, under the
command of Captain Heany, to clear the road.   As the entire
column of over eighty waggons, one following the other in
single file, straggled out to a length of sometimes over two
miles, it was decided to cut two parallel roads from this point,
upon which the column moved in two divisions ; and, as the
plan was found to answer well, a double road was cut from the
Umshabetsi right up to Fort Salisbury.   Our advance party,
now augmented by a contingent of Khama's men, who proved
of great assistance in carrying out the heavy work of cutting a
double road, now kept in touch with the column, but always
managed to open up a road faster than the column could
travel.   The management of the waggons and oxen and the
daily formation of the "laagers" was entirely in the hands of
Messrs. Edward and George Burnett, two most energetic and
experienced colonists, and most admirably, I think, they per-
formed their very arduous duties.

Steadily and uneventfully we advanced, till on 1st August
we reached the Lunti river.   Up to this point I had always
had local natives to assist me in guiding the expedition—first
from Tuli to Sitoutsi's ; from there to Matipi's, and then on to
the Lunti, which we crossed by a ford which had been used
in former years by Boer hunters from the Northern Transvaal.
Beyond the River Lunti, except for the first few miles, as far as
Chibi's brother's kraal, I had no natives to assist me in the
guidance of the expedition.   As I knew that the broken
country which skirts the edge of the plateau began not far
beyond Chibi's, I asked Colonel Pennefather to give me four
days to examine the country on ahead and look out a good
line for a waggon road ; and as the cattle required a rest, and
there was a lot of heavy work to be done before a practicable
ford could be made across the Lunti river, he made no
difficulty about giving me the time I required ; so on 2nd

August I set out on my journey, accompanied by Lieutenant Nicholson, an experienced frontiersman, a young Transvaaler named Borius, my Hottentot boy John, and one of Khama's mounted scouts. We carried nothing with us but our rifles and half rations of biscuit and meat for four days.

On the first evening we slept at the foot of Silogwi hill, where a brother of Chibi was then living, and on the following day, holding a north-easterly course, reached another small native village perched on the shoulder of a conspicuous granite hill named Zamamba. We here off-saddled the horses, and whilst Nicholson and Borius were buying a little maize for the horses and boiling some water to make a cup of tea, I climbed to the top of the hill in order to scan the country on ahead. I obtained a splendid view over a great extent of country. For some miles ahead on the line I wished to travel the ground was level and covered with open forest, and, winding through this level forest-covered expanse, could be traced the course of the River Tukwi, and its tributary the Tukwan. Beyond the Tukwi the country, though rising gradually, continued level for a distance of eight or ten miles, but then became very broken and hilly, the hills rising higher and higher, one beyond another, to the distant horizon. Viewed from the summit of Zamamba, this rugged broken country extended north and south as far as the eye could reach. Beyond the farthest ridges to the north-east lay, as I knew well, the open downs of Mashunaland ; but, at first sight, it looked as if it would be no easy matter to find a practicable waggon track through the broken country that intervened. I could see one opening indeed, leading straight into the hills exactly on the line that I wanted to take, but from the top of Zamamba it was impossible to tell how far it would take one. However, as it ran up just beneath and parallel with a high range of hills, the name of which I afterwards found to be Inyaguzwi, and looked as though it might take one far into the broken country, I resolved to explore it forthwith.

On reaching the Tukwi river we again off-saddled, after having first discovered a suitable ford for the waggon train. From there Nicholson and I rode on soon after mid-day, taking Khama's man with us, but leaving Borius and my boy John to await our return, as their horses were not in very good condition. It was late in the afternoon when we rode into the entrance to the valley I had seen from the top of Zamamba, just where it narrowed in beneath the shadow of Inyaguzwi. Down its centre ran a fine clear stream of water—the Godobgay. This valley we now followed up, and as it led us mile after mile into the broken country, always ascending gently and regularly, and always running exactly in the right direction, my heart beat high with hope that it would lead me right on to the open downs of Mashunaland, and thus prove to be an easy open pass through the only piece of country in which I had anticipated any difficulty in finding a road for heavy waggons.

When the sun went down we were still in the pass, but as I felt sure from the appearance of the surrounding hills that we were now only just below the edge of the plateau, I asked Nicholson to look for a suitable spot to pass the night, close to one of the springs of the Godobgay, and leaving Khama's man to assist him in collecting wood enough to keep up a good fire all night, cantered on by myself up the pass. About a mile ahead stood a small rocky hill whose summit rose well above the broken ridges by which it was surrounded. This hill I climbed, and my feelings may be better imagined than described when I say that I saw stretched out before me, as far as the eye could reach, a wide expanse of open grassy country, and knew that I was looking over the south-western portion of the high plateau of Mashunaland.

As I stood alone on that little hill on the evening of 3rd August 1890, and looked first forwards across the grassy downs, in the middle of which the thriving township of Victoria now stands, and then backwards down the easy pass by which I had ascended from the Tukwi, a weight of responsibility, that had at times become almost unbearable, fell from my shoulders, and I breathed a deep sigh of relief. It must be remembered that the guidance of the expedition to Mashunaland had been entrusted entirely to me, and had any bungling taken place, causing delay, there is no telling what might have happened, for we were cutting a road

round the flank of Matabililand, in the teeth of the remonstrances and very unequivocal threats of Lo Bengula.   Now,
however, I felt that my task was practically over.   The
expedition was camped at the Lunti river.   Between there and
where I stood there would be no difficulty in cutting a good
road, whilst farther on to the north-east I had an intimate
knowledge of the whole country, and knew that I could take
the expedition with ease and comfort along the great divide
which forms the watershed from which the innumerable streams
run westwards into the Zambesi, and eastwards to the Sabi,
as far as the source of the Umgezi river, from whence I
could follow the line of the waggon track I had cut from
the neighbourhood of Mount Hampden to that spot in 1887.

On the afternoon of 5th August I got back to the camp on
the Lunti, and was assailed with innumerable questions, such
as " Well, Selous, have you got a good road for us ?   When are
you going to take us into the open country?" etc. etc., and when
I told every one that I had found a good easy road right on to the
plateau, and said that within a week the expedition would be
there, and practically safe in the open country from any attack
the Matabili might make, I think that a very general sense of
relief spread right through the camp.   Later on I gave my
intimate friend, Mr. Christopher Harrison, who was then
secretary to Mr. Colquhoun, a detailed description of the pass
I had hit upon beyond the Tukwi, and showed him the sketch
map I had made of it.   Mr. Harrison then said we must give
it a name, and suggested Providential Pass, as implying good
fortune in finding such an easy ascent ; and this name I wrote
down in my sketch map, which was handed in, in due course,
to Colonel Pennefather.   A year later Mr. Theodore Bent
travelled up the pass, which he considers a very commonplace portion of a commonplace country.   In his interesting
book, *The Ruined Cities of Mashunaland*, page 48, he says
" Providential Pass is distinctly commonplace."   To Mr. Bent
Providential Pass was but one dreary stage of a long
tedious journey, and no doubt his verdict will be that of all
those for whom the vast expanse of the African veld is but a
hideous wilderness only fit for wild beasts and savage men.
More primitive natures are, however, more emotional, and a

Transvaal Boer, when talking to me last year about the ascent
by Providential Pass from the bush country to the open plateau,
said, " When I came to the head of the pass, and looked over
the open grass land before me, I felt as if I had come into the
light out of a dark chamber," and he further said that he felt
inclined to sing and to shout and to gallop his horse away
across the open downs.

However, the name of Providential Pass will soon be
entirely forgotten.   It was a name that appealed to the
feelings and imaginations of the pioneers who were cutting a
road through an unknown country in the face of unknown
dangers.   The existence of the pass, occurring as it did exactly
on the right line and affording an easy exit from the low-lying
bush country to the open plateau of Mashunaland, thus
allowing the expedition to travel easily and quickly through
that portion of the route in which it would have been most
difficult to resist an attack by the Matabili, was such an
unexpected and singular piece of good fortune that it might
well be called Providential.   But the casual tourist of to-day
who travels without danger or difficulty up the broad waggon
track which the first pioneers cut through the pass, who knows
nothing about the surrounding country, and who is not sufficiently imaginative to reflect how difficult it would have been
to have found a road through the broken country on either side
if the pass had not existed, may perhaps agree with Mr. Bent
that the scenery of Providential Pass is " commonplace " and
the name ridiculous.

There is now no necessity for me to give a detailed account
of the further progress of the expedition to Mashunaland, as it
was entirely uneventful, and, moreover, several other accounts of
it have been written.   Suffice it to say that on the evening of
13th August the whole expedition camped close to the head
of Providential Pass, and on the following day trekked on to
the open country.   Here Fort Victoria was established, but has
since been abandoned : the township of Victoria—the site of
which I myself selected—having been laid out on the high
ground between the Umchegi and Umshagashi rivers.

It was here that Sir John Willoughby, who had left Tuli some
time after the main column in command of a small detachment

of police who were acting as escort to a convoy of waggons, caught us up. Previous to this time Sir John Willoughby had made a name for himself as a successful sportsman in England and East Africa, but henceforward he must take an honourable place amongst those to whose energy and capacity the present rapid development of Mashunaland is due. I was always struck not only with Sir John's energy and activity, but also with the thoroughness with which he always carried out whatever he was engaged upon; and I feel sure that if Mashunaland is the country we believe it to be, he will bring to a successful issue the great enterprises on which he is now engaged. No one has a firmer belief in his integrity, energy, and ability than myself, and I trust that he may one day reap a rich reward for the faith that is in him, and the way he has backed it.

Whilst we were cutting the road from the Lunti river to Fort Victoria, an ultimatum was received from Lo Bengula ordering Colonel Pennefather to turn back at once, "unless he thought he was strong enough to go on," but warning him that he might expect trouble if he did so. This letter was brought by my friend Mr. Johan Colenbrander, who had been first sent with it, accompanied by four headmen, to Fort Tuli. To my mind there is no doubt that when the king dictated this letter he thought the expedition was still at Tuli, and when his headmen, after a twelve days' tramp from Bulawayo, found that we were gone, they asked Mr. Colenbrander to ride on as hard as he could on our track and deliver the letter to Colonel Pennefather. This he did, and having received a suitable reply, returned at once to the king's ambassadors at Tuli, and from thence to Bulawayo. But when Lo Bengula received Colonel Pennefather's answer to his ultimatum he knew that we must have reached the open plateau of Mashunaland, and at once recognised that the time for attacking us had gone by, for on the open downs, with our force of five hundred mounted men, we would most certainly have cut up any force he could have sent against us. Personally Lo Bengula probably never wanted to fight, though it is the most absolute nonsense to talk of his ever having been friendly to the expedition. But he had a very difficult part to play, and it is wonderful that he managed to restrain his people as he did. Had any delay taken place at Tuli, as the king evidently expected, or had the expedition got into any difficulty whilst cutting the road from Tuli to the open country, it is my belief that we should most certainly have been attacked by a large Matabili army; and had such an attack been made in the bush country, the expedition to Mashunaland, even if it had not been overwhelmed and annihilated, would probably have been so crippled by loss of cattle that it would not have been able to proceed.

During the progress of the expedition the most intense excitement prevailed in Matabililand. Large numbers of new shields were made by the king's command, and the order was also given to the whole nation—men and women— to make new sandals. This order, by the way, is always given to the men on the eve of a large military expedition, and was probably given on this occasion to the women as well because the king had an idea that his country was about to be invaded by the pioneer expedition on one side, and the Bechwanaland Border Police on the other. In that case, he must have thought that the plan of cutting a road to Mashunaland, to which he had been asked to give his consent, was only a blind. The fact, however, that besides ordering the women to make sandals, he sent all the cattle in the country up to the northern districts on the very edge of the "fly" infested forests of the Zambesi valley, seems to prove conclusively that some idea of the sort was in his mind. Mr. Colenbrander told me that day after day bodies of men fully equipped for war, numbering sometimes several hundreds strong, came up and reported themselves to the king, and then did not return home, but went into encampments on the eastern border of the country. But all the time the Matabili did not know exactly where the white men were, or what they were going to do, until at last it became known that the pioneer expedition had passed Matabililand, and were still travelling north-eastwards across the open downs of Mashunaland. Then two things must have become apparent to them. Firstly, that the white men had no intention of interfering with Matabililand, but were really engaged in cutting a road to the Mazoe river, and secondly, that were they to make an attack upon a force of mounted men in the open country they were likely to come off second best.

A feeling of relief was probably very general throughout the country, for even the most savage and ferocious amongst them would hesitate to engage in a war with Europeans unnecessarily, as they know what a serious business it would be ; whilst the king, and the greater part of the elder members of his tribe, who know all about the history of the recent Kafir and Zulu wars, not to mention their own defeat by the Boers in 1836, are fully convinced that no successes they might gain at first against white men would save them from ultimate destruction. I have heard it stated that it was only the

ROAD FROM SALISBURY TO MANICA.

extreme friendliness of Lo Bengula and the Matabili people that made the expedition to Mashunaland possible. That is not my view. We cut the road to Mashunaland in defiance of them, and our advance would most certainly have been resisted but for two circumstances. The first was the fact that during the progress of the expedition a well-equipped force of five hundred mounted men of the Bechwanaland Border Police were encamped on the south-western border of Matabililand, and the second, that after the expedition crossed the Tuli, and until it reached the plateau of Mashunaland, Lo Bengula and his people never knew where we were.

Upon reaching the open country I asked Colonel Penne-father to allow me to change the line of route and strike direct to the source of the Umgezi river, instead of passing to the east of Gutu's and Umtigeza's villages, as I had originally intended doing, out of deference to Lo Bengula's feelings, as these two chiefs pay him tribute. After his last ultimatum, however, I did not think we owed him much consideration, and as the cattle and horses were now getting into low condition it was absolutely necessary to proceed by the shortest and easiest route. Having consulted Dr. Jameson, Colonel Pennefather, whom I always found a most considerate and obliging officer to work with, gave me leave to make the alteration I desired. On 1st September the expedition reached the source of the Umgezi, near where Fort Charter was established. In this district the soil is very sandy, and the tracks made by my waggon-train in the light ground three years previously, when in 1887 I cut a road, as I have already related, from Mount Hampden to this very spot, were plainly visible.

We were now within fifty miles of Mount Hampden, which had been named as the goal of the expedition, and in which district it was intended that a township should be established. Naturally, having guided the expedition so far without assistance and without a mistake, and having borne as it were the heat and burden of the day, I was anxious to conduct it to its destination ; but Mr. Colquhoun was also most anxious to proceed at once to Umtasa's, the chief of Manica, in order to conclude a treaty with that potentate in favour of the British South Africa Company, and as I was the only man in the expedition who knew anything about the intervening country, or had ever been to Manicaland, he wanted me to accompany him, and I at last agreed to do so. I gave the best instructions I could to Mr. Nicholson and Mr. Edward Burnett, supplied them with the sketch maps I had made of this part of the country in former years, and handed over the guidance of the expedition to them. It is a matter of history that on the 11th of September 1890 the British flag was hoisted at Fort Salisbury, on the banks of the Makubisi river, and the expedition to Mashunaland thus satisfactorily brought to an end.

CHAPTER XXII

ON 14th September 1890 a treaty was concluded between Mr. A. R. Colquhoun, as the representative of the British South Africa Company, and Umtasa, the chief of Manica, by virtue of which the British Company acquired and took possession of a large slice of very valuable auriferous country, to which the Portuguese had previously laid claim. This treaty and the subsequent events in Manica called forth indignant remonstrances from the Portuguese, and a certain amount of adverse criticism in England, though I am bound to say that with few exceptions the press of England, Scotland, and South Africa stood staunchly by their countrymen. My idea of the whole controversy is this. On the one hand the Portuguese claim to Manica was a very hazy and unsubstantial one, much more so than I had previously believed ; besides which, having held the country, as they said, for four hundred years and done so little with it, they had forfeited all right to be allowed to hold it any longer. On the other hand, the British Company knew that they could colonise the country, and develop its great natural resources, and being determined to take possession of it, were anxious to do so legally, if possible, under the rights acquired by a treaty with Umtasa ; though possibly, had no such treaty existed, the British flag would still have waved on the hills of Manica.

Such undertakings as the expedition to and occupation of Mashunaland cannot but foster the love of adventure and enterprise, and tend to keep our national spirit young and vigorous. Like an individual, a nation must in time grow old and decay ; and when once the love of adventure is so far

dead within the breasts of young Englishmen that tales of
dangers and difficulties successfully overcome no longer fire
their, blood, and induce a large percentage of them to give up
ease and comfort at home and seek their fortunes in wild and
distant lands, then will the decadence of England have set in.
As a nation we are probably already past our prime ; but that
we still possess a vast fund of vigour and energy there can be
no doubt.   Nothing has gratified me more than the way I have
seen young English and Scottish gentlemen, including officers
in the Guards and other crack regiments, after having been
brought up in the lap of luxury, turn to and rough it in
Mashunaland with the patient equanimity and steady determination which deserves, if it does not always win, success.   I
never realised, however, how strongly the blood of the old Norse
pirates—I beg pardon, I mean Vikings—runs in the veins of
the modern Briton until my visit to Captain Heyman's camp,
two days after he had, with only fifty men of the police and
pioneers, beaten off an attack made on his position by the
Portuguese, and afterwards captured the fort of Massi Kessi.
Whatever was in the fort of course fell into the hands of our
men.   It was not very much—with the exception of eleven
machine guns which the Portuguese had abandoned—but
sufficient to whet their appetites, and there was not a man
amongst them who did not look forward with the greatest
satisfaction to the speedy advent of the large force of six hundred
Portuguese troops which was supposed to be advancing from
the east coast to drive the British out of Manica.   The spirit
of our men was splendid.   They never doubted but that they
would rout the Portuguese and win a rich loot.   However, there
was no more fighting, and an arrangement was soon afterwards
arrived at between the British and Portuguese Governments, by
which it was decided that the disputed boundary line between
the territories of the British South Africa and Mozambique
Companies should be settled definitively by a joint commission
of the two nationalities.   I am afraid that this disputed
boundary line has not even yet been settled definitely.

    After the conclusion of the treaty with Umtasa, Lieutenant
Adair Campbell of the pioneers, Mr. Christopher Harrison,
secretary to Mr. Colquhoun (who was at that time Administrator

of the Chartered Company's territories), and myself, rode over the mountain chain which divides the valley of the Umtali river from the Revui, and presented ourselves at Massi Kessi, the headquarters of the Portuguese in Manica. This part of the country is without exception the most mountainous and broken and withal the most beautiful, that I have yet seen in Africa. It is simply a mass of rugged hills rising to a height of over six thousand feet above sea-level, among which there are many fine open valleys, watered by rushing streams of the clearest water, all of which are fed by the innumerable little burns that, rising amongst the summits of the mountains, have cut deep fissures for themselves down every hillside. Many of the ravines thus formed are clothed with clusters of banana-trees, especially on the southern slopes of the mountains. Lemons of excellent flavour also grow wild in these ravines, as they do on the eastern and northern slopes of Mashunaland.

Arrived at Massi Kessi, we were not received with any excessive cordiality by the Baron de Rezende, who was at that time the Managing Director of the Mozambique Company in Manica. He not only objected to our having made a treaty with Umtasa, but also maintained that the occupation of Mashunaland by the British South Africa Company was an invasion of Portuguese territory. The object of our visit had been to try to buy provisions and trading goods from the Mozambique Company, as we had been practically living on our rifles for some time past, and knew that the Portuguese had plenty of provisions and stores in Massi Kessi. The Baron's sympathies, however, were not sufficiently cosmopolitan to induce him to assist men whom he looked upon as his country's enemies, and no doubt considering our visit as the addition of insult to injury, he refused point-blank to help us in any way ; and had it not been for the kindness of two of our countrymen, the members of a syndicate that had obtained a sub-concession from the Mozambique Company, and who were at this time at Massi Kessi, we should have got nothing to eat at all. But Mr. George Crampton and Mr. Harrison, the two gentlemen above referred to, supplied us with the best meal we had had for many a long day, after discussing which we at once started on the return journey to our camp near Umtasa's.

Shortly afterwards Mr. Colquhoun, having left Mr. Trevor and a sharp semi-civilised native, named Jonas, at Umtasa's village to watch events, returned to Salisbury to take over the administration of Mashunaland ; whilst I, accompanied by a small escort under the command of Lieutenant Adair Campbell, made a journey amongst the independent chiefs living on the southern and eastern borders of Mashunaland. I had a most excellent interpreter in Zwartland, a Makalaka subject of Khama's, with whom I spoke in Sintabili, he translating what I said into the various dialects of Chiswina used in Mashunaland, all of which are thoroughly comprehensible to a Makalaka, whose language is practically the same. I explained to all the chiefs that the white men had come into Mashunaland and meant to stop there ; but assured them that they wished to live at peace with and deal justly by the native inhabitants of the country. I also told them that should they enter into treaties of friendship with the British, they would be protected from Lo Bengula and Gungunyan on the one side, and from Gouveia on the other, by one or other of which chiefs their territories had been previously continually devastated. With the exception of Motoko, with whom I found it most difficult to arrange a treaty, one and all the chiefs whom I interviewed expressed their gratification that the white men had come into the country. They frequently used such expressions as " Now we shall sleep," " We shall reap the corn we sow," " We shall see our cattle increase." In November 1890 I visited Motoko's country, but was unable on this occasion to see the aged chief. Indeed, I found the people so suspicious, they never having had any previous intercourse with Europeans, that I determined to take my escort back to Salisbury, and then return alone and see if I could not overcome the fears of the people.

On 27th November we reached Salisbury, where many huts had already been put up. At this time events were happening in Manica, in which I am sorry to say that I took no part, of the gravest importance to the future of the country.

Of these events, which form a very interesting portion of the early history of the colonisation of Mashunaland, I will now give a short account. This account, which I wrote at the request of the Administrator, and which I believe to be

absolutely impartial and accurate, was published in the *Man-chester Guardian* for 20th January 1891, and ran as follows :—
    " During the past two months, events of the greatest im-portance to the future welfare of Mashunaland have followed one upon another with the most startling rapidity, and one more page of the deepest interest has been added to the history of British enterprise.   Before, however, proceeding to give an account of what has lately happened in Manica, it will be necessary for me to recall to your readers the preliminary steps which have led up to the present situation.   It will be remembered that on the 14th of September last a treaty was concluded between Mr. A. R. Colquhoun, the Administrator of Mashunaland, and Umtasa, the chief of Manica, by which that chief ceded all the mineral rights of his country to the British South Africa Company, and at the same time placed himself under the Company's protection.   Before this important treaty was concluded, Umtasa was repeatedly asked whether at any time he had ever ceded his country, either to the Portuguese Government, or to the Directors of the Company of Mozambique, and he as repeatedly denied ever having done so, as also did his chief councillors.   When asked on what terms he was with the Baron de Rezende, the local representative of the Company of Mozambique at Massi Kessi, he said, ' I allow him to live there.   He sometimes gives me presents, but I have not given him my country, nor have I ever concluded any treaty with him.'   Later on, he said repeatedly that the Portuguese held an assegai at his heart, and when pressed for an explanation of this statement said that he was terrorised and compelled to do what the Baron required of him by the threat that if he gave any trouble, Gouveia, the Capitão Mor of Gorongoza, would be called in to invade his territory with a large armed force.   Now it must be understood that amongst the weak and unwarlike tribes of South-Eastern Africa this Goanese adventurer, Gouveia, otherwise known as Manoel Antonio de Souza, is regarded with much the same feelings of mingled terror and detestation as, two centuries ago, rankled in the breasts of the pious peasantry of the Western Lowlands of Scotland against their powerful and unscrupulous oppressor, John Graham of

Claverhouse. And it is surely a matter of deep reproach to
a nation which makes loud boast of its enlightenment and
civilisation, that the terror inspired by such an agent should
be the sole machinery which they possess to govern and
control (and apparently shut off from all the ameliorating
influences of trade and commerce) many small tribes of unwarlike natives, who, powerless to resist, groan under the
present oppression, and who would welcome with open arms
the influx of British settlers and miners, or indeed any other
change that would alter the present state of things and give
them security of life and property. However, for the present
I shall have to leave this subject. As I have said above, a
treaty was concluded between Umtasa and the British South
Africa Company, and at the chief's urgent request one police-
man and a native interpreter were left with him, as representatives of the Company, pending the establishment later on
of a regular police post to safeguard the Company's interests
in the Manica country, and to protect Umtasa against any
attack that might be made upon him in revenge for his assertion of his independence of Portuguese rule. On 25th October,
in consequence of reports from native sources that Colonel
Paiva d'Andrada, accompanied by Gouveia, with a large force
of armed natives, was approaching the Manica country from
the east, Sergeant - Major Montgomery, with a small force
consisting of only ten men of the British South Africa Company's Police, was despatched from Fort Salisbury to Umtasa's,
and two days later, Lieutenant Graham, accompanied by Sub-
Lieutenant Shepstone, followed to take command of this small
detachment. At the same time Lieutenant the Hon. Eustace
Fiennes was ordered to proceed to Umtasa's from Fort Charter
with a portion of 'A' troop of the Company's police, but
owing to the difficulty that was experienced in taking waggons
through a roadless country, this detachment did not reach
Umtasa's until 15th November.

"In the meantime Captain Forbes,[1] leaving Fort Salisbury
on 31st October, reached Umtasa's kraal on the morning of
5th November, and assumed the command of all the Company's
forces in the Manica country. Definite information had now

---

[1] Now Major Forbes, and at present magistrate at Fort Salisbury.

reached Umtasa that Colonel Paiva d'Andrada and Gouveia
had invaded his country, and were already at Massi Kessi, or
within a short distance of that place. Captain Forbes therefore
at once sent Lieutenant Graham, accompanied by two troopers,
over to Massi Kessi, with a letter to Colonel Paiva d'Andrada
remonstrating strongly against the invasion of the territory
of a chief who had lately concluded a treaty of friendship

MAJOR P. W. FORBES.

with the British South Africa Company, and warning them
that such an action was likely to lead to grave complications,
as he (Captain Forbes, commanding the British South Africa
Company's forces in Manica) was determined to resist force
with force. This letter, which was handed to him by Lieutenant Graham on 6th November, Colonel d'Andrada declined
to answer, affecting to treat the whole thing as a *mauvaise
plaisanterie*. Lieutenant Graham and his two troopers were,

however, treated with the greatest kindness and courtesy by
Colonel d'Andrada and the Baron de Rezende.   On 8th
November, Gouveia, accompanied by seventy men, all armed
with rifles and side arms, arrived at Umtasa's kraal, Captain
Forbes at the time only having ten men at his disposal, as
Lieutenant Fiennes had not yet arrived with the men of ' A '
troop.   A letter of remonstrance was, however, sent to Gouveia,
which he affected to treat with contempt and derision, waxing
very wroth at the statement that if he did not leave Umtasa's
country he would be put out of it.   From the 8th to the 15th
Umtasa was frequently interviewed by Gouveia, and by the
end of that time, though Captain Forbes did his best to re-
assure him, there is no doubt that he was in a state of extreme
terror, and might possibly have been frightened into making
any statements that Gouveia chose to dictate to him, as he
knew that the armed force that had already occupied his
kraal would very soon be augmented by reinforcements under
the command of Colonel d'Andrada and the Baron de Rezende,
whilst the handful of Englishmen under Captain Forbes, he
imagined, would be powerless to assist him.   However, he
little knew the gallant young officer who commanded the
British South Africa Company's forces in Manica at this
critical juncture, and to whose good judgment, pluck, and
determination it is due that a most important crisis in the
history of the British occupation of Mashunaland has been
passed, not only without bloodshed, but in a way that will
raise the prestige of Englishmen all over South-Eastern Africa,
whilst at the same time a death-blow has been dealt to the
second-hand influence of Portugal in the same regions through
such men as Gouveia.

      " Captain Forbes could not venture, indeed, to make a move
with his ten men, but he despatched two of them on horseback to look for Lieutenant Fiennes, urging that officer to
leave the waggons and push on without delay on horseback.
Luckily he was not far off, and, pushing forward, was enabled
to reach Umtasa's kraal in the very nick of time with twenty
troopers.   Mr. Dennis Doyle, superintendent of native affairs
for the Company, together with Captain Hoste and Lieutenant
Biscoe, lately officers of the pioneer corps, also reached

Umtasa's just about the same time—that is, on 15th November, a day after the arrival of Colonel d'Andrada and Baron de Rezende, who, with the whole of their followers, all well armed, were inside Umtasa's stockaded kraal. Captain Forbes had received information from some of Umtasa's people that Colonel d'Andrada had given orders that if any Englishmen were seen approaching the kraal the entrances were to be blockaded, and that resistance was to be made. However, Jonas, the native interpreter, who had been with Trooper Trevor (the acting representative already referred to) from the first, was able to introduce them into the kraal by a back entrance, and also to show them the huts in which Colonel d'Andrada and his officers had taken up their quarters, and also those in which the greatest number of Gouveia's followers were collected ; and a couple of hours after Lieutenant Fiennes arrived Captain Forbes suddenly entered the kraal, and with ten men proceeded to arrest Colonel d'Andrada, the Baron de Rezende, and Gouveia. At the same time Lieutenants Fiennes and Biscoe, with the rest of the men, were rapidly disarming Gouveia's retainers. Mr. Doyle and Captain Hoste had entered the kraal with Captain Forbes, and the former, who is a proficient in native languages, went about warning Umtasa's people not to take any part in the proceedings, which were, he told them, entirely between the Portuguese and the English. In this work he was ably assisted by Umtasa's head enduna (councillor), who did his best to quiet the excited people. Gouveia's men were taken entirely by surprise, and offered no resistance. Many of them delivered up their arms, and the rest fled, and thus Colonel d'Andrada, De Rezende, and Gouveia were arrested without bloodshed. Immediately after the arrest Captain Forbes, with admirable judgment, despatched Colonel d'Andrada and Gouveia, with an escort of ten men, under command of Lieutenant Fiennes, to Fort Salisbury, for to have released them upon parole in the Manica country would have been a fatal mistake, as such an action would have been attributed by the natives to weakness, and would infallibly have led to a dangerous rising among Gouveia's people in the Gorongoza province ; whilst the arrest and deportation of the much-dreaded Gouveia by a handful of the British South Africa Company's policemen cannot but raise British prestige not only in Manica but throughout the whole of South-Eastern Africa.

"Colonel d'Andrada protested that he and his friends, Gouveia and the Baron de Rezende, were at Umtasa's kraal on the most pacific of missions, namely, to discuss certain mining questions on behalf of the Companha de Mozambique, of which he was the director, the Baron the local agent, and Gouveia the employé (the supplier of labour), and that though the large body of porters and 'bearers' with them were certainly armed, they were only armed against attacks from wild beasts. A couple of days after the arrest, Captain Forbes pushed on to Massi Kessi, taking the Baron de Rezende with him, and also M. de Llamby, the engineer of the Company of Mozambique, who had accompanied the Portuguese expedition to Umtasa's kraal.   On their arrival at Massi Kessi both these gentlemen were released on parole, and Massi Kessi was formally taken possession of by a small detachment of the British South Africa Company's forces.   Massi Kessi, it may here be said, is nothing but a trading station and stockaded compound, built by the Baron de Rezende in his capacity of local representative of the Mozambique Company.   There is no Portuguese garrison there, and not even one single native soldier, nor is there any large native town in the vicinity.   All the Europeans in the province of Manica, with the exception of the Baron de Rezende, and two other Portuguese traders, are either English or American prospectors, or the employés of the Mozambique Company, who are Frenchmen, Spaniards, and Italians.   A tide of immigration has now, however, set in towards the Manica country which, if the gold-fields are as rich as they are supposed to be, nothing will be able to stem ; for as soon as it became known in Mashunaland that a treaty had been effected between Umtasa and the British South Africa Company, by which the Company had secured all the mineral rights in that country, a large number of the prospectors and disbanded members of the pioneer force, which had formed part of the expedition to Mashunaland, at once made their way towards the new El Dorado, and now, in addition to the effective occupation of the country by a strong force of the

Company's police, the country is being thoroughly explored by a hardy, enterprising, and energetic band of Englishmen, Scotsmen, and British South Africans—men well calculated to uphold the traditions of their race, and not at all likely to relinquish the firm grip they now have of the Manica country.

" Nor must it be thought that in this matter of the occupation of Manica the British South Africa Company has done anything more than assert the rights fairly obtained from Umtasa, the hereditary chief of the country, through the treaty recently concluded with him. He entirely repudiates the Portuguese claim to sovereign rights over his country, nor does either Colonel d'Andrada or the Baron de Rezende contend that Umtasa himself ever ceded his country to their Government or the Mozambique Company ; and whilst the Baron de Rezende, in an interview with myself last September, based the claims of his Government to Manica on the assumption that Umtasa's country formed part of Gungunyan's dominions— which, however, Umtasa stoutly denies—and therefore belonged to Portugal, because that powerful chief was a vassal of the King of Portugal—a proposition which Gungunyan denies,— Colonel d'Andrada now for the first time tells a story of Umtasa having ceded his country to Gouveia some twenty years ago, and maintains that the mineral rights of Manica were ceded to the Company of Mozambique by Gouveia. Now, not only do these two stories not agree, but each fully discredits the other ; for if Colonel d'Andrada really believes that Umtasa gave his country to Gouveia, he must acknowledge that he is entirely independent of Gungunyan. On the other hand, if, as Baron de Rezende asserts, Umtasa is really tributary to Gungunyan, he never could have given his country to Gouveia. The true facts of the case are easy to see. Certain Portuguese officials have coerced Umtasa into an unwilling acceptance of the Portuguese flag, by threatening to set either Gungunyan or Gouveia into motion against him should he refuse to accede to their demands.

" Thanks in the first place to the treaty concluded between Mr. Colquhoun and Umtasa last September, and again to the able way in which Captain Forbes recently checkmated the last and desperate attempt at intimidation on the part of the Portuguese, this reign of terror is now over, and under the auspices of the British South Africa Company the gold-fields of Manica have been opened to the world.   Next year thousands of eager, pushing, energetic men will flock into Mashunaland and into Manica (which is racially and territorially, be it noted, a part of Mashunaland), and more will be done towards opening up and developing this, the fairest portion of South Africa, in six short months than has been effected by Portugal in the whole of the three or four centuries during which she claims to have possessed the country.   One cannot but feel sorry for the chagrin and mortification which recent events must have caused to two Portuguese gentlemen, of whose courtesy and kindness all Englishmen who have ever met them speak with one accord in the highest terms.   I refer to Colonel Paiva d'Andrada and Baron de Rezende, men imbued with the spirit of the old Portuguese navigators, a spirit which now only flickers up occasionally in the breasts of their descendants like flame among the embers of a dying fire.   But a few such men cannot regenerate a decaying nation.   The sun of Portugal's glory has set never to rise again in Eastern Africa, and it is time that this feeble nerveless power ceased its endeavours to stem the tide of enterprise which has already opened up Mashunaland and Manica to the world, and now demands an outlet to the Indian Ocean."

SALISBURY, MASHUNALAND.

CHAPTER XXIII

Reach Fort Salisbury—Write a supplement for the *Graphic*—Its fate—Report of a journey to Motoko's country, and the conclusion of a treaty with that chief

As related in the last chapter, I reached Fort Salisbury on 27th November 1890, after having spent three months in journeying through the southern and eastern districts of Mashunaland, and concluding treaties of amity with all the principal native chiefs living in those districts.

Arrived at Salisbury, I at once set to work to put all my various surveys together on one map, adopting the large scale of five miles to the inch in order to get in all the numerous small streams whose courses I had carefully sketched from the tops of hills. This map I went on adding to as long as I remained in the country, and by the middle of 1892 I had made a careful compass survey of nearly the whole of Mashunaland, which is now in the hands of the Royal Geographical Society.

Besides this mapping work, I did a good deal of writing at Mr. Colquhoun's request, and amongst other things wrote a descriptive account of Mashunaland, its past history and present condition. This article, at which I worked hard for at least a week, was sent home, together with a large number of photographs, and had it ever reached its destination would probably have appeared as a supplement to the *Graphic* newspaper. However, it never reached England, and as the accident which prevented its doing so forms an interesting episode in the early history of the colonisation of Mashunaland I will here give a short account of it.

During the first few months after the occupation of the country the weekly mail was carried from Salisbury to Tuli by post riders, post stations having been established all along the line of route, at distances varying from twenty-five to forty miles one from another. At each of these posts two or three men of the British South Africa Company's Police and as many horses were stationed, and the light mail-bag was carried rapidly over the four hundred miles of road by relays of men and horses. The post riders always rode day and night, and on one occasion a despatch was handed in to Colonel Penne-father at Salisbury eighty-four hours after it had been de-spatched from Tuli.

Well, the mail-bag which left Salisbury on 18th December 1890, carrying letters to anxious friends from the little band of British pioneers in Mashunaland, also bore my supplement to the *Graphic*. Late on the evening of Christmas Day a young fellow named Thomas, belonging, I think, to " D " troop of the Company's police, started southwards from Matipi's post station with the same mail-bag. He rode one horse, and led a second that carried the mail-bag on a pack saddle. The sky was cloudy and overcast, drizzly rain soon commenced to fall, and when night set in the darkness became intense. A ride on such a night, alone, through the endless silent woods of the African wilderness, would be depressing at any time, but more particularly so on Christmas night, and especially so after a Christmas dinner of " bully beef " and hard biscuit. However, young Thomas—he was but a lad, not long out from home, —soon had something more enlivening to think about than the Christmas dinner he had not eaten ; for suddenly both the horse he was riding and the pack animal he was leading commenced to snort and plunge, and then galloped forwards in the darkness along the waggon track, and Mr. Thomas immediately became aware that a lion was close behind them, as every stride was accompanied by a hoarse grating growl, that, heard at close quarters on a dark night, is not a reassuring sound. In this weird chase the darkness no doubt favoured the lion, and probably the horses never got properly into their stride. In any case, it was but a matter of a second or two before the lion sprang up and seized the horse Thomas was riding, clasping it from each side with its massive legs, and digging its cruel claws deep into either quarter. The horse was checked, and the jerk threw Thomas from the saddle ; but the sharpness of the lion's claws, aided by the pace at which the horse was going, made them cut through skin and flesh like so many knives, so that the grim beast lost his hold and fell to the ground, whilst the horse rushed madly forwards along the road. The lion at once took up the chase again, neglecting to notice Thomas, who ran to the nearest tree, which he climbed without any unnecessary dawdling. Before long the lion, not having been able to again overtake either of the horses, came back to where he had made his first spring, and then, probably scenting Thomas in the tree, walked up and lay down at the foot of it. Here he remained the entire night, sometimes lying down, and at others walking about round the tree. Thomas had no rifle with him, but carried a revolver slung over his shoulder. He was, however, afraid to fire at the lion with this weapon, as the tree in which he had taken refuge was but a small one, and he feared that the dangerous beast beneath him might, if irritated by a wound, spring up and possibly succeed in clawing him out of the tree.

It was broad daylight next morning when Thomas heard the crack of a whip, and presently was rejoiced to see a waggon train coming along the road. Then the lion got up and walked sulkily away into the bush, and Thomas came down the tree and told his strange story to the people with the waggons, with whom he returned to Matipi's. Both horses turned up early in the night at the next post station. The flanks of the one that had been attacked were badly lacerated by the claws of the lion, but it eventually recovered. The horse which carried the mail-bag seems to have left the road and dashed away into the bush when its companion was seized by the lion, and eventually turned up at the post station minus the mail-bag, which had been doubtless torn off by the bushes through which the terrified animal rushed. I have given this story in some detail, as it is an interesting one, just as I heard it from my friend, Mr. Jesser Coope, who was in command at Matipi's post station, and who started Thomas off with the mail on Christmas night, and heard the tale of his misadventure on his return to

the station the following morning. Four months later, after it
had lain on the ground during the greater part of the rainy
season, the lost mail-bag was picked up by Mr. Gourlay, who
was on his way up to Mashunaland, and who came upon it a
short distance away from the road when he was out shooting. It
was brought back to Salisbury, and its contents handed back
to their owners. My supplement to the *Graphic* had, however, been a good deal injured by long exposure to the rain,
and I had no spare time just then to rewrite it, so that, thanks
to the lion, it never appeared in print.

As soon as ever I had finished my writing and mapping
work in Salisbury I made preparations to revisit Motoko's
country in order to conclude a treaty with him on behalf of
the British South Africa Company. Of this journey I wrote
the following report, which I now reproduce, by the kind permission of the Directors :—

To His Honour
    The Administrator of Mashunaland.

SIR—I have the honour to report that on 19th December
1890 I left Fort Salisbury in order to conclude the negotiations
opened with Motoko, paramount chief of the Mabudja, during
the previous month, to get a mineral concession from him in
favour of the British South Africa Company, and at the same
time to obtain his signature to a treaty of alliance with the
British in Mashunaland.

I travelled with a waggon, and was accompanied by Mr. W.
Leslie Armstrong, an employé of the British South Africa
Company, a young man whose services have been of the
greatest assistance to me during the whole trip.

After leaving Fort Salisbury I followed the waggon road to
Mangwendi's as far as the eastern branch of the Makubisi
river (about four miles distant from the Fort), after crossing
which I left it, and took a more easterly course towards
Sikadoro's town, which I reached early the next morning.

The country between Fort Salisbury and Sikadoro's town
is magnificent, and appears possessed of every requisite for
agriculture or stock farming. Starting from Fort Salisbury at
a height of four thousand nine hundred and sixty feet above sea

level, we travelled over gently undulating downs, down every hollow in which ran a stream of the clearest water, and over which were scattered patches of forest of small extent, yet sufficient to shelter cattle during cold weather, until, when within three miles of Sikadoro's hill, we had attained an altitude of five thousand three hundred feet. From this point we obtained a magnificent view over the country to the north-east, which lay spread out before us in a series of green, well-watered valleys, interspersed with granite hills, until hill and valley became blended into one blue mist in the far distance.

After leaving Sikadoro's town we travelled nearly due east, and crossing the rivers Nola, Inyagui, Inyakambiri, Shabanoghwi, Ungurughwi, Monyokwi, and a multitude of smaller streams, reached Rusungwi hill, which is about thirty miles distant from Motoko's kraal, on 26th December. The previous day, which, although unaccompanied by snow or plum-pudding, was nevertheless Christmas Day, we spent near the source of the river Monyokwi, at an altitude of about four thousand seven hundred feet above sea-level. The day was a hot one for Mashunaland, as the sun shone out strongly from amongst scattered clouds charged with rain, yet I could not help contrasting it and the following night with those of Christmas 1889, which I spent in Cape Town. I still have a lively remembrance of the broiling heat of that day, aggravated by the necessity of wearing coat, collar, and necktie, and the stuffy closeness of the night that followed. But how different was my experience on Christmas Day 1890 on the breezy downs of Mashunaland. Up till eleven o'clock the almost constant south-easterly breeze kept the air delightfully cool and pleasant. From that time till 4 P.M. the wind fell and the sun was certainly hot, but by no means oppressively so. After that the breeze sprang up again, and reduced the evening air to a temperature as near perfection as possible, whilst during the night it became cold enough to justify the use of a couple of blankets. And this, let me remark, is the normal summer climate of the Mashuna uplands, where hot nights are almost if not entirely unknown.

After passing Rusungwi hill we had to do a good deal of chopping to make a passage for the waggon through thick groves of mahobo-hobo trees, and on the 27th of December crossed the Inyamashupa river (a tributary of the Inyadiri), which forms the boundary between the territories ruled over by Mangwendi and Motoko.

The following day, after travelling through a well-wooded country intersected by numerous streams, we reached our old camp near Kalimazondo's town, which is about six miles to the south-east of Motoko's. Here I was delayed four days whilst communications were opened with the " Mondoro " or " Lion-God," a sort of high priest who appears to have more power in the country than Motoko himself. This high priest's office is hereditary, and no step of any importance is ever taken in the country until this " Lion-God " has been consulted. He is the only god the people know of or worship. They pray to him and make him propitiatory offerings, and the place where he lives is called " Zimbabwi," which practically means " a place of prayer and sacrifice." All the tribes living in the neighbourhood of the River Mazoe, both north and south of it, have a " Mondoro" or " Lion-God " or high priest, whose office is hereditary, and who has really more power than the chief ; but all these tribes, with the exception of the Mabudja, have been so broken up, that the chiefs have probably lost all belief in their gods, and the gods in themselves, and neither the one nor the other any longer attempt to stand on their dignity when visited by strangers. With the Mabudja, however, it is different. They are still a nation, and, what is more, a warlike nation, capable of putting several thousands of warriors into the field, and they still believe in themselves and in their god. Just now they are particularly self-satisfied, as, last year, after refusing to accept the Portuguese flag, they were able to beat off the attack that was made upon them by a large and well-armed force under Manoel Antonio de Souza, the well-known Capitão Mor of Gorongoza, who was despatched against them by the Portuguese in order to persuade them to a better state of mind.

In consequence of the consultations between Motoko and his god as to the advisability of concluding a treaty with the British in Mashunaland, we were delayed for four days at Kalimazondo's kraal. As, however, it rained almost incessantly during that time, both day and night, in such a manner as to render travelling with a waggon impossible, this did not very much matter. At length a message came, telling Kalimazondo that he was to take the white man by the hand and bring him to Motoko. A wish was also expressed that I should bring the waggon and the big oxen and the horses.

So on the following morning I inspanned, and reached Motoko's kraal on 2nd January. I was under the impression that I should be able to see Motoko on the following day. But in this I was mistaken, for it was not until some days later, on 6th January, that I was at last permitted to interview the venerable old chief. During the four days previous to this I held many meetings with large numbers of the elders of the tribe, to whom I had to explain the purport of my mission. They one and all agreed that Motoko would be only too happy to make friends with the British, and to allow them to look for gold in his country, make roads through it, etc., but they seemed very suspicious about his putting his name on a paper. After four days' constant interviewing my diplomacy and my patience were wellnigh exhausted, and I was still kept at arm's-length from Motoko. During these four days hundreds upon hundreds of natives, men and women, boys and girls, came daily to see the white men, the waggon, the large oxen (their own breed of cattle are very small), the horses, and the donkeys. The crowd, however, that all day long surrounded us was always a good-tempered one. At last, on 6th January, Siteo, the eldest son, I believe, of Motoko, came and said that Motoko was ready to see me, so I at once sent for the horses, not knowing exactly how far off Motoko's village actually was ; but, as it turned out, he was not half a mile away, on the top of an enormous gently-sloping mass of granite rock. At the foot of this rock I left the horses, and then accompanied by Mr. Armstrong and William Hokogazi, my Zulu servant, made my way through a dense mass of people to near the top of the granite rock. During our progress up the rock, a distance of perhaps two hundred yards, we walked along a lane, left for us amongst a dense mass of natives, who were packed tightly all over the open granite slab, nearly all squatted down. It is difficult to estimate numbers, but I am sure that at this interview Motoko

was surrounded by far over a thousand men, all fully armed, a
large number of them with guns, the rest with assegais, battle-
axes, and bows and arrows.   When we reached the highest
portion of the granite slab (which it must be remembered was
a naked rock some acres in extent) we found that a kind of
arbour of boughs had been erected, beneath which sat Motoko,
the aged chief of the Mabudja, with two marimba players behind
him and a few old men on either hand.   All round the arbour
the older and more important members of the tribe were
squatted.   None of these men carried arms, and I saw that
their assegais were all tied up in bundles and laid outside the
arbour.

And now without any delay I was introduced into the
presence of Motoko.   He is the oldest man, I feel sure, that I
have ever seen, and must be nearly if not quite a hundred years
old.   William declared that he was so old he must be the
contemporary of Chaka.   As soon as I had seated myself a
man rushed forward and shouted out a few words in praise of
Motoko, and immediately afterwards a crowd of women who
were standing in the background broke out into a shrill quaver-
ing cry, which is meant as a welcome to strangers.   As soon
as the noise had subsided, I told Motoko, through William
Hokogazi and Sipiro, my interpreters, the purport of my visit,
the meaning of the writing on the paper to which I wished him
to put his name, and the reasons why it was absolutely necessary
that he should sign his name if he was willing to grant the
concession asked for, and to conclude a treaty with his new
neighbours the British.   He listened very attentively to all that
was said, made some intelligent comments, referring to the fear
he entertained of being attacked by the Portuguese ; said that
messengers from Umtasa had lately informed him of all that
the British South Africa Company had done in Manica ; and
finally said that he was very glad of the opportunity of concluding a treaty of friendship with the British ; that his country
was theirs, and that Englishmen might go where they liked in
it to look for gold.   I then said, " If the words you have spoken
come from your heart, I will write your name and my own
on the paper which has been translated to you, and you must
make an ' x ' behind your name."   He then placed his hand on

mine whilst I wrote his name and made the " x," as his hand
was too old and shaky to actually hold the pen.   Siteo and
Kalimazondo then made crosses as witnesses for Motoko,
whilst Mr. Armstrong and William Hokogazi did the same on
behalf of the Company, and the treaty between Motoko and
the British South Africa Company was concluded.

As the old man was evidently fatigued with the interview,
my party and I now shook hands with him and bade him
good-bye.   On our way back to the waggon we were escorted
by at least a thousand men, all in a state of great excitement.
On arriving at the foot of the rock they asked me to let them
see the horse gallop, which I did.   This apparently excited
them, and then in their turn they gave me a very interesting
exhibition, something equivalent to a sham fight.   They made
charges upon an imaginary enemy, brandishing spears, knives,
battle-axes, and bows and arrows.   Two men devoted themselves entirely to making a shrill whistling noise with a kind
of reed flute, a sort of pibroch, with which, I suppose, a real
charge would be accompanied.   It was a very savage scene,
and I must say the performers looked as if they would
thoroughly enjoy sticking an assegai into somebody or anybody,
and I have no doubt they would.   To Mr. Armstrong and
myself, however, they evinced great friendship, constantly
rushing up and shouting out " Shamari a Motoko " (" Friend of
Motoko ").

Altogether I consider that the signing of the concession and
the treaty of alliance by Motoko is a very satisfactory business,
although it took a long time and the exercise of much patience
to obtain ; for it was done in full council and in the presence
of a large number of his people.

In conclusion I will say that Motoko's country is of great
extent, and comprises all the territory west of Mangwendi's and
Umsawasha's that lies between the Ruenya and Mazoe rivers,
and that the gold-fields visited by Mauch, and called by him
the Kaiser Wilhelm Gold-Fields, are within his dominions.   The
whole of his country in the neighbourhood of the Lower Mazoe
and the Ruenya, none of which has ever been visited by a white
man, will also probably prove to be auriferous.   A large portion
of Motoko's country lies at an altitude of about four thousand

feet above sea-level, and seems very fertile. His people are wonderfully well supplied with all kinds of vegetable food, and in no part of the country have I seen such fine rice as is here grown, of very large grain and beautifully white. The Mabudja people are entirely different in appearance, manners, and disposition from all the other tribes inhabiting the British South Africa Company's territory in Mashunaland. Physically they are a fine race, and in disposition they are undoubtedly warlike and ferocious. From what I saw and heard I feel sure that Motoko could muster at least five thousand fighting men, and in a short space of time.

The language they speak is merely a dialect of the language spoken by all the other tribes in this part of South-Eastern Africa. Motoko's country has been constantly raided by the Abagaza, with whom they say they used to have periodical encounters; but the majority of them do not even know the name of Lo Bengula or the Amandibili, which is not very surprising, considering that no impi of Lo Bengula has ever penetrated to within several days' journey of even the western border of Motoko's country.

UMTALI VALLEY.

CHAPTER XXIV

AFTER having concluded the treaty with Motoko early in January 1891, as I have related in the last chapter, I piloted my waggon over the high plateau, and passing through the countries of Mangwendi and Makoni, made my way down to the British South Africa Company's camp at Umtali. At that time it was not known whether the better route to the east coast would be by the Pungwi or the Buzi rivers, and before leaving Motoko's I had received instructions from Salisbury to first of all assist Lieutenant Bruce to cut a road from Umtali to Umliwan's kraal on the Lower Revui, and then to lay out an entirely new road from the Odzi river to Salisbury, as the one that had first been made *via* Mangwendi's and Makoni's stations at the latter end of the previous dry season had proved very unsatisfactory as soon as the rains set in. I reached the Odzi river in the middle of February, and found it in flood, and quite impassable for waggons. I remained on the river's bank for fourteen days, and during that time twice visited Captain Heyman's camp at Umtali, swimming my old shooting pony through the Odzi without difficulty. As at the end of this period, however, the river showed no sign of running down, I thought it would be better to waste no more time doing nothing, and so resolved to set about cutting the new road to Salisbury without any further delay. I had no white companion but my cheerful, willing, and intelligent lieutenant, Mr. W. L. Armstrong ; but as he and I got on very well together, neither of us ever felt lonely or got downhearted. Although Armstrong and I were out in a waggon during the whole of this very severe rainy season, and were much exposed to wet, and during the latter part of it were working day after day on the road, standing often for hours together barefooted in mud and water, and in the full heat of the sun, whilst laying the corduroys across the bogs, neither he nor I ever had an hour's headache, much less an attack of fever. People said that I was acclimatised, but that cannot have accounted for Armstrong's immunity from illness, as he had only left his native town of Harrogate a few months before. The fact is that having plenty to do, and keeping one's mind and body both constantly occupied, helps to keep a man in good health. Once get into a low and despondent frame of mind, and you become predisposed to contract fever or any other disease that is going round. I must say that I have been most fortunate in the two young Englishmen who were assigned to me to assist me in my road-making work. First I had Mr. Armstrong, and then later on Mr. Jesser Coope, both most excellent young fellows, and the stamp of young Englishmen one wants in a new country—good-tempered and forbearing with the natives, not afraid to soil their hands by handling axe or spade, always ready to set an example of hard work, conscientious and intelligent, and taking everything as it came without grumbling. There are dozens more young Englishmen and Scotsmen like them in Mashunaland, but I cannot forbear paying a just tribute of praise to the two young men who were of so much assistance to me.

On 3rd May I reached Salisbury, having laid out one hundred and fifty miles of new road through a very difficult country, owing to the enormous number of bogs in which the innumerable streams which water the high plateau of Mashunaland take their rise. I did an immense deal of riding to pick out this line, and gave three strong well-fed horses all the work they wanted. Sometimes I would get a good line for twelve or fifteen miles, but then got amongst bogs that it would have taken endless time and labour to corduroy, and had to give it up and find another. I never moved the waggon until I had got a good line for at least twenty miles on ahead. In one place I was six days, riding over forty miles every day, before I could find a route to my satisfaction. My object was to select a line as direct as possible, that would cross a minimum of boggy ground, and could thus be made into a good permanent road at the smallest possible expense to the Company. Such a road I think I found. It looks simple enough now, but it took a lot of riding to find it, and if any one rides out on either side of it towards the end of the rainy season he will find out what the country on each side of the road is like.

When I reached Salisbury, early in May, the corduroying work along the road had not all been completed, and it had been my intention to get a fresh supply of trading goods with which to pay native labour, and to then return and finish the road forthwith. However, just before my arrival news had reached the Administrator that a Portuguese expedition was on its way up to Manica from the east coast, with the intention of driving the British out of Umtali, and Mr. Colquhoun asked me to take down a contingent of men and two waggon loads of stores and ammunition to the assistance of the little garrison of our countrymen in Manica. Now I am not a fighting man, and neither look forward with enthusiasm to the prospect of being shot, nor feel any strong desire to shoot any one else ; but under the circumstances I was of course prepared to lend a hand in the coming struggle if necessary. I was joined by Lieutenant Adair Campbell and twenty more ex-pioneers, and we made a start for Manica on the 5th of May. Nobody thought that anything would happen before 15th May, which was the date on which the *modus vivendi* between the British and Portuguese expired. Before we reached the Odzi, Borrow overtook us, having come down, like a good fellow, to take part if necessary in resisting the Portuguese attack. On 13th May we reached Umtali, having brought two heavily-laden waggons over the uncompleted road from Salisbury, at the end of a very severe rainy season, in the short space of eight

days.   We were astounded, and I must say disappointed and
disgusted, to find that on the 11th of May, four days before
the expiration of the *modus vivendi*, the Portuguese had
made a sortie from Massi Kessi and attacked Captain Heyman's
camp near Chua.

It is unnecessary for me to say more than a few words
about this affair, as it is a matter of history.   The Portuguese
probably did not know that their opponents had a seven-
pounder cannon in position on the hill they occupied.
Captain Heyman, an old Cape Mounted Rifleman and a good
artilleryman, handled his men with his accustomed coolness and
good judgment, and our men shot well and steadily.   The
Portuguese force, on the contrary, only one hundred of whom
were white men, the remainder being black levies from Angola,
shot very badly, not one of our men having been hit.   When
they found that they were getting within range of the canister
shot, which began to drop amongst them, it may well be
understood that these black levies, who did not care one brass
farthing whether the British or the Portuguese flag waved
over the hills of Manica, felt more inclined to retreat than to
advance ; and soon, in spite of the utmost efforts of the two
Portuguese officers who were leading them, they bolted back
to Massi Kessi, followed by the Portuguese.   The attack
appears to have been ill planned and badly managed in every
way.   All our men agreed in praising the bravery shown by
the two Portuguese officers, who evidently did their best to
bring their men on.   That night Massi Kessi was abandoned,
and, as I have already related, was taken possession of the
following morning by Captain Heyman and his men.

It was shortly after the capture of Massi Kessi that I was
sent down to Umliwan's to fetch away two waggons and some
men of the British South Africa Company's Police who had
been left in charge there.

Umliwan is one of the small semi-independent chiefs living
between the Pungwi and Buzi rivers.   I say semi-independent,
as he has been the victim of numberless raids by the Gaza
Zulus, and, I think, pays tribute to Gungunyan ; but he
entirely denies the justice of the four-hundred-year-old claim
to sovereignty over his territory put forward by the Portuguese.

With this chief (Umliwan) the British South Africa Company had concluded a treaty towards the end of 1890 ; and as his country lies within sixty miles of the junction of the Revui and Buzi rivers—up to which point the latter river was said to be navigable for boats of light draught—Lieutenant Bruce was despatched with twenty men to cut a waggon road from Manica to his chief kraal, and to form a station there. This arduous undertaking was accomplished during the worst months of the rainy season ; and the men suffered much from fever, the natural result of exposure and bad food. Many oxen were killed by falling into old game pits, and those that reached Umliwan's were so reduced in condition by excessive hard work

BATHING IN THE PUNGWI RIVER.

that the greater part of them subsequently died. Thus when the news reached the British South Africa Company's agents in Mashunaland that the Portuguese were advancing from the coast in force with the intention of driving us out of South-Eastern Africa, and Lieutenant Bruce and his men were recalled to strengthen the little garrison at Umtali in Manica, he was obliged to abandon the waggons, and come on with his men on foot, leaving directions with Sergeant Stanley and four men, who had been down to the Buzi river, to follow as soon as possible.

It was to bring in these men and the abandoned waggons that I was despatched to Umliwan's, and, as the journey was in some ways an interesting one, I will give an account of it. Besides my own waggon and oxen, I took down two spare spans and gear, and two drivers. I was accompanied by Mr.

W. L. Armstrong.   As it turned out, I met Sergeant Stanley
and his men three days after leaving Umtali, between the
Mineni and Uzonway rivers, all of them being fairly well,
though they had evidently suffered from fever.   I took my
waggon a few miles beyond Umbayu's kraal, and then, leaving
it and my cattle in charge of my Zulu driver, Armstrong and
I went on with the horses to Umliwan's, taking the spare
cattle, drivers, and half-a-dozen Kafirs with us.   We reached
Umliwan's on 31st May, and the following day, whilst the
drivers were getting the waggons in order for trekking, we
went down to the Revui with a lot of Umliwan's men to look
for hippopotami.   The pools they took us to were eight or
nine miles down the river to the south-east, just below a pretty
cataract, which must be a fine sight when the river is in flood.
As Umliwan assured me that the tse-tse fly did not exist on
this side of the Revui, I took my three horses down with me,
in order to be able to bring as much meat back as possible.
On reaching the pools where our guides had expected to find
the hippopotami, we found them untenanted, and an inspection
of the footpaths along the bank showed us that the game we
were in search of had gone up stream, whither we at once prepared to follow them.

The morning had been cool and cloudy, but the sun was
now shining brightly, and seemed warm for the time of year.
I was driving the horses along a hippopotamus footpath leading through the dense bush on the river's bank, when, coming
to a little clearing, I saw a lot of flies settling on them.   Being
fearful that, in spite of what the Kafirs said, there might possibly be " fly " near the river, I at once took a good look, and to
my horror saw that my two priceless shooting-horses were
covered with tse-tse flies, or, at any rate, that there were at
least twenty on them ; the third horse was still behind.   Armstrong now coming up, we set to work catching the flies, he
and I pinning their feet with a knife blade (the best way of
catching them, as they are as quick as lightning), and the
Kafirs securing some with their hands.   We had soon caught
ten, and frightened off the rest, and I then led the horses forward, the Kafirs continually flicking them with boughs and
keeping a sharp look-out.   Every now and again a fly settled,

and I then caught him with my knife.   Altogether I caught
sixteen flies on the horses, the last not a mile and a half from
Umliwan's kraal.   I did not think my horses would be
affected, as it takes several flies to kill a horse,[1] and not
many got time to inject their poison.   Some did, and filled
themselves with blood, but the greater part were caught
before doing any damage.   So much for Kafir information.
When I showed the flies to Umliwan, the old brute said, in the
most unconcerned way, " Yes, they are the impugan (tse-tse
fly) ; they must have come from the buffaloes beyond the
Revui," quite forgetting that he had assured me most solemnly
that very morning that there was no " fly " whatever on this side
of the river.   But that is the character of the untutored savage.
Without   malice   prepense,   but   just   through   carelessness,
ignorance, or cussedness, he will do you an irreparable injury,
or, at any rate, allow you to do yourself one, and remain all
the time perfectly unconcerned either at his own fault or your
misfortune.   The best way to avoid trouble and loss is to
regard in cold blood all savages in Africa as David in his
wrath regarded the Jews of old—believe them all to be liars,
and never take their word for anything until you have verified
their information.   You will sometimes give yourself needless
trouble, but, on the other hand, you will sometimes avoid heavy
loss.

On the following day, 2nd June, as the waggons were not
yet ready to start, Armstrong and I went down again on foot
to some pools in the Revui above Umliwan's, and shot three
hippopotami.   On 6th June we got back to our own waggon,
and found everything all right, my Zulu driver reporting that,
although hyænas came round the camp nightly, he had neither
seen nor heard anything of lions.   All the time we had been
away the oxen had not been tied up, but had lain loose round
the waggon at night, and on the day of my return they again
did so, the horses being tied to the waggon wheels.   A hyæna
came prowling round, keeping the dogs barking continually,
but being just the day before new moon, and the night
absolutely dark, it was impossible to see to shoot.   I may here
say our waggon was standing just at the base of a low line of

---

[1] They were never any the worse.

hills, covered with forest and dense undergrowth ; below lay a valley, intersected by two streams, stretching up to a high range of hills some three miles distant. The waggon track crossed the nearest stream—a little deep ravine, with steep banks and small pools of water—about one hundred and fifty yards below our camp, and here there was an open space of ground some two hundred yards square, but everywhere else the country was covered with dense bush, or with grass seven or eight feet long—an impossible country in which to hunt.

On 8th June the empty waggons had not yet come up from Umliwan's, and I was utterly weary of the monotony of the enforced delay in a country where, owing to the density of the bush and the length of the grass, it was impossible at that time of the year to move out of the native footpaths.   On this evening we saw for the first time the new moon, which soon sank behind the range of hills to the west. Before turning in I looked round the camp, and saw that the oxen were all lying close up round the waggon, entirely surrounding the horses, which were fastened, as usual, to the wheels.   Armstrong lay in the afterpart of the waggon, I in the front.   The Kafirs smoked "dacha," and were as noisy and talkative as usual, but at length everything was quiet.

About four o'clock in the morning—some two hours before daylight—I was awakened suddenly by the noise of a stampede amongst the cattle.   In an instant Armstrong was out of the waggon and round at the horses' heads, and I followed as quickly as possible.   Two of the horses were still lying down, and the panic that had seized the oxen had evidently not affected them, but not a single ox was to be seen near the waggon.   The Kafirs were now throwing fire-sticks in all directions, and calling out "Shumba, shumba!" (lions, lions!). Everything was, however, perfectly still.   The frightened oxen must have made a rush, and then stood listening.   My Zulu driver now fired two shots into the bush above the camp, and said he could see a lion, but as the night was absolutely dark I do not think he could possibly have seen anything. The Kafirs had by this time all got blazing torches of long grass, which lighted up our little camp but only rendered the surrounding darkness the more intense.   Suddenly the silence was again disturbed by the sound of the trampling and rushing of the oxen, as, mad with fear, they crashed through the underwood towards the open ground to our right, each panic-stricken beast no doubt believing that it was a case of "the devil take the hindmost." And so it was, for before they had run one hundred yards the lions had got hold of one (presumably the hindmost), and the poor brute's agonised bellowings echoed and re-echoed from hill to hill across the narrow valley. I would that that distinguished naturalist, Mr. A. R. Wallace, could hear the piteous cries of an ox being slowly bitten to death by lions, or of a donkey being vivisected by hyænas. Such cries are terrible to listen to, and revealing, as they but too surely do, the frenzy of fear and agony of a dying brute, are a powerful appeal against the cold cruelty of nature's inexorable laws.

My driver and I, accompanied by some of the Kafirs carrying torches of blazing grass, now ran down to where the ox was bellowing, and coming pretty close to it must have scared off the lions, one of which growled, though none showed themselves within the circle of light. I think we must have frightened them off, as the ox broke away from them and rushed down towards the stream. He was soon caught again, and bellowed terribly, poor brute; but the lions did their butcher's work without uttering a growl; they were several minutes killing him. The loud bellowings at length died away in low moans, then everything was once more still. When the ox was caught the second time I made no further attempt at a rescue, as I wanted to get a shot at the lions, and judged that the less they were disturbed the better my chance would be of finding them at daylight; and, for another thing, had they been driven off the ox they had already maimed, they would most certainly have followed up the herd and killed another.

There was now nothing for it, after having made up the fires and put double "reims"[1] on the horses, but to wait for dawn. The lions were singularly quiet, although every now and again we could hear them crunching the bones of their victim. At length the partridges began to call, and a faint

[1] Raw hide thongs, with which horses are tied to a waggon wheel or a tree at night.

roseate flush in the eastern sky told us the day was about to
break.   Whilst waiting for it to get light enough to shoot, we
had a cup of coffee, as the morning was cold and damp, everything, especially the long grass, being saturated with dew.   As
the lions had killed the ox so late in the night I had every
hope of finding them at the carcase at daylight, and relied, too,
on a big dog I had to rush in and bay at least one of them
after I fired.   I had three dogs, two of which I knew were
useless, but the third, which had been lent me by a friend at
Fort Salisbury, came of a good stock, and was a very likely-
looking tyke.   The dense bush and long grass rendered it useless attempting to do anything with a horse.

The red dawn now began to give place to a dull gray light,
and at last I was able to see the ivory sight of my rifle.   Then
Armstrong and I, accompanied by my Zulu driver leading the
big dog Tiger, ready to slip at a moment's notice, advanced
down the waggon track towards the drift, through the little
gully below our camp, in the near neighbourhood of which the
crunching of bones told us that the carcase of the dead ox
lay.   Moving slowly and cautiously forwards, we were soon
within thirty yards of the drift, but being enveloped in long
grass, could still see nothing, although we could now hear very
plainly what I thought was the lions crunching bones, apparently
just beyond the ford.   Again advancing, I had almost reached
the near bank of the stream before I came in sight of the
carcase of the ox lying in the waggon track some fifteen yards
beyond the farther bank.   Two animals were tearing away at
the meat, and, to my surprise, I saw at once, although the light
was still dim in the shadow of the forest, that they were
hyænas.   As I saw them, they saw me and beat a precipitate
retreat.   Had I wished to do so, I could not have got a shot
at them, but as I felt sure the lions were still close at hand, I
had no thought of interfering with them.

We now all three crossed the stream and went up to
the carcase of the ox, so much of which had been eaten
that I knew several lions must have been at work on it.
As is so often the case with these wily animals, they
had retired just at daylight, giving the hyænas a chance
to get a snack before sunrise.   The bush in front was now

excessively thick, and I felt sure the lions were still close at hand, very likely watching us.   I now slipped Tiger, encouraging him to take the spoor into the bush.   But the dog was evidently cowed and frightened, and proved himself utterly useless, as were also the other two.   All this time we were beating the bush round about the carcase.   At this time the lions were close to us, as one of them gave a loud growl not far in front of myself, to the left of the road, and another close to Armstrong and the driver, in the bush on the other side of it.   The covert was, however, too dense to allow us to see anything, and the dog in whom I had put my trust would not run in and bay the lion.   Once or twice he barked, and then came running back to us, but on these occasions I think he had no clear idea of why he was barking.   Oh for one short hour of Ruby and Punch, and the rest of the pack that had formed part of my old hunting outfit !   Then, indeed, had I told a different tale of this morning's work.   As it was, we soon had to give up all hope of coming to conclusions with the lions, for after the two growls above referred to we heard nothing more of them ; and the density of the covert rendered all further pursuit useless.   So, in no very good humour, we returned to the waggon without having fired a shot.

The fire which had cleared the grass off to the left front of the waggon had crossed the stream just above the road and burnt an open place just round the patch of bush in which one of the lions had growled at Armstrong and my driver.   On our arrival at the waggon, which was not more than two hundred yards from the carcase of the ox, our Kafirs, none of whom had accompanied us, told us they had seen four lions break across this piece of open ground and enter the bush beyond.   From knowledge gained later I think there were five lions—a large male, two large females, and two younger females, not quite full grown ; and as the Kafirs did not seem clear as to whether any of the lions they saw were males or not, I think these four animals were the females, and that the old lion must have been by himself, and was probably the one that growled near me. He must then have gone round in the bush and joined the others beyond the open ground.   I now saddled up my horse, and rode into the bush on the track of the lions, which I could

plainly see on the ashes of the burnt grass.   As, however, the
bush and grass rendered it impossible to see anything at a
distance of a few feet, I soon gave it up.   I now called out the
Kafirs and followed up the spoor of my stampeded cattle.   I
was afraid they might have gone a long distance, and was
agreeably surprised to find that they had not run more than five
hundred yards, and we found them feeding quietly, as if nothing
had happened, within half a mile of the waggon.   The lions
had not shown much discrimination, as they had caught and
killed one of the leanest oxen in the herd.

What was to be done now?   I felt pretty sure the lions
would return in the night, and felt a strong and natural desire
to come to terms with them if possible.   Moreover, it was
absolutely necessary to do so, for a party of five lions are
dangerous neighbours, and, besides my oxen and cows, I had
valuable horses I could not afford to lose.   But what to do?—
that was the point.   The dense covert with which all this
country is covered at this season of the year rendered it next
to impossible, without dogs, to obtain a view of them by day,
and unluckily, as we had only seen the new moon for the first
time on the previous evening, the nights were just now
extremely dark.   At first I thought of setting guns ; but
besides that this seems a mean way of killing lions if it can
be avoided, I had only three rifles altogether at the waggon,
and could not afford to set more than two of them, which
might very likely be discharged by hyænas before the lions
came, as has happened to me before now.

After turning various plans over in my mind and carefully
re-examining the ground round the carcase, I determined to sit
up for the marauders in spite of the darkness.   There was no
tree near the kill large enough to support a platform, so I
resolved to build a shelter on the ground.   With the help of
the Kafirs I soon put up a sort of small hut, made by first
leaning three forked poles together in the shape of a tripod,
the prongs naturally supporting one another, and then filling
in the interstices with stout saplings, all meeting at the common
apex.   As none of the poles were planted in the ground, the
structure was by no means a strong one.   When the Kafirs
had nearly completed the work I went up to the waggon for a

short time, and on my return found that they had covered the
hut with light boughs, leaving two holes to fire through on the
side facing the carcase, and a small opening between the poles
at the other side by way of entrance.   I had not intended to
have the hut covered with boughs, and in future will take care
to have nothing but the bare poles, so that I can fire through
them all round ; but thinking that in all probability I should
only get one shot when the lions first came to the carcase, I
made no alteration.   The hut stood amongst some small trees
and saplings on the edge of the waggon track, and two or
three yards from the steep bank of the stream I have spoken
of before.   There was no water, however, just where the
waggon track crossed the stream, though there were pools both
above and below.   From the side of the hut on which were
our shooting holes it was just nine and a half paces to the
nearest part of the ox's carcase, which lay across the roadway.
The distance, I thought, was so short that, no matter how dark
it might be, a lion could not be altogether invisible.   I did
not take into consideration the gloom of the surrounding bush
and the thick mist which rose nightly from the bottom of the
valley.

Our hut being ready, there was nothing more to be done
till the evening ; and about six o'clock, having finished dinner
and made everything snug for the night at the waggon, Armstrong and I took our rifles and blankets and went down to
take our places in the hut.   The sun had not been long down,
but it was quite dusk already in the gloom of the forest beyond
the stream, and nearly dark inside our shelter.   The Kafirs
had cut a few short poles to block up the entrance, which
Armstrong set about doing as soon as we were inside, whilst
I was clearing some leaves away from my shooting hole.   It
now became dark with astonishing rapidity, and by the time
we had got everything in order it would have been absolutely
so had it not been for the faint light cast through the shadows
of the forest by the new moon, which was, however, but two
days old.

It was not yet seven o'clock, I think, when we both heard
some animals treading on the large crisp dry mahobo-hobo
leaves with which the ground was covered in the bush beyond

the waggon track. As they reached the roadway, which was
nearly clear of leaves, their steps became noiseless. We were
now intensely on the alert, and almost immediately a something
loomed up, like a dark shadow, beyond the carcase of the ox.
At first I could not tell whether it was a lion or hyæna, and
until I felt sure on that point I determined not to fire. The
moon's thin crescent still showed above the hills, but its light
was but feeble, and, in spite of it, it was now very dark beneath
the trees. Whilst I was speculating as to its identity, with
noiseless tread the shadowy form had advanced down the roadway, till it stood alongside the carcase of the ox. It held its
head up, which, despite the size, made me think it was a
hyæna, as a lion usually holds its head low. When, however,
after a moment's pause, it passed the dead ox and stood
within a few yards of us, evidently looking suspiciously at the
hut, the boldness of the beast made me think it must be a lion.
At this instant two more vague and misty forms loomed up to
my right, and the foremost at once came towards the hut.
From its size I knew it must be a lion, and so whispered to
Armstrong, " I'm going to fire." From his position on my
left he could not see these two lions from his window, but was
watching the one that had first come up to the carcase.
Unfortunately he misunderstood my low whisper, thinking I
had said, " Don't fire," or he might have fired at this animal.

And now there was a dark something coming noiselessly
up towards where I sat, and actually within three yards of
the muzzle of my rifle, though it was so dark that the sense
of its nearness was lost. It was impossible to miss it, but I
wanted to give it a dead shot, and so, pointing my little rifle
towards the front part of the hazy form before me, I pulled
the trigger. The report of the rifle, loudly as it should have
sounded in the silence of the night, was instantly dwarfed and
drowned by the terrific roaring grunts of the wounded lion,
wounded unto death indeed, for it just rolled or fell down the
steep bank of the stream, and lay moaning at the bottom,
within a few yards of us. After a few seconds a gurgling
noise, as of an animal choking, told me that it was at the
very point of death. I had scarcely got another cartridge
into my rifle, and as far as I remember the lion just shot was

still moaning within a few yards, when a second animal appeared in the darkness to my right. It looked much lower than the first, and I thought it must be a hyæna. It was invisible to Armstrong, but as it was very close to me I at once fired into it, and instantly the hoarse grunting roars that followed the shot would have let any one within a mile know it was a lion that had received the bullet. The animal must have been coming forward to reconnoitre, and was, I suppose, in a crouching position. When hit, she (for it was a lioness) was probably knocked over, and then, like the first one shot, either rushed or fell down the steep bank below into the bed of the stream. She just managed to crawl up the farther bank, and we could hear her, evidently dying, just beyond, the first furious grunts being succeeded by low moans. Soon all again was still, and I knew that two lions lay dead.

Scarcely another minute had passed, and I had just whispered to Armstrong that I thought our sport with the lions was over for the night, when we both heard an animal breathing alongside of our shelter, within a few feet of us, and the next instant a gentle shake given to the hut, and a noise as of one of the loose branches with which it was covered being torn off, let us know there was another lion in our neighbourhood even more enterprising than the two that had been shot. It was soon evident to me that the animal was looking for an entrance to our shelter, for, after tearing off a few more boughs, it got to the place where we had crept in, but which was now blocked up with poles. Here it halted, and, from the way it kept touching the poles, seemed to be trying to get its paw through. This was a little more than I had bargained for, and, at the risk of incurring the charge of inhospitality, I resolved to try to keep our visitor outside in the cold. Of course, whilst the lion was acting in the manner I have described, I, on my side, was not idle. As soon as I realised what our visitor was trying to do, I turned round, and, lying on the ground, tried to look between the interstices of the poles forming the entrance to our hut. It was, however, so absolutely dark that I could see nothing. Instant action was nevertheless necessary, for, as the poles forming our hut were not fixed in the ground, the lion might

have got its paw between two of them and pulled them out
at any moment, and then, by pushing its head and shoulders
through, would have infallibly overturned the whole structure.
To prevent such a consummation I now pushed the muzzle
of my rifle between the poles, just where my ears told me
my would-be interviewer was moving them, and, pointing it
upwards, holding the stock on the ground, pulled the trigger.
Once more, and for the third time that night, the report of
the rifle was answered by the most terrific grunting roars it is
possible to conceive, uttered, as they were, within six feet of
our ears.   I am sorry I had not a phonograph with me in
order to preserve these powerful expressions of the feelings of
a wounded lion.   Suddenly released in a London drawing-
room, I feel sure they could not fail to produce a very marked
effect.   Well, the expanding Metford bullet, received at such
close quarters, must have given the lion a very nasty jar.   I
fancy that it fell over, and was rolling on the ground when
Armstrong fired through another opening at the sound of the
roars.   Whether this second bullet hit it or not I cannot say,
but immediately after the shot the wounded beast, still grunting
loudly, made a rush through the bushes behind the hut to the
edge of the bank above the stream, which was quite precipitous, and then fell headlong with a loud splash right into
a shallow pool of water.   Here it lay for some time splashing
the water slightly—by moving its tail, I fancy—and moaning
in a way that made us feel very happy ; for no one who
heard it could have imagined there was half an hour's life left
in the beast.   We thought we had got three lions in about
five minutes, and felt very pleased with ourselves.   There
were two more about, I knew, but I had very little fear of
another attack, and very slight hopes of getting another shot,
as I imagined, after the misfortunes of their relatives, the
remainder of the family would move off.

We now spread our blankets and lay down—not to sleep,
but in order to keep our vigil with the greatest possible comfort.   From this time until about midnight we were several
times disturbed by an animal sniffing round the back of our
hut.   It never came on to the road in front of our shooting
holes, and we could never see anything through the poles at

the back.   Sometimes these sniffings were very loud, or
sounded very loud in the silence of the night, and came
right up to our hut ; but nothing ever touched the poles or
the branches that covered them.   Thinking that the remaining lions must have retreated, I put these sniffings down
to hyænas, and wondered they did not come round to the
carcase of the ox.   I may here say I was entirely mistaken
in my surmise, as, on examination next morning, we found
no hyæna spoor at the back of our hut, whilst lions had walked
round and about in all directions, making a regular path
between the hut and the bank of the stream.   However, to
thoroughly understand the character of the African lion one

A SLUMBERING LION.

must live and learn.   On a dark night these animals are
undoubtedly very bold and fearless.   From time to time the
wounded lion, which seemed to have dragged itself out of the
pool of water into which it had first fallen, and to be now
lying on the farther bank, moaned in a very pitiful way ; it
might have been a human being in the last extremity.
These moans and groans, however, came at longer and longer
intervals, and at last we made sure the lion last hit was as
dead as its comrades.   The sniffings, if they did nothing else,
served to keep us wide awake, and the constant strain on our
nerves made the time pass very slowly.

It must have been some time between midnight and two
o'clock in the morning that we heard an animal at the carcase
of the ox ; and, from its very noisy way of feeding, I soon
felt sure that it was a lion.   We now raised ourselves noise-

lessly from the ground and looked out of our shooting holes, but could see nothing. It very soon became evident, however, that there were two lions, as every now and again one—which, I think, was the big male of the party—gave a most prodigious snarl at its comrade. These lions, it must be remembered, were less than ten yards from the muzzles of our rifles ; yet so intense was the darkness that we could see absolutely nothing. One might just as well have held one's face in a basin of ink and endeavoured to read the future of Mashunaland. And now for hours these lions lay, "so near and yet so far," tearing at the meaty portions of the carcase, and crunching up the breast bones and the ends of the ribs. Every now and again they would rest from feeding and then lay breathing with a loud blowing noise ; then the tearing and crunching would recommence. Every now and again the big lion, as I guessed, would awake the echoes of the night with a loud grunting snarl, to which the dogs at the waggon always replied with angry barkings.

It would be supposed that to lie thus in the wilds of Africa, within ten yards of a couple of lions feeding noisily, and sometimes snarling loudly, would be a sufficiently novel experience to keep one awake ; yet to show how "familiarity breeds contempt," I may mention that I twice had to wake my young companion, and tell him not to snore, as the noise might disturb the lions. And now over and over again I looked and looked towards where the lions were feeding, until my eyes ached, but in vain. Several times I thought of firing at the sound. However, as lions feeding at a carcase are nearly always lying down, and as in the present instance they might have been on the farther side, there was only a chance of hitting, and only a small chance of mortally wounding, one of them. After some doubt I resolved to wait, in the hope that they would remain until the first streak of dawn. Being so near, I only wanted light enough to see the lions, and could have dispensed with the necessity of looking at the sights of my rifle. The veriest trifle of moon would have sufficed, or even a decent shooting-star ; but the darkness that fell upon Egypt could not have been more intense than the unfathomable gloom of this African night.

Slowly, very slowly, the night wore on, and still the lions munched and crunched and the darkness held. And now hyænas commenced to howl around, apparently answering one another. There is something so weird and wild in the varied cries of the African laughing hyæna when meat is about that I have ever loved to listen to them. No wonder this animal is so intimately connected with all the superstitions of the Kafir tribes of South Africa. About an hour before day-break the lions commenced to drag the remains of the carcase through the bush beyond the waggon track, and shortly after-wards they suddenly left it—so suddenly indeed that it seemed as if something had startled them, as they made a regular rush through the bush, trampling loudly on the mahobo-hobo leaves. To this day I am at a loss to understand why they retired in such haste, as the whole night through they had treated the barking of the dogs and the talking of the Kafirs at the waggon with the most sublime contempt. However, they were gone, and all chance of a shot at them was gone too, as the surrounding cover was so thick as to render it almost impos-sible to get a sight of them in the morning.

A little before the lions left the carcase, the animal that had tried to get into our hut, and which we thought had been lying dead for some hours, commenced to groan again, and then, moaning all the time, evidently crawled out of the stream, and moving slowly through the bush at the back of the hut, passed close to where its comrades were munching at the remains of the carcase. It then came slowly back towards the stream, and then the moaning ceased. These groans and moans had no effect on the lions at the carcase; they ate away the whole time, undisturbed by the thought of their two dead comrades lying stiff and stark within a few yards of them, or by the piteous moans of the remaining member of their family which was evidently in a dying condition. Truly they possessed two requisites of terrestrial happiness—a good appetite and no conscience.

At last the day began to break, and a cold gray dawn revealed to us that the whole valley in which we were was enveloped in a dense mist, so dense indeed that the rosy flush in the eastern sky that usually heralds the approach of light had been entirely

hidden from us. The hyænas, which had kept their distance
while the lions were at the carcase, now commenced to
approach, and soon a band of four came walking down the
roadway, looming large in the misty light. Holding their
heads high, and craning their necks from side to side, on they
came, until they reached the spot from which the remains of
the carcase had been dragged. Here they halted a minute and
gazed curiously at our hut, from which the rifle barrels protruded ominously. Then, with a series of wild howls, they
swerved off to the spot where the lions had left little more than
the head and a few bones of the ox, and were soon tearing
away at what remained. I might have shot any one of them as
they stood in the roadway, but I cherished a hope that the
lions were still close at hand, and would return and drive the
hyænas off their kill. When, however, half an hour more had
passed, and the hyænas were still crunching away undisturbed,
I knew our chance of getting another shot at the lions was a
very small one, and was just on the point of leaving the hut to
examine our victims when a fifth hyæna came walking down
the road. I could by this time see the sights of my rifle, and
as the brute stood about fifteen yards off looking curiously at
the hut, I planted an expanding bullet in the centre of its
chest. Armstrong fired at the same time, and his bullet broke
one of its hind legs low down. A spotted hyæna is a very
tough beast, as any one knows who has shot many ; but this
one only gave a jump backwards, and lay dead on the edge of
the road, not four yards from the spot where it was standing
when hit.

We now crawled out of our hut and looked around us.
The first thing that we saw was the carcase of the lion first
shot ; it was lying on its back at the bottom of the little river
bed below our huts. This proved to be a very big old lioness,
in fine order, and excessively fat. I preserved the skin for
setting up. The expanding Metford bullet had struck her
right on the point of the shoulder, smashed the bone to pieces,
and, as we found on cutting her up, had gone right through the
centre of her heart. From the place where she was hit she
had done nothing more than roll down the steep bank to the
stream. The second animal hit was also a lioness, not

nearly so large as the first, but yet a fine animal, perhaps not quite full grown.   She lay on the bank just beyond the stream, having had strength to crawl out of the river bed, into which she had rushed or fallen when hit.   The expanding bullet had caught her just behind the shoulders and had gone right through.

We never got the last lion hit, although I think there can be no doubt that it lay dead within a few hundred yards.   The blood lay in pools where it had been lying moaning during the greater part of the night, and it must have changed its position several times.   When, however, it moved away towards morning, the blood must have ceased to run, and we could not follow the spoor.   The dogs were useless, and the bush and grass terribly thick, and so we lost her.   I say " her," as I believe the party consisted of a large lion, two big lionesses, and two younger ones ; for the boys said there were two large ones and two smaller animals amongst the four they saw in the morning after the ox was killed.   One of the big lionesses we killed, and the other, I think, was the one that tried to get at us in the hut.   The survivors, I imagine, were the lion and one of the younger females.   Our bag for the night was, therefore, two lionesses and one large spotted hyæna. With a little light and a little luck it might easily have been four lions.

I may mention that the place where our waggon was standing was within fifty yards of where some of Lieutenant Bruce's men were encamped about two months earlier, when one of their boys (who hailed from the Orange Free State, and came up with the expedition last year) was dragged by a lion from under one of the waggons, and carried off and devoured in the bush close at hand.   The same night a second attempt was made to obtain another victim, but fortunately it was unsuccessful.   I have no doubt that the same party of lions that visited my waggon was responsible for the death of Lieutenant Bruce's servant ; and after seeing what they did with the carcase of an ox, I can understand their not being altogether satisfied with a Hottentot boy.   I should say it was the lioness we wounded, but did not get, that actually collared him ; and if that is so she will never taste human flesh again.

On my return to Umtali from Umliwan's I at once set
about completing the work on the road between that place and
Salisbury, and early in July had the entire road in good
order for heavy waggons, all the bogs being corduroyed and
the streams bridged.   After this I was sent by the Company
to try to find a route to the coast along the watershed
between the Pungwi and Buzi rivers, free of " fly " and therefore suitable for a waggon road.   But in this I was unsuccessful, as I found the whole of the low country between the
Buzi and Pungwi rivers to be infested with tse-tse fly.   I
reached M'panda's, on the Pungwi, in the end of August and
returned to Salisbury in September.[1]   Shortly afterwards I was
sent down to Tuli with instructions to overhaul the " weigh
bills " of all the waggons I met on the road, in order to find
out whether a sufficient supply of food was likely to reach
Salisbury before the rainy season set in, to provision the country
during the time that communication with the outside world was
likely to be interrupted, owing to the large rivers becoming
impassable.   I rode down alone on horseback, and finding that
an ample supply of food to meet all possible contingencies was
on the road at various points between Tuli and Salisbury, I
returned at once to Mashunaland.   When near Charter I met
Mr. Rhodes, Mr. De Waal, and Dr. Jameson, and again
returned with them to Victoria, and afterwards accompanied
them on a visit to the head kraal of the chief, Chibi, on a
diplomatic mission.   After this Messrs. Rhodes and De Waal
went south, whilst Dr. Jameson and I returned to Salisbury.
Here I was once more employed by the Company in laying
out and making roads, and continued at this work until May
1892, when, there being no more work for me to do, I termi-
nated my engagement with the British South Africa Company,
and after spending two or three months shooting, and collecting
specimens of natural history in various parts of the country,
made my way down to Beira on the east coast.   On 3rd
October I shot my last lion, a fine large male, and on 7th

---

[1] As I have lately been accused of slaughtering game for sport, I will take this
opportunity of saying that during this journey, though I walked for days amongst
innumerable herds of wild animals, I only fired away twelve cartridges from the day
I left Salisbury until the date of my return there, and that, as is my usual practice, I
never fired a shot except for the purpose of supplying myself and my party with meat.

October my last elephant, a splendid old bull with tusks weighing 108 lbs. the pair.   On 19th October I left Beira for Cape
Town, and after a visit to the Transvaal started for England,
where I landed once more, safe and sound, on 17th December
1892.

CHAPTER XXV

Remarks concerning the relative merits of large and small bore rifles—
Some hunting reminiscences

HAVING now briefly related the sequence of events which led up to the occupation of Mashunaland by the British South Africa Company's pioneer expedition, and told my readers something concerning the early history of the colonisation of that country, I will, before bringing my narrative to a close, add some hunting reminiscences, culled from my diaries of years ago, at a time when I still wandered and hunted in solitary contentment, little dreaming that in a few short years a British colony would be established in the midst of my old hunting grounds.

Before commencing these, I will, however, first say a few words concerning the relative merits of big and small bore rifles, and the reasons which have led me to discard the former and trust entirely to the latter.

I first gave up the use of large-bore rifles and enormous charges of powder when I left off hunting elephants as a business; for I found it too much trouble to carry these weighty weapons about the country with a supply of heavy ammunition in districts where there was only an off chance of meeting with elephants. But the more experience I had in shooting heavy animals like giraffes, buffaloes, rhinoceroses, and hippopotami with a 450-bore rifle, by Gibbs of Bristol, the more confidence I gained in its efficiency, till at last one day I tried it on elephants. On that day I killed six of these animals, under by no means favourable circumstances, and since that time I have killed four more with the same kind of rifle, using of course the long, solid, hardened bullet of 540 grains, and a powder charge of only 75 grains.

I do not, however, advise any of my readers who may be about to adopt elephant-hunting as a profession to entirely exclude large-bore rifles from their battery. Not at all. If a man is going to make a business of elephant-hunting he wants the most deadly weapon he can get, and I think there is no doubt that under many circumstances, especially in thick bush, a heavy large-bore rifle would be far more effective than a small-bore for elephant-shooting. On the other hand, I think that if a man is going on a long journey of exploration, when every pound weight of his outfit is of importance, and hopes to kill an elephant or two, but would not feel that his life was embittered if he did not do so, there is no necessity that he should burden himself with anything larger than a 450-bore rifle of the right kind, with the long solid bullets for heavy game, and expanding bullets for soft-skinned animals. So many elephants have been killed of late years with 450-bore rifles, principally Martini-Henry's of the Government pattern, that it is no longer possible to regard such an occurrence as a mere lucky accident. Put your long solid 450-bore bullet through the upper part of an elephant's heart, or through the big blood-vessels of both his lungs, and you will kill him nearly as quickly as if you inflicted the same wound with a 4-ounce spherical ball. Hit him in the ear and put your bullet into his brain, and you will drop him as dead as if you had blown his head off with the 81-ton gun.

Of course if a man goes out to Africa with nothing but a small-bore rifle, and happens to fall in with elephants, and does not manage to kill one, he will all his life believe that had he only had a heavy rifle he would have bagged his animal. However, it is only necessary to read Gordon-Cumming's accounts of elephant-shooting with heavy rifles to see how difficult it sometimes is to kill these animals. If my memory serves me, he relates having fired thirty-seven bullets from a heavy 10-bore rifle into one elephant after it had been crippled by a broken shoulder. I have known personally many of the old Boer elephant-hunters of the last generation, and there was not one of them who had not endless stories of

the elephants he had lost, after firing many shots into them
with heavy smooth-bore guns.   On the other hand, I remember
Jan Engelbrecht, a son of old Michael Engelbrecht, telling me
quite a different experience.   He happened to be at Mr.
Collison's waggon one day without a heavy rifle, when a herd
of elephants was sighted close at hand.   Mr. Collison lent
Jan a horse and one of his own rifles, a double 500-bore, by
Holland and Holland, the well-known firm of Bond Street.
Jan Engelbrecht of course used heavy solid bullets, and he
killed four good elephants.   In describing the incident to me
afterwards, and telling me how surprised he was at killing
the elephants so easily with a small-bore rifle, he concluded by
saying, " Mijn magthet, nooit zaal ik wieder en groet roer en
mijn hand vaat" (" By jove, I'll never take a big gun in my
hand again ").   Now Jan Engelbrecht was born and brought up
in the hunting veld, and had been shooting elephants all his
life with large smooth-bore guns, and would never have thought
of trying a small-bore if he had had his own old " roer " ; but
the one experiment converted him.   However, I will content
myself by saying that to my mind it has been clearly proved
that elephants can be killed without any great difficulty with
450-bore rifles, provided long, heavy, solid bullets are used.
But to the professional elephant-hunter I say, give yourself
every chance, and take the heaviest rifle you can stand up to
for shots in dense bush, and when you cannot get a fair shot at
a vital part.   As for buffaloes, which are acknowledged by Sir
Samuel Baker and other writers to be excessively tenacious of
life, they are easily killed with a 450-bore rifle.   During the
past two years, 1891 and 1892, some hundreds of buffaloes
have been killed on the Lower Pungwi river, near Beira.
Quite nine out of every ten of these have been killed with
sporting Martini-Henry rifles, which are of course of 450-bore.
   Some years ago at the Umfuli river, in Mashunaland, a
young Free State Boer named Montgomery, who was shooting
for hides, killed sixteen buffaloes out of a herd with the same
kind of rifle.   These facts, I think, speak for themselves.   You
can kill anything that walks this earth with a 450-bore
Metford rifle, by Gibbs of Bristol, or with a good rifle of
the same bore by any other good maker.   Having used

Gibbs's Metford rifles for the last twelve years with the most complete satisfaction to myself, I naturally swear by Gibbs ; but I have of course seen many other splendid rifles by other makers, notably by Rigby, and Holland and Holland. Naturally every one believes in the weapon that has done him good service. My friend Cornelis van Rooyen, who is as good a hunter as South Africa can produce, and a right good fellow to boot, uses nothing but a double 500-bore rifle, by Holland and Holland, which was given him some years ago by his friend and companion, the late Mr. H. C. Collison. With this rifle he has shot every kind of game in Africa, from a steinbuck to an elephant, and he will not believe that the world can produce its equal, though he acknowledges that my Metford is a good little weapon in its way.

Should any of my readers, acting on my advice, determine to try a 450-bore rifle, let them be very careful about the kind of bullets they use. For large game, as I have already said, you want a long, heavy, solid bullet, and for large antelopes and lions the best kind of bullet is one weighing about 360 grains, with a small hollow at the point, good thick walls round the hollow part, and a heavy solid end. Such a bullet will mushroom on striking an animal, but will also have great penetrating power. The small, light Express bullets, with scarcely any base, a large hollow in the point, and thin walls, are useless for anything but very small animals, as, being driven at an immense velocity by a heavy charge of powder, they break all to pieces on impact, and merely inflict surface wounds on such animals as the larger African antelopes. These are the projectiles which Sir Samuel Baker, in his most interesting and useful book, *Wild Beasts and their Ways*, condemns in such unqualified terms, and I am quite of his opinion concerning them ; but the bullets used in such a rifle as Mr. Gibbs's 461-Metford, taking the No. 2 cartridge, have a very different effect. These 461-bore rifles shoot either a 570-grain bullet propelled by 80 grains of powder, or a 360-grain expanding bullet with a small hollow at the point, propelled by 100 grains of powder.

In conclusion, I do not say that a man who happened to get killed through failing to stop the charge of a wounded buffalo, elephant, or lion with a 450-bore rifle might not possibly have saved his life if he had had a heavy rifle in his hands.   But any one who hunts big game ought to be prepared to take some chances ; and after all, if the element of danger were entirely eliminated, where would the fun come in? It must be borne in mind that my remarks only refer to African shooting, where much of the country is very open, so open indeed *that one's rifles ought to be carefully sighted up to at least four hundred yards.*

In the dense grass jungles of the East no doubt heavy rifles are far more necessary than in many parts of Africa.   I have of late years lost my interest in large-bore rifles, but I would advise any one desirous of investing in such weapons to have a look at Holland and Holland's new 10 and 8 bore Paradox guns, shooting 8 to 10 drams of powder and a steel bullet coated with lead.   I happened to see some shot the other day at the shooting ground, and was much struck by their great accuracy.   The penetration too, I was assured, was very great, and these weapons are of course much lighter than rifles of the same calibre.

Having said my say about rifles, I will now proceed to relate a few hunting reminiscences.

It was on the Chobi that, one morning in September 1877, being in want of meat for my men, I followed the fresh spoor of a large herd of buffaloes from the river, and in due course came up with them.   Just as I sighted them they got my wind and came galloping out obliquely past me in a dense black mass and well within shot.   I fired at a cow with a single 10-bore rifle I was then using, and knew that I had hit her about the right place.   I then ran on after the herd, but the wounded cow could not keep up with her companions for more than one hundred yards, after which she slowed down to a trot, and then, stopping, turned and looked at me, the blood streaming from her mouth and nostrils.   She was quite done for, and as I approached lay down, and commenced to bellow, as these animals so often do when dying.   As she did so, the herd, now about one hundred and fifty yards from her, stopped, and the buffaloes all stood closely packed together gazing towards where I stood, close to the still bellowing cow.   I had pushed

another cartridge into my rifle whilst running, and now hastily
fired at another buffalo whose head and shoulders protruded from
the confused black mass of the herd.   The animal, a fine young
bull, fell to the shot in its tracks, and the herd again galloped
off.   The cow was by this time dead, so, accompanied by my
boys, I walked leisurely towards my second victim, which still lay
perfectly still and apparently dead.   When quite close I saw
the bullet wound in his neck, and knew that his sudden fall
had been produced by the shock to the spinal column, from
which, if it is only a jar and the bones are not broken, an
animal will recover as suddenly as he collapses on receiving the
wound.   I was close in front of the seemingly dead animal
when he commenced to struggle and at once endeavoured to
stand up, first getting on to his hind legs whilst still kneeling, as
is the way with all bovine animals.   I was standing within a
yard of his nose, so, hastily firing into his chest, I sprang past
his head and made for a small tree behind him.   In spite of
the terrible wound he had just received, the sturdy beast
struggled to his feet, and, catching sight of some of my Kafirs
who were already some distance off and in full retreat, at once
charged after them, grunting furiously.

I was now by my tree, watching events and putting
another cartridge into my rifle.   The buffalo having missed
my boys, who had all climbed into or were standing behind
trees, soon slowed down to a trot, but was evidently still
eager for revenge, as he came round in a half-circle with
nose upraised and horns laid back.   I was just going to
fire at him, when he must have got my wind, for he suddenly swung round and, seeing me, came on at a gallop as
hard as he could.   He was about one hundred yards off when
he started, and when he was some sixty yards from me I fired
for his throat; but he neither stopped nor swerved, nor showed in
any way that he was hit, but came straight on.   I had plenty
of time and could have swarmed up the branchless stem of the
sapling by which I was standing, and got out of his reach with
the greatest ease ; but as my legs were bare I knew that such
a course meant the loss of a lot of skin, so I determined to
dodge him.   I was young and active in those days, and full of
confidence in my nerve, so, holding the stem of the tree in my

left hand, I leant out as far as possible and awaited the onset. When he was very near me—so close indeed as to preclude the possibility of his being able to swerve and pass on the other side of the tree—I pulled my body with a sudden jerk up to and beyond the stem, and, shooting past the buffalo's hind quarters, ran as hard as ever I could to another tree standing in the direction from which he had come. I knew that by this manœuvre I should gain a good deal of ground, as, even if my adversary had followed me, the pace at which he was going was such that he would not have been able to turn till he had got some way past the tree where I had given him the slip. Had he come round after me I should have now climbed for it ; but, as I expected, when I dodged from under his very nose and shot past behind him he lost me entirely and ran straight on. He did not, however, go far, but stopped and lay down, and I killed him with another bullet. On examining him I found that the shot I had fired at him as he was charging had struck him in the gristle of the nose (which was, of course, outstretched, as it always is when a buffalo charges), and, passing through the back of his tongue, had entered his vitals and inflicted a mortal wound from which he would soon have died without another shot.

As with the African elephant, so with the buffalo it is almost impossible to kill either the one or the other with a shot in the front of the head when charging, owing to the position in which the head is then held, though both may be easily killed by a shot in the front of the head when standing at rest.

In 1879, when hunting near Linyanti, on the eastern bank of the Chobi, I took a stroll from camp one evening with my gun carrier and wounded a buffalo bull, which I followed through some rather open bush. I sighted him several times, but as the bush was by no means thick, he always saw me coming on, and galloped off before I got within shot. At length the covert grew denser, and on the edge of an open valley became very thick indeed. Here I took my rifle and followed the spoor myself slowly and cautiously. However, the wounded animal went right through the bush into the open, so I handed the rifle back to my boy, and told him to take

the spoor again.   He almost immediately lost it, but we soon
found that it had just gone into the open, and then turned
short round and entered the bush again.   Just in front of us
was a large mass of evergreen shrubs, and as my boy, who still
had the rifle, got round it he started back.   As he did so I caught
the rifle from his shoulder with my left hand, and at the same
instant saw the wounded buffalo, which had been standing
just behind the bushes, coming on with loud grunts, and
literally within ten yards of me.   I had no time to raise the
rifle to my shoulder, but, swinging it round to my hips, just
pulled the trigger, and at the same time sprang to one side.
At the same moment I was covered with a shower of sand, and
some part of the buffalo, nose or horn or shoulder, touched my
thigh with sufficient force to overturn me, but without hurting
me in the least.   I was on my feet again in a moment, ready
to run for it, but saw that my adversary was on the ground
bellowing, with a hind leg, evidently broken, dragging out behind him.   Before he recovered himself I despatched him with
a bullet through the lungs.   My random shot must have passed
under his chest, between his forelegs, and had broken his
right hind leg just above the hock, bringing him down suddenly
and covering me with a shower of sand.   As there were no
trees about, but only scrubby bush, if it had not been for this
lucky shot disabling him he would probably have got me.

As much of our South African hunting is still done on
horseback, and one gallops after game at a break-neck pace
over all sorts of rough ground, the true nature of which is often
concealed by long grass, it is not to be wondered at if one gets
a good many spills.   I, myself, have had my share of these,
but I have seldom hurt myself.

Late one evening in September 1883 I was riding over
to my camp on the Manyami river, Mashunaland, and was
quite alone, as I had left my boys about thirty miles off in the
morning and ridden on.   I had entered an open valley which
ran down to within a short distance of my camp, when, from
the bush I had just left, a black rhinoceros trotted out into the
open, having no doubt got my wind as I passed.   At first I
had no intention of meddling with him, as I had no Kafirs
with me to cut him up if I shot him, but before he had

got far I bethought me that his skull would be worth something to me as a museum specimen, and at once galloped up and gave him a good shot with a small 450-bore rifle I was carrying. He had broken from a trot into a gallop before I fired, but on receiving the shot went a good deal faster, at the same time snorting violently. The ground was now perfectly open and first-rate for galloping, as the long summer grass had been burnt off; so, hastily remounting and pushing in another cartridge, I put on the pace in order to get a second shot before reaching the belt of timber which skirted the open valley.

A black rhinoceros can gallop at an extraordinary pace

BLACK RHINOCEROS DRINKING.

for so heavy a beast; indeed, it is just as much as a good horse can do to overtake one, so that as I ranged alongside, my horse, a powerful stallion, was going at his utmost speed. I was just going to rein in for another shot when he either crossed his forelegs or trod on his own front foot, and came down all of a heap with tremendous force, shooting me far over his head. I felt great pain in the groin at once, but nothing else; but as I got on my feet, doubled up and groaning and pressing my right hand to where I felt the pain, I heard the unmistakable sound of bone rubbing on bone—crepitating, I think, is the word—and raising my hand found that my left collar-bone was badly fractured, the one broken end sticking up in a point under the skin. It seems that the stock of the rifle had caught me a severe blow in the groin, and the barrel, coming up across my chest, had broken my collar-bone. In addition to this I had fallen on my right shoulder, and so was sore all over. I did not trouble any more about the rhinoceros, but getting on my horse, which was not materially damaged by the fall, rode slowly down to my camp a much sadder man than I had been before I saw the rhinoceros. I was alone that year in the veld, and so had nobody but my Kafirs to help me to set my broken collar-bone. However, I knew pretty well what to do, but spent a tedious time in camp waiting for the bone to set. On the twenty-third day I shot a Tsessebe ante-lope, the following day two elands, and the next three sable antelopes. The bone was not then properly set and hardened, and ached so at nights, owing to the strain on it from guiding my horse with the left hand through the bush, that I got but little sleep ; but it got better every day, and was soon all right.

One day in 1887 I was riding with Mr. J. A. Jameson (brother of the Mr. James S. Jameson who, to the infinite regret of all who ever knew him, lately lost his life on the Congo), when, near a place called Pondoro's, we espied four splendid koodoo bulls coming down from some rocky hills to drink in the stream below. As soon as they saw us they halted and, after gazing towards us for a few moments, turned and cantered heavily towards the hills, and we at once galloped in pursuit. They gained the rocks before we could get within shot, and, when just on the ridge, stood amongst some great boulders of stone and again looked back at us. My friend here dismounted for a shot, but as he could see nothing but the head and- horns of the largest bull, its body being covered by a rock, only got a very bad chance, and fired without effect. The koodoos at once disappeared and entered the thick bush behind the ridge of rocks, and I galloped in close behind them. Of the four two were very large bulls, one of which had a magnificent pair of horns—long, well twisted, and perfectly symmetrical. The bush was now so thick that it was impossible to dismount in it and get a shot, so I resolved to stick close to them until they got into more open ground. Being mounted on a quick active pony, I was able to press them pretty hard and keep close to them. They soon separated, two going off to the

left, one of the young bulls remaining with the big one I
wanted.   Very soon these two again separated, and I was left
alone with the biggest bull.

We were now going down a gentle slope, still very thickly
covered with bush ; but I knew that we should soon emerge
upon one of the open valleys between the wooded hills, and,
once there, the koodoo bull would have been mine.   However,
it was not to be.   Suddenly I came upon a row of open
pitfalls, old ones certainly, but still pretty deep, and some
eight or ten feet long.   I nearly went into one, but just missed
doing so, and, thinking the danger past, stuck the spurs in
and pushed my pony to his greatest speed in order to get
close up to the koodoo, and have a shot at him as soon as he
got into the open.   Suddenly I found myself on the edge of
another row of pitfalls, and on the very brink of one, at which
I was going obliquely and at full speed.   It was impossible to
wrench the pony's head round and pass the pitfall, as I had
done before.   We were too near before I saw it, and the only
thing was to stick the spurs in and hope my horse would
jump.   However, an African hunting-horse, though he will
usually jump well at timber, will seldom negotiate an open
ditch, and on this occasion my pony went full tilt right into
the pitfall and the next instant I was on the other side of it
with the saddle.   The pace at which he was going had carried
him the whole length of the pitfall, the opposite end of which
he had struck with his chest with great violence and then
fallen back into it, I myself going on with the saddle over his
head.   I could see at once that the poor brute's back was
broken, though he was still alive.

As soon as Jameson came up with the Kafirs we got him
out of the hole, and I at once shot him.   We then cut him
open and found that the backbone was broken, one rib broken
off close up to the vertebræ and two more forced out of their
sockets—altogether a pretty good smash.   I myself had hurt
my foot, which must have got in between the horse's chest
and the side of the pitfall, and strained some of the tendons so
that I could not walk for some three weeks afterwards.

On 4th October 1880 I rode out from my camp on the
Umfuli river, Mashunaland, and crossing the Lundaza, one of

its tributaries, came across a herd of elands, and shot the two bulls. I had a lot of Kafirs with me, so that I was able to carry nearly all the meat back to camp, and bushed up the remainder, including the necks, heads, and skins, to be fetched on the morrow. The next day I rode back with my boys to our *cache*, thinking I might possibly find a lion there ; but nothing had been touched, so, sending the Kafirs back to camp with the skins and heads and all the meat that was left, I took a round by myself, hoping to come across ostriches, the feathers of which giant birds were then valuable. I had not ridden a couple of miles after leaving my boys when I came upon a herd of some sixty or seventy elands, with three enormous old bulls amongst them. An eland bull is not an animal that an African hunter likes to pass by, as the fat that can be obtained in large quantities from one in good condition is most useful in cooking the dry meat of the smaller antelopes. However, to have shot one there and then would have been to have destroyed a magnificent beast for the benefit of the vultures, which would have devoured the carcase before I could have brought boys from camp to cut up the meat. After a little thought, and seeing the direction the elands took as they trotted away, I determined to drive the biggest bull out of the herd and try to take him to our camp on the Umfuli. With this intention I galloped up to the herd, and was soon close behind an immense old bull.

But few people in England probably have any idea what a magnificent animal an eland bull really is. That the bull now in the Gardens of the Zoological Society is not equal in size to a large wild specimen may be at once seen by comparing him with the animal now on view in the Mammalia Gallery of the Natural History Museum at Kensington. However, the bull about which I was talking, in spite of his great weight and size, went off at once into a springing gallop, which kept him in front of my horse for half a mile or so, when he broke into a trot, and I came alongside and took him away from the herd. He then made a fresh spurt, but this time could not keep it up for more than two hundred yards, and after that never broke from his trot again. As he had headed of his own accord for my camp, I had little difficulty in keeping him to the right course, and had only to be careful not to press him too hard, as in that case a tired eland

bull will stop and refuse to go any farther. The country being
very open, I let my splendid victim trot quietly on some two
hundred yards in front of me, the foam flying in flakes from his
mouth, and besmirching his broad chest and low hanging
dewlap. We soon reached the Lundaza, the banks of which
are high and steep, so, being afraid that if he saw me near him
he would stand in the water and refuse to go any farther, I held
in to give him time to pass it, but then galloped down as hard
as I could, as there were some wooded ridges just beyond in
which I might easily have lost him if he had got too far ahead.
As I reached the river I did not see him, and thought he had
walked down the bed of the stream, and so continued to canter
along the bank.

Thinking he might possibly have gone up stream, I turned
in the saddle to look behind me, but without checking the
horse. Not seeing the eland, I brought my head round again,
and got a fearful blow in the right eye from the point of the
overhanging branch of a dead tree under which my horse had
taken me. The blow half stunned me and knocked me right
out of the saddle on to my horse's quarters. At once checking
him, I regained my seat, and putting my hand up to my eye,
which was closed, found I was bleeding pretty freely. At the
same time I felt very sick, but saw with my left eye the eland
bull trotting away about two hundred yards off on the other
side of the river, and still making straight for our camp. I at
once got my horse down the bank, crossed the stream, and was
soon once more close behind the eland. I felt very sick, but as our
camp was now not more than two miles off, and he was going
straight to it of his own accord, I determined to try to get him in.
He went steadily on till within five hundred yards, when I think he
must have winded something, as he suddenly stopped and would
not go a step farther. Feeling that I should soon faint, I dismounted and, looking at the eland with my left eye, raised my
rifle and sent a bullet through his lungs, and then remounting
galloped into camp, where there were several Europeans. Mr.
Tainton went out with Kafirs and got in the eland meat, and
Mr. Ronkesley and my old friend Mr. Thomas Ayres, the well-
known South African ornithologist, looked after me. I must
have had concussion of the brain, as I became half unconscious

and vomited up everything that they gave me, even tea, so they got frightened, and the following morning sent boys to call Dr. Crook, who was hunting with Mr. J. S. Jameson at the distance of a day's journey to the north. As soon as the message reached them they most kindly came to my assistance, though they were having great sport with rhinoceroses, Mr. Jameson having only the previous day shot three of these animals— bull, cow, and half-grown calf—in one run.

Well, Dr. Crook doctored me *secundum artem,* and the wound in the corner of my eye healed up. It was, however, more than a month before I could see properly with my right eye. From time to time the wound opened and then healed up again, but the Doctor could find no dead bone in it. Time went on, and early the following year I returned to England, and one June morning was walking down Bond Street with Mr. Rowland Ward, the well-known naturalist of Piccadilly, when I 'began to sneeze and he accused me of having a cold. I denied the soft

FACSIMILE OF THE PIECE OF WOOD WHICH ENTERED THE AUTHOR'S FACE (ACTUAL SIZE).

impeachment, and presently felt something come down one of the ducts into the back of my mouth and spat it into my hand, and there was a piece of hard African wood, the end of the dry branch which, eight months previously, had struck me in the eye on the bank of the Lundaza river in Mashunaland, and, having passed right through the bone with the force of the blow, had lain perdu in my head all that time, till at last, having got into one of the ducts at the back of the nose, it had passed down into my mouth. This piece of wood was not a splinter, but a solid bit of hard wood quite three-quarters of an inch long and of a very considerable thickness.

In the end of October 1887, whilst travelling in company with a party of English sportsmen, Messrs. J. A. Jameson, A. C. Fountaine, and F. Cooper, I crossed the Sebakwi river, not very far from its source, on the Mashuna plateau, and the following day camped near the head waters of a small stream, a tributary of that river. As we knew that herds of blue wilde-beests frequented the open grassy downs that stretched away to the south-west as far as we could see, and my friends were anxious to secure a few heads of these curious-looking animals, we intended to remain where we were for a couple of days, and hunt the surrounding country in search of them. The next day, Cooper being laid up with a bad foot, and Fountaine having something to do in camp, Jameson and I rode out together. The first thing we espied was a pair of ostriches, but, the country being very open, they saw us and made off when we were still far away ; and though we galloped some distance after them, we never got a shot. Soon after this we came across a herd of Tsessebe antelopes, one of which Jameson shot. I galloped after the herd, and on topping a ridge came in sight of some wilde-beests in the valley beyond. Reining in, I was just about to turn my horse's head and ride back to call my friend, when the wary beasts, having probably winded me, galloped off in a long line, swinging their bushy black tails as they ran. The only thing to do now was to pursue them, which I did, and soon wounded a fine old bull, the biggest animal in the herd. He at once left the others and went off alone, and I thought he was done for. However, I was mistaken, for upon seeing me approach he went off at a tremendous pace, and finally ran right away from me ; so after firing a long shot at, and missing him as he crossed a small stream, I pulled in and off-saddled my tired horse.

After waiting for more than an hour, and none of my Kafirs appearing, I again saddled up, and, as a heavy thunderstorm was threatening, rode straight back for the waggons, thinking that my friend Jameson would do the same with his boys. Before reaching camp a heavy shower fell, accompanied with much thunder and lightning, which soon drenched me—the first rain of the season. On riding up to my waggon, which was standing a little apart from the others, I was informed that during my absence our oxen had been attacked by lions, and two of them killed, amongst some large thorn-trees less than half a mile from our camp ; and that Fountaine, accompanied by Cooper's English servant, Philip, had saddled up and gone after them with all the dogs ; and as several shots had been heard, there was no doubt that they had come to close quarters with the bold marauders. As I was told that shots had been heard only just before my arrival, I at once caught another horse, and

hastily transferring the saddle, galloped as hard as I could in
the direction pointed out to me. Just where the lions had
killed the oxen lay a piece of rising ground, on which grew
some large thorn-trees, without, however, there being any
underwood below them ; and beyond this lay an open valley,
bounded on its farther side by a series of rocky ridges, thickly
covered with forest and underwood.   In the valley stood here
and there a single large thorn-tree, beneath one of which
were gathered a knot of Kafirs ; and upon riding up to them
I found that they were standing round the carcase of a fine old
lioness.   They informed me that the white men had killed three
lions, but that one was still alive, and that the dogs were after
him in one of the wooded hills beyond the open ground.   Just
as they were speaking I saw Fountaine come galloping into
view, closely pursued by a fine lion, who in his turn was
accompanied by our whole pack of dogs.   The lion soon gave
up the pursuit, and, with all the dogs barking round him,
retreated into the wooded ridge to his right, where he became
invisible, though his angry growls were plainly audible.   The
dogs stuck to him well, and, working our way towards the
growling and barking, we presently got a view of him, standing
on a large rock, twitching his tail angrily from side to side, but
his attention thoroughly engaged by my plucky pack of mongrel
hounds by which he was surrounded.   Here we killed him
without any further difficulty.

A lot of the Kafirs and waggon drivers having now come up,
we lifted this lion on to Fountaine's horse, and balancing it over
the saddle, with a man holding it in position on each side, had
the horse led off to camp—not a mile distant—in order to
weigh the animal just as he was.   Fountaine and I, with Philip,
now went with the rest of the boys to skin the other three lions,
while the first drops of a tremendous storm of rain commenced
to fall.   We were just skinning the last carcase (that of the lioness
I had first ridden past) when the storm burst upon us with the
most terrific violence.   The rain came down in a way I have
seldom seen equalled, making it impossible to distinguish anything at a distance of over twenty yards, and the level ground
on which we were standing was soon covered with water a
couple of inches deep.   Our rifles and the Kafirs' assegais were

standing against the trunk of the thorn-tree beneath which the lioness lay, but luckily they did not appear to attract the lightning, which was playing all round us in a very disagreeable manner, whilst the terrific crashes of thunder by which it was accompanied assured us that the storm was raging directly overhead.

As soon as we had got the lioness's skin off we returned to camp, and directly the storm was over set to work to weigh the carcase of the lion. We rigged our scale on to a strong horizontal branch, and slinging the heavy body in a couple of strong thongs, hitched them on to the hook depending from it ;

LIONESS WATCHING HERD OF ANTELOPES.

but as our scale would not weigh anything over 300 lbs., we found the lion was much too heavy. We now skinned him, leaving the head, paws, and tail in the skin ; but even then the carcase was too heavy. We then cut off the one shoulder, and what was left still weighed 285 lbs. ; and the shoulder, together with the skin, with head, feet, and tail attached, weighed 100 lbs. more, giving 385 lbs. as the weight of the animal just as he lay. This lion, though a fine massively-built animal, was still not quite full grown, as his mane was only just commencing to appear, and, though not in low condition, had yet not an ounce of fat upon him. I have seen old full-grown lions very much more bulky, and sometimes in such high condition that their bellies were covered with a layer of fat nearly, if not quite, an inch thick, and I feel sure that such lions must have weighed very much more than the young animal whose weight I have recorded.   In fact, I now believe that a large full-grown South African lion, when in high condition, will weigh from 400 to 500 lbs.[1]   Dr. Livingstone, amongst other unfairly depreciative remarks concerning the lion, speaks of him as "somewhat larger than the biggest dog."

In the evening, finding that my best dog, Punch (a grandson of the Punch previously mentioned, and a rare good dog with a lion), was absent, I made inquiries about him, and heard from one of my boys that he had been shot by accident while engaged in baying the lions, and that he had been seen lying under a bush close to where the first lioness was killed.   As it was already getting dark before I found this out, I could do nothing that evening, but at daylight the next morning, saddling up a horse and taking the boy with me who had last seen him, I went to look for my poor old dog.   However, we could find no traces of him whatever, although, owing to the previous day's heavy rain, the ground was everywhere soft and muddy, and it was impossible to miss the spoor of anything that had passed after the rain had ceased to fall.   After looking in vain for some trace of the poor animal whose pluck and devotion to duty had cost him his life, we came round to the large thorn-tree beneath which we had skinned the lioness, and at once saw that the carcase was gone, and on examining the ground found that it had been dragged away by two more lions during the night.   The footprints, which were very plainly discernible in the soft ground, were those of a large animal, probably an old lioness, and a half-grown cub.

After following the trail for some little distance, and finding that the carcase was being dragged to the wooded ridge where we had shot the last lion, I galloped back to camp to call my friends and get the dogs, without whose help I knew that we should have had but little chance of killing the lions, or even sighting them at all in the thick forest that backed the rocky ridges.   My friends did not take long to saddle up, and we were soon back again with all the dogs and Kafirs, and at

[1] Since writing the above I have weighed another large lion, and found that it turned the scale at 408 lbs.

once took up the spoor. The carcase had been dragged right amongst the trees on the edge of the rocky ground, and there partially devoured, all the meat of the hind quarters having been torn from the bones. This is the only case that has actually come under my notice of lions feeding upon the flesh of their own kind, but it is one that admits of no doubt whatever, and I have heard of other instances of the same kind.

Although we had seen nothing of the lions on approaching across the open, I felt sure that they had seen us, and had only just moved off, as their scent was so warm that the dogs whined with excitement as they sniffed about round the carcase. Very soon old Ruby and her daughter Fanny got the spoor away, and, followed by the rèst of the pack, took it up at such a pace that we had all our work to do to keep them in sight amongst the thickly-growing trees. We had not far to go, however, for soon a few sharp barks, quickly followed by the deep-toned growls of an angry lion, let us know that our quarry was at bay, and almost immediately we sighted a fine old lioness standing on a large block of stone amongst the trees, with our whole pack yelping round her. Cooper, who, despite his bad foot, had this morning joined the hunt, was the first up, and, dismounting quickly, at once gave the beautiful though dangerous beast a shot in the middle of the chest with a 500-bore Winchester, which, passing through her heart, killed her almost instantaneously, as she just gave one sweep with her tail and came tumbling head foremost off the rock, and never stirred from where she lay on the ground at its foot. As the shot was fired poor old Ruby, mad with excitement, rushed in, and was just in time to get a severe bite in the hind quarters, the last expiring effort of the dying lioness. This was a very fine animal, very thick-set and heavy, and with a very good coat. Of the half-grown cub that must have been somewhere about we could see nothing, but as he was a young animal we did not bother much about him. I had to have poor Ruby carried home. She had four nasty holes through the fleshy parts of her hind quarters, but no bones were broken, and as I had the wounds washed out with strong carbolic lotion, they soon healed, and the old dog was all right again in a month's time.

In going back to camp we noticed that a large thorn-tree, standing about sixty yards from the one beneath which we had stood whilst skinning the lioness during the terrific thunderstorm of the day before, had been shattered by lightning. As there were several rifles and assegais standing round our tree, I think we may consider it a fortunate circumstance that it was not struck as well as, or instead of, the other one.

In December 1882 I was travelling south from the Matabili country, and was in charge of about a hundred head of cattle belonging to Mr. Fairbairn, a well-known trader. I was just inspanning the waggons one afternoon amongst the hills skirting the Inkwesi river when a heavy storm of rain came on, accompanied by much thunder and lightning. The boys herding Mr. Fairbairn's cattle now drove them up alongside of the waggons, and they stood thickly clustered together amongst the trees. Suddenly, from where I stood in front of my waggon, I saw some splinters of wood fly from a tree near me —about sixty yards off—whilst all the cattle standing beneath it fell to the ground. On going up to see what had happened I found thirteen fine oxen lying dead. Most of them must have had their heads down feeding, and had been struck dead so instantaneously, and fallen so suddenly, that their necks and heads were bent in under their bodies. I could not get a Kafir to come near the dead animals, and they seemed quite frightened at what had occurred. I turned all the carcases over, but could find no mark of any kind upon any of them.

Some years ago I lost one of my best friends by lightning. In March 1879 I left Klerksdorp in the Transvaal, and my friends Messrs. Clarkson, Collison, and French were to follow me as quickly as possible, and we then intended to hunt together in the Mababi country. Clarkson was struck by lightning near Klerksdorp, and French, poor fellow, still more unfortunate, lost his life in the waterless forests between the Chobi and the Zambesi. Since then Collison and I have had many a good day together in the wilds, and now he, too, has gone. He was with Clarkson when he was struck, and has often told me how it happened. The weather had been very wet, and the ground was consequently in a very bad condition for waggon travelling. My friends one evening had got through a very bad bit of ground, and outspanned on the farther side just as a heavy thunderstorm came up. Having tied up the oxen and horses, and made all snug for the night, Clarkson went over to Collison's waggon, and getting up in front, so that he sat half on the side and half on the fore box, commenced to talk to his friend, who was inside, when the storm burst upon them, and the lightning played all round, whilst the thunder crashed overhead. Suddenly Collison felt himself pushed backwards, and lost consciousness for a short time. When he came to himself he was aware of a sulphurous smell, and raising himself called out, " Hallo, Mat, what's up ? " But poor Mat Clarkson never spoke again, for he lay dead across the fore box of the waggon. He had been struck in the head, and the electric fluid had passed out through his side down the iron " rung " at the side of the waggon, a small round hole like that made by a Martini-Henry bullet having been drilled through his broad-brimmed felt hat, which hung in Mr. Leask's office in Klerksdorp for some time after the accident.

CHAPTER XXVI

Further hunting reminiscences

On the 17th April 1879 I left Bamangwato with two waggons, taking with me two young colonists in my employ as elephant hunters, and started for the Mababi river, which I eventually reached early in June, after a very difficult journey owing to the extreme scarcity of water in the desert wastes lying between the Botletli and Mababi rivers. A few days later I was joined by Collison and French, two old acquaintances who had also come in on an elephant-hunting expedition. These gentlemen lost ten of their oxen by thirst in crossing the waterless country south of the Mababi.

After forming a main camp, in which we placed all our waggons, and having made strong kraals for our oxen and horses, we left everything in charge of some of our native servants, and started on foot on 18th June in search of elephants, which animals we hoped to fall in with in the country immediately to the north-west of the Mababi, or else in the neighbourhood of the Chobi and Sunta rivers.

During the following six months I hunted sometimes in company with one or more of my companions, at others alone, with only my own native followers.

On 1st July, having crossed the desert country which lies between the Machabi and Chobi rivers, Collison and I fell in with our friends French and Miller, whom we had not seen since the day after we left the waggons. The following morning we all joined company, and held to the north and west along the river's bank, or rather along the edge of the lagoons and swamps through which the river here runs. During the course of the forenoon we passed several herds of blue wildebeests, tsessebe antelopes, and Burchell's zebras, scattered over the open alluvial flats which form the intermediate space between the marsh and the forest-clad sand-belts to the south ; whilst the fresh spoor of numerous buffaloes, elands, and giraffes showed where herds of those animals had passed on their way to and from the water during the preceding night. Glancing across the lagoons and flooded meadows to our right, large herds of the graceful water-loving leechwe antelopes were constantly in view, and often allowed us to approach to within two hundred yards of them before taking to flight. These beautiful animals are exceedingly numerous on all this part of the Chobi, and the elegant lyrate horns of the males are amongst the handsomest of the trophies to be won by a sportsman in this part of the world. When pursued they usually take to the water, dashing through the shallow lagoons, amongst which they love to dwell, with a series of plunges, each fresh spring being taken from the bottom, even when the water is almost up to their necks. The splashing and commotion made by a herd of a hundred leechwe antelopes crossing a sheet of shallow water may therefore be better imagined than described. Having plenty of meat we none of us fired a shot the whole morning, though we were often sorely tempted to do so by sundry old leechwe rams that stood looking curiously at us, sometimes within one hundred and fifty yards. When at last they did take themselves off, they invariably thrust their noses forwards and trotted away with their horns laid back on their necks, soon, however, changing their pace to a heavy gallop, and occasionally bounding high into the air, apparently out of sheer exuberance of spirits.

About noon we came suddenly upon the river itself, which here flowed in a deep channel, about one hundred and twenty yards broad, and with a current of at least five miles an hour. We had just reached the verge of the steep bank, when, with a loud snort as it blew the water from its nostrils, an immense hippopotamus bull raised its head above the surface. Not expecting anything of the sort, none of us had our rifles ready, and before we could get hold of them the monster had once more vanished from the scene. Behemoth had, however, thoroughly grasped the situation before retiring, for he did not again rise to breathe for several minutes, and then appeared nearly two hundred yards farther down the stream. We then separated and took up positions above and below the spot where he had last gone down. He was, however, thoroughly alarmed, and showed so little of his head above water, and that for so short a space of time, that it was some while before any one got a shot at him. At last Collison fired, but a little too late, striking him in the nose after the vital portion of his head was already out of sight. This wound, however, caused him to leave the water and take to an impenetrable bed of reeds on the farther side of the river, in which we heard him crashing about and grunting for some time. As he left the river in the shelter of a small reedy creek, we did not get the chance of a shot at him, and, not having a canoe, were unable to follow him.

Just then we heard three shots fired in succession by Miller, who had strolled a little higher up the river, and upon going to see what he had fired at, found that he had come across five more hippopotami, two of which he thought he had killed. As several, however, continued to rise at intervals, on the head of one of which I could see the white bullet mark a little above the eye, I suspected that he had only wounded them. Shortly afterwards I struck one in the side of the head with a bullet from my 10-bore. It was a ricochet shot, as I saw the bullet strike the water just too short ; but, as we afterwards found out, it entered the skull with the rebound just at the root of the ear. I felt sure I had killed it, however, as a few seconds after my shot two of the animal's feet just appeared above the surface of the water, showing that the dying beast must have rolled over as it sank. Then everything disappeared. I now sent two Kafirs to watch for the body to come up, which I thought would happen before very long ; but hour after hour passed, and still nothing appeared. At last, just as it was growing dusk, the carcase rose, having been at least five hours under water. The current soon brought it to our side of the river, and we got it to a shallow place and cut it up at once. The victim was an old cow ;

she was not in good condition, as we had hoped would be the case, and the meat was most villainously tough, though very well flavoured.

I forgot to mention that, whilst passing through a patch of bush on the river's edge, trying to get a shot at the first hippopotamus, I came right on to a young buffalo bull lying down, which at once jumped up and came trotting towards me, grunting furiously. My shouts, however, mingled with the strong language I at the same time freely bestowed upon the Kafir who carried my rifle, and who, being a few yards behind me, would not come any nearer, changed the animal's seemingly aggressive intentions, and after eyeing me for a moment he turned, and dashing out of the little patch of bush into the open, nearly ran over the Kafirs who were in charge of our baggage. As he turned I saw that he had recently been mauled by lions, open wounds, still running, being plainly visible on his shoulder and quarters. A boy of French's, who carried a rifle, pursued and shot him. I did not go and look at the carcase, but the Kafirs, who only brought back the tongue and some marrow bones, said the poor beast had been so torn and bitten that the meat was uneatable—meaning, I suppose, uneatable for men who were looking forward to a gorge of hippopotamus, which they of course thought would be rolling in fat.

The following day we did not move camp, but occupied the morning in drying the meat of the hippopotamus, and cutting the hide into long strips suitable for sjamboks. In the afternoon Miller went out and shot two buffaloes, having fallen in with a large herd, whilst I took a stroll down the river and knocked over an impala ram with a pretty head.

On 4th July we again pushed on, still following the course of the river towards the north-west. The country through which we passed, if not in any way grand or picturesque, was yet far from being so monotonous and uninteresting as are many parts of the interior of Africa. Scattered here and there over the alluvial plains skirting the marsh were patches of sandy soil, of from an acre to three or four acres in extent, all of which were covered with bush and tall forest trees, amongst which the dark-foliaged evergreens which grow so thickly on the brink of the Victoria Falls were conspicuous.   Here and there, too, a fantastic baobab, with its huge gouty-looking stem and long leafless limbs, met the eye, whilst clusters of tall feathery palms came in sight at every turn.   We passed game of several varieties, and hundreds of leechwe antelopes, large herds of which were to be seen feeding round the edge of every lagoon.   Some of them were very tame, and several times large herds crossed just in front of us, within a hundred yards, usually running one behind another in a long straggling line. One herd consisted entirely of males, and, as they filed past, I counted fifty-two.   Some of these were little more than kids, with horns only a few inches in length, but there was not a single ewe amongst the lot.   Amongst other animals we passed close to six old buffalo bulls that were feeding slowly away from the river on their way to some shady patch of bush, in which they intended to pass the heat of the day.   So intent did they appear to be upon cropping the short grass that we were close upon them before one of their number, raising his ponderous head, noticed us.   After staring at us inquisitively for some seconds, he stretched out his nose and went off at a heavy lumbering gallop, closely followed by his five companions. After running a hundred yards or so, they all pulled up, and, turning about, stood eyeing us, and then, once more betaking themselves to flight, crashed through a thick patch of bush and disappeared from view.

Early in the afternoon we reached a spot where a cluster of large thorn-trees came down to the water's edge.   Here a small herd of elephant cows had been in the habit of drinking lately, and, as they had not drunk during the preceding night, it seemed probable that they would do so during the coming hours of darkness.   As we had none of us yet seen an elephant since leaving the waggons, we determined to camp a short distance on ahead, in the hope that they would come down to the river again that night.

Beneath a fine wide-branching tree, growing upon a knoll some quarter of a mile ahead, and close to the water's edge, we accordingly pitched our camp.   In the early part of the night we sat round the fire conversing, and discussing the chances of the elephants coming down to drink.   Every

moment we expected to hear the shrill trumpet of one of
those animals ; but the night wore on, and no sound broke
the perfect stillness but the loud howl of a hyæna that had
winded our hippopotamus meat. At length we all fell asleep.
At daylight next morning we sent a Kafir to see if the
elephants had been down to the water, and he soon returned
with the news that they had, and brought with him a large
thorn branch freshly broken off to support his statement.   He
reported that as far as he could gather from the spoor the herd
consisted of a young bull, two large cows, and some half-dozen
small animals.   As it would have been ridiculous for all four
of us to follow so small a lot of elephants, we resolved that
two should take their spoor, whilst the other two should proceed
farther up the river ; and we cast lots for choice.   Fortune
decided that French and I should follow the elephants ; so,
leaving two Kafirs to look after our traps—not forgetting to
put a pot of hippopotamus meat on the fire, with a view to a
dish of rich thick soup on our return in the evening— and
bidding good-bye for the present to our companions, we made
a move without further delay.

Soon after leaving the river and entering the sand-belt we
came upon a large herd of zebras and sable antelopes feeding
together.   Amongst the latter was one remarkably handsome
bull with long sweeping horns.   I longed to try a shot at him,
and was sorry afterwards that I had not done so, but in the
early morning a rifle shot can be heard at a great distance,
and as we did not know how near the elephants might be to
us, we were afraid to run any risk of disturbing them.   Although
the sable antelope is far from numerous along the Chobi, it
is to be met with sparsely, as far as I have been, all along the
banks of that river ; and it appears to me that the horns of
the males in that district attain to a greater size than in any
other part of the country.   After passing the sable antelopes,
we tramped steadily on the elephants' spoor for several hours
without a halt, seeing nothing but a small herd of eland cows,
which wary animals sighted us when we were still several
hundred yards distant, and at once trotted still farther out of
harm's way.   All this time the spoor had taken us continually
down wind ; so that, had we got near the elephants, they would

infallibly have scented us and bolted, probably before we caught sight of them. As, however, they were still far ahead, we always hoped they might change their course and give us a chance of approaching them ; but shortly after mid-day, as they showed no signs of doing so, and were miles ahead of us, we called a halt, and coming to the conclusion that it was not worth while following such a worthless lot of elephants any farther under such unfavourable circumstances, we turned about and retraced our steps towards the river.

About an hour later two of our Kafirs, who had gone off in pursuit of a honey-bird, came rushing back, saying they had come upon a rhinoceros lying asleep, though they were afraid that the birds which were upon it had noticed them, and would give the slumbering beast the alarm. Clutching our heavy elephant rifles, we advanced silently and swiftly towards where the monster lay. "There he is, there he is!" suddenly exclaimed one of the Kafirs, and at the same instant I, too, caught sight of a black or prehensile-lipped rhinoceros, standing broadside on about a hundred yards off, though almost hidden from view by a thick bush. He evidently suspected danger, and stood with his head held high, listening intently. I was trying to point him out to French, whom I wished to have first shot, when, without more ado, the beast started off at a great pace through the bushes. There was then no time to wait for my friend ; so, taking a hasty aim with my single-4, I fired, and striking the rhinoceros, as it afterwards appeared, high behind the shoulder, and in all probability grazing the back-bone, rolled him over in his tracks like a rabbit. Running up, we found him floundering about on the ground, twisting up his great ugly head, and then dashing it sideways against the earth, squealing repeatedly the while. Another bullet in the chest, from my friend's heavy single-8, settled him. He was as lean as a crow, and though the Kafirs cut some of the meat for themselves, we only kept a small piece of the heart, trusting to fall in with something more tasty later on. This was a large, full-grown prehensile-lipped bull rhinoceros. I measured him carefully with my tape-line, and found, by planting an assegai at his shoulder, and another parallel to it at his forefoot, and then taking a straight line between the

two, that he stood 5 feet 8 inches in vertical height.   His
anterior horn measured 1 foot 11 inches in length, and the
posterior 8 inches.

A little later on, having resumed our march, we sighted a
herd of giraffes stalking quietly through the forest in front of
us.   There were sixteen of these stately beasts in all, and a
grand sight it was to view so many of them together.   They
were much tamer than is usually the case with these shy and
long-sighted animals, and allowed us to approach to within
two hundred yards of them, before starting off at their peculiar
gallop.   (N.B.—Giraffes never trot, as they are so often represented to do in drawings.   They have but two paces, a walk
and a gallop or canter, and break at once from the one into the
other.)   As these giraffes, upon taking to flight, made straight
towards the river, holding the same course as we ourselves were
pursuing, we soon sighted them again.   This occurred several
times, and upon each occasion they allowed us to approach a
little nearer, till at last French tried a couple of shots at them,
after which we saw them no more.

It must have been about two hours later, and when we were
not more than two or three miles from the water, that, upon
emerging from a patch of thick bush, we found ourselves in
full view of an immense herd of buffaloes.   They were feeding
down an open glade in the forest, and coming obliquely towards
us, so, as we had no good meat, we resolved to try to shoot
a couple of fat cows.   About a hundred yards to our right was
a large ant-heap, within shot of which it seemed that some of
the buffaloes would pass if they held on their course.   The
ground was rather open, but by creeping cautiously forwards
on our hands and knees, pushing our rifles in front of us, and
remaining perfectly still whenever one of the buffaloes raised its
head and looked in our direction, we at length managed to gain
its shelter unobserved.   The foremost animal, an old cow, was
now almost within shot ; but, as she was a lean-looking beast,
we resolved to let her pass, and devoted our attention to a
round, sleek-looking heifer that was coming along on the near
side of the troop some fifty yards behind.   Before this latter
animal, however, was well within shot the old cow, who had got
past the ant-heap, raised her head and must have made us out,

"A little later on, having resumed our march, we sighted a herd of giraffes stalking quietly through the forest in front of us. There were sixteen of these stately beasts in all, and a grand sight it was to view so many of them together."

as she stood with her eyes intently fixed upon us. Seeing that there was no time to be lost, French then fired at the heifer, and, striking her on the point of the shoulder, brought her bellowing to the ground. At the report every buffalo wheeled round with astonishing quickness, and the whole herd dashed off, enshrouded in a dense cloud of dust.

Directly my friend fired, I put a bullet into another cow just as she turned, but it failed to stop her. Leaving French to administer the *coup de grâce* to his animal, I ran on after the herd. As is usual in such cases, the foremost buffaloes, not knowing what the deuce was the matter, very soon pulled up, compelling those behind to follow their example, and the whole herd thus stood crowded together in a compact mass, the rearmost animals all looking anxiously towards where I stood. Being within fifty yards of them, I might have picked my animal ; but as I felt sure that by following its blood-spoor I should get the one I had already wounded, and as I could not see a bull with a very fine pair of horns, I did not fire, but waited until the herd again took to flight—about which they were most expeditious. Then I went to look for the spoor of my wounded cow. We soon found it, and as the blood was flowing freely, had no difficulty in following it at a good round pace. The wounded beast soon left the herd, and, as its track was still bespattered with its gore, I had no doubt we should very soon overhaul it ; in point of fact, a minute or two later we saw it walking slowly along with lowered head. Not thinking it had much strength left, I ran towards it without any attempt at concealment. I had reckoned without my host, however, for the buffalo turned and saw me before I was well within shot, and, sorely wounded though she was, after eyeing me for a second, the blood streaming from her nostrils, dashed off again at a gallop, as if unhurt. I might have given her a shot from behind, but I knew she was mine and determined not to waste cartridges unnecessarily. After trotting along for another quarter of a mile on her spoor we saw her again, walking very slowly, and at the same instant sighted two old buffalo bulls standing a little to one side of her. The wounded animal did not pay any attention to them, but held slowly and dejectedly on her way. The old bulls must, I fancy, have smelt the blood as she passed, for, stretching out their noses, they came trotting straight towards where we stood.

Ever since a buffalo bull once killed a favourite horse of mine I must confess to having nourished a spite against these old fellows, and as I knew that the meat would be most welcome to the Makubas living on the river, I prepared to give the two patriarchs a warm reception. When they were about eighty yards off they halted, and one of them, turning broadside to me, stood looking in the direction taken by the cow. This was my opportunity, and in another instant a bullet from my single 10-bore struck him fair in the shoulder, and brought him to his knees. His comrade, after staring for a few moments towards me, came running obliquely past at a heavy lumbering gallop. I just got another cartridge in in time, and firing when he was a little past me, caught him on the ribs high behind the shoulder. The one first hit had recovered his legs, and made off for a short distance, but now stood beneath a small thorn-tree, and I saw that his hours were numbered. At this instant the death bellow—so well known to every sportsman who has shot the African buffalo—of the second bull greeted my ears, and, running towards the sound, I found the great beast stretched upon the ground, and upon the point of expiring. My bullet had struck him high up, about a foot behind the shoulder, and gone through both lungs. He had nevertheless managed to run nearly three hundred yards before falling. Hastily cutting out his tongue and opening him, we returned to the one first hit. He was still standing, but, just as we neared him, he lay down and commenced to bellow. Upon our approaching he tried to rise, but had not the strength to do so, and we despatched him with assegais. Leaving two of the Kafirs who were with me to cut out the tongue and remove the intestines—in order that the meat should not go bad during the night—I went on with the rest, and again took up the spoor of the wounded cow, as I felt sure she had not gone very far. Nor was I mistaken, for in less than five minutes we came upon her lying down. She jumped up when she saw us, but I was then close to her, and killed her with a shot through the heart.

It was now quite late, the sun having been some time down,

so, after cutting out the tongue and stomach, as we had done with the bulls, and trusting that the lions and hyænas would not smell out and devour the carcases during the night, I hurried back to where I had left my friend.   As he and his Kafirs had already cut up his buffalo—a nice fat young cow— and were only waiting for me to start for the river, we set off at once, and reached our camp soon after dusk.   The pot of hippopotamus soup which we had put on the fire before starting in the morning turned out a great success, and off it and some fat juicy buffalo steaks we made a most excellent supper.

Early next morning I sent one of my Kafirs to call the Makubas from the neighbouring village, and show them where the buffaloes lay.   They turned out *en masse*—men, women, and children—overjoyed at the prospect of such a feast.   I went with them, hoping I might find lions at one of the carcases.   However, we found them untouched.   I gave the Makubas the two bulls, just as they were, and they also got all but the choicest parts of the cow, which my boys and I kept for ourselves.

Having in the foregoing pages given an account of a few days' sport on the River Chobi, north of the Sunta outlet, which will give an idea of what that part of the country was like some fourteen years ago, let me now transport my readers once more to the well-watered and well-wooded slopes of North-Western Mashunaland.

Early in June 1880, in company with Collison, Jameson, and Dr. Crook, I left Bulawayo.   Our intention was to travel steadily on to the River Umfuli (about three weeks' journey to the north-west) and there form a central camp, from which we could make hunting expeditions in various directions during the continuance of the dry season.

At Inyati we were joined by Fathers Law and Wehl, members of the Society of Jesus, who were on their way to Umzila's country to found a mission station.   These gentlemen travelled with us as far as the River Umniati, where we separated with mutual good wishes for one another's success, their route lying to the south-east, whilst ours lay to the north-east.   Space will not allow me to do anything more than briefly touch upon the disastrous result of the difficult enterprise undertaken by the Jesuit fathers. Having crossed the River Sabi, after a most arduous journey, they were obliged, owing to the hostility of the natives, to abandon their waggon and start on foot, with little more than the clothes they stood in, for Umzila's kraal, which it took them, as far as I can remember, thirteen days to reach. During this period they subsisted upon the game they shot, which fortunately was very plentiful. They do not seem to have been kindly or hospitably received by Umzila, and poor Father Law, after dreadful sufferings from fever and starvation, at last died early in November. Father Wehl subsequently died at Sofala, and the two lay brothers who accompanied the expedition were the only survivors of the party.

Between Inyati and the Umniati river we did not find very much game. Still, after the first two days, we always got enough to keep all our large party—natives and dogs included—in meat. Just after crossing the River Vungo, Jameson and I, having taken a ride round, came upon a hen ostrich on her nest. As she left it at full speed my friend fired both barrels at her, but missed. We then went up to the nest, which was just a large shallow hole scratched in the sandy soil, and found that it contained twelve eggs. Thinking that either the cock or the hen ostrich would put in an appearance just at sunset, which is the time these birds relieve one another whilst incubating, we cleared out a little place in the centre of a small thick bush, about thirty yards from the nest, in which my friend took up his position. I then took his horse, and leaving him with one Kafir, rode on, having arranged to return for him a little after dark. After a two hours' ride I reached the River Gwelo, where I shot a water-buck. Leaving the Kafirs to cut it up, I rode down the river towards the drift, where I knew I should find the waggons outspanned. On my way I saw a great many more water-bucks, besides koodoos and reed-bucks. At dusk I saddled up my own and my friend's horse, and, leading the latter, rode back along the road to where I had agreed to meet him, as the ostrich's nest was not very far away from the waggon track. It was quite dark, though the night was clear and starlit when I met him. He had shot the hen bird as she was returning to the nest just at sunset. She was in very good plumage, and worth about £10, the feathers of a fine cock being worth about £25 at that time. The next day we sent some Kafirs back for the eggs, of which we afterwards made some very good omelettes and pancakes.

After this something or other fell to our rifles almost daily—water-bucks, koodoos, sable antelopes, tsessebes, and zebras being the game most frequently met with. Our mode of travelling was as follows :—At daylight every morning we saddled up our horses, and, after having seen the bullocks in-spanned, and the waggons started, rode out in search of game, returning to the waggon track in three or four hours, by which time we usually found the waggons outspanned and breakfast ready. In the afternoon we made a second trek with the waggons, and took another round on horseback, outspanning sufficiently early to allow time to form a camp and give the bullocks an opportunity of filling themselves before they were tied up for the night. Collison, Jameson, and myself always slept in an open "scherm," in front of the bullocks, with a roaring wood-fire at our feet, for the nights were very cold.

On 24th June, just before reaching the River Umgezi, I had the luck to shoot a lion. On the morning of that day Jameson and I had ridden out early as usual, and having made a round, were nearing the River Umgezi, where we expected to find the waggons already outspanned, when Jameson thought he caught a glimpse of something running through the forest in front of us. As we wanted meat we at once took our rifles and cantered forwards, and almost immediately emerged upon a narrow open glade. Seeing no sign of any game, I thought, as we had lost so little time, that my friend had been mistaken ; but, as he felt sure he had seen something, I proposed that we should separate and gallop through the next patch of forest. I had hardly entered the bush, my friend then being a couple of hundred yards to my right, when I saw four koodoo cows crossing obliquely in front of me, and making, it seemed, for the opening I had just left. With a quick wrench of the bridle I turned my horse's head and galloped at full speed along the edge of the bush, so as to intercept them just as they emerged from the forest. In this I succeeded perfectly, and was just pulling in to jump off and have a shot, as the beautiful beasts passed out into the open at a long springing gallop, when I caught sight of an animal following hard in their wake, and coming along at a great pace through the bushes.   I saw instantly that it was a lion, and in the same moment of time the beast noticed me.   He instantly stopped dead, glanced towards me for just a second of time, and then, turning about, took himself off through the bush at an astonishing rate.   I thought no more of the koodoos.   All I wanted was to possess myself of that lion's skin.   Luckily I was very well mounted, or he would have saved his hide.   The forest was not the easiest sort of country to gallop through, the large trees growing pretty close together, though the underwood was luckily not very thick.   The grass, too, had not yet been burned off, and here and there grew in large thick patches higher than the back of a lion.   For some distance I only just managed to hold my own, sometimes indeed losing sight of the faint-hearted king of beasts for a considerable time in places where the grass was rather thick.   But when I did so I put the spurs into my nag, and let him out as hard as he could go through bushes and over fallen timber until I caught sight of the lion again.

At length I began to gain upon him.   He was going along at a heavy gallop, just like an immense dog, but did not appear to be covering the ground so fast as was really the case. When we now came to patches of grass I was rather afraid he might crouch and either attack me as I passed or else break back.   However, keeping a sharp look-out, I rushed my horse through such places at full speed.   Coming suddenly to a more open part of the forest, and when I was within fifty yards of him, the lion pulled up, and, facing round, stood with lowered head and open mouth, growling savagely and switching his tail from side to side.   So suddenly did he change his tactics that, as I was galloping hard, I could not pull up quickly enough, but had to swerve off and ride right past him.   As I did so he stood on the same spot, but turned as I passed him, always keeping his head towards me.   When I pulled my horse in and was about to dismount for a shot he came walking towards me, holding his head very low between his shoulders and growling hoarsely. From my previous experiences with lions I felt sure he was on the point of charging, so, as I was very near him, I fired a quick shot from the saddle and struck him nicely, just between the neck and the shoulder, bringing him on to his head, roaring loudly. Quickly slipping in another cartridge, I jumped to the ground and gave him another shot, which smashed his shoulder and put him quite *hors de combat.*

At this moment Jameson came galloping up. The lion now lay on the ground growling. When we came near him he raised himself on his hind legs and threw his body towards us, but seemed quite paralysed in the fore quarters. My friend then gave him a shot, and another bullet behind the ear at once ended his career. This was the smallest full-grown male lion I have seen, but he was in good condition and in perfect hair. Like the generality of wild lions, he had very little mane. His skin, when pegged out to dry, though not unduly stretched, measured 9 feet 7 inches. I have shot lionesses whose pegged-out skins measured as much, though I do not think they were so thick-set and heavy as this lion. Many people may feel surprised at a lion hunting in broad daylight. It is the only case of the sort that has come within my own personal knowledge, but I do not think it in any way remarkable, as it was still early in the morning, and a very cold, cloudy day. This lion was the most cowardly of his species that I have yet met with, and his conduct afforded me another proof of how impossible it is to judge of the probable behaviour of any dangerous animal by drawing conclusions from the attitude shown by a single beast of the same kind previously shot. Before a man asserts that, speaking generally, a certain animal is dangerous or not, he should have had a large experience of the beasts in question.

Just after I had shot the lion, and whilst we were outspanned at the River Umgezi, Jugu, the eldest son of a Mashuna chief who was credited by the Amandibili with supernatural powers, and held in great reverence accordingly, came up, accompanied by a few followers. He was on his way to Lo Bengula to ask him to send an army to attack several Mashuna chiefs living beyond the Manyami river with whom his father was at feud, and who, he said, possessed large herds of cattle.   He was only too successful in his mission, and a few months later scores of villages, whose inhabitants had for some years been living in peace and prosperity, were burnt to the ground, the male inhabitants and the married women either assegaied or dispersed over the country, their large herds of cattle and goats driven off, and their children carried away into captivity by a large army of the cruel and blood-thirsty marauders who own allegiance to Lo Bengula.   Jugu expressed himself as very pleased at our having killed the lion.   He said he thought that it was one that had been haunting the Umgezi river lately, and had killed several people journeying backwards and forwards between his father's villages and the Matabili country.   These people had been dragged off and killed at night whilst encamped on the banks of the river.

Seeing that our Kafirs paid him great respect, Master Jugu commenced to put on a lot of side, asking us if we did not know that we were in the country of the mighty wizard of Situngweesa.   When I told him that I only knew of one king, Lo Bengula, from whom we had purchased the right to hunt through the whole country westward of the Manyami river, and further expressed my opinion that his father was a witch (umtagati), he waxed very wroth, and, jumping up, poured forth a torrent of prophetic warnings in his own language. Presently after, having cooled down, he came and begged for beads, calico, brass wire, anything and everything in fact for which he knew the name in the Matabili language.   He got nothing from us, but each and every one of our boys reverently placed a piece of meat beside him on the large rock on which he was sitting.

One of my boys, who understood the Mashuna language, told me afterwards that Jugu, during his oration, had said that his father would now show Lo Bengula that the country beyond the Umniati river belonged to him, Chameluga ; that the white men whom he had sent to hunt there should have no sport, for he would cause the elephants and all other game to retire before them wherever they went, so that they should starve for want of meat ; and that finally, when in disgust they wanted to leave the country, he would cause the rains to fall and the rivers to overflow their banks, so as to be impassable, and that they would then die of fever and famine. Happily for us these dire predictions were not altogether verified, though we certainly had very bad luck with elephants.

The following day (25th June) Collison fell in with two lionesses, the larger of which he killed ; her skin, when pegged out, measured 9 feet 4 inches. The same morning I shot a fine water-buck bull and two tsessebe antelopes, whilst Jameson bagged a blue wildebeest and a tsessebe.

It was not until 30th June that we fell in with rhinoceroses, though we had seen and followed without success the fresh spoor of those animals on two occasions previously. On the evening of the day in question, however, Jameson and I shot two of those animals of the prehensile-lipped or so-called black species. On the 31st of August Jameson and I returned to our waggons on the Upper Umfuli, after a six weeks' hunting expedition on foot, which we had made into the " fly " country north of our camp.

The following morning, as we were short of meat, I saddled up my best pony, who was fat and frisky after his long rest, and rode out to look for a head of game. I had ridden for about an hour towards the north-west, and had just emerged from a belt of open forest upon a broad valley, when I per-ceived two large animals standing in the shade of a single small tree, about four hundred yards up the valley. " Impofo, impofo ! " (Elands, elands !) cried my Kafir attendants excitedly, visions of fat meat floating before their mind's eye. The beasts looked so large and of such a deep gray colour that I, too, at first thought they were elands, though I very soon found out my mistake ; for one of them, noticing our approach, moved clear of the small tree beneath which he had been standing and gazed towards us, when his magnificent spiral horns at once made me aware that I beheld a pair of old koodoo bulls, which animals, in common with the eland, become, when aged, of a deep bluish-gray colour, the thinness of their coats in both cases allowing the dark colour of the hide beneath to show through the scanty hairs.

Taking my little 450 Express from the hands of the

Kafir who had been carrying it, I now cantered towards them, on which they at once made across the open towards a narrow belt of forest at the head of the valley. They ran at a heavy gallop, carrying their splendid horns nearly upright, but sloping slightly backwards. I saw at a glance that they were two bulls of the largest size, magnificent specimens of one of Africa's noblest game animals ; and inwardly registering a vow that I would add at least one of their heads to my collection of hunting trophies, I pressed my stout little nag to his utmost speed, in order to get as near them as possible before they gained the shelter of the forest. They had, however, a long start, and entered the bush some way ahead of me. For a short time I lost sight of them, but, galloping hard in the direction they had taken, soon made up the ground between us. My two bulls, I found, had joined a large herd, of which they were no doubt the lords, and which must have been lying just within the edge of the bush. When I say large herd I mean a large herd for koodoos, more than a dozen of which animals are seldom found together. Upon this occasion there must have been at least twenty-five, besides the two original patriarchs. Several were fine young bulls, with horns measuring from two to nearly three feet in length. I was very glad to see that the old bulls had joined a herd, as I knew they would be more easily shot than if they had held on by themselves. As the patch of forest through which the chase led was, I knew, of small extent, I did not press my game, but just kept about one hundred and fifty yards in their rear, having determined not to fire until they left the bush and made across the open country beyond.

They had scarcely left the shelter of the forest when the foremost cows, which probably had never yet fully compre-hended the cause of the disturbance of their mid-day slumbers, came to a halt, and the whole herd following their example, they all stood with their great ears cocked, looking back towards the bush. One of the big bulls was on the outside of the herd, and within one hundred yards of where I already stood dismounted beside my pony, and still within the shelter of the forest. What a magnificent beast he was, to be sure ! grandly and symmetrically proportioned in body and limbs, the graceful head seeming almost too small for the mighty horns by which it was surmounted. Beneath his throat and reaching from the jaw to the chest, a long fawn-coloured beard waved to and fro in the breeze, whilst a mane of white hair ran all along his back almost to his quarters. As I raised my rifle, taking a hasty though careful aim for his shoulder, a feeling of exultation possessed me ; for I felt that he was mine. Imagine, then, the intensity of my disgust when the hammer descended on the cap without exploding it. The next instant the koodoos again bolted. I hastily re-cocked the rifle, and for the second time aimed at the bull as he was running a little to one side of the herd, and at about a hundred and twenty yards' distance. The cap, however, again failed to explode ; so, throwing the cartridge out of the rifle, I pushed in a fresh one, and remounting, again galloped in pursuit. One of the two big bulls now left the herd, and went off by himself, making in the direction of the river, which was about two miles distant. I looked first at his horns, and then at those of the other old patriarch that still kept with the cows ; but, as they appeared equally fine in both, I pursued the latter, and very soon gave him a shot obliquely from behind, which, entering just behind his ribs, penetrated right into his chest. He at once left his comrades, and cantering heavily to a small patch of bush stood with lowered head beneath a small tree. I quickly gave him another shot in the centre of the shoulder, and then galloped away again at right angles, in the hope of catching sight of his companion in one of the large openings through which I knew he would have to pass.

I crossed in front of the herd, and galloped hard for about a mile, edging towards the river ; but, seeing nothing of him, turned and galloped back on the other tack, and, again coming in sight of the herd, shot one of the young bulls. I then returned to the big bull I had first killed, and, as my Kafirs were already there before me, at once cut off his head, and broke him up. We then bushed up the carcase of the young bull, as my Kafirs could not carry all the meat, and returned to camp. I was not very well pleased with my success, for I felt sure that, had it not been for my cartridge missing fire, I should have killed the other old bull with my first shot, and bagged

both of them.   As it was, the horns of the one I did get were
a beautiful pair, very prettily twisted and perfectly even.   They
measured in a straight line from point to base 3 feet 5 inches,
and round the spiral turn of the horn 5 feet 3 inches.   I have
shot a koodoo bull with horns nearly five inches longer than
this, in a straight line, but never one with so much twist.

The following day I again rode out, taking a pack bullock
with me to carry the meat of the koodoo whose carcase I had
bushed up the preceding day.   As lions were fairly numerous
about our camp, I cherished a hope that some of these carnivora might have smelt it out and uncovered it, in which case
there would have been a good chance of getting a shot at one,
as it was still very early.   However, my *cache* had been
quite undisturbed ; so, leaving a couple of boys with the pack
bullock to cut up the meat and get it back to camp, I rode on
with the rest.   After a time I saw a herd of tsessebe antelopes,
but did not go after them, and a little later came across an
old wart-hog, routing up the ground in search of roots, and
got two shots at him, missing both times.   I certainly ought
to have hit him, and probably should have done so, but that a
perfect hurricane of wind was blowing, which made it very
difficult to hold a light rifle steadily.

Not long after this I spied a little oribi antelope lying
down in the middle of a broad open valley from which the
grass had all been burned off.   About one hundred and fifty
yards from where the graceful little animal lay stood a single
thorn-tree, beside which I dismounted, the oribi having all this
time lain quite still.   I tried to rest my rifle against the trunk
of the tree to steady it, but it moved so much, owing to the
strong wind swaying the branches, that I could not avail myself of its support.   When I did fire I missed, upon which the
pretty little antelope at once jumped up and took itself off,
but, after running for about fifty yards, again stopped and
stood looking at me.   Having slipped in another cartridge, I
then fired a second shot, and this time struck it in the hind
quarters.   Although the expanding bullet smashed one haunch
all to atoms, and the solid end tore right through its entrails,
the fragile-looking animal ran at least three hundred yards
before my Kafirs secured and killed it.   The tenacity of life of

all the African antelopes with which I am acquainted is most
remarkable.   As I wanted the skin of one of these antelopes I
off-saddled and flayed it carefully, and then, saddling up once
more, turned my face homewards, as the high wind made the
shooting very unsatisfactory.   When about four miles from
camp I sighted two ostriches, a cock and a hen, running
leisurely along about half a mile in front of me.   As the
country was perfectly open here, I hardly thought I should be
able to get within shot of them, but, as the feathers of a good
cock ostrich were at that time worth £20, I determined to
have a try.   As, when I first saw them, the ostriches were
running at right angles to my course, I galloped obliquely
towards them, and was rather surprised to find that, upon my
nearing them, they did not increase their speed.   When, however,
I had approached to within about three hundred yards I saw
that the reason of this was that they had a lot of chicks with
them, which their parental instincts prompted them not to
desert.   As the grass had all been burnt off here, the ground
was as bare as a billiard table, and I could see the young
ostriches quite plainly.   It was astonishing how fast the little
creatures ran.   The old cock was much bolder than the hen,
and kept much nearer to the chicks.   I could easily have
galloped right up to the latter, but I was afraid that, if I did
so, the cock would run clean away and leave them to their
fate.   I had six cartridges with me, and missed him with the
first five ; these were, however, all rather long running shots, and
the wind was still blowing hard.   With the sixth and last shot
I struck the devoted bird just at the junction of the neck with
the body, killing him on the spot.   I felt rather sorry to have
shot him ; however, £20 is £20 all the world over, and I am
afraid I should have been less pleased if I had missed him
altogether.

.When I shot the cock, the chicks were on the edge of
some long grass that had not been burnt off, and most of them
ran into it before I could intercept them.   Three, however, lay
down outside in the open, with their little necks stretched along
the ground, and I kept guard over them until my Kafirs came
up, when we secured them.   Two of them died from the cold
the first night, as, not understanding their requirements, I had

neglected to cover them with a blanket. The third lived for two months and was doing well, when it met with an accident and was killed. The old cock was a splendid bird, but unfortunately the ends of the white and most valuable feathers had been worn down and soiled during incubation. The black and tail feathers were, however, very fine. Had this bird been shot three months earlier in the season, he would have been worth at least £25. As it was I got £18 for him.

On 4th September I again rode out in the early morning and shot two sable antelopes, the one a very fine bull with a beautifully-curved pair of horns measuring forty-two inches over the curve. The following day, there being now a fair supply of meat in camp, Jameson and I started on a trip to Lo Magondi's kraals, which lay amongst the hills about fifty miles to the north-west of our camp, and just on the verge of the "fly" country. As we expected to be away from the waggons for a fortnight or so, we took supplies of tea, flour, etc., for ourselves, and maize for our horses, sufficient to last that time. Late on the afternoon of the first day's ride we sighted three sable antelopes and a herd of impalas, and giving chase to the former, I shot one of them, a fine male.

Early on the morning of 6th September we came upon the carcase of a white rhinoceros that our mutual friend Collison had shot a few days previously. A little later we saw a large herd of roan antelopes near the River Umsengaisi, amongst them one old bull with a very fine pair of horns. I did my best to get a shot at him, but he was very wide awake, and always kept well in front of the herd ; so that, although I might have shot one or two of the cows, I could not get a chance at him, and finally lost sight of the herd in a thick grove of mahobo-hobo trees. During the day we saw the recent spoors of several rhinoceroses, both of the black and white species, but nothing of the beasts themselves ; nor indeed did we meet with any game whatever, with the exception of three zebras (Burchell's), one of which I shot, as our boys were without meat. Jameson also wounded one of the others, but lost it in the bush.

That evening we slept on a Kafir footpath, not far from Lo Magondi's kraals. About two hours after sunrise on the morrow, when we were quite close to the foot of the hills amongst which the kraals are situated, we met a fine old eland bull face to face, coming from the opposite direction, upon which we at once shot him. As we had a little business to transact with Lo Magondi, in whose charge we had left several trophies of the chase in the previous July, and from whom I expected to be able to buy some ivory, this supply of meat, so near his town, was very opportune. We at once sent two Kafirs on, to apprise the old fellow of our arrival, and then off-saddling the horses (there was a beautiful running stream of water in the valley just below us), set to work to cut up the eland and make a camp.

In the afternoon our messengers returned, accompanied by Lo Magondi and about twenty of his followers. We at once presented the old fellow with a hind quarter and half of the heart fat of the eland, whilst on his side he gave us a large pot of beer, a basket of ground nuts, and some pogo meal. That night there was great feasting and rejoicing in our camp, our own boys, who had long been living upon meat and longed for a little vegetable diet, buying large supplies of maize, beans, meal, beer, and tobacco from the equally meat-hungry Mashunas. Lo Magondi had brought with him all the hippopotamus tusks, rhinoceros horns, etc., that we had left in his charge, but no ivory. He, however, said that he would send for two tusks the following day, upon which I showed him my stock-in-trade, consisting of cotton shirts, beads, coloured handkerchiefs, etc.

At the old man's request we rode out the next day under the guidance of some of his people to try to shoot him some more meat, he at the same time sending men to fetch his ivory. We rode a long way without seeing any game at all, but at last sighted a small herd of roan antelopes, one of which, a fine bull with a remarkably handsome pair of horns, I shot. On our way back to camp we crossed the spoor of some bull elephants that had been about here not many days before us. They had broken the trees down in all directions, and peeled the bark off scores of machabel saplings, making the sur- rounding forest look quite white.

Upon returning to camp I set to work to do a trade with

Lo Magondi, but found him a terribly hard nail. He had been accustomed to dealing in former years with Portuguese traders from the Zambesi ; and as these men got their merchandise by water carriage from Europe right up to Tete, and then employed slave labour to have it carried up country, they could afford to sell very cheap. It was quite late when I at last concluded the purchase of the larger tusk, weighing about 30 lbs., and I was then tired of haggling, and would not bargain for the other.

As soon as day broke the following morning we saddled up, and in spite of Lo Magondi's entreaties that we should buy the other tusk, broke up our camp and rode away to the eastward, intending to cross the Manyami river and look for elephants amongst the machabel forest beyond. We had been riding for about two hours, when we crossed elephant spoor that appeared quite fresh. A careful inspection showed us that the tracks were those of a few old bulls, and that they must have passed early the preceding night ; so, as elephant bulls are at the present day exceedingly *raræ aves in terris* anywhere south of the Zambesi river, we at once followed them. The country about here consisted of alternate open valleys, from which the long grass had all been burnt off, and machabel forests, in some of which the young saplings grew very close together, rendering the riding rather awkward, though there was no underwood. I was armed with a little double 12 smooth-bore by W. W. Greener, the cartridges being loaded with 4 drams of powder and spherical bullets. Although this was a very excellent and hard-shooting little weapon, it did not take a sufficiently heavy charge for elephants ; but, as a single 10-bore rifle which had been sent me from England the preceding year, and upon which I had relied, had turned out a very bad and unreliable weapon, it was the only breech-loader I was able to get. After following the elephants for about an hour, we came to a stream of water, a tributary of the Manyami, where the mighty beasts had drunk. Here we off-saddled, and whilst the horses were having a roll and a drink, boiled a kettle of tea and made a hasty breakfast off some cold eland's breast which we were carrying with us ; then again saddling up, and leaving all our baggage in charge of two of our Kafirs, we once more took up the spoor, attended by all the rest in light marching order.

The spoor was easy enough to follow, as the elephants had broken the trees down in all directions and stripped the bark from hundreds of saplings, so that we could often see their white, freshly-peeled stems more than a hundred yards on ahead. The giant beasts must have been undisturbed for some time, and had evidently been feeding along very slowly, and utterly inapprehensive of any danger. Notwithstanding the slow rate at which they had been travelling, however, it took us another three hours before we came up with them. At last we sighted them standing quietly in the full enjoyment of their mid-day sleep amongst a rather thick grove of machabel trees, not far from the base of a range of small stony hills. Before we fired at them they got our wind and ran. There were five of them, all immense old bulls, and, as is usual in such cases, they at once separated, each one taking his own course. I tried to keep them together, but could not manage it, and as the largest tusker was passing me for the third time, I jumped off and gave him both barrels behind the shoulder, Jameson at the same time saluting another monster. Suffice to say, we each killed our animal, the other three having in the meantime made their escape. I very nearly got a second elephant, for he was in sight just before I despatched the first ; but though I galloped hard in the direction he had taken, in the hope of catching a glimpse of him as he was cross-ing one of the numerous open glades, I never again set eyes on him. I gave the elephant I killed twelve shots, and believe that the first two were both through his heart, as I saw the blood running down behind his shoulder directly after I fired, exactly in the right place ; and as he did not fall—although he at once slackened his pace—I thought the bullet had possibly not driven through the thick mass of flesh just behind the shoulder, and so fired the next eight shots for his lungs, which are the least protected vital part in any animal. At the tenth shot he turned and faced me, throwing the blood in streams from his trunk. I then fired two more shots into his chest, when he reeled backwards, shook his head, making his huge ears rattle against his sides, and then fell heavily to the earth.

Upon cutting out this elephant's heart I found that three bullets had gone clean through it, and that a fourth was still in it, whilst his lungs had been riddled. I laid the heart upon the carcase, and made a drawing of it on the spot, showing the position of the four bullet holes on the one side. This statement will, I am afraid, be looked upon with suspicion by the generality of my readers, though all those who have shot much large game will probably be able to call to mind similar experiences. There are, however, no animals with which I am acquainted so extraordinarily tenacious of life, speaking generally, as old elephant bulls, and it is quite a mistake to suppose that they will succumb to body shots as quickly as younger animals or females of their own species.

My elephant carried a fine even pair of tusks, weighing exactly 100 lbs. the two, whilst those of the one shot by my friend weighed 41 lbs. and 31 lbs. respectively, the one tusk being broken. I took some measurements of these two elephants very carefully with a tape-line, which were as follows :—

Elephant shot by Jameson—Vertical height at shoulder, 10 feet 4 inches ; size of ear, 5 feet $6\frac{1}{2}$ inches long, by 3 feet 4 inches broad ; girth of forefoot, 4 feet $7\frac{1}{2}$ inches ; length of tusk beyond the lip, 3 feet 1 inch ; girth outside lip, 1 foot 3 inches. My elephant—Vertical height at shoulder, 10 feet ; size of ear, 5 feet 5 inches long, 3 feet 3 inches broad ; girth of forefoot, 4 feet $4\frac{1}{2}$ inches ; length of each tusk beyond the lip, 3 feet 8 inches ; girth outside lip, 1 foot 4 inches ; length of whole tusk measured over the outside curve, 5 feet $10\frac{1}{2}$ inches ; weight, 50 lbs.

The measurements for vertical height represent the distance in a straight line between two assegais held parallel to one another, the one having been placed at the sole of the foot, the other at the shoulder. In India, twice the girth of the forefoot gives the height of an elephant ; but this measurement is taken, I believe, from the living animal, when the foot is expanded by the weight of the animal's body resting upon it, which, of course, very much increases the size. These elephants were both old bulls that had long attained their full stature ; and, although it is possible that some animals attain to a much greater size, I fear that it will not be easy to find one which, if honestly measured, would have stood eleven feet at the shoulder. As Mr. Sanderson remarks in his most excellent book upon the wild beasts of India, it is astonishing how the length of horns, skins, etc., and the heights of animals shrink before a tape-measure.

NATIVE STOOLS AND MEAT DISHES FROM THE BAROTSI VALLEY.
UPPER ZAMBESI.

INDEX

in the author's experience to the general hospitality of the Boers, 5

Boers, remarks concerning their hospitality and kindness, 5, 9 ; Mr. G. Macall Theal's work, *History of the Boers in South Africa*, referred to, 8 ; Matabili attack on the, at Vechtkop in 1836, 102

Bonga's stockade at Masangano, capture of, by Portuguese, 316

Borius, a Transvaaler, of the pioneer expedition, 375

Borrow, ——, overtakes author's party on way to Umtali to take part with British against Portuguese, 407

Botletli river, crocodiles in, 17 ; Batauwani women and children cross the, in canoes when raided by Matabili, 101 ; Matabili trying to cross the, on water-plants, are drowned, 103 ; scarcity of water between the, and the Mababi river, 449

British Museum, author starts to collect large animals for the, 3

British South Africa Company (see also under *Mashunaland*, etc.), author terminates his engagement with, 426

Bruce, Lieutenant, author sent to assist him in making roads, 405 ; making waggon road from Manica to Umliwan's, 409

Buck-waggon, description and arrangement of, 24

Buffalo, in the neighbourhood of the Kadzi, 55 ; rifles used for shooting, 430 ; narrow escapes from wounded, 433, 434 ; difficult to kill with shot in front of head when charging, *ibid.* ; charged by one that had previously been bitten by lion, 452 ; shooting, near Chobi river, 459

Bukwela's town, guides procured from, 141

Bulawayo, captive Bushman children brought to the king at, their escape, 110 ; visit Lo Bengula at, over the "Sea-Cow Row," 135-138 ; journey to, with Mr. W. Montagu Kerr, 139 ; start from Tati for, after hunting expedition to the Mababi, 155 ; visit to Lo Bengula at, to confer with him about pioneer expedition, 360 ; leave, on shooting expedition with Messrs. Collison, Jameson, and Crook, 461

Bullets used in killing large game (see under *Rifle*)

Burchell's zebras, shooting, near Golodaima's town, 183 ; plentiful north of Zambesi on road to Monzi's, 211 ; near Chobi river, 450

Burnett, Mr., one of the gold-prospecting party to the head of the Mazoe river, 265 ; comes upon a party of lions near Kansawa river, 279 ; he accompanies author on visit to sources of the Mazoe, 292 ; lion and hippopotamus shooting, 299 ; on pioneer expedition to Mashunaland, 313

Bushman assegaied by Matabili after he had shown them the way to Pandama-tenka, 104 ; Bushman woman and child killed by Matabili warriors, 105

Bushman woman, old captive, her escape from the Matabili, 111

Bushmen (Masarwas or Amasiri) from Khama's country, good at finding the way, 88 ; murdered by Matabili raiders, 101 ; and Makalaka, Khama's man, fleeing from Matabili raiders, well received by, 104 ; origin, language allied to Korana, physical characteristics, weapons, etc., 106, 107 ; probably allied to the Niam-niam dwarfs of Schweinfurth, the pigmy races, etc., 107 ; excellent as trackers and assistants in the hunting veld, 109 ; their remarkable faculty for finding their way through forests, etc., 110, 186 ; children of, captured by Matabili warriors, the escape of six from the king's courtyard, 110

Butterflies, caught during travels, presented to South African Museum, Cape Town, 16 ; several supposed new species caught, 54 ; catching, at the Umsengaisi river, 55 ; catching, north of Zambesi river, 210

Buzi, attempt to find waggon road to the coast, free from tse-tse fly, along the watershed of the, and the Pungwi, 426

CAMPBELL, Lieutenant Adair, with Mr. C. Harrison and author, visits the Portuguese at Massi Kessi, 385 ; joins author to take part with British at Umtali against Portuguese, 407

Canoe, upset by hippopotamus in the Zambesi, 259 ; it is recovered, but ivory tusk, etc. lost, 261

Cape Colony, "Klipspringer" antelopes found in, 162

wrongly laid down on Mr. Ravenstein's map, 215; roan antelopes at the, 245

"Unkwila mondo," native name for Lichtenstein's hartebeest (*which see*)

Ushamba hill, encampment at foot of, 49

VAN ROOYEN, Cornelis, return to Matabililand with, in 1885, 184; his valuable dog killed by wounded sable antelope, 191; respected by the natives in Mashunaland, 332

Vechtkop, Matabili attack on the Boer camp of, in 1836, 102

"Veldschoon," repairing worn-out, before starting for Zumbo, 57

Vermaak, Solomon, with Berns Niemand when he was killed by crocodile, 81

Vicenti, on Zambesi, African Lakes Company's station at, 270; arrive at, on boat journey down Zambesi, 307

Victoria, building going on at, 351; site of the township of, 378

Victoria Falls, the main range of hills running from, to the Kafukwi, 210; visit to the, 263; dark-foliaged evergreens on the brink of, 452

Vultures, large number in neighbourhood of elephants that had been shot, 180

Vunga hills, arrive at Inya-tsu-tsu near the, 280

Vunge on Livingstone's map, probably the present Inya-tsu-tsu, 280

WAHLBERG, Professor, killed by an elephant, 359

Wainji river, its junction with the Umrodzi, 291; crossing the, on journey from Mount Hampden to Inyota, 295

Wallace, Mr. A. R., his theory of the origin of the primitive races of men in Africa, 108

Wankie's Town, arrival at, when endeavouring to reach the Garanganzi country, 201; breadth of Zambesi near, *ibid.*; character of country near, *ibid.*; return to, with survivors of party, after the flight from the Mashukulumbwi, 241

Ward, Mr. Rowland, his book, *Horn Measurements of Great Game*, 367; referred to, 441

Wardell, Mr., of Mr. Coillard's Barotsi Valley mission, 251

Ware, Mr. Harry, meeting with, 245

Wart-hog seen near Umvukwi Mountains, 53; chased by "Punch," the dog, is shot after wounding "Punch," and sent to Cape Town Museum, flesh of a fat, good eating, 79

Wata and his people driven by Matabili from hill near Gurumapudzi river in 1868, 295

Water, party suffering from want of, 66

Water-plants, Matabili trying to cross the Botletli river on, are drowned, 103

Watson, Mr. Frank, pleasant meeting with, at Horn's Vley, 153

Wedza, peaks of, seen from top of Dombo hill, 328

Wehl and Law, Fathers, their ill-fated journey to Umzila's kraal, 97; travelling with, on their journey to Umzila's, 461

Weinen (the place of weeping), 7

Westbeech, George ("Georos"), his travels in the Hanyani river district referred to, 47; Matabili warriors visit his man "Africa's" camp at Gazuma, 105; meeting with Mr. Frank Watson at Horn's Vley, who is taking goods to, at the Zambesi, 153; meet him at Gazuma, discussion with him on prospect of getting into the Barotsi valley, he shows Mr. F. Arnot's letter written in Garanganzi country, 198; Marancinyan, a friend of, 243

Weyand, Karl, and Jan Engelbrecht, white rhinoceroses killed by, 158

Weyers, John, meeting with at Pandama-tenka in 1888, 197; accompanies author to Wankie's Town on his proposed journey to Garanganzi country, 198

Wheel of waggon breaks whilst crossing the Sarua river, 118

White rhinoceros, on the verge of extinction, where found, 58; prepare for a journey to the Mazoe and Sabi in search of, 73; probably not to be obtained outside the fly country, 100; shooting a pair of, referred to, speedy extinction of, 158; ten killed by Weyand and Engelbrecht in 1886, and five others by natives, *ibid.*; shot by Mr. Collison near the Umsengaisi river, 472

Wild Beasts and their Ways, Sir Samuel

THE END